Killing Children in British Fiction

Killing Children in British Fiction
Thatcherism to Brexit

DOMINIC DEAN

SUNY PRESS

Dusk on the Hove Seafront, photograph by Dominic Dean, 2024.

Published by State University of New York Press, Albany

© 2024 State University of New York

All rights reserved

Printed in the United States of America

No part of this book may be used or reproduced in any manner whatsoever without written permission. No part of this book may be stored in a retrieval system or transmitted in any form or by any means including electronic, electrostatic, magnetic tape, mechanical, photocopying, recording, or otherwise without the prior permission in writing of the publisher.

Links to third-party websites are provided as a convenience and for informational purposes only. They do not constitute an endorsement or an approval of any of the products, services, or opinions of the organization, companies, or individuals. SUNY Press bears no responsibility for the accuracy, legality, or content of a URL, the external website, or for that of subsequent websites.

For information, contact State University of New York Press, Albany, NY www.sunypress.edu

Library of Congress Cataloging-in-Publication Data

Name: Dean, Dominic, author.
Title: Killing children in British fiction : Thatcherism to Brexit / Dominic Dean.
Description: Albany : State University of New York Press, [2024] | Includes bibliographical references and index.
Identifiers: ISBN 9781438499550 (hardcover : alk. paper) | ISBN 9781438499574 (ebook) | ISBN 9781438499567 (pbk. : alk. paper)
Further information is available at the Library of Congress.

For Hilmi

Contents

List of Illustrations ix

Acknowledgments xi

Chapter 1 Creative Destruction: Brexit and Britain's
          Future Past   1

Chapter 2 Thatcher's Demons and Maggie's Boys:
          Children and Youth in Thatcherism's Hinterlands   39

Chapter 3 Boy Kings, Queerness, and Radical Nostalgia   109

Chapter 4 Abduction and Abuse: Disappearing Children
          in the 1980s and 1990s   135

Chapter 5 Children of Nowhere: Migration and Haunted
          Futures in Ishiguro's *A Pale View of Hills*   173

Chapter 6 Migrant Children and Mobile Youth in
          Twenty-First Century British Fiction   197

Conclusions and Speculations: Reading the Child-as-Future
in the Twenty-First Century   249

Notes   261

Works Cited   269

Index   285

Illustrations

Figure 2.1 In *The Innocents*, the face of the perverse adult, Quint, appears behind the dangerous child, Miles, of whom he is suspected of taking possession.   60

Figure 2.2 Christine, in her distinctive red coat, slips under the water in the opening sequence of *Don't Look Now*.   61

Figure 2.3 A picture of innocence: the image of Rowan carried by Sargeant Howie in *The Wicker Man*.   62

Figure 2.4 The postwar institution: the Ludovico Medical Center in *A Clockwork Orange*.   71

Figure 2.5 The desired house: the Cat Lady at home in *A Clockwork Orange*.   72

Figure 2.6 Hundreds Hall in its better days, during Faraday's childhood visit to the fête in the 2018 film adaptation of *The Little Stranger*.   94

Figure 2.7 During the fête, the young Faraday turns away from his parents to gaze longingly upon the house.   94

Figure 2.8 In the final moments of the 2018 film adaptation of *The Little Stranger*, the adult Faraday is watched by his childhood self at the center of Hundreds Hall.   96

Figure 2.9 The young Faraday, now elevated to the position of power at the center of the Hall, gazes down on his adult self.   97

Figure 3.1 By the film's conclusion, the young prince has been transformed into an agent of queer triumph. 119

Figure 3.2 Prince Edward appears initially as a curious and sometimes as a horrified witness to adult misdeeds in Jarman's *Edward II*. 120

Acknowledgments

I believe that academic literary studies depends on the creativity of literary authors, as film studies depends on that of filmmakers, and produces the best fruit when it accepts, embraces, and—above all—enjoys this unequal relationship. I would like, therefore, to first thank the authors and filmmakers, many of them still living, whose work is explored in this book. I hope I have done justice to both its power and its pleasure. Amongst the authors, special thanks go to Melissa Harrison for her kind and helpful interactions.

I would like to express my sincere gratitude to Rebecca Colesworthy and all her colleagues at SUNY Press. Rebecca is both the most supportive editor anyone could wish for and rightly recognized as a leading voice on issues in scholarly publishing and its relationship with the academy and society. It is a huge privilege to have worked with her to bring this project to fruition, and I thank her for her patience and, especially, for her initial and encouraging confidence in the work. I would also like to thank the peer reviewers for giving rigorous but immensely supportive and thoughtful feedback.

I owe huge debts of personal gratitude to many colleagues, friends, and family in the preparation of this book, whether their support was intellectual, moral, or both.

Thanks to Hilmi, who supports me every day and consistently inspires me with his creativity and high standards, and whose curiosity about art and narrative of all genres keeps my own fueled and sparked. I owe him many debts beyond what I can express here.

I would like to thank all my family for their love and support, starting with my parents for nourishing and encouraging me throughout my childhood and life to date and for encouraging a child to read when he was reluctant. Thanks to Jess, Oli, Callum, Asha, Yasmin, Aaron, Izyan, Amal, little Adam, and all my extended family.

This book is the product of many wonderful working relationships and intellectual collaborations with the many fine scholars I have been privileged to interact with. Special thanks go to Thomas Docherty, who supervised the doctoral research that provided the genesis for this book. Thomas's scholarship and intellectual example have inspired me with their ambition, rigor, and ethical commitment since my undergraduate years, when he consolidated my love of literary studies in his role as a much-loved Head of the Department of English at Warwick. Thomas has always remained supportive and committed throughout every challenge. I also thank the secondary supervisors for my PhD, Tina Lupton and the late Christina Britzolakis, who were always thoughtful and supportive, and the examiners, Carol Chillington Rutter and Josh Cohen, who gave me a stimulating, rigorous, and intellectually encouraging viva, despite it taking place the day before the Brexit vote. Thanks also to Jeremy Treglown, who supervised my master's dissertation, where I developed my early work on Peter Ackroyd, and who first introduced me to Ishiguro's work.

I am grateful to a number of colleagues and friends who discussed the early work for this book with me and/or read drafts, especially Pam Thurschwell, Vicky Lebeau, Chris Vardy, Ben Liberatore, Feras Alkabani, and Peter Cherry. Thanks to Stephen Guy-Bray for a valuable conversation regarding the chapter on *Edward II*. Particular thanks to Alex Henke for editorial support with the initial proposal. The sections on Ishiguro have also benefited from engagement with the many wonderful Ishiguro scholars I am privileged to know, amongst whom Bas Groes, Peter Sloane, Ivan Stacy, Catherine Charlwood, Richard Robinson, and Yugin Teo have been particularly important collaborators.

It is impossible to include all those others who have supported me during the production of this book, but some are listed below.

There are many colleagues and friends in academia and higher education who have offered much-valued personal, professional, and/or intellectual support along the way, including Peter Boxall, Lucy Arnold, David James, Michael Jonik, Ronnie Barnsley, Edwin Coomasaru, Luke Seaber, Charlotte Lydia Riley, Nick Taylor-Collins, Louis Goddard, Doug Battersby, Gianni Sara, Leonardo Carella, Jo Moran-Ellis, Alison Phipps, Janet Boddy, Elaine Sharland, Rachel Thomson, the late Christian Smith, Jen Baker, Liz Barry, Emma Mason, Claire Langhamer, Clive Webb, Fiona Mathews, Peter Matthews, Mark Walters, Sandro Eich, Matthew

Dimmock, Andrew Hadfield, Tom Healy, Madhu Krishnan, Richard Schoch, Catherine Pope, Chris Hewson, V. Joshua Adams, Iain McDaniel, Dion Georgiou, James Sumner, Becky Guest, Chris Louttit, Paul Veyret, Anna Grey, Natalia Cecire, Leon Betsworth, Leslie Mabon, Jami Rogers, Katie Tobin, Mark Carrigan, Ed Owens, Rameez Ahmed Bhat, Gav Maclean, Anne-Marie Angelo, Hannah Mason-Bish, Andy Kesson, Nick Hubble, Wouter Woltering, Michael Docherty, Michelle Lefevre, Jackie Cassell, Dylan Lewis, Damien Jarvis, Martin Paul Eve, James Wilsdon, Catherine Sloan, Katherine Kruger, Mariadele Boccardi, Bob Eaglestone, Ödül Bozkurt, Jordan Welsh, Rachele Dini, Phoenix Andrews, and Sarah Lee.

I have benefited from the support of many personal friends, whose kindness and encouragement and shared interests have kept me going throughout the project. They include Peter Cherry, Feras Alkabani, Kirsty Bennett, Stuart LaCroix, James Beaumont, Paul Davidson, Alex Aghajanian, Amira Abdelhamid, Zacharias Semler, Nat Cameron Robertson, A. J. Nadim, Carlos Orozco, Lucinda Neal and Ryan Fordham, Sean Kelly, Andrew Rosser, Esther MacInnes and Anne-Marie Murphy, Carl Beasley, Sam Woolway and Ana Sparbel, Kirsty Bridger and Greg Stroud, Clare and Steve Hunt, Holly and Ben Ashmore, Lucy Crick and Ben Butt, George Eaton and Jen Johnson, Kieron and Janice Clement-Smith, Reehan Miah, Eleanor Turney, Rob Marks and Isi Genn-Bash, Zainab Juma, James Pelling and Emily Dimer, Alexander Ghionis, Laura Lundahl, David Ivanyan, Laveen Ladharam, Neil Bastian, Gareth Roberts, Chris Whitehouse, Jared Goode, Abhay Sandhu, Will Goddard, Ryan Macbeth, Sean Tyler, Ivo Damme, Louis Goddard, Matt Turner, Fr. Colin Wolczak, and Mgr. Michael Jackson. Special thanks to Helen Knight, who first welcomed me to the English department as an eighteen-year-old undergraduate and who has been a good friend ever since.

I have also benefited from the support of wonderful colleagues currently or formerly at the University of Sussex, throughout many areas of the University and at all levels of the hierarchy. They include Mark Chee, Simon Lascelles, Debbie Foy, Keith Jones, Michael Davies, Seb Oliver, Vanessa Cuthill, Michelle Stonestreet, Hayley Cordingley, Rebecca Downing, James Morland, Katherine Blackadder, Rob Witts, Gill Watson, Lorna Hards, Laura Vellacott, Liane Wrigg, Deeptima Massey, Christina Miariti, Suzanne Fisher-Murray, Megan McMichael, Nora Davies, Pascale Fanning-Tichborne, Ian Carter, Simone Robinson, Ian Sinclair, Isla-Kate Morris, Nicola Ashton, Stacey Moon, Saskia Gent, Felix Rehnberg, Sue

Angulatta, Alice Robertson, Angela Pater, Owen Richards, Laurence Pearl, Steve McGuire, Sahar Abuelbashar, Richard Taylor, the late Joy Blake, Sui-Mee Chan, Amy Waldron, Sam Nesbitt, Beth Logan, and Jane Harvell.

Images are reproduced with the kind permission of Donnacha Coffey for Filmgrab.

Chapter 1

Creative Destruction

Brexit and Britain's Future Past

Killing Children from Thatcherism to Brexit

As the twentieth century entered its closing decades and the twenty-first began, British fiction was full of children killing, or being killed, or both. British politics of the period, meanwhile, has been replete with futures being destroyed, contested and recreated on competing models. This book explores some of the scenes and themes of child-killing and children killing that appear in British literature, film, and culture from the rise of Thatcherism in the 1970s to "Brexit"—the political phenomenon dominating British public life in the late second and early third decades of the twenty-first century—which frame Britain's recent and continuing conflicts over competing futures. These conflicts share, this book argues, an underlying attempt to avoid historically situated and institutionalized politics in favor of seeking an essential and permanent reality (often accompanied by an ideal of an organic British nation and society), driven by desire to secure the future and erase its uncomfortably unknown character—the character assumed by the child. In the child, an ultimately unknown future nevertheless possesses a material presence in need of institutional and domestic accommodation, education, and affective and political attention. It is the challenge of accommodating this child, who is materially present yet represents a future that is impossible to fully secure or even confidently envisage, that provokes—this book argues—relentlessly imagined, and sometimes realized, violence from adults. The intensity and breadth of this phenomenon makes recent British fiction a powerful collective case study for a broader argument for the child's material alterity and for such alterity's political, epistemological, and critical implications.

Carol Chillington Rutter calls child-killing "the last taboo, the practice Britain still called 'evil'" in the 1980s and 1990s (176). Yet, although in killing a child adults destroy a future, often, in the cases explored here, adults regard this as a *preventative* killing that avoids the child destroying the future or erasing a (re)productive relationship between the future and the past. These child-killings thus often appear as *creative* destruction, securing the future by destroying the child who embodies a future latently or blatantly going wrong. An equivalent destructive creativity often appears, conversely, in the child's own real or imagined acts of destruction or disruption against a denuded adult social order, itself a repeated motif in late twentieth and early twenty-first-century British fiction (and other cultural forms, particularly film). The language of imagination and literary motif should not imply that this destruction is necessarily less than material: as we shall see, the killing children of recent British literature and culture intersect with real history and, even in their fictional forms, invoke real risks.

The idea of killing a child—as a taboo broken frequently in unconscious fantasy, occasionally in reality, and often in literature—has a substantial heritage in psychoanalytic theory. Serge Leclaire even claimed that "there is for everyone, always, a child to kill" (3), referring to the ghostly child within, formed by parental investment, who haunts and troubles the adult self. This is an important idea—later, I describe Kathryn Bond Stockton's powerful queer revision of it—and such a child does feature in many of the literary texts discussed here. However, this framing risks too quickly confining dangerous children (relatively) safely within a space of adult interiority; often, in the texts explored here, we are dealing not just with a problem child-as-past haunting adult memory but with a very material and very much "other" child-as-future that is under the adult gaze but not wholly secure in their perception. Nor is this perceptual insecurity readily or necessarily eased by recourse to interpretative frameworks available from psychoanalysis or queer theory, despite their value and richness when applied to literary case studies.

The notion of "creative" destruction of either past or future—a destruction that might be symbolically or materially directed toward, or from, the child—has broad and deep resonances in British cultural and political history since the mid-1970s, the period primarily covered here (although this perspective is extended by how Britain has obsessively engaged in rewriting its own recent history, particularly the postwar period from 1945 and the "progressive" 1960s and 1970s). This book's premise is that scenes and themes of children killing or being killed in acts of creative destruction are noticeably prevalent and carry intense signifying power in British literature and culture from the rise of Thatcherism to the period of Brexit—despite Chillington Rutter's contention, mentioned previously, that such killing remained a powerful moral taboo even while other ideas of moral value were undermined or revised. In fact, the taboo often operated alongside its breaking, as we shall see.

We shall find here children killing for access to power, security, beautiful things, and even (a particularly British passion, this) grand country houses; children who must be killed because they embody the traumas of migration and globalization; children who lure adults into deadly traps; and children who disappear without trace, destroying or restoring adult British society in the process. These children appear in works from major late twentieth and early twenty-first-century British authors including Kazuo Ishiguro, Ian McEwan, Doris Lessing, Sarah Waters, Alan Hollinghurst, Peter Ackroyd, and Jim Crace; from earlier writers who influenced them, such as Rose Macaulay, Graham Greene, and William Golding; from filmmakers including Stanley Kubrick, Nicholas Roeg, Robin Hardy, Derek Jarman, and Remi Weekes; and from more recently emerging British writers such as David Szalay and Melissa Harrison.

Of course, dangerous children do not originate in narratives of this period. Henry James's influentially ambiguous 1898 novella *The Turn of the Screw* is arguably the archetypal modern literary narrative of child-killing, where an adult's paranoid belief that the children in her care are falling under malevolent influence—an influence attributed to dark external forces but which ultimately threatens any secure distinction between them and the child's interiority or between a perverse past and the children's future—eventually leads to a child being killed in the very attempt to "save" him. When James's novella was turned into the 1961 movie *The Innocents*, the threat this child posed to the adult (and vice-versa) was made visibly explicit.[1] This change placed the film as an early case of the trend that exploded in horror movies from the 1960s onwards, where children appeared as sources of violence and objects of fear (discussed in chapter 2).

This change also reflected some of the characteristics of the children and their circumstances that I explore here, which are, at least to some extent, distinctive to the period studied in this book and its particular obsessions, such as the intensive materialism of the child's interests and its context in the politics of "aspiration." Beyond this, we shall find that, in such cases, the child comes to represent a general threat to the perceived organic integrity of the adult social and epistemological order, a threat that surpasses (even if it still emerges within) the risk of particular children going awry. Dominic Lennard, in his study of horror movie children, *Bad Seeds and Holy Terrors*, describes "the child villain [. . .] as a side effect of the ideological colonisation of childhood" (2) through the increased protection of "childhood" as a legally and economically secured category in the twentieth century, a framing that reflects the focus of much scholarship on dangerous children in literature and film. Although I accept this framing and expand its application here, the dangerous children considered in this book not only reveal the perversities and repressions within mainstream models of childhood; they also threaten the nation's entire epistemological stability, its sense of relationship between past and future.

I read the texts explored in *Killing Children* within—but also often as challenging—the existing and continually growing body of historical and theoretical scholarship on children in modern and contemporary literature and culture. I engage several major theorists in this field directly, including Lee Edelman, Kathryn Bond Stockton, Jacqueline Rose, Vicky Lebeau, Adam Phillips, Natasha Hurley, Rebekah Sheldon, and Steven Bruhm; however, the literary children encountered here are as resistant to theoretical categorization (even categorization *as* resistance, or as queer) as they are materially demanding and destructive. Some of this resistance reflects the fact that contemporary theory on children is primarily, though not exclusively, driven from within North America, and British futures offer some distinct problems—though they also often possess uncanny, ironic, and sometimes obsessive relationships with America, as we shall see.

The opening context for this book is the politics of Thatcherism: the political movement that gained governing power with Margaret Thatcher's victory in the United Kingdom's general election of 1979, directly retained such power until 1990, and largely sustained its political and cultural dominance well into the early twenty-first century (Mullen et al. 8–10). As we shall see, a central strand across Thatcherite ideology, rhetoric, and policy involved affirming the nascent aspirational qualities in the child—even (in the view of Thatcherism's opponents, but sometimes also in that of its supporters) in their apparently destructive forms. Yet,

Thatcherism's attitude toward this latent quality in the child was fraught with suppressed conflicts and contradictions, arising from its attempt to repudiate postwar and progressive futures and replace them with an alternative future secured through retrieving one version of the child and destroying another. Along the way, this would establish the socially conservative futurism, located in the child's image, that was explicitly mobilized against queer and radical attitudes to the ideological and experiential position of children (as influentially described by Lee Edelman in the North American context). This "reproductive futurism" has, however, come under pressure from the emergence of more open political hostility toward children and youth in the second decade of the twenty-first century. As my final chapter explores, this is especially the case in relation to migrant children and mobile youth.

The period of British history covered by *Killing Children* begins with a sharp turn toward neoliberal capitalism and rhetorical nationalism, combined as the foundations of Thatcherism, yet ends with the union of these forces being subject to severe challenges and unstable reconfigurations in Brexit-Era Britain. Ishiguro's *A Pale View of Hills*, discussed in chapter 5, is one example of a phenomenon repeatedly seen in the works explored here, where contradictions and problems over the-child-as-future are used to recognize the full ideological, epistemological, and affective force of the contradictions in Thatcherite Britain and, in key respects, to *anticipate* the disintegration of Thatcherism's account of the future, a disintegration given new visibility in the Brexit era.

I position and read Brexit, the second historical-ideological bracket for this study, as—among other things—exactly this disintegration of the Thatcherite future, with the latter based in an optimistic combination of neoliberalism and nationalism that sustained its political and cultural dominance, albeit with some revisions of its original features, into the 2010s. The Brexit vote of 2016 erupted in the middle of that decade as an unusually (and for some, almost unthinkably) emphatic instance of a wealthy country rejecting one version of the future and adopting another explicitly for reasons concerned with identity, culture, and narratives of the nation's position in the world. Crucially, the economic rationalism of the "Remain" side was defeated by "Leave" campaigns that spoke to these themes (Eatwell and Goodwin). (In this sense, whatever else it may have been, Brexit was something of a gift to cultural historians and, indeed, to psychocultural theorists.)

Brexit operates in this account not as the single event of the vote, or of the United Kingdom ultimately leaving the European Union,[2] but rather as a distinctive *period* in British political history, beginning in early 2016 and continuing well into the early 2020s, defined by the political, cultural, and generational conflicts invested in it. These conflicts involved significantly different views of the relationship between the past and the future—which Robert Eaglestone has glossed as the "cruel nostalgia" that emerged on both the Remain and Leave sides of the Brexit referendum (92)—and of intergenerational divides. To pro-Brexit Leavers, the attitudes and interests of children and youth often represented an alien, unstable, and undesirable future (Bristow 7), while Remainer campaigns, both before and after the referendum, repeatedly emphasized Brexit as a perverse threat to the young, wantonly destroying the generational contract.[3] Although anxiety over generational conflicts of values and attitudes is obviously not a new phenomenon,[4] Brexit has given it renewed drive and focus and a more prominent place in British public discourse. The Brexit-Era Right has also largely abandoned the optimistic and affirmative discourses of children and youth that Thatcherism set in opposition to dangerous postwar and progressive children and youth in the 1980s. The Brexit Era has nevertheless seen a significant revival and reinvigoration of Thatcher-Era and earlier anxieties about children, youth, and institutions as sources of an emerging dangerous future (explored further in chapter 2), particularly via a heavy association with migration (explored especially in chapter 6).

As Britain's long post-Thatcherism disintegrated into Brexit, then, the future embodied in the child became less an object of celebration than of paranoia and hostility. Yet, British fiction anticipated this, particularly through the imagined killings of children, long before it became politically explicit. Through this fiction and the histories that it reflects, parodies, interrogates, and queers, *Killing Children* explores how Britain has experienced, and continues to face, a series of intersecting crises of the future—all of them refracted through the child. Though these crises are peculiar to Britain in their specific forms, they reflect issues of relevance far beyond the UK—as well as issues of relevance for literary and cultural theory, where the issue of the child-as-future is by no means an easy or settled one, despite the ambitious and valuable theoretical and textual scholarship on this subject in recent decades. Theory (and the professedly radical political projects with which it is often aligned) faces a persistent problem, I suggest, in analyzing the difficulty of the child-as-future without reducing it to a series of consistent signifiers that ultimately risk making the future almost as knowable as in the most conservative reproductive futurism. Insofar as such practices of recognition emerge through my own close readings of children in particular texts—exactly the activity that forms much of my content—I am interested here in how textual children work to confound overly safe or satisfying readings and how this points to the greater ethical and political question of how to accommodate the child and protect their rights while recognizing their alterity, their resistance to recognition itself.

This book's project, then, can be analogized geologically, where, in the recent strata near the surface, child-killings represent powerful conflicts over British futures in the late twentieth and early twenty-first centuries, with Thatcherism as one version of the future and Brexit as its disintegration. In the substrata, these killings signify broader and deeper, more psychosocially and epistemologically fundamental, difficulties in adult acceptance of the child as embodiment of the future in the present—difficulties that challenge critical theories and theorists as much as political conservatives or anyone else. As Kathryn Bond Stockton says, the problem child[5] of literature illuminates "why our notions of history are challenged by the waywardness of fictions" (*The Queer Child*, 9). Accordingly, the body of fiction, film, and other cultural material that responds to Britain's history from Thatcherism to Brexit by imagining the child who must kill or be killed explores both a strain of anxiety within this history—the severity of which other kinds of text cannot as fully describe—and an epistemological dimension of historical crisis that only the child can properly embody.

Creative Destruction

Creative destruction: a destruction in the present, promising a renewed future. The phrase evokes innovation, revolution. Joseph Schumpeter theorized creative destruction out of Marx's argument that capitalism's periodic financial crises will finally produce its own annihilation. The phrase later became more associated with capitalist innovation[6] that claims to produce future value by disrupting the present.

The child and the youth are associated with creative destruction, or at least disruption, because of their embodiment of the future in the present. The cultural authority of this embodiment has a recent example in Greta Thunberg (Kverndokk 145, 155), who at the age of fifteen began publicly demanding that adults *protect* a future value at risk of being destroyed in the present by destroying the current carbon-based economy. The authority of this creative destruction relies on the idea of the child or youth as creative, prophetic, and energetic, but it is also dismissed or mocked as childish because of the same qualities. Behind this lies adult fears that the capacity for creative destruction might not be securely channeled for the purposes that conservative or mainstream adult culture finds acceptable, like productive innovation or patriotic endeavor (the kinds of creative destruction that Thatcherism's combination of neoliberalism and nationalism celebrated and that feature again in Brexit rhetoric).

Creative destruction in these senses is an important theme in radical childhood studies, which find their intellectual origins in Freud's claims to have identified aggression and the desire to violently remake as a central to "normal" childhoods. More recent childhood theorists, like Adam Phillips and Kathryn Bond Stockton, have found radically disruptive forms of "growth" and future-making within the child's perversely destructive, or at least apparently unproductive, creativities. The contemporary political Right, however—in the UK as elsewhere—offers renewed fears of children and youth engaged in disturbance of generational responsibilities and national allegiance. Global crises of the future have produced new protest movements, themselves often mocked as childish; yet, alongside their radicalism, children and youth are accused of being hopelessly sheltered "snowflakes" (Alyeksyeyeva 7–10) and as hopelessly consumerist and individualist even in their apparently radical politics (Nicholas and Clark 39, 41–45).

Throughout the period discussed in this book, we shall see the creatively destructive child emerging through access to new material times and spaces as well as to institutions. Although Thatcherism attacked the supposed danger represented by these phenomena (while developing a version of the creatively destructive child for its own purposes), it did so through an economically naturalistic and nationalistic discourse that ultimately fell out of step with its own institutional and economic consequences. The post-Thatcherite Britain of neoliberal consensus, envisaged by proponents as a source of a stable movement into the future, became increasingly perceived (and not only on the Left) as itself representing a destruction rather less creative than it promised, as secure identification with a national community and confidence in a secure future were challenged by globalization, transnational institutions, and immigration.

The resulting intergenerational conflict of values has led to renewed fears of the creatively destructive child and youth. Moral panics in media and political rhetoric recognize youthful potential for creative destruction through exaggeration and exploitation; literature, film, and other cultural forms recognize it by taking the substance betrayed by these exaggerations more seriously than mainstream politics and culture are prepared to. All this reflects an underlying perpetual challenge: How, and on what terms, are we to make space for the unknown future as a present child? Recent British history shows a society repeatedly struggling to effectively negotiate such questions.

Brexit as Creative Destruction

Margaret Thatcher's first general election victory in 1979 was widely, and particularly for its cheerleaders, attributed to the Left's alleged complacency toward the failures and fissures in the postwar future it had attempted to introduce, which became a future *past*.[7] The crisis of 1979 went on to introduce not only a new government but also a radical new future and, eventually, a neoliberal consensus that substantively endured until the Brexit vote of 2016 introduced a new period of British crisis.

Brexit itself involved competing invocations of future and past, with each side accusing its opponents of sacrificing one to serve the other and of seeking fantasies of one, the other, or both. It has also seen both sides accusing the other of engaging in destruction that only pretends to be creative.[8] Brexiteers seek escape from transnational institutions, aiming to rebuild a unified nation-state imagined as operating organically in the global marketplace. Viewed by progressives and liberals, however, Brexit is a nostalgic, identitarian, ultimately deluded attempt to retrieve a lost national glory and imagined ethno-social unity. Its Britain is clearly not the country produced, historically, by Thatcherism (even though some leading Brexiteers are Thatcherites) but rather an attempt to dismantle it.[9] Whereas Thatcherism combined aspirational neoliberalism and xenophobic nationalism, Brexit suggests that their relationship must be fundamentally renegotiated to ensure the former serves the latter—and thus is aligned with a surge of anti-globalist politics in the later 2010s (see Barnett; Norris; Eatwell and Goodwin).

The Brexit period has seen the rhetorical invocation of several historical analogues for British separation from European institutions (Kettle; Patient). The most frequently cited Britain to which Brexit seeks to return is a version of the country during the Second World War or immediate postwar period; Brexiteers have repeatedly evoked a heroic narrative of British independence against a quasi-Nazi EU to the fury of opponents who deplore the suggestion of equivalence (Stratton 245–46). Despite this implying a repudiation of Britain's participation in the European single market in particular and enthusiasm for transnational globalization in general—the former a specific achievement of the Thatcher governments, the latter reflective of their overall orientation—it nevertheless shares with Thatcherism the attempt to fundamentally revise and reconfigure Britain's postwar trajectory. British political rhetoric and popular culture is, as critical commentators have widely argued, stuck in nostalgia for the war and the immediate postwar period as the basis for a rhetorical recourse to social cohesion and national purpose. As Owen Hatherley put it, early 2010s "austerity" Britain was so suffused in the cultural imagery of wartime and immediate postwar Britain that "parts of the country began to resemble a strange, dreamlike reconstruction of the 1940s and 1950s, reassembled in the wrong order" (4).

Although most influential pro-Brexit figures can be roughly divided between economic nationalists and a "free-market" faction (including self-defined Thatcherites) seeking to make Britain an increasingly deregulated competitor on the global marketplace, both sides share a rhetorical and ideological hostility to institutions—particularly, but not only, international institutions—*as institutions* subject to historical development and political negotiation rather than embodiments of an organic reality. The most far-reaching arguments for Brexit similarly regarded it not merely as the correct policy response to a specific set of challenges at a particular historical moment but as a restoration of an organic and teleological account of British, and especially English, history as a whole—of national history as, in fact, ultimately existing beyond, even if it might be realized within, the contingencies, complexities, and chaos of historical events and processes. The UK's integration into the European Union, with its pooling of sovereignty and weakening of national borders for Europeans (though not, crucially, for those from outside the EU) was regarded as an aberration from this essential British story, its correction well overdue. This could involve, for example, regarding Brexit as the successor and logical conclusion of the English Reformation (Kettle), with its split from European Catholicism and role in accelerating modern capitalism, and the "Glorious Revolution" of 1689 when this status outside Catholic Europe was reinforced (Patient).

More skeptical voices interpreted Brexit's attempt to recreate the organic British nation and its borders in light of later imperial history and its continuing legacies for late twentieth and early twenty-first-century Britain. Peter Mitchell's *Imperial Nostalgia* (2021) treats Brexit as a sign of a nation stuck in its imperial past, part of a broader reactionary turn involving many countries in the early twenty-first century but with specific British characteristics directly related to the legacy of the Empire. This legacy was responsible, Mitchell argues, for shaping codes for the expression of apparently organic, essential values that dominate national self-understanding and public discourse and directly shape the political events of recent history, while the EU is seen as a rival against which Brexit is understood by proponents as "an anticolonial revolt, in that it allows Britain to assume her proper place as a natural leader of empires rather than a subject of them" (95). David Edgerton, meanwhile, has audaciously argued in *The Rise and Fall of the British Nation* (2019) that contemporary British nationalism was forged by the only period in which "Britain" has truly been a nation-state rather than an empire or part of a transnational European polity, the period roughly between the end of the Second World War and the mid-1970s. This resonates with the powerful and complicated relationship of that postwar period with Thatcherism and with the Brexit era—both of which constitute, as I argue here, attempts to reconfigure and rewrite its history in the interests of renewing the British future. Across these readings of recent history and its contexts, it is migration that consistently and particularly provokes fraught confrontations with the legacies of the past and anxieties over the possibilities for future change.

Brexit Britain's Moving Children

My treatment of Brexit as period rather than event underlines intergenerational division and historical revision as its core features. This follows an increasing trend in literary scholarship and cultural history where Brexit is read as condensing a contest of British futures and accelerating attempts to retrieve futures past (see Eaglestone, ed., *Brexit and Literature*, 2018; Meek, *Dreams of Leaving and Remaining*, 2019; O'Rourke, *A Short History of Brexit*, 2019; Shaw, *BrexLit*, 2021). If young people are one prominent target of these endeavors, an even more obvious target is the migrant, and these two objects of hostility have parallels and connections with each other. The conflict of values and perceptions involved in interactions between generations, exposed and accelerated by Brexit, itself echoes the hostility toward migration in pro-Brexit rhetoric (J. Morrison 594–95) and in motivations for the Brexit vote itself (Goodwin and Milazzo 450–52). In Brexiteer rhetoric, young and mobile British people are presented as naive cosmopolitans, enablers of globalized migration; young males relentlessly appear as the most dangerous migrants, particularly economically mobile, young, male Eastern Europeans (Veličković 71–103) and young male Muslims (Cherry, " 'I'd Rather My Brother' " 270–71).

As I discuss in chapter 6, Brexit was preceded by a period of remarkable prominence of migrant youth and children as objects of anxiety in British public discourse. As conflict and instability deepened in Syria, Libya, and other Middle Eastern and North African countries, refugee movement and irregular migration into Europe significantly increased in the mid-2010s, attracting overwhelming coverage in British media (Griessler 337–56). As we shall see later, this involved circulation of images of children, deployed as interventions and reactions to the crisis—children like Alan Kurdi, whose dead body, photographed lying on a beach, prompted renewed promises of safe channels for refugees in the UK. However, this apparently successful use of affective images of the child was accompanied by a strain of paranoia. Rightwing politicians queried the interpretation of Kurdi's image (Sehmer) and British tabloids published lurid headlines about young men in Calais falsely claiming to be children to gain access to the UK, displaying photographs of individuals supposedly brought under legislation for transfer of unaccompanied child refugees who, these newspapers asserted, looked like adults, not children; this coverage "coded [them] as deceptive figures," even potential abusers (Ibrahim 9). These assertions were powerfully contested by experts and advocates, who attributed the apparent signs of age to, in part, the experiences to which these children had been exposed (Coram 2017).

This panic reflected the basic fact that the child, their status defined by vulnerability and the need for protection, constitutes an inherently unstable category caught between essentialist and conditional framings of a fraught reality where the child's development, experiences, and intentions are always at least partly obscured to the adult's gaze. The migrant or refugee child, caught between the absolute imperative—codified into international law—to protect the innocent child and the phobic paranoia of the unknown outsider, condenses these features of children and youth in general.

Institutions, the Organic, and Child-Killing

Problems of managing children and the inchoate future they embody are often also problems of institutions faced with the challenge of accommodating and educating them. I argue that British fictions of violence toward the child also often reflect an intense anxiety over institutions—even reaching a wish to eradicate the institutional as such—that directly relates to this function. The mid-twentieth-century development of postwar British institutions in education, housing, and social care and the establishment of the NHS represented a significant expansion of institutional access for the British public as a whole, while the expansion of access to secondary and higher education gradually extended the period before the entrance of young people into the adult workforce. However, many recent child-abuse scandals have involved the profound failings of particular institutions; in one of the most notorious recent British child-abuse scandals, discussed in chapter 4, this encompassed major national institutions like the BBC and NHS. Even before this, Thatcherism had attacked postwar and progressive-influenced institutions as sites of perversion that, in their alleged distance from the essential facts of social and economic life, were accused of creating generations of misguided children and dangerous youth.

The Oxford English Dictionary definitions for an *institution* include:

> The giving of form or order to a thing; orderly arrangement; regulation.
> Training, instruction, education, teaching.
> A regulative principle or convention subservient to the needs of an organized community or the general ends of civilization.
> An establishment, organization, or association, instituted for the promotion of some object [. . .] e.g., a church, school, college, hospital, asylum, reformatory, mission, or the like [. . .] The name is often popularly applied to the building appropriated to the work of a benevolent or educational institution.

An institution, then, seeks to make the future, typically alongside administering the material conditions, the times and spaces, serving this mission. Here, I accordingly treat an institution as a site of deliberative regulation and specific historical purpose and, therefore, not natural or organic. An institution is in this sense artificial; an educational institution, in particular, must often acknowledge its forms and regulations as temporary and is typically marked by substantial separation from the surrounding society.[10] Such an institution must accept significant uncertainty in its attempts to shape the future. Literary tradition has children accessing institutions only to dramatically confound their programs and predictions, from Charles Dickens's Oliver Twist demanding "more," to the heroic children of the nineteenth-century Bildungsroman, to Roald Dahl's Matilda, and J. K. Rowling's Harry Potter. All these narratives attest to the unpredictable potential and material risk in opening an institution to and for the child who embodies the future—a future that adults seek to influence through their educational programs, but which remains finally uncertain in the present presence of the child. This also reflects a possible ambivalence in the institution's mission: Is it to make the future merely by fully revealing and expounding the essential nature of the world (and of its students)? Or is its relationship to history more contingent, or more agentic, than that? The institution's intervention in history might be both its own and not its own—because it is also dependent on the development and agency of the children it protects. This is a central issue for some institutions featured in this book.

In the contemporary United Kingdom, most major institutions—including most educational institutions—are attached to the British state through direct management, regulation, and/or funding control. This does not mean that they lack institutional characteristics; however, their status as institutions in the terms defined previously is often in actual or latent conflict with politics dominated by organicist and essentialist ideas of the state and national community. Such discourses, never far from the center of modern British politics, reemerged with a vengeance in Brexit. The NHS featured heavily in the 2016 campaign for the UK to leave the EU, most notoriously in a factually dubious advertisement displayed on buses, which read "We send the EU £350 million a week / Let's fund our NHS instead / Vote Leave / Take back control." The rhetorical use of the NHS in this and other pro-Leave campaigning specifically posed the health service as an organic national entity in conflict with the EU as transnational and parasitical foreign institution. It echoes claims about "health tourism," supposedly enabled by weak immigration controls related to Britain's EU membership, as a threat that would drain the service's resources—assumed, in this rhetoric, to be a natural match to the British people's contributions to its funding. Here, an issue of limited financial or material significance (Oliver) gained substantial political and media attention because it impinged on an organicist framing of what a national institution should be and do. This framing is obviously dubious, since the NHS emerged, far from organically, from a dramatic political intervention within British history; nevertheless, it remains both rhetorically powerful and politically effective. (The NHS was perhaps most spectacularly and famously framed as part of the national teleology in the opening ceremony of the 2012 London Olympics, which communicated that "along with James Bond, Mr. Bean, William Shakespeare, cricket, David Beckham, the Queen and heroic failure, the NHS is a peculiarly British institution" [Abbasi 321].)

Brexit was concerned with the supposed subjugation of the British nation—imagined in essentialist and organicist terms—by a transnational institution. But it was also, as the bus advertisement suggested, equally concerned with Britain's own internal institutions, even if Leave rhetoric implied that they shouldn't really be institutions in the terms I am using. Similarly organicist understandings pervade discourse around schools and their particular role in raising the nation's children and youth, where moral panics around progressive approaches to the teaching of British and colonial history, and around the influence of Islam in certain areas of the country, have led to a recurrent and intensifying insistence on "British values," presented as recourse against activist institutional change and against the dangers of children being corrupted by un-British influence. As Lockley-Scott notes, "'Fundamental British Values' is [. . .] a label, developed in the wake of the 'end of multiculturalism' rhetoric" (354), intended to preempt the attractions of Islamist and other extremist ideology for young people and central to Conservative school policy in the 2010s. The same tendency to frame the teaching of history and citizenship, and the curriculum as a whole, around identifying and celebrating British values and achievements tightly hedges issues around the teaching of colonial and imperial history and associated debates, where rightwing moral panics tend to regard correct history as established, known, and beyond significant revision, treating any attempts at revision as identitarian betrayals of moral truth and historical fact rather than attempts to better reach them (Riley 292–94).

In studies of British nationalism since Benedict Anderson's influential *Imagined Communities* (1983), nostalgic organicism has been widely identified as integral to Britain's cultural imaginary, and this theme has only gained wider prominence in the early twenty-first century. Owen Hatherley's *The Ministry of Nostalgia* (2016), for example, provocatively describes how this intensified during the 2010s through a spurious but pervasive narrative equivalence, in political and media rhetoric, between the neoliberal austerity and revived nationalism of the 2010s and the sacrifices of the Second World War and social democracy of the postwar period. In *Killing Children*, I do not attempt any kind of comprehensive mapping of this organicism. Yet, I try to show just how vigorously, and with how much cultural breadth and depth, it fights against the nation's changing historical position in the late twentieth and early twenty-first centuries. I also aim to demonstrate how this organicism works against the institutional as an expression of a contingent (thus inorganic) future and a potential accommodation of the child who embodies that future. In exploring how this repression is worked through in imagined killings by and of that child, we find the psychocultural force behind the politics.

Institutions attract profound and consistent hostility, I argue, when they threaten to approach or expose the world as historical, contingent, and political rather than guaranteed by essentialist and ultimately atemporal principles. The child is also, of course, a reminder that such principles do not hold, in their embodied temporality, their status as a physical trace of the future in the present who nevertheless stubbornly refuses to disclose that future to the adult's gaze. This combination means that the child who has, or might gain, institutional access and protection can become a profoundly difficult figure for the adults we encounter in this book, from the real Margaret Thatcher (and her fictional incarnations) to the "Guardians" of Hailsham in *Never Let Me Go*. Since the child never fully discloses the future to adults in the present, access to educational and other institutions has to be given to the child as both a free gift and an investment based on calculated risk. In late modern Britain, neoliberal, socially conservative, and ethno-national imperatives clash over the terms of this investment.

Yet, as the British psychoanalytic theorist Adam Phillips points out, "it is not the child [. . .] who believes in something called development" (21). Phillips means that, rather than striving painfully toward the future, the child may be satisfied with a provisional or even, to the adult world, trivial present—of the kind that the protected space of the institution has the potential to accommodate—full of "the pleasures of interest" (21). As when the child indulges in roleplaying their future as an astronaut or a nurse, play may be good enough for the child; but from an adult perspective, certainly under contemporary neoliberalism, such play is perverse when it ceases to be productive, even if only on a promissory basis. The issue is not that the indulgence and perversity of child's play will never have an impact on the "real" adult world but rather that the nature of such impact is neither guaranteed nor predictable. The resulting adult uncertainty often emerges, inter alia, in the political reception of "youth cultures," themselves often perceived by older generations as the products of childish play threatening to carry over into "adult" culture. This scenario has repeatedly arisen in late modern Britain, particularly when youth cultures emerge within or demand access to institutions. There is always the possibility that the gift of institutional access might be withdrawn from children, the investment regarded as too risky. In chapter 6, this plays out in the perverse educational institution in *Never Let Me Go*, a dramatic and uncanny alternative history of these conflicts in Britain that imagines them through children who are reared to be killed.

Behind the scenes and themes of violence toward and from children explored in *Killing Children* lies a persistent desire to eradicate the inscrutable, uncertain, and provisional qualities the child presents to the paranoid adult gaze; and it is the same violent impulse toward the child that emerges within the fear that the institution protecting and accommodating the child's development might be permitting and generating fantasies that flourish within, but nevertheless threaten to overspill, their institutional boundaries. This fear appears (often disguised as mockery) in Brexit rhetoric. As noted previously, prominent Leavers tend to present their opponents as the products of an institutionally protected, privileged, and childish class: "snowflake" youth. Brexit rhetoric is marked by conflicts over which generation is entitled to define fantasy versus reality. Behind the mockery, fetishes, and phobias, there lies—as I argue throughout this book—a common profound fear of the uncertainty embodied by the child-as-future. Killings of and by children, apparently such unnatural acts, are regularly imagined to promise to naturalize and stabilize this—a promise pursued within various dehistoricizing, racializing, and other essentialist terms.

I have attempted to introduce this book's historical and cultural context; we need this context to understand the real and imagined killings of and by children that are the book's focus. Yet, we also need these "killing children" to understand the context—to register its severity, depth, and breadth. Profound conflicts over the future, its proper relationship to the past, and the uncertainty represented by the child are not unique to Britain. They are accelerating across a world currently facing serious challenges over the planetary and global future and over the relations between international institutions, nation-states, and nationalisms. However, *Killing Children* tries to show, through its thematic strands and detailed case studies, why the British case is of acute significance in the series of such conflicts it presents. Although the chapter sequence is not strictly chronological, the chapters nevertheless cumulatively develop a reading of Britain's recent cultural and political history alongside an argument over the challenges this provokes for reading the child-as-future.

Summary of Chapters

Chapter 2, "Thatcher's Demons and Maggie's Boys: Children and Youth in Thatcherism's Hinterland," provides a long and broad historical backstory for my themes and arguments, initially through exploring the postwar tendency toward fear of dangerous children and youth across politics and popular and literary cultures. This tendency became crucial to Thatcherism's later rhetorical demand to halt postwar and "progressive" futures and replace them by simultaneously saving the innocent child and co-opting the male child's aggressive energies into legitimized entrepreneurial aspiration. The first part of the chapter surveys these developments: from early postwar work by Rose Macaulay, Graham Greene, and William Golding; to 1960s and '70s horror films and the influential Stanley Kubrick adaptation of Anthony Burgess's *A Clockwork Orange*; to Thatcher-Era novels by Doris Lessing, Alan Hollinghurst, and Peter Ackroyd. Across these works, I argue, the aspirational yet violent male youth acts as a consistent trope for an ambivalent yet urgent threat to adult British society. Meanwhile, the child in horror films—an increasingly prevalent figure from the 1960s onwards—emerges as an important parallel to dangerous children in literature. I go on to explore how the figures of the queer child and youth further develop this sense of threat while exposing some of the contradictions of conservative reactions. For all these children and youth, their willed access to material spaces and material objects of desire appears as a persistent target of fearful anxiety throughout the texts explored in this chapter, which concludes by reading Sarah Waters's 2011 novel *The Little Stranger* as a retrospective, haunted play on overinvestment in the child in early postwar England while foreshadowing the paradoxes of Thatcher-Era aspiration in the later twentieth century. I use both *The Little Stranger* and the earlier material in the chapter to argue that queer readings often struggle as much with accommodating the risk presented by the child as do conservative reactions to the dangerous child and youth.

Chapter 3, "Boy Kings, Queerness, and Radical Nostalgia" sustains this theme while turning from broad history to examine a single case study, an anti-Thatcherite reconfiguration of British history with a child as its center: Derek Jarman's 1991 queer movie *Edward II*, a reworking of Christopher Marlowe's sixteenth-century play of the same name. This chapter explores ambivalences involved in queer retrieval of English history; it also argues that Jarman's erasure of the deadly child written by Marlowe, who was replaced by a more visibly queer but (I argue) ultimately less dangerous boy, underlines the material challenge presented by the child-as-future to progressives and conservatives alike. This chapter thus shows how peculiarly British problems over the child, rooted in the UK's late twentieth-century history and in its relationships to earlier histories and national heritage, also have fundamental and wide-ranging implications for the theory and political or critical practice of interpreting and accommodating the child-as-future.

Chapter 4, "Abduction and Abuse: Disappearing Children in the 1980s and 1990s," considers the prevalence of narratives of child abduction and abuse in the 1980s and early 1990s alongside Thatcherite ideas of organic social order and interests in child protection—retrospectively rendered macabre following the identification of major figures of the era, notably the entertainer Jimmy Savile, as child abusers. I read Ian McEwan's 1987 novel of child disappearance, *The Child in Time*, as combining an elegy for a lost child with an attack on Thatcherism's destruction—rhetorically creative but, in McEwan's telling, materially, spiritually and ecologically brutal—of the postwar future. Tracing connections between this and McEwan's later work on the film *The Good Son* (1991) and the novel *The Children Act* (2014), I argue that he shows a growing willingness to imagine the child's death as a solution to the political and personal problems of adults. I also explore Blake Morrison's extended essay, *As If* (1997), on the real murder of James Bulger—a child killed by other children—as crucial context for discourses on the child and violence as Thatcher-Era Britain transitioned into post-Thatcherism. Throughout this chapter, I consider the paradox—used by McEwan as the central conceit of *The Child in Time*—that efforts to secure the child from disappearance by making their innocence and vulnerability transparently visible increasingly disappears the real and integral opacity of children and childhood, an opacity that paradoxically emphasizes their materiality.

Chapter 5, "Children of Nowhere: Migration and Haunted Futures in Ishiguro's *A Pale View of Hills*," explores Kazuo Ishiguro's early 1980s debut novel, reading a series of ambivalent scenes and themes of child-killing haunting the book as they respond to Thatcherism's negotiation with postwar history and attempt to maintain an essentialist ethnonationalism alongside intensified participation in neoliberal globalization. *A Pale View*—through its unbearable refusal to disclose the reality of the child-killings on which it pivots—anticipates, I argue, the later disintegration of Thatcherism's competing imperatives for the future. Ishiguro's use of the migrant child as a particular object of paradoxical, paranoid adult attempts to variously protect and destroy the future is of critical significance here, and my reading further develops the themes of visibility and materiality established in the earlier chapter.

Chapter 6, "Migrant Children and Mobile Youth in Twenty-First Century British Fiction," returns to the migrant child imagined as vulnerable and to the mobile youth imagined as dangerous. The fraught, ambivalent relationship between migrant children and mobile youth allows British political and media culture, I argue, to imagine breaking the taboo on killing children with increasing openness; and early twenty-first-century British literature and film provide powerful reflections on this disturbing phenomenon. Returning to Ishiguro and his novels *When We Were Orphans* (2000) and *Never Let Me Go* (2005), alongside 2010s British fiction from Jim Crace, Melissa Harrison, and David Szalay and film from Remi Weekes, the final chapter finds children killing and being killed in fictional responses to Britain's crises over migration in the 2000s and 2010s. I argue that the migrant child's role for an adult British audience intersects with the alterity of the child in general and with the mobile generations that threaten any sense of organic stability in the early twenty-first-century UK. The figure of the migrant child helps to clarify both contemporary conflicts over interpretation and protection of children in general and the particular paradoxes of recent British history, especially in the Brexit Era, significantly defined by hostility to migration and conflict over the national position within a globalized, postcolonial, post-Empire world.

Children, in Theory

The prevailing theoretical scholarship on children in literature, film, and culture today derives from a range of psychoanalytic frameworks and from queer, gender, and broader cultural and critical theory. *Killing Children* draws heavily upon this continuing tradition while exploring features of dangerous children in recent British literature and culture that complicate and challenge it. Arguably, these British cases have not been subject to as forceful and extended theoretical treatment as the (largely) American material explored by Edelman, Bond Stockton, and Sheldon (though there is a rich body of British scholarship on children in fiction, mostly somewhat more Freudian in orientation, as I describe further later in this chapter).

Contemporary queer theory is, in key respects, a product of the 1980s. Although drawing on an older psychoanalytic legacy that reached back to Sigmund Freud's early twentieth-century innovations in theorizing sexuality and family relations, it principally grew out of 1980s developments, where the peak of what can be loosely called *post-structuralism*, especially the works of Michel Foucault and Jacques Derrida, combined with the maturing of feminist and sexuality-focused political-intellectual movements that had arisen in the 1960s and '70s and their encounters with reinvigorated rightwing counterattack during the HIV-AIDS pandemic. As the 1980s turned to the '90s, scholars such as Eve Kosofsky Sedgwick and Judith Butler began to explore the implications of queer theory for understanding childhood and adult attitudes toward it; they would later be joined by James Kincaid (with *Erotic Innocence: The Culture of Child Molesting*, published in 1998) and Lee Edelman (with his highly influential *No Future: Queer Theory and the Death Drive* in 2004). Much of this work reacted to the moral panics of 1980s and 1990s American conservatism and to Clinton-Blair Third Way neoliberalism, where conservative precepts were shorn of their surface toxicity—including, initially to a limited and later to a greater extent, toward LGBTQ+ people—while retaining their substantive ideological and political assumptions. Edelman indignantly captures a resulting intellectual hollowness:

> In its coercive universalisation [. . .] the image of the Child, not to be confused with the lived experiences of any historical children, serves to regulate political discourse [. . .] That figural Child alone embodies the citizen as an ideal, entitled to claim

full rights to its future share in the nation's good, though always at the cost of limiting the rights "real" citizens are allowed. For the social order exists to preserve for this universalised subject, this fantasmatic Child [. . .] (11)

For Edelman, the symbolic function of the Child as political-rhetorical figure is to embody the future as reproduction of a (heterosexual, nuclear-family-based) present, in terms held to be above and beyond politics and therefore open to neither challenge nor refusal: "That Child remains the perpetual horizon of every acknowledged politics, the fantasmatic beneficiary of every political intervention" (3). The purpose of this child-as-future, through whose image society is coerced, is, then, to foreclose political possibility, producing instead a "reproductive futurism." Edelman argues that the figure of the adult queer is used—most openly, but certainly not only, by homophobic rightwingers—as the opposite to this reproductive futurism, functioning instead as an embodiment of the "death drive," to use the influential, controversial explanation for perversely destructive behavior first developed by Freud in *Beyond the Pleasure Principle* (1920), refined by Jacques Lacan, and thoroughly queered by Edelman with conceptual support from Judith Butler and Leo Bersani. Edelman argues, provocatively and influentially, that resistance to reproductive futurism requires fully accepting and embracing the queer death drive (this is his "antisocial thesis") and refusing the supposedly unrefusable figure of the Child. Complicating this formulation, Edelman also argues that reproductive futurism itself contains a concealed and repressed operation of the death drive. In reducing the future to a kind of living death, its possibilities are neutered. Edelman argues, therefore, that "queerness attains its ethical value precisely insofar as it accedes to [. . .] its figural status as resistance to the viability of the social while insisting on the inextricability of such resistance from every social structure" (3). Edelman's goal is not to reshape futurism on progressive lines but to reject it utterly as keeping, in Lacanian terms, the symbolic order attached to an Imaginary that refuses access to *jouissance*, with the future marking "the impossible place of an Imaginary past [. . .] as the site at which being and meaning are joined as One" (10).

Edelman's cultural context and political framing is specifically American; his intellectual context, however, is drawn primarily from Lacanian psychoanalysis, which is both abstract and Eurocentric. This is somewhat characteristic of much of the theoretical work on childhood in the past few decades, which tends to be referentially American but somewhat vague in delimiting its geographic and cultural scope, moving between an overwhelmingly US-based frame of cultural reference and a body of theory that originates in Europe and which, particularly in its earlier twentieth-century versions, freely made universalist claims through a casual imperialism (this is certainly true of Freud, who is an ancestor of most modern theoretical work on childhood). Recent theoretical scholarship on children from Bond Stockton, Breslow, and Sheldon has begun to engage more deeply and expansively, and with more careful historical specificity, with issues of postcolonial and global childhoods and migration (the latter being the major focus of my final two chapters), but perhaps inevitably still with primarily North American and Anglocentric orientations and frames of reference. My own focus on the UK is, of course, only a relatively marginal expansion of this in global terms; but the migration theme (the framing through which issues of race and postcolonialism tend to be addressed within mainstream British politics and public discourse) hopefully at least introduces issues of significance for how Western, Anglocentric countries—and specifically the UK, with certain characteristics not straightforwardly shared on the other side of the Atlantic—relate to the rest of the world, especially via the fraught figures of the migrant child and mobile youth.

The cultural context of the late twentieth-century US does, of course, have significant elements in common with the UK during the same period (though every parallel deserves many caveats): both countries saw powerful conservative ascendancies in the 1980s, reacting explicitly against the postwar expansion of state welfare and progressive social movements, with this later dividing into a dominant neoliberalism centrist faction and a socially conservative faction. These contexts are reflected in the material covered by this book; Jarman's *Edward II*, for example, is thoroughly reactive to the homophobic politics of the 1980s. In both countries, the collapse of the Soviet Union in the 1990s and subsequent neoliberal consensus under American hegemony led to a certain complacency regarding further historical change, infamously captured by Francis Fukuyama's thesis in *The End of History and the Last Man* (1992). (Ishiguro's millennial novel *When We Were Orphans* (2000), discussed in chapter 6, reflects this period in depicting hegemonic globalizations and their crises.) Both countries saw the interruption of their unequally shared hegemony in a spate of post-Cold War conflicts during the 1990s, which significantly accelerated after 9/11 (with the UK effectively serving as the US's first partner in the War on Terror). Both were major international actors in the global financial crisis of 2007–2008, and both have experienced long political effects from that crisis. Both saw the presumed interests of the child and youth prioritized under the neoliberal consensus, with 1980s conservative panics over the implications for children of progressive movements on sexuality and gender moving slowly away from the mainstream under the 1990s to 2000s neoliberal ascendancy only to be dramatically revived in the 2010s and early 2020s (Rozsa; Armitage, 22–23). Even though these moral panics have ebbed and flowed in the UK, the popular obsessions with child abuse and abduction that became established during the 1980s influenced literature and culture throughout the subsequent period, as I argue in chapter 4.

Scholarship on children and their representation during this period has been influenced by all these developments, though it is only starting to grapple with the most recent phenomena, particularly the increasingly explicit rejection of the child-as-future as moral imperative in 2010s and early 2020s rightwing politics. Edelman's *No Future* came at a particular point within this history, when neoliberal centrism had peaked in the Clinton Era but seemed to be under renewed rightwing—and in the US, specifically conservative evangelical—assault. Edelman's identification of the opposition between the celebrated, innocent child-as-future and the queer death drive has justifiably influenced subsequent scholarship on childhood (including this book). His basic theses are persuasive, at least for *No Future*'s own moment, and have considerable explanatory and interpretative power. His work emphasizes the moral and political absolutism surrounding the image of the child and its resulting close relationship to both material and symbolic violence—a major concern of *Killing Children*. Despite this, I argue that the material explored in this book leads us, in its final analysis, to significantly diverge from Edelman's conclusions, particularly regarding the child's place in history, which I read as being more complicated, ambiguous, and dangerous than the reproductive futurism thesis acknowledges.

Edelman advocates for queerness as "a refusal [. . .] of every substantialisation of identity [. . .] and, by extension, of history as linear narrative (the poor man's teleology) in which meaning succeeds in revealing itself—*as itself*—through time" (4). But there is another way of understanding history, rather than through the terms of teleology or negation; this would emphasize historical contingency alongside risk and uncertainty as preconditions of historical phenomena that have constantly reshaped and undermined the neoliberal certainties, whose dominance Edelman seems to regard as total (implicitly, he seems to have accepted the end of history diagnosis that later twenty-first-century events would frustrate). For all the brilliance of Edelman's theorization of the Child as figure, the future is not merely rhetorically or figuratively embodied in children but materially embodied in them too; we cannot know it, but we have to make time and space for it. The future's materiality in the child inhabits it not as teleology, but alterity.

Edelman acknowledges the distance between the figure of the Child and actual children but crucially does not seem to attribute significant agency to the latter in challenging the former. Building upon more recent scholarship from theorists such as Kathryn Bond Stockton, Stephen Bruhm, and Rebekah Sheldon, and taking my cue from the fictional children who are persistently stranger than any theoretical framing can fully capture, I avowedly *do* attribute such agency to them. I also insist on their ambiguity and fundamental opacity toward adults. As Bruhm says:

> While Edelman's incisive analysis offers us purchase on many kinds of normalizing representations of the Child, it imagines children as ostensibly stable and promissory figures who will always seduce us to fighting on their side. Put in other terms, Edelman's Child is always only sentimental, never belonging to any other representational category. And while such a stabilizing move is ultimately necessary for his profoundly destabilizing argument, students of genres like science fiction or the gothic know otherwise: those readers habitually encounter children who are as likely to sterilize, poison, or explosively decimate the future as they are to ensure it. (Bruhm, "The Global Village of the Damned," 157)

I would take the critique further here: Edelman's argument may be destabilizing, yet it is ultimately not clear that the schema it sets out is. Edelman's goal is, by encouraging refusal of reproductive futurism, to access jouissance. But jouissance, as formulated by Lacan, cannot function as a steady-state entity; it arises as an excess that can neither be embraced nor refused,[11] contrary to Edelman's advocacy for access to it via simultaneous refusal of reproductive futurism and accession to the queer death drive. It is neither the product of teleological history, nor of an end of history. Ironically, children themselves, certainly on the evidence considered in this book, reflect and seek these qualities of jouissance. A revealed teleology promotes stability—and, certainly, many of the adults in the narratives explored here try to achieve this by securing the image of the child to circumscribe the politics of the future in much the way Edelman describes (though these are also often stories of such attempts coming unstuck). But the children explored here accelerate and interrupt the flow of adult time; they seize objects, times, and spaces from adult society prematurely and perversely. In doing so, they are, of course, trying to secure a different future for themselves, though often this future takes the form of the immediate present (reflecting Phillips's sense of the ambivalent relationship between play and development, 21).

Some of the ambivalences and contradictions over the child's place in a psychoanalytic schema and theoretical framework derive from the original conception of the death drive in *Beyond the Pleasure Principle*, where Freud famously refers to the child who plays the repetitious Fort/Da game to cope with maternal absence while setting up the observational and theoretical basis for his case for a death drive. In this game, a boy's repeated throwing away and retrieval of a small object is interpreted by Freud as the child's attempt to consolingly restore his mastery of an environment in which the mother is not continuously present. Though Freud ostensibly uses this game as a contrast to the conditions for the death drive—and as an example of how, in many contexts, repetition of an apparently painful experience does ultimately produce a pleasurable outcome—he returns to it in ways that imply an underlying ambivalence about the relationship between the child's creative actions and motivations and the destructions of the death drive (which, according to him, do not rationally return to pleasure but rather to the stability of death).[12] Many of the children I explore in this book not only reflect these ambivalences and general resistance to fully secure theorization, but they also question the substitutive tendency in psychoanalytic interpretation of childhood ambitions and satisfactions that Freud expresses so clearly in his account of the Fort/Da game. As we shall see, even when material objects appear to be bound up in the deaths of adults, these children use them in ways that undermine this comforting, if gothic, adult understanding of their significance.

Although Freud's idea of the death drive is useful for my readings here, they also often confound or at least query it. In this, they reflect how the death drive has long, as Todd Dufresne points out (20), been surrounded by psychoanalytic debates over the fundamental role of instinctual drives (as Freud favored) versus that of external conditions (as favored by, for example, Alfred Adler). In the literary and film texts considered here, the protagonists (often, of course, a child, a youth, or an adult driven by motivations derived from childhood) combine the perversity and force of an instinctual, obscure, and seemingly inescapable drive with its direction toward a particular material or spatial object (often exposing a very different fault line, between organicist security and neoliberal mobility, along the way). For this reason, I use my readings not to offer a comprehensive psycho-theoretical schema in the way Edelman does, but rather to show the role of the text in combining obscure motivation and material object to expose an alterity in the child, an alterity of real political and historical consequence.

Are these protagonists, for all their apparent obscurity, perhaps nevertheless ultimately trying to achieve what Edelman characterizes as the "fantasmatic order of reality in which the subject's alienation would vanish into the seamlessness of identity" (8)? Certainly, the attempt to achieve a unified selfhood on better terms than those offered by the adult world is a common motivation of the dangerous children studied here. Things are often more complicated than this, though, as at the end of Sarah Waters's 2011 novel *The Little Stranger* (explored in chapter 2), where the protagonist Faraday, deeply affected by the intersection between the memory of his deceased mother and his class insecurities, finally achieves control over the grand house he has sought throughout the narrative, having been implicated in killings along the way. There are powerful hints that this "taking of control"—a "retrieval" of a control that previously only existed as fantasy—to use Brexit-esque language, heals, albeit on the most perverse terms, his original childhood alienation. So, in a sense, Edelman's thesis is fulfilled in this vision of unity between self and world and between Symbolic and Imaginary. However, in *The Little Stranger* this vision is achieved through violent disruption of the established order, in ways that fundamentally challenge the stability of neoliberal teleology, revealing the roiling, chaotic aggression underneath it; and Faraday's drive finally finds stable investment not in political narrative or teleological category but in possession of a material object that is also a material and temporal space (the house itself). If this possession is to be sustained, it will be necessarily in actual history, with all its contingencies. In reading this novel, the child's obsession with the grand house (a surprisingly common object of desire in the texts explored here) and its adult aftermath shows the depth and power of modern British conflicts between neoliberalism and nationalism, especially when they invest in the same object. While the satisfaction Faraday finds in the house exposes its own conceptual ambiguity, for the theory-minded reader, between the theoretical pillars of the death drive and the pleasure principle, there is an unresolved ambivalence that finally affirms, again, the alterity of the child—an alterity itself threatened by both neoliberalism and nationalism. So, with this narrative as with others considered here, an immediate historicist reading is underpinned by a broader and more fundamental theoretical significance, which leads in turn to a more fundamental reading of the stakes implicated in the political history.

Edelman's argument in *No Future* is based on the idea that the queer always persists as a constitutive excess outside futurist teleology, the part of existence that this teleological vision can never either absorb or erase. Arguably, Faraday's object here (the house) becomes *too* satisfying for Edelman's theory, replacing queerness as the deliverer of jouissance in that it provides a pleasure beyond that available through the Symbolic order, even if it certainly incorporates such pleasure. (The house and the protagonist are themselves in many respects queer, but neither are totally or unambiguously so, as we shall see.) In this book, we find the child (including the child persisting within the adult) often being a little stranger than any category of queerness, signaling the challenge to all secure theoretical categorization that the child presents.

As Kathryn Bond Stockton points out in *The Queer Child* (2009), much as the queerness Edelman describes may be in opposition to the figure of the Child, it is not something securely separate from actual children—quite the contrary. But as soon as we acknowledge actual children's possession of this queerness, they complicate it. Edelman tacitly takes the queer (identified with the death drive) as a site of stability; arguably, nothing is ultimately so stable or substantial as negation because negation always does the same work, irrespective of historical circumstances. But if the Child and its opposite, the queer, are stable positions on the theoretical compass, actual children are never so stable; the idea of a queer child merely (ironically) clarifies this reality.

This is the point at which Bond Stockton, also drawing on scholars of childhood Steven Bruhm and Natasha Hurley, picks up from Edelman to explore the children he mentions only in passing: the children "that must live inside the figure of the child" (*The Queer Child*, 5) and trouble it with a form of living that conflicts with both reproductive futurism and the queer death drive Edelman posits against it. Arguing that the queer child distils and thereby exposes qualities that actually apply to every child (3), and drawing on Freud's framing of homosexuality as an arrested development (23–24), Bond Stockton finds an alternative model in "sideways growth":

children's "supposed gradual growth, their suggested slow unfolding [. . .] has been relentlessly figured as vertical movement upwards (hence, 'growing up') toward full stature, marriage, work, reproduction, and the loss of childishness." Against this, Bond Stockton is interested in "the horizontal—what spreads sideways—or sideways and backwards—more than a simple thrust toward height and forward time" (4). This has a parallel with how fiction itself operates as a kind of sideways growth relative to history. Hence, the queer child in literature and film "illuminates [. . .] why our notions of history are challenged by the waywardness of fictions" (9). Even the fetishized, innocent Child critiqued by Edelman tends to eventually show signs of such waywardness, Bond Stockton claims (29–33)—a claim borne out by several fictional children described in this book, too, from Prince Edward in *Edward II*, to Rowan Morrison in *The Wicker Man* (1973), to the ghostly Susan Ayres in *The Little Stranger*.

Whereas Edelman, despite his protests to the contrary, in practice relies on positivistic recognition of the queer—which has recognizable qualities as a social force, according to his case studies—and on the affirmation and embrace of these qualities, Bond Stockton is concerned, as am I, with what is opaque and troubling even in the categories such qualities produce. Of course, pragmatically, we are still bound to define, recognize, and analyze through categories and case studies (on the model Freud first established for narrative interpretation of troubling children); but the ultimate purpose of this, at least here, is not to affirm a knowable quality behind or within the opacity but to consider the historical and political consequences this opacity produces and what we might do with them, intellectually, politically, and ethically.

I seek to achieve this purpose by exploring a wide range of literature, film, and cultural material that features children killing or being killed in late twentieth- and early twenty-first-century Britain. In doing so, I build on those who have responded to or followed Edelman with studies that draw attention to the opacity, complexity, and variety of the child beyond the figure of the Child deployed in reproductive futurism. Bond Stockton does this in relation to (mostly) modern American queer fiction and film. Steven Bruhm does it in relation to the gothic tradition, the horror genre, and to aspects of postwar history that predate and complicate the moment of all-encompassing neoliberal hegemony that so dominates in *No Future*. His work has taken these issues into the British context, noticeably in relation to the disturbing utopian children in the British sci-fi-horror movie *Village of the Damned* (1960), which has influenced my discussion of children in the horror genre in the next chapter (and which, in turn, influences readings throughout this book). Rebekah Sheldon, meanwhile, has explored children as the future in contemporary eco-apocalyptic literature through a feminist, queer, and ecocritical reading in *The Child to Come: Life After the Human Catastrophe* (2016), which critically considers how eco-futurism repeats some of the same fundamentally defensive and essentialist beliefs seen in reproductive futurism—and how fictional children challenge this tendency.

Another important insight Bond Stockton provides—channeling Freud's original version—is that the queer child and the adult this child becomes are not securely distinct from heterosexuals, whose development ostensibly takes a more normal path (both are haunted by their "ghostly child" within). If, in this account, all children are thoroughly queer, they are also a little stranger, and certainly more dangerous, than "queer" is typically taken to imply, as I argue in this book. There is a complicated nexus between queerness, violence, and theory at work here. The death drive, as theorized by Edelman, seems like an indisputably radical, and indeed destructive, force. Its power derives partly from how Edelman refuses to contemplate creativity before destruction; the latter must be embraced fully, not in the hope of any (re)productibility. However, the gesture of embrace is a much more reassuring and less costly demand, I suggest, than giving up time and space to the child whose ambition, whether we theorize it in opposition or alignment to the death drive, may more prosaically turn out to be to our material, political, or epistemological detriment (to some extent it *must* be so since the immediate interests of different generations inevitably vary). In effectively allowing us to escape not only neoliberal teleology but also history as a process of political and generational conflict and negotiation, the queer death drive as theorized by Edelman offers us, in the final instance, a surprisingly cozy deal. I argue that the child who is potentially but not securely or exclusively queer, who offers violence to adults in ways that invoke but also destabilize formulations of a death drive, and who seeks to achieve satisfaction in time rather than outside it works to challenge this deal. This child demands attention because, for one thing, the Child is no longer securely or unequivocally the figure of conservative-centrist celebratory futurism in the way that they were in the 1990s and early 2000s (a point I expand upon later, especially in chapter 6).

In this context, the child embodies the future—not in a teleological sense but in a material, mundane, and yet utterly opaque way. This opacity is so troubling that it sometimes leads adults to kill, and far more often to imagine killing, the child, as we shall see throughout the texts considered here. It also means that the child can kill, or be imagined to kill, to achieve the future they want (or just the time and space to create it) on a different path or more accelerated timetable than the adult order permits. I describe these issues as both historical—in the sense that they are concerned with historical, not teleological, time—and institutional—in that institutions formalize and regulate the time and space given to the child-as-future and seek to provide the objects and texts to shape the nature of that future.

In developing this argument, I draw on a psychoanalytically driven body of British scholarship on children, which differs somewhat from the American tradition of Edelman, Bond Stockton, Hurley, Bruhm, Sheldon, and others in that it tends to be more Freudian than Lacanian and is less wholly embedded in—though always relevant, and sometimes related, to—queer theory. A powerful early example is Jacqueline Rose's *The Case of Peter Pan, or the Impossibility of Children's Fiction* (first published 1984, revised 1992). Here, Rose uses the complicated textual, performance, and rhetorical history of Peter Pan—both the texts and the character—to create a virtuoso investigation of childhood in (adult) culture informed by Freud and applied to late twentieth-century British cultural history. Arguing that "*Peter Pan* lays bare a basic social and psychic structure—that so-called perversion resides in the house of innocence, alarming not because it is alien to innocence but because it is already there" (xii), Rose develops her case against this recent history and particularly against the hypocrisies and repressed contradictions in Thatcherite attitudes toward and policies for children. She highlights how organicist ideas about childhood have been invested in nationalism and in Thatcherite attacks on public institutions.

Rose connects her themes to crises over childhood innocence and pedophilia, identified as "one of the traumas of the 1980s" (xi). Her approach broadly aligns with those later taken by Kincaid, Edelman, and Bond Stockton in identifying ideas of the child's absolute "innocence[,] not as a property of childhood but as a portion of adult desire," revived in the 1980s via "myths of primordial innocence, racial purity, [and] Victorian values" (xii). Rose links this to Thatcher-Era homophobic policy (xiii). Throughout, she insists on the ultimate opacity of children and childhood, a theme she elucidates through the peculiar tradition of constant rewriting of *Peter Pan* such that it is, unusually, a canonical narrative without a fixed text. Rose insists, though, that this opacity—from the gaze of adults—is not merely a theoretical issue but one of material and historical import with acute significance in late twentieth-century (as well as earlier) British history. She also warns against simply translating *Peter Pan* from affirmation of conservative innocence into a radical text by diagnosing its transgressive qualities, noting that if it is "read today as pure transgression, the risk is that it will simply re-emerge on the other side of its more familiar mythology" (xiii), while its essential legibility to the adult gaze remains constant, merely reframed. This radicalism-by-recognition, Rose implies, is a route into unwitting conservatism, a contention I develop in this book.

Rose's study is echoed in the psychoanalytic theorist Adam Phillips's *The Beast in the Nursery* (1998). Both of these works share a commitment to appreciating the ambiguity and opacity of the child's ambitions, creating theoretical space for them without containing or theorizing them away. Phillips achieves this by advancing a certain skepticism toward the death drive, while both he and Rose return instead to Freud's earlier interests in the child's capacity for pleasure and satisfaction (especially in *Three Essays on the Theory of Sexuality*, 1905). As Phillips puts it, critiquing the legacy of Freud's work on childhood under Winnicott, Klein, and Lacan (with the latter, as we have seen, becoming a particular influence on queer-theoretical accounts of children):

> The theoretical vogue for lack and insufficiency has become a perverse boast; a way of disqualifying the child's very real imaginative achievements. As though the child is somehow cursed by what he doesn't have, by what's missing (competence, sexual maturity, independence and so on). [. . .]
>
> If there is a vividly frustrated child at the heart of psychoanalysis—a child that has stolen the show with his anguish, a child whose abject resourcelessness is somehow exemplary—there is another Freudian child who has been mislaid [. . .] with an astonishing capacity for pleasures and, indeed, the pleasures of interest [. . .] This child who can be deranged by hope and anticipation—by an ice-cream—seems to have a passionate love of life, a curiosity about life [. . .] a kind of ecstasy of opportunity. (21)

I agree with Philips's diagnosis here; yet, the qualities he identifies are no less difficult or dangerous for adults than queerness and the death drive.

Their satisfaction requires access to material objects and resources, and the times and spaces on which to use them, on terms that the adult may struggle to reconcile with their own version of the future. Phillips captures this when advocating for an anti-reductionist psychoanalysis: "We don't," he observes, "believe that the football fan isn't really interested in football; we believe that he is far more interested in football than he can let himself know" (14). Similarly, many of the dangerous children in *Killing Children* cause trouble for adult society by being excessively interested in things for which their age, class, gender, nationality, migration status, or race would constrain the fulfilment of that interest; often, these things are even quite conservative objects of political, aesthetic, and material value. Phillips, in contrast to Edelman, thinks that objects of desire can be satisfying: indeed, sometimes—from the perspective of adults—dangerously satisfying. I agree, and we shall see multiple examples with (desired and material) objects that support this case, from the house in *The Little Stranger* to the severed heads handled by the child-king Edward III in *Edward II*.

I am influenced, then, by the theorizations of children and childhood offered by Rose and Phillips and by other scholars working in their British psychoanalytic tradition, such as Vicky Lebeau with her study *Childhood and Cinema* (2008). Both this British tradition and its North American parallel have a shared basis in psychoanalytic theory and in cultural histories of childhood that chart the long legacies of earlier modern, and especially Romantic and Victorian, ideals for understanding children in the twentieth and twenty-first centuries: notably Philipp Ariès's *l'enfant et la Vie Familiale Sous l'Ancien Regime*, translated as *Centuries of Childhood: A Social History of Family Life* (1962), Reinhard Kuhn's *Corruption in Paradise: The Child in Western Literature* (1983), Carolyn Steedman's *Strange Dislocations: Childhood and the Idea of Human Interiority 1780–1930* (1998), and Anne Higonnet's *Pictures of Innocence: The History and Crisis of Ideal Childhood* (1998).

I have also used work by UK-based scholars whose relationship with psychoanalytic and queer theories is looser but who nevertheless overlap with their approaches in exploring children's role in recent British cultural history. Particularly important instances are Carol Chillington Rutter's *Shakespeare and Child's Play: Performing Lost Boys on Stage and Screen* (2007) and Geraldine Cousin's *Playing for Time: Stories of Lost Children, Ghosts and the Endangered Present in Contemporary Theatre* (2007); although both of these have primarily a theatrical focus, they are ambitious, wide-ranging studies of representations of children in the period with which I am concerned. These studies, like Rose's, Phillips's and Lebeau's more directly psychoanalytical work, emphasize the persistent opacity and ambiguity of children that hedges the politics of their representation. The American sense of a dominant centrist celebration of the child as the presumed universalizing goal of politics and culture is on shakier ground on the other side of the Atlantic, and children as objects of real or imagined adult violence is a consistent theme in this body of UK-based scholarship. With this book, of course, I sustain this emphasis. I have also been influenced by dialogue with new and emerging scholarship on children in literature and culture from Chris Vardy, Katherine Kruger, Jen Baker, Catherine Sloan, Ben Liberatore, and other early-career colleagues working in the field.

The British Case

Throughout *Killing Children*, we shall see some potential explanations emerge for the prevalence of adult interest in imagining the child who kills or must be killed in British histories between Thatcherism and Brexit. With a phenomenon so culturally, psychosocially, and politically complex, no single exclusive and definitive answer will be forthcoming. I will argue, however, that British politics and culture during this period retains a persistent tendency toward organicist ideology, and its celebration of neoliberal aspiration—which naturally has recourse to the figure of the child-as-future—is much less easily integrated into this organicist tendency (despite Thatcherism's vigorous attempt) than is arguably the case in the USA.

My comparisons to American contexts here are driven by two factors: Firstly, because North American scholarship dominates in contemporary critical childhood studies, and the fact that British fiction on killing children challenges (as I argue) some of the arguments and assumptions made by that scholarship shows the value of this comparative exercise. Secondly, because the relationship with the USA as the global hegemon has framed and sometimes dominated British national identity formulation and international positioning since the Second World War, particularly in the era between Thatcherism's rise and the Brexit referendum; this is an important contextual theme in its own right.

The postimperial British context[13] of migration and exposure to transnational institutions, the context that Brexit attempts to resolve and reset, has repeatedly brought a pressure that exposes this gap between the organicist and the aspirational. This, I argue, leads to a hostility toward institutions in general as historical and political, rather than organic, entities, reflecting the indeterminacy—and thus the risk—of the children they accommodate.

To summarize the political backdrop to these phenomena requires almost infinite caveats; whereas in the USA the idea of a necessary structural conflict between nationalism and cosmopolitanism is clearly aligned with the political Right and is challenged by some powerful counternarratives about the role of immigration in American national identity, in the UK the suspicion of such a conflict has arguably never been far from the political center ground (hence, for example, "Euroskepticism" remaining a significant force even during the premiership of the rhetorically internationalist Tony Blair), and the available counternarratives have less established purchase upon mainstream ideas of national identity. Simultaneously, even at the high point of "end of history" neoliberal Anglo-American ascendancy from the late 1980s to the early 2000s, the UK's position as a postimperial country seeking a compensatory role that could never match the global power with which it entered the twentieth century clearly placed it in a different historical position to that held by the USA. Both countries have defined their later modern role in part by their victory in the Second World War, but in the British case, this was also marked by being both an achievement against historic rivals (the continental European powers) and the largest-scale enterprise undertaken by the British Empire, with Brexiteer rhetoric strongly emphasizing the former. For the UK, the postwar period's economic and social changes were also marked by more radical political change (in the shape of the postwar institutions introduced by Clement Attlee's Labour government of 1945–1951 and the social-democratic consensus that prevailed for some time afterwards) and less secure economic prosperity relative to the same period in the USA as well as by the accelerated dissolution of empire.

There were significant consequences of this for the risks that the child-as-future was taken to present, as we shall see throughout *Killing Children*. It is in their shared orientation toward these risks that theoretical and literary scholarship and political history provide a combined explanatory framework for the intensity with which adults imagined children killing and needing to be killed. The characteristics of the British case I have outlined in this chapter could and did lead to a more zero-sum attitude toward the future, a sense that the ambition of the young might *necessarily* be a danger to adults and the order of things they cherished, leading children's imaginations—as expressed through political rhetoric, literature, film, and culture as a whole—more readily toward violence, even the most taboo forms of violence.

These are, I suggest, important issues to return to during a period when intergenerational conflict is ever-intensifying and the moral status conventionally attributed to the figure of the child increasingly fails to hold, its function as a political guarantee no longer secure. This is a period when earlier panics over children's knowledge of LGBTQ+ existence have been revived and redirected toward transgender children accused of prematurely wanting to take agency to change their own bodies; a period when the ambitions of children are threatened by intensifying international emergencies and renewed nationalisms; a period when all forms of pleasure and access to pleasure are relentlessly politicized. Focusing on scenes and themes of children killing and needing to be killed in British culture from Thatcherism to Brexit is to create a very narrow snapshot of the contexts for these developments—but it is a telling one.

There are certain dimensions of these issues and their contexts that I am not able to cover in detail in this book or whose representation here is constrained by my own limitations. The history of the UK during the late twentieth and early twenty-first centuries has been significantly shaped by the devolution of government in Scotland and Wales and by conflict, post-conflict evolution, and continuing instabilities in Northern Ireland. Unfortunately, these developments have little direct representation in the body of material I explore here, and this book has a strong Anglocentrism; the monarchy, aristocrats, villages, country houses, boarding schools, and strong presence of London in the texts explored here all signify a hegemonic Englishness, one weighted toward southern and upper-class objects of authority and desire. These are important, of course, precisely because children and youth access and use them in ways that develop tensions, or worse, with the dominant adult culture. On the other hand, as I shall argue, we shouldn't necessarily adopt overly quick or complacent notions of children and youth queering or otherwise radicalizing these objects and spaces, many of which remain fundamentally conservative in nature.

Another major context for the UK in this period that mainly appears here as a parallel or contextual concern rather than the overwhelming focus is the legacy of the British Empire. Though the bulk of legal and constitutional decolonization preceded the rise of Thatcherism, elements of it were ongoing into the core period covered by this book (notably with the handover of Hong Kong in 1997). Although some of this remains ostensibly in the background rather than the foreground in my readings, this is partly because public discourse in the UK tends to acknowledge and explore these issues primarily through arguments over (im)migration, which forms the focus of my penultimate and final chapters, and latterly through the battles over national identity and understanding of Britain's historical position created by Brexit. The UK's postimperial realities receive wide-ranging if subtle treatments from Kazuo Ishiguro in *A Pale View of Hills* (1982) and *When We Were Orphans* (2000), considered in my penultimate and final chapters respectively.

I have been unable to encompass any detailed reading of the COVID-19 era—when the UK, like almost every country, experienced a dramatic rupture in public and everyday life, the political and sociocultural consequences of which are still playing out—though I do refer to the increased prevalence of conspiracy theories about children during this period early in chapter 4.

In my readings of children, childhood, and youth, boys and young men tend to feature somewhat more frequently than girls and young women, though this is by no means exclusively the case: the first textual reading in the next chapter features a dangerous girl, Rose Macaulay's Barbary, and girls feature prominently as threats to adults in the horror movies considered later in that chapter; McEwan's novel *The Child in Time*, discussed in chapter 4, focuses on a girl's disappearance; and girls play important roles as objects of adult paranoia over migration and its traumas in the Ishiguro, Harrison, Crace, and Weekes texts explored in chapters 5 and 6. The preponderance of males should be understood in relation to how competing visions of neoliberalism and nationalism during the period have introduced obsessions with entrepreneurial, aspirational, and fearful qualities, as well as with a capacity for violence, stereotypically associated with boys and male youths. I have generally allowed the gender dynamics involved in all this to emerge implicitly rather than forming a primary or explicit object of my analysis.

Despite these and other limitations, I hope that *Killing Children* provides a compelling picture of children who must kill or be killed in the interests of the future in British fiction from Thatcherism to Brexit and that it stimulates more of the curiosity about this field that first provoked it.

Chapter 2

Thatcher's Demons and Maggie's Boys
Children and Youth in Thatcherism's Hinterlands

Thatcherism and the End of the Postwar Future

> Children are at risk, criminals prosper, men of violence flourish, the nightmare world of *A Clockwork Orange* becomes a reality.
>
> —Margaret Thatcher, "Speech to the Conservative Party Conference, October 13, 1978"

> Indeed, this was a period of obsessive and naïve interest in "youth."
>
> —Margaret Thatcher on the 1960s, *The Path to Power*, 153

On reaching power in 1979, the leaders of the political project known as Thatcherism attempted to halt the futures that had been pursued in postwar Britain—from the immediate postwar period to 1960s and '70s progressive movements—and to replace them with an alternative of their own making. This political and economic project was also profoundly cultural. Its eponymous leader established her *-ism* in part by drawing upon a series of powerful tropes—often derived from literary, film, and popular culture—that associated the postwar and progressive futures with dangerous children and youth, confirming that these futures were (as the Sex Pistols infamously claimed in 1977, long before Lee Edelman) really "no future" at all.

This chapter reviews the depth and breadth of the obsession with dangerous children and youth in Thatcherism's hinterlands and considers its implications; it explores the ambivalent relationship, between condemnation and absorption, of children and youth with the cultural politics of Thatcherism itself; and, finally, it turns to a twenty-first-century novel, set in the early postwar period, that redraws their danger from a post-Thatcherite lens. This is deliberately a panoramic chapter, seeking to convey the extent and variety—but also the underlying connectedness—of representations of children and youth as violently dangerous, if also energetic and aspirational, during this period. Here, the creatively destructive child exposes the close lines between Thatcher's favored youth and fetishized children and their abject doppelgängers and finds in them a highly consequential traffic between popular and literary culture, theory, and politics. Throughout, the will to imagine killing of or by the child underlines the severity of the anxieties at stake.

I have described Brexit as a dissolution and renegotiation of a union between nationalism, social conservatism, and neoliberalism. This chapter describes how fears and fetishes of children and youth earlier formed an important backdrop and series of overinvested figures in the forging of that union within the evolving, long-running political project known as Thatcherism. Reaching back to the early postwar period, and through the 1960s and '70s, we see Thatcherism's revision of the future fundamentally shaped and framed by a later twentieth-century history where the child became a source of horror and the youth a figure of fearful violence—if also one often vested with aspirations and ambitions. These figures attracted powerful responses from (and were sometimes already shaped by) theory, especially via the postwar spread of psychoanalytically underpinned approaches to childhood, and from conservative countertheories or anti-theories. The literary examples considered here not only register, parody, and interrogate this, they also, I argue, present the child as fundamentally challenging for any theoretical capture.

A key aspect of this argument involves considering the relationship between the child—typically presumed to be innocent, vulnerable and in need of protection, though the children here of course threaten such expectations—and the youth, especially the male youth, in the in-between age bracketed by childhood and adulthood. Margaret Thatcher herself regarded addressing the threat of dangerous youth as central to her political mission, focusing on their alleged capacity for a social destruction, always with potential for actual violence, that began in childhood and in the fracturing of the nuclear family (and, by extension, of contained and civilized masculinity). Thatcher acknowledged no border between morality and politics, articulating her economic and social agendas as a single project rooted in the values inculcated in her own childhood.[1] She regarded the children of single mothers, alongside other diverse family models emerging from 1960s and '70s social change, as generating "graffiti, drug trafficking, vandalism and youth gangs" (*Path to Power* 549). However, if youth culture was dangerous, it was also trivial: a "world of make-believe" and "perverse pride" (153). Behind a social threat lies an epistemological one, a risk to reality itself, in the form of dangerous *pleasure*, whose attractiveness to the young seems contagious—and the pleasures of drugs, sex, and violence were only the most vivid manifestations of this. Conservative fears over the future often emerged in this period, as they still do, through imagining children's fantasies going out of control and beginning to occupy a dangerous amount of real space, even finding themselves—in the youth—on the cusp of adult realization.

The risk of the dangerous child-as-future repeatedly takes on a very real and material form in the texts considered here and in the spaces and objects for which the child demands access or possession—often in ways that are illicit, illegitimate, or illegal from an adult perspective. This is tied, we shall find, to such material spaces, particularly houses, being ambivalent embodiments of both aspirational social mobility and organicist beliefs about social and national value. Often, the attempts by children and youth to access these assets also complicate any straightforward theoretical categorization or affirmation of their own desires. Suggestively, several texts here include various failed theorists alongside their dangerous children.

In Thatcherite rhetoric, the progressive and radical left of the 1960s, '70s, and '80s was itself a monstrous child of its postwar heritage, the grotesque growth from a corrupted seed. This attitude was particularly directed toward LGBTQ+ and antiracist activists, both cast as the "Loony Left" and as threats to children's integrity and innocence. Alongside these targets, and supposedly causally related to them, fears of "delinquent" children and youth—already a staple trope for fears of social breakdown since the 1950s, aligned with the increasing presence of teenagers with leisure time and spending power (Campbell 101-03)—grew. These dangerous youngsters (overwhelmingly, but not exclusively, young men) were Thatcherism's permanent horror figures: always attacked, yet never successfully erased (as we shall see, their function as Thatcherism's foil endured even beyond the Thatcher governments). They repeatedly featured in Thatcher's 1970s speeches and interviews on the denuded and perverse future supposedly emerging under "socialist" Britain and encouraged by leftwing theorists.

This often involved recourse to motifs from popular and indeed literary culture, as in Thatcher's speech to her 1978 party conference: "When a rule of law breaks down, fear takes over [. . .] families feel unsafe even in their own homes, children are at risk, criminals prosper, men of violence flourish, the nightmare world of *A Clockwork Orange* becomes a reality." Building on this invocation, Thatcher continued on to refer to "young thugs attacking the elderly." It is perhaps unlikely that she actually read or viewed *A Clockwork Orange*,[2] but her speech nevertheless indicates how literary and popular culture operated in a symbiotic relationship with "real" politics, as did non-literary social theorizing. A few months before the aforementioned speech, Thatcher appears to have read Patricia Morgan's *Delinquent Fantasies* (Joseph), an anti-Theory work of theory driven by hostility to Freudian psychoanalysis and to "the rapid dissemination of the latter as Psychology in the social science boom of the sixties, with its enormous influence on child-rearing, education and social work" (Morgan 38) having become perniciously combined with "a vague Marxism" (39). Morgan sought to challenge all of this with a brisk essentialism that considered social relations as inevitably reflecting permanent human flaws and that was skeptical about the role of institutions as distinct from mainstream society (126–27).

Later, when Thatcherism reached the zenith of its political power, two quite different pieces of legislation, passed only months apart, underlined its sustained interest in the child at threat—and, latent behind them, the child *as* threat. The 1989 Children Act (after which Ian McEwan would later name his 2014 novel, explored in chapter 4), required that the child's interests take priority in every situation where the authorities are required to determine them. Another law, the Local Government Act 1988, notoriously prohibited the "teaching of the acceptability of homosexuality as a pretended family relationship" in its Clause 28. The loaded use of *pretended* indicated that this was part of a battle over reality itself—not a dispute merely over policy, but rather over the natural, inherent value of the heterosexual family that the Loony Left was ludicrously and dangerously attempting to suppress. This battle was over recognition of reality and, thus, framed in quasi-visual and essentialist terms rather than as a matter of democratic political choice or of the legitimate autonomy of institutional policies. The proximate cause of the moral panic that produced this legislation concerned certain books being provided to schools controlled by the leftist Inner London Education Authority (Gillan). Baroness Knight, who introduced Clause 28 in Parliament, emphasized her concern about "brightly coloured pictures of little stick men [that] showed all about homosexuality and how it was done" ("Section 28" 2). Knight's perception was that the visual domain risks influencing the child irretrievably; rather than regarding education as a discursive, reflective, and gradual process, she framed the child's encounter with text and image as a *Turn of the Screw*-like scene of irremediable corruption and possession.

The clause generated impassioned leftwing (and, later, increasingly mainstream) opposition from its initial proposal until its repeal in 2003. Both it and the Children Act of 1989 were concerned with how the future would be affected by the child's encounters with the adult world—encounters either educational or physical, the latter imagined at worst as the child's abduction or abuse—and both sought to recognize and promote the child's interests in the future. The context for this was frequently and expansively articulated by Thatcher herself:

> To compete successfully in tomorrow's world—against Japan, Germany and the United States—we need well-educated, well-trained, creative young people. [. . .] But [. . .] too often, our children don't get the education they need [. . .] children who need to be able to count and multiply are learning anti-racist mathematics—whatever that may be. [. . .] Children who need to be taught to respect traditional moral values are being taught that they have an inalienable right to be gay. And children who need encouragement [. . .] are being taught that our society offers them no future. ("Speech to the Conservative Party Conference, October 9, 1987")

Economics, morality, Britain's relationship to globalization, and "the future" are all consolidated and reified here as interests of the child. Here, the child's energies and potential are the source of competitive national advantage; yet, the child is also profoundly, disturbingly, vulnerable. This child-at-risk is subtly posed as the child who might *become* a risk—through the agenda of the left but also through the child's apparent susceptibility to that agenda. Thatcher argued in her speech that "the great majority of crimes are committed by young people, in their teens and early twenties.

It is on such impressionable young people that [. . .] the glamorisation of crime can have the most deadly effect," a glamorization she attributed to "left-wing councils and left-wing teachers" and to broadcasters who "flout their own standards on violent television programmes," risking "a brutalising effect on the morally unstable" (Thatcher, "Speech to the Conservative Party Conference, October 9, 1987").

This rhetoric was often not only lurid but also profoundly nostalgic in the way it imagined the child as product of a traditional nuclear family (Samuel 11–14). This strongly echoed the function of "Victorian values"—a phrase heavily invested with socially conservative attitudes to class, sexuality, and gender—in Thatcher's rhetoric and worldview, acting as an internal counterweight to Thatcherism's own narratives of productive creative destruction and the potential of those narratives to disrupt Thatcherism's claims to conservative stability. This delicate balance pervaded its rhetorical discourses over the child and the youth respectively, with the former presented as vulnerable, innocent, and in need of protection and the latter as both a potential threat and a source of aspirational and entrepreneurial energy. The gap between these two figures was bridged with an obsessive concern with education and exposure to potential influence from "anti-racist mathematics" or gay-themed books.

For Thatcher's opponents, the relationship between the vulnerable child and the dangerous yet aspirational youth gave scope for accusations of fundamental hypocrisy in the government's program, producing a rich target for satire. On the night of the 1987 general election, a few months prior to the speech quoted previously, ITV's popular puppet-based TV satire *Spitting Image* parodied *Cabaret*'s (1972) scene, where a handsome Nazi youth sings the anthemic "Tomorrow Belongs to Me." In *Spitting Image*'s version, the boy—prepubescent, but dressed as a City banker, the image of Thatcherism's materialistic, masculine-aspirational promise—fades disturbingly into the show's grotesque puppet-Thatcher before a series of cuts to images of environmental degradation, economic chaos, and closing hospitals. Finally, Thatcher repeats, voice echoing, "tomorrow belongs to me." Thatcher's demand to recognize a vision of "tomorrow," the sketch indicates, depends upon *not* recognizing the future actually emerging, replacing it with the sinister, uncanny fantasy-child vision of "tomorrow." Here, the Thatcherite future, the supposed object of the child's fascination, transforms him, embodiment of that future, into becoming himself the object of adult fascinations (a hypocritical transference dramatized as the grotesque Thatcher/child juxtaposition). This circular fantasy imagines Thatcherism successfully, yet monstrously, channeling the child's own imagining of "tomorrow"; this was both an actual child and, as his adult attire suggested, a fantasy of an essential inner child behind the ambitious male youth whose ambitions Thatcher, as grotesque oedipal mother, uniquely offered to fulfil. This scene was reflective of a whole genre of anti-Thatcherite satire, found across literary fiction—as in McEwan's *The Child in Time*, discussed in chapter 4—and popular culture—as here in *Spitting Image* and in the comedian Harry Enfield's character Loadsamoney, a boorishly childish, nouveau-riche young man from South East England, the region that generally most prospered under Thatcherism.

These themes had not only cultural and economic dimensions but also spatial and material (and materialistic) ones. Thatcherite rhetoric often associated violence from and toward children and youth with the "inner city"—code for urban areas, typically including estates and tower blocks, reconstructed in the postwar period under broadly socialist principles. By the 1970s, such areas had become associated with deprivation and crime (as they are in *A Clockwork Orange* itself), targeted by the 1980s "New Right counter-reaction to post-war dreams" (Luckhurst 98). Yet, even as the "inner city" became ever more damned by association with violent young males, the City—London's financial district—became associated with young "yuppie" men, who were socially and financially mobile and increasingly unrestrained in pursuit of wealth thanks to Thatcher's government (particularly via 1986's "Big Bang" financial deregulation) and who came to be popularly regarded as emblematic of Thatcherism's ambivalent generational consequences: of the gap between its socially conservative rhetoric and the future it actually produced. Alan Hollinghurst's *The Line of Beauty* (2004) depicts these tensions at a late 1980s City restaurant, where older men are "harassed by the speed and noise, their dignity threatened by the ferocious youngsters who already had their hands on a new kind of success. Some of the young men were beautiful and exciting [. . .] It wasn't so much a public-school thing. As everyone had to shout there seemed to be one great rough syllable in the air, a sort of 'wow' or 'yow' " (204–05).

The same gap was more brutally distilled later in the opening sequence of the biopic *The Iron Lady* (2011), which imagines the consequences of Thatcherism's neoliberal deregulation through the figure of the male youth. The film follows the afterlife of Thatcherite dominance in the New Labour era, which retained Thatcher's neoliberalism and limited aspects of her social conservatism but tied them to a more cosmopolitan liberal agenda that was especially visible in an increasingly globalized, transnational London. As this film opens, an elderly, now-senile Thatcher escapes her police-protected home to purchase some milk; the ironic echo of the Grantham grocery shop of her childhood cues a macabre vision of an uncomprehending Thatcher traveling through a late 2000s London that is saturated in her legacy yet utterly alien to her. As Thatcher approaches the young immigrant or second-generation man at the counter, an obnoxious City man cuts ahead of her, talking aggressively into his mobile. While the unrecognized old lady waits, a young black man approaches behind her. He listens to loud music through headphones—atomized like the City man—and impatiently pushes past Thatcher. The unintended consequences of Thatcherism here seemingly include irresponsible, antisocial norms of young male behavior and immigration to the neoliberal metropolis, an important driver of the Brexit vote and a long-term consequence of Thatcherite economic change, despite the Thatcher government's hostility toward non-white immigration. The financier on his mobile echoes the City boys who appear later in a montage representing Thatcherism's late 1980s peak, where flushed young men on the trading floor, then partying, are juxtaposed with headlines: "Business is Booming," "Profits, Profits, Profits," and "Maggie's Millionaires." A boorish song repeatedly yells: "I'm in love with Margaret Thatcher; I'm in love with Maggie T."

Ironically, the Notsensibles' song was originally intended as a piece of punk provocation[3] against the Thatcher of the 1970s; its re-use here is suggestive of the ironies and contradictions of Thatcherism's relationship with youth cultures. This becomes evident if we notice how aspects of the aesthetic signifiers of the Thatcher-Era yuppie and of the materialistic young (especially southern English) males, whose aspirations Thatcherism was popularly regarded as encouraging, had been shared by earlier groups, notably the Teddy Boys. The latter constituted an urban subculture that originated in the United Kingdom in the 1950s and had revivals from the 1970s to the 1990s—influencing the aesthetics of *A Clockwork Orange* (Goh 265)—which combined elegant Edwardian-style attire with openness to American-influenced consumerism and involvement in violence against outsiders (sometimes racist violence, as notably dramatized in Colin MacInnes's 1959 novel *Absolute Beginners*). As Stephen Ross notes:

> Teddy boys articulated a complicated cultural moment. For

> many members of the British public, the Teds presented a menacing view of the future arriving just a bit too early for comfort. [. . .] Refusing to go back to pre-war social distinctions, the Teds mobilised their unprecedented prosperity [. . .] and increased urban mobility to assert their agency in the streets, flaunted their affluence and embraced aspects of American culture [. . .] And yet the Teds were not by any means only a forward-looking group. The moral panic they provoked had as much to do with their invocation of a past that was gone for good as it did with a heady vision of the future. (28)

As with many of the children and youth I explore in this chapter, the Teddy Boys were paradoxical, disrupting traditional class hierarchies with aggressive demands to access desired spaces and possess desired objects and being implicated in violence against the peace and stability of the adult order. Yet, the objects of their desire were also fundamentally conservative in their source and coding. One reason the Teddy Boys and other youth cultures received hostility from mainstream adult society lay in their demanding access to material and social pleasures—claimed aesthetically by their exhibitionist self-presentation, physically by their occupation of new urban and consumer spaces—without the delay and mediation involved in more sanctioned forms of aspirational social mobility (as Bond Stockton argues, the enforced delay in children's normative economic participation makes the forms of consumption and investment they do engage in prone to fantasy and excess, *The Queer Child*, 222–23).

Later parodies of Thatcherism's own favored young men (such as Enfield's Loadsamoney and literary versions from McEwan and Hollinghurst) presented it as indulging and accelerating childish materialism and antisocial aspiration just as much as these youth cultures. As we shall see, Thatcherism, while deploying dangerous postwar children and youth as figures of fear to consolidate conservative reaction, nevertheless incorporated some of these youth's characteristics into its project for a new future.

In the texts I explore here, the dangerous youth is related to the child in multiple ways. The child might be threatened by the youth, or they might show the latter's destructive tendencies already in gestation, perhaps in danger of ever-earlier eruptions. Certainly, they might demonstrate their fundamental formation, perhaps becoming fixed too early to stop them, not least because adult violence toward the child is of a different moral status than violence toward the dangerous youth—or is it, always? In considering these questions, we shall not only trace a backstory through the origins of Thatcherism in Britain from the late 1940s onward; we shall also find how the anxieties, agendas, and figures involved have even broader and deeper significance for reading the child-as-future in late twentieth- and early twenty-first-century Britain.

The rest of this chapter is divided into four sections. The first considers the rise of the child as a figure increasingly invested as an explicit source of violent threat in fiction and film of the 1950s, '60s, '70s, and into the Thatcher-Era 1980s. I often refer to this as the *horror child* because of its strong connection with the horror film genre, the tropes of which literary fiction begins to adopt and adapt—though such fiction also anticipates them, I suggest, from an early stage. The second section explores the figure of the dangerous youth in Thatcherism's hinterlands, particularly through examining how *A Clockwork Orange* itself anticipates Thatcherism's ambivalence between abjection and absorption of this youth's qualities. The third section turns to direct representations of and responses to the dangerous child and youth as well as the rise of the queer child and youth as a further object of horror during the Thatcherite 1980s, with reference to work from Doris Lessing, Peter Ackroyd, and Alan Hollinghurst. I suggest that the rise of the queer child or youth draws renewed attention to the ambivalence and insecurity of Thatcherism's claims. Finally, I explore Sarah Waters's 2009 novel *The Little Stranger* as a retrospective, anticipatory fiction on the relationship between the dangerous child and the ambitious youth in the second half of Britain's twentieth century. I make the case throughout for the children and youth of Thatcherism's hinterlands being of both historical significance for British narratives of history, nation, society, and self-understanding during this period and broader theoretical and critical significance for our practices of reading the child in all their materiality, materialism, aspiration, and opacity.

Horror Children

Early Postwar Horror Children

I turn next to some children imagined within the period between the late 1940s and the late 1970s, where Thatcherism found the dangerous children against which it ultimately would plan a new future in the 1980s. This was a period of repeated anxiety over the rise of various youth cultures, from the Teddy Boys to Punks, and of contest over the health of childhood and its relationship to social, domestic, and national security. It is also, certainly from 1960 onward, a period when the child as an explicit source of fear found a new place in popular culture, especially via the horror movie genre. Although this was principally a Hollywood phenomenon, it also included some distinctive, and notably early, British contributions, revealing the willingness to attribute horrific danger even to very young children. I discuss some of the films involved later; but first, I want to observe that closely related children emerged in literary fiction even earlier, in the immediate postwar period, and that their examples display themes relevant not only to the anxieties of their own period but also to the long-running fears of dangerous children and youth that would ultimately become central to the cultural politics of Thatcherism.

The United Kingdom's early postwar period was characterized by severe social anxiety and fatigue over the war's continuing legacy, coexisting with expressions of often-utopian optimism. The Cold War and the nuclear threat were rapidly accelerating. Alongside ambitious developments in housing, education, and the National Health Service (in 1948), painful rationing of basic goods was extended (Kynaston 117) while class, gender, and racial structures were disrupted by the war and, though at first only gradually, through non-white Commonwealth immigration (Kynaston 270–77). Against this backdrop, a newly marked emphasis on the importance of children and childhood for a socially healthy future was increasingly established—including, for example, through the BBC's popularization of the psychoanalyst Donald Winnicott's theories:

> Through radio broadcasting, psychoanalysis reached the hearts and minds of millions of British people [linking] citizenship, home, and the notion of the child as a future citizen whose stable mental health, "normalcy," and ability to collaborate democratically with others were dependent on good parenthood and family dynamics.
>
> Winnicott's radio talks were broadcast in a time when [. . .] there was also a growing anxiety about the fragility of the family [. . .] and fears of "war babies" turning into "juvenile delinquents" due to the wartime absence of their fathers or the working hours of their mothers. (Shapira 113–14)

This was a society under pressure, newly informed by popular theory, to protect and nourish children and simultaneously frightened of the implications of moral abnormality among them. This concern would be a sustained feature of the United Kingdom's later twentieth century. Although Thatcher rhetorically invoked Victorian values, she sometimes varied this with references to returning to the values of the 1950s (qtd. in Sinfield, *Literature, Politics and Culture*, 4); her first political experiences took place during the '50s, and her idea of both the healthy family and its adversaries were heavily informed by the postwar context Shapira describes.

Continuing within this context—and while looking forward to how they prefigure literary, cinematic, cultural, and political developments between the 1950s and 1979—I consider three pieces of early postwar literature that make the violent, even deadly, child an essential sign of their times.

The World My Wilderness (1950), *The Destructors* (1954) and *Lord of the Flies* (1954)

Rose Macaulay's novel *The World My Wilderness* shows, as Beryl Pong observes, "war's lasting, destructive effects on children's maturation," producing "a distorted [. . .] novel of formation" (92–93). Macaulay's children have participated in murder even before the narrative begins. In 1945, Barbary and Raoul live in southern France with Helen Michel, their mother and stepmother respectively. These children were part of the local *Maquis* (resistance) attacking occupiers and collaborators; they seem to have been involved in the murder of Maurice, Helen's late husband and Raoul's father, himself a collaborator. Barbary was also the bait to lure an infatuated German soldier to his death. Barbary is seventeen; Raoul, just fifteen. Helen also has a two-year-old son, Roland. Macaulay teases a heroic framing for these difficult children only for it to dissipate into ambiguity after Helen sends both Barbary and Raoul back to England, where Barbary is supposed to attend the Slade School but instead explores, with Raoul, City of London bombsites, especially ruined churches—spaces they share with young petty criminals. There, Barbary develops her own childish but authoritarian vision: "I shall preach [. . .] how divorced people can't really marry again. And I shall preach about hell" (50–51). The children's mix of fundamentalism and nihilism sharply contrasts with their parents' respective cold conservatism and louche liberalism, and ultimately leads to scandal, exposure of family secrets, and Barbary's exile from her London home.

The World includes several typical mid-century tropes surrounding the dangerous child, including an ineffective psychologist (88–89)—which registers the rise of Freudian ideas while indicating skepticism over their efficacy in controlling children—and an almost-cinematic gaze on and from the child that is tinged with menace:

> Roland's cot was low [. . .] The room was dim; in the first moment [Helen] did not see Barbary crouched by the cot, still in her wet frock, her draggled hair drooping like dank seaweed around her face. She got up, startled, defensive, pushing her hair from her eyes.
> "I didn't disturb him," she whispered. "I only wanted to look at him."
> Helen gave her across the sleeping child her withdrawn, enigmatic glance [. . .]
> For a moment Barbary paused, a hesitant shadow in the shadowed room. Her lips moved, forming a word—mother, mummy, it might have been; but now Helen's glance had left her, she was leaning over Roland picking him up to set him on his pot. Replacing him, she [. . .] made the little adjustments that one makes in the night lives of infants lest some ill befall them [. . .] Roland was a placid and cheerful sleeper; not like Barbary had been at his age, all nerves, waking in terror, screaming at shadows, then, when her mother arrived, hiding her face in her breast. (12–13)

These visual dynamics, with their "cuts" from one gaze to another, anticipate the horror films that would obsess over children in the coming decades. The dangers that befall infants extend by association to Barbary herself; nevertheless, "I only wanted to look at him"—what is the harm, after all, in just looking? (Much potential harm, in a post-Freudian culture.) Helen's turn away when her daughter is trying to vocalize her own gaze as maternal attachment invites a Freudian reading of the scene while echoing, and perhaps undermining, Winnicott's idea of the "good enough mother" who gradually allows her child to experience frustration and separation, adjusting toward autonomy. Barbary's excesses and her premature quasi-maternal gaze toward her infant half-brother, as well as Helen's own "withdrawn, enigmatic" glance, suggest this process going awry as the gazes between adult, child, and child attempt to focalize on the suspected risks between each other but confront mutual alterity.

The World, in its relentless emphasis on Barbary's alterity and the materiality and intensity of the child's own future-making, is skeptical over whether any political or epistemological project *can* know the child sufficiently to secure the future from risk. When her uncle, a "consulting specialist in nerve ailments" (88) with a belief in the talking cure, attempts to "probe the dark places in [her] obviously disarranged mind" (99), Barbary's response is to steal from his wife and run away.

The possibility that the risks all this reflects could prove deadly for adults is, Macaulay suggests, to be taken seriously; *The World* depicts children creating a new future of uncertain realism, but its present threat to the adult order is certainly real enough. In this depiction, and in the centrality of material spaces and objects—as well as the time in which to explore and use them—to it, Macaulay's novel anticipates important aspects of the presentation of the child-as-future as current threat that would repeatedly recur in later twentieth-century British fiction and film, and it shows any postwar optimism as haunted by this threat from its beginnings. These aspects include the repeatedly stated fear that the delinquencies of particular children with particular experiences of the war might indicate a general generational trend and societal decline; the proximity of young children to dangerous youth (in the ruined churches where Barbary and Raoul hang out with young criminals); and the suggestion that, while this proximity certainly indicates the possibility of "development" going wrong, the child is also dangerous on their own terms. Barbary's moral and political naivety derives from a childishness reflected in her distaste for sexuality (68–70) and immature attitude toward family relations (44). We shall often find that, at least in the perception of writers and filmmakers from this period and beyond, children with conservative tastes can be as dangerous as those with radical potential, and nor are the two always categorically distinct.

Four years later, Grahame Greene's short story *The Destructors* introduced more children who occupied London's postwar wreckage. A boys' gang is taken over by the oddball Trevor, who initiates a plan to destroy a local London townhouse, supposedly designed by Christopher Wren, that stands alongside a desolate area flattened by German bombing—an architectural survivor attracting attention from the young and unoccupied, like the ruined churches of *The World*. Under Trevor's charismatic leadership, the gang follow through when the house's owner, "Old Misery," is away, burgling then gradually destroying the house progressively from the inside until the structure is fatally compromised: "The skirting was up, the door had been taken off its hinges, and the destroyers had moved up a floor [. . .] they worked with the seriousness of creators—and destruction after all is a form of creation. A kind of imagination had seen this house as it had now become" (15). When Old Misery returns, the boys lock him in an outhouse while they use their cunning to engineer for a truck to pull a support pole from the house's side, causing the walls to fall; the (adult) truck driver cannot help laughing.

This destruction arises from a peculiar kind of aesthetic consumption, and Trevor's own consumerism is directed toward a disconcertingly elite object: the townhouse, whose faded beauty only a refined taste would savor. Trevor, an architect's son (7), possesses such taste, savoring details like the "floating" staircase "like a corkscrew" (10). (The perverse child with a love of architecture is a surprisingly common trope in the texts explored here; the violent youth with a love of high culture appears even more widely.) Yet, despite this sophisticated interest, Trevor wants to possess the building immediately, absolutely, deliciously: "T. said, 'It's a beautiful house,' and [. . .] meeting no one's eyes, he licked his lips" (10). He exemplifies, in a most unusual context, Bond Stockton's characterizations[4] of "children's unedited pleasure in obvious extremes of consumption and destruction" and "create-in-order-to-destroy: the dream of manufacturing what you will profusely and on the spot consume, not as a necessity but strictly as a luxury" (238).

Trevor rejects the deferred, mediated access to material pleasures on offer from adult-governed society; he even insists that the gang burn Old Misery's cash savings rather than steal or spare them. This rejection of deferred satisfaction registers through a class framing; Trevor's parents present socioeconomic mobility in reverse, confounding both postwar optimism[5] and traditional hierarchy: "His father, a former architect and present clerk, had 'come down in the world'" (7). A society where access to material pleasures—including beautiful things previously reserved for higher classes—has become unmoored from either hierarchical stability or controlled mobility is, Greene implies, a society with reason to fear its younger generations, with their intensity of desire all the more dangerous for its fundamental childishness.

A psychoanalytic or queer-minded reader might readily identify Trevor's compulsive creative destruction with the death drive, clearly incompatible as it is with the most basic principles of social order or (re)productive economy; this boy is surely not going to become a good 1950s family man. In these characteristics, Trevor seems to embody the death drive as formulated by Freud and reworked by Edelman. Yet, his preferred creative destruction has to be planned and implemented as an act within the material and social world—driven, but also negotiated. Paradoxically, the rejection of all deferral of pleasure requires a bit of forward thinking (that is, deferral!). His death drive plays out as mundane social structure; it becomes the organizing principle of a group, a distinct organization in potential conflict with other dangerous youth groups. As much as it perfectly embodies the Freudian death drive, it lacks its singularity. More importantly, Trevor and his gang are simply too difficult and too dangerous for even any queer adult to comfortably affirm or accept them (Old Misery himself, their victim, is notably queer-coded, fitting Edelman's sinthomosexual figure), and the laughter that is the final adult response to these children's actions—which Old Misery resents—registers their unassimilable position. Their destruction is nevertheless both a creative act of visionary imagination and a material product of children being given time and space with no demands for moral or economic productivity.

William Golding's infamous novel *Lord of the Flies*, published in the same year as *The Destructors*, has a British airplane crash—during an unexplained disaster, perhaps an outbreak of nuclear conflict—on a lonely Pacific island. All survivors are young boys. One of these, Ralph, is elected as chief and requires the boys to constantly maintain a smoke signal to alert passing ships. Another boy, Jack, organizes a hunting party to find food. Ralph, Jack, and the quiet Simon all act as leaders, while the asthmatic Piggy is increasingly bullied. The attempt to build a rational economy of food gathering and distribution rapidly falls apart, as the boys fail to complete allotted labor, pursue unproductive play, and develop paranoid beliefs about a "beast" inhabiting the island. Jack gains renewed support by promising to kill the beast and summons his hunters to hunt down a wild pig, even those assigned to maintain the fire—thus causing a passing ship to fail to stop. As tensions escalate, the boys split between Ralph's loyal followers and Jack's gang. Simon, alone, encounters a pig's head that the latter have erected as an offering to the beast. Simon speaks with this "Lord of the Flies," who asserts that the boys themselves are the beast and warns Simon that he risks being killed by the other children. Both Simon and Piggy are, indeed, soon killed by Jack's gang; Ralph escapes but is almost hunted down before he suddenly encounters an adult—a British naval officer, landed from a passing ship. Ralph bursts into tears, then the boys hunting him appear and do likewise. The officer expresses his disappointment at their behavior.

Lord of the Flies invokes both Britain as island nation and Britain as empire (one already disintegrating by 1950), particularly via the linking of British imperial values to children's virtues in R. M. Ballantyne's *The Coral Island* (1857), which Golding parodies (having both the boys [33] and the officer [224] explicitly reference Ballantyne). Golding, like Macaulay and Greene, explores postwar British children being given their own time and space outside adult expectations against the backdrop of sudden national and social disorientation; all three narratives end with the children's violence putting the ability of adult society to accommodate them into serious question. There is a subtextual hint here that in certain circumstances the adult might even need to kill these children, lest they kill. Surely, Jack's gang could be countered by force to prevent them murdering another child—with the officer's revolver subtly indicating this possibility. Barbary and Raoul are already complicit in murder, a proven danger to adults. And the sheer irrationality and physical scale of Trevor's creative destruction underlines the scope of his potential risk to society. This suggests an underlying threat to break the taboo on child-killing, even while the postwar British order—as with its adoption of Winnicott as authoritative voice—made new assertions of children's centrality to national wellbeing.

Yet, powerful though this hint is, Golding—like Macaulay and Greene—does not allow his dangerous children to become unambiguously the abject embodiment of a darkness that the adult world might legitimately destroy. Barbary and Raoul may have committed murder in France, but their criminality in London is far pettier; Trevor and his gang are more perverse than deadly; Jack's gang may play at being a "savage" tribe—and the play may even extend, horrifically, to the murder of other children—but they crumble instantaneously before an adult in authority. All of these children are both dangerous and profoundly difficult for adult society, but they are not yet the monstrous children of later twentieth-century horror movies, whose threat often directly and explicitly justifies adult violence against them.

The ambiguity in these dangerous children underlines rather than mitigates, though, the inscrutable risks they present to the adult world, an inscrutability that continues to challenge claims to comprehensive critical interpretation. In both *The Destructors* and *Lord of the Flies*, children seek to escape the adult-legitimated economy of discipline and delay controlling access to objects of desire. In Freudian terms, they reject the pleasure principle, and in their failure to accept the heterosexist and reproductive—as well as the economic—delays and discipline required by adult society, and in the very senselessness of some of the projects they embark upon, these children arguably occupy the queer version of the death drive as advanced by Edelman. Yet, their mix of organization and (paradoxically) delayed gratification as well as their internal complexities, conflicts, and rivalries—and, not least, their status as children in the midst of uncertain developments rather than holders of a fixed psychosocial position—works against the identification of them with such a singular drive. Their categorical and theoretical difficulty is reinforced by the complexities in their relationship to adult violence. True, Barbary and Raoul are sustaining the anti-authoritarianism of the adult-led Resistance, but no adults tell them to combine this with quasi-religious fundamentalism. True, too, Greene's Destructors are finishing off the German bombers' job when they destroy Old Misery's home, but they are apparently not (yet) adult enough to actually take life down with the house. Both Macaulay's and Greene's children have strikingly conservative objects of desire, taken from an authoritative adult world that the war has disrupted and made more available to them through the legacies of that war's violence; yet, the uncompromising and creatively destructive ways in which they pursue this desire make their relationship to the actually existing, current adult world ambivalent and hedged with risk. *Lord of the Flies* is framed by a possible outbreak of large-scale conflict, but the boys are isolated from it; it does not provoke their crimes. The children's danger and difficulty in these cases may reflect a broader postwar condition, but it also has its own discrete character; it is not merely allegorical or supplementary to adult harms and failings.

Significantly for this difficulty in categorizing or theorizing these children, *Lord of the Flies* resists discourses of organic and authentic human (or British) nature. In the boys' failure to create a stable society in their new island nation, the novel instead insists on the power of historical contingency: The boys arrive as the result of an accident. Their survival is also dependent more on luck than anything else. Recognizing this, Ralph prioritizes maximizing their chances of attracting attention from a randomly passing ship. By chance, a ship is passing precisely when the light is allowed to go out; and by later chance, an uncontrolled fire alerts the naval vessel. The significance of such chance events is only emphasized by how Golding's novel plays with contrasting teleologies of biological, environmental, and psychic essentialism, both in its own literary allusions and in the boys' ideas. The contingency involved in whether or not a ship will pass by becomes an intolerable reality for most of the boys, who turn to the security of invented rituals enacted as "though repetition would achieve safety of itself" (168), a notion echoing Freud's Fort/Da.

I dissent from Julian Lovelock's conclusion that "the disintegration of the society on the island because of the 'beast' within is also an allegory for the disintegration of the outside world that has chosen war over peace" (104); the boys' recourse to allegory—via the beast itself, and in literature like *The Coral Island, Treasure Island,* and *Swallows and Amazons* (33)—is misleading (for both them and the reader) because such allegorical cohesion, implicitly allied to teleology as it is, is persistently undermined by Golding's subtle emphasis on acceptance of historical contingency as central to any rational or humane society. The novel raises the difficult question of whether we can tolerate such contingency in the actions of children as the embodiments of the future, as signifiers of our continued collective survival. How can we sufficiently tolerate the risk the child presents to give them their own time and space, especially when the established economy of delayed gratification for socially sanctioned return is absent or undermined? *Lord of the Flies* warns against turning to an essentialist idea of the true value or motivations of children as an answer—against trying to absorb the capacity of children to cause violent destruction into either a celebratory or an abject account of their (or Britain's) essence.

Dangerous Postwar Children and Theory

These narratives reflect both the anxieties of their postwar period and the fears of dangerous children and youth that would become sustained throughout the later twentieth century. They register the early rise of the horror child in postwar literary fiction even before its later prominence in popular culture (albeit, the figure is much less fixed and more ambiguous than it would become later), marked by the threat this child poses to the adult order. Macaulay, Greene, and Golding introduce themes that will remain important throughout the texts I explore, notably the desire of children to access material objects and protected times and spaces in which to construct an alternative future to that offered by adults (even when the future involves pure creative destruction for present satisfaction, as in *The Destructors*). For Macaulay and Greene, at least, it is partly the completeness of that satisfaction that makes the children's actions so unnerving, so unassimilable to adult characters—and to adult readers, including those seeking to generate authoritative interpretations of their significance. Security against instability and contingency is a goal for these children, underlining the uncanny relationship between their desires and the failures of an adult world that seeks the same. These narratives demonstrate the paradoxes of children desiring relatively conservative objects but creating an anxiety, even a danger, for adults by desiring them too much or too soon, outside sanctioned channels of social, economic, and educational mobility. Already, we see a latent tension for regimes that seek both social stability and to indulge the aspirations of youth; this is exactly the tension that featured so powerfully in Thatcherism's later relationship with the young.

These narratives reflect the popularization of psychoanalytically influenced concerns about childhood in 1950s Britain, with their obsessive and fetishistic treatments of particular objects, homosocial relationships and absent heterosexual development, and violent resentment of parental figures. Psychoanalytic ideas had been spread by publication of James Strachey's *Standard Edition* of Freud beginning in 1953 and, probably more widely, by Donald Winnicott's public work, especially his BBC radio talks, which lasted from 1943 into the 1960s.

Although the dangerous children of Macaulay, Greene, and Golding register these developments, they are also not wholly contained by the Freudian themes they invoke. All these children form personal projects and social groupings beyond the conventional family and are often more concerned with the physical spaces and material assets available to them than with either their families or chosen groupings. In their perversity and rejection of socially sanctioned delay in favor of some more immediate access to material pleasure or the jouissance of purposeless destruction, these children evoke aspects of Freud's death drive. Yet, the fact that pleasure is still often present in their drive and its objects—as in Trevor's aesthetic enthusiasm, for example—complicates the picture since Freud made a strong distinction between the death drive as operating wholly *beyond* the pleasure principle and perverse object attachments and behaviors that merely translate an unpleasurable reality into a pleasurable one (*Beyond* 17). Trevor's gang observes the reality principle—they defer satisfaction while painstakingly deconstructing the house—but then satisfaction, achieved at the moment of destruction, fulfils the pleasure principle while simultaneously being as destructive as Freud imagined the death drive to be. Such a creative destruction is perhaps even more perverse than Freud's theory, and its later queer reformulations, are primed to accommodate. These children's actions are organized in their particular social contexts and bear idiosyncratic traces from them that complicate theorizing; they sometimes develop noticeably conservative fantasies from those contexts; and the moral fundamentalism or authoritarianism sometimes behind their violence cannot be straightforwardly assimilated into affirmative identification of queerness. The satisfaction they achieve from their objects of desire—especially in Trevor's case—also challenges both queer and psychoanalytic readings that are essentially substitutive in structure, typically regarding particular material objects of desire as more symptomatic of repression and displacement than genuinely satisfying.

Progressive Britain's Horror Children

The literary examples explored previously show postwar British literature developing tropes and themes around dangerous children that would in time explode into popular culture in a much more explicit—and often exploitative—form. The 1960s and '70s saw a spate of British horror movies that were not only willing to invite—and sometimes to compel—adults to imagine killing the dangerous child but also to use this child to work through progressive Britain's threats and traumas. Viewed in retrospect, they expose the essential cultural preparation for the more lurid and paranoid elements in Thatcherite reaction over the family, children, and their alleged threats, yet they also point toward contradictions and problems that would persist within this reaction.

These emerged within a horror movie genre that was increasingly willing to make children the objects of audience fear. British cinema was an early participant in this phenomenon, through films such as *Village of the Damned* (1960, an adaptation of John Wyndham's 1957 novel *The Midwitch Cuckoos*) and *The Innocents* (1961, an adaptation of Henry James's *The Turn of the Screw*). These films were linked by starring a successfully creepy child actor, Martin Stephens, and both were marked by a willingness to imagine killing the child in order to save a broader social and epistemological order. While *Village of the Damned* uses its horror children to register Cold War fears of mass destruction and mind control through powerful weapons and infiltration by aliens, *The Innocents*—which remolds James's dangerous boy, Miles, to be a far more explicit physical and sexual threat than in the original novella[6]—codes fears over breakdown of the sexual and moral order, expressed through a Freudian framing. Miles, a prematurely adult-styled little boy, dresses (in a sense not unlike the Teddy Boys, though the context is very different) in a flamboyant but conservative style, embodying patriarchal and masculinist values in a way that makes them more uncanny than straightforwardly conservative, coming from such a young boy who uses them to undermine adult authority. *The Innocents* is also a story based on both home invasion and class transgression, where the deviant servants Quint and Jessel infiltrate Bly Manor and corrupt the upper-class progeny who live there, sustaining their intrusion through the children (as visualized in fig. 2.1) even after their own deaths, in an ultimate corruption of the child's role of embodying the future—which leads to Miss Giddens killing Miles in order to save him.

The Innocents was an early contribution to establishing the paradigm where horror movies use the unknown qualities of children as objects for projecting the most extreme anxieties over fragmentation in the social and moral order. Hollywood would go on to produce several horror classics on this model, notably *Rosemary's Baby* (1968), *The Exorcist* (1973), and *The Omen* (1976, notably primarily set in the UK).

Alongside the 1980s rise of the slasher genre, which took fear of the violent male youth to lurid extremes, the figure of the horror child would continue to appear frequently in popular horror movies; this has persisted to the present day. (The young child was, in fact, present at the birth of the slasher subgenre in the six-year-old Michael Myers's act of oedipal violence opening John Carpenter's *Halloween* [1978], a backstory that establishes that if the male youth is the source of social violence, the child is the original and inner source of his own violence. *Halloween* is also notable for featuring a Freudian psychiatrist who abandons

Figure 2.1. In *The Innocents*, the face of the perverse adult, Quint, appears behind the dangerous child, Miles, of whom he is suspected of taking possession. From *The Innocents*, directed by Jack Clayton, Achilles Film Productions/Twentieth Century Fox, 1961. Screenshot courtesy of Filmgrab.

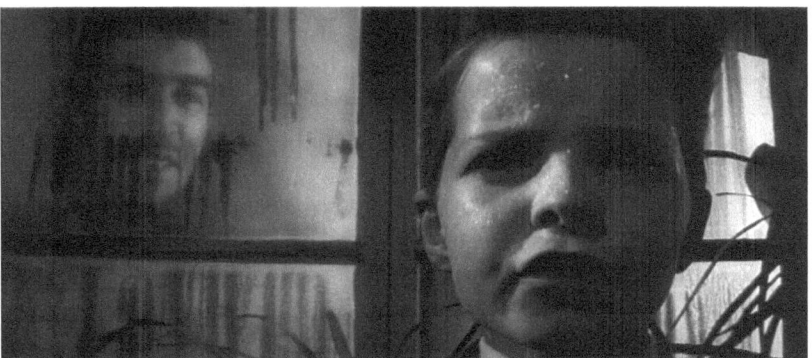

his psychoanalytic theories for a discourse of inherent evil in the boy). Although many horror child movies are heavily conservative in their ethics, the 1960s and '70s British examples sometimes—without losing the lurid reactionary potential of their themes—work through severe social and epistemological anxieties in quite sophisticated and subtle ways.

The Wicker Man (1973) and *Don't Look Now* (1973)

In 1973, two British horror films featured a lost child as fatal trap for adults: Nicholas Roeg's *Don't Look Now* (released October 1973, adapted from Daphne DuMaurier's 1971 short story) and Robin Hardy's *The Wicker Man* (December 1973). Each shows an adult male haunted by a lost child who leads him into grave danger; in each case, an apparent threat *to* the child is ultimately revealed as a threat *from* the child.

Don't Look Now opens with a young girl, Christine, who drowns in the grounds of her parents' English country home (fig. 2.2). Traumatized parents John (Donald Sutherland) and Laura Baxter (Julie Christie) travel to Venice, where John, an architect, has been commissioned to restore a church. They soon encounter two elderly sisters, one of whom claims to be psychic and tells Laura that she can see the dead Christine. John

Figure 2.2. Christine, in her distinctive red coat, slips under the water in the opening sequence of *Don't Look Now*. From *Don't Look Now*, directed by Nicholas Roeg, Casey Productions/Eldorado Films/British Lion Films, 1973. Screenshot courtesy of Filmgrab.

remains skeptical yet begins to repeatedly catch obscured glimpses of a child, wearing a red coat similar to Christine's, around Venice—where a real serial killer is also reportedly at large. Following news that their son, at boarding school, has been injured, Laura returns to England; John remains. His self-assurance disintegrates, and he pursues the red-coated child when he sees her again. He eventually corners her in a deserted palazzo, but she is suddenly revealed to be an adult dwarf and cuts his throat. Dying, John realizes that he had multiple premonitions of these events, but he—and we—failed to see properly. *Don't Look Now* is obsessed with seeing—and particularly seeing the child—correctly, as emphasized in details such as Laura playing a peek-a-boo game with some children in the hospital; John's accumulating misidentifications; and the paradox of the blind sister who possesses truer, fuller sight than visible reality affords to John. The film's obsessive focus on visual knowledge, a theme embodied in the spectral lost child, implies that the reality connoted by this child is ultimately to be recognized correctly rather than rationally parsed or analyzed.[7]

Another deadly failure to see the child and read her significance correctly befalls Sergeant Howie, protagonist of *The Wicker Man*. Howie is called to Summerisle, an isolated Hebridean island, to investigate the disappearance of a young girl, Rowan Morrison (fig. 2.3). Howie becomes

Figure 2.3. A picture of innocence: the image of Rowan carried by Sargeant Howie in *The Wicker Man*. From *The Wicker Man*, directed by Robin Hardy, British Lion Films, 1973. Screenshot courtesy of Filmgrab.

increasingly disturbed by the revived pagan religion to which the island community has subscribed and horrified by the frank sex education offered to Summerisle's children. (His reactions to Summerisle's decadent, hippie-ish, sexually liberated, police-unfriendly society reads like a parody of conservative hostility toward 1970s countercultures.) Howie meets the island's magistrate, Lord Summerisle, descendant of a Victorian agronomist, who explains that his grandfather developed strains of fruit to prosper in the island's climate and encouraged the belief that old gods would deliver this prosperity. Howie comes to believe that Rowan has been selected for sacrifice on May Day to secure an improved harvest after recent disappointments. He infiltrates the May celebration; yet, while "rescuing" Rowan, he discovers that this child has been a trap all along—Howie himself is the intended sacrifice. The islanders burn him alive inside a giant wicker man.

The rationalist, authoritative adult male is drawn into a deadly trap; attempting to save the lost child, he is himself murdered. Both Howie and Baxter are curiously trapped by their refusal to accept the death of the child (a refusal driven respectively by the demands of socio-legal authority and rationalism), and the ambivalence between life and death surrounding each girl parallels the ambivalence of the category of childhood itself between innocence and experience, a theme with which both films morbidly toy. If the living child—on the inevitable path toward no longer being a child—is recalcitrant to the adult gaze, the securely dead child provides a potentially more reassuring presence, a fact highlighted by both men's obsessive recourse to the dead child's image; Howie carries a picture of Rowan to cross-check against, while Baxter chases his daughter's image around Venice.

An impulse toward violence against the aberrant child is subtly both coded and given cover here. In *Don't Look Now* the child is already dead, so whatever Baxter does, he cannot kill Christine again; and if he had preempted the dwarf's violence by attacking his apparent daughter, he could have saved his own life. In *The Wicker Man*, Howie only needed to have passively accepted Rowan's presumed murder in order to save himself. If subtextually these films encourage adult viewers—who identify with, yet are more perceptive than, the protagonists—to accept the loss of the child, they are nevertheless absolutely required to retrieve the child in another sense: *Don't Look Now* and *The Wicker Man* tell us that the adult *must*, on pain of death, discover the true position of their own life within a broader historical and epistemological reality and must do so *through the child.* The lost child becomes a scapegoat. Though Rowan was not actually sacrificed by her community, her status as a child—with the special moral imperatives children hold for adults—is used for a purpose that sacrifices the claim to innocence that it manipulates.

The demand to recognize an essential underlying and permanent reality is, paradoxically, itself prompted by social change. Summerisle, with its sexual liberation, collectivized community, rejection of state authority for charismatic cult leadership, derelict Christianity, and defiant neo-paganism, is a provocative refraction of 1970s cultural changes (largely of the varieties against which Thatcherite socially conservatism reacted). Summerisle also satirizes both the proudly independent island of British nationalism (as did *Lord of the Flies*) and the conservative identification of rural communities with the authentic essence of the nation.[8] (Hughes observes that Summerisle's apparent collectivism is actually neo-feudalism, its veneer of organicism actually a cover for scientific manipulation of commercial agriculture [63–66]; he persuasively argues that, here, apparently radical social change perversely produces an organicist essentialism, which in turn covers for a renewed, conservative, and patriarchal power hierarchy.)

The lost child luring the sacrificial victim to his death to protect this perverse operation (a sacrifice that, Howie suggests with belated cunning, may not be sufficient—maybe Lord Summerisle himself will be sacrificed next year) gives the whole structure a layered ambiguity. The child, figure of innocence, has knowingly participated in a scheme to entrap and murder. How much do Summerisle's adults really know of the interior life of Rowan, who is simultaneously central and marginal to these events? If she trapped Howie once, could she entrap Lord Summerisle (who has a voyeuristic interest in young women) in the future? Howie's final prediction implies that the material and teleological immediacy represented by the human sacrifice—expected, until the final moments, to be a child-sacrifice—is itself a dangerously childish attempt to control the future, not least when it relies on the child playing a predictable part.

Social change is present, too, in *Don't Look Now*, "a horror film for 1970s Britain: a nation in social, economic and political turmoil [where] certainty has been lost" (Gildersleeve 7). The Baxters are a cosmopolitan transnational couple,[9] moving freely between England and Italy—reflecting the UK's accession to the European Communities in January 1973 that established the basis for the freer movement between Britain and Europe against which Brexit would react four decades later. Theirs is a modern marriage, full of argument, banter, and sex, as in the notorious scene where their lovemaking is preceded by Laura's acceptance that their ghostly daughter is present with them (the specter of the dead child perversely enabling, as Vicky Lebeau points out [125], adult sexual release). Social change is closely tied to ideological and even epistemological flux in both films, represented through the decline of British Protestant Christianity[10] and its various threatened replacements: Howie is a devout virgin horrified by the open pre- and extra-marital sexuality of Summerisle; Laura is unsure whether she is a Christian but is "kind to children and animals"; John is an assertive atheist who is, nevertheless, expert on the physical fabric of churches.

Both protagonists stay in an inn or hotel—transitional locations contrasting with the Baxters' own English gentry home and Lord Summerisle's spectacular Baronial residence. These, like the country houses in *A Clockwork Orange* (and that in *The Little Stranger*, discussed later) embody the aesthetic and material objects of social mobility and masculine aspiration as well as the conflict between conservative bourgeois social mobility and less restrained, less "rational," more decadent—and, counterintuitively, more childish—alternatives. Both the Baxters' house and Lord Summerisle's mansion are marked by adult indulgence and failures of conventional adult responsibility. As gentry-style and aristocratic residences respectively, they also connote the possibility of a reproductive order—for knowledge, capital, and children—beyond that offered by capitalist modernity or postwar social change.

Both Howie and Baxter are haunted by spectral yet material objects associated with children, like the balls and dolls that echo Christine's play immediately before her death and lure John toward his fate, or the odd candied creations that greet Howie at Rowan's mother's sweetshop. On Summerisle, child's play is also associated with the pagan (or countercultural) pleasures that Howie finds absurd, frivolous, and infantile. The connection is emphasized by the prominence of children in the dances around the maypole and at the stone circle and by how Howie's death depends—in the final moments, when it perhaps could have been averted—on a child's play-acting. These men fail, in part, because they misread child's play and childish pleasures and because they fail to read visual clues accurately; seeing and believing have gone adrift here. In taking the child-as-threat as a signifier for challenges to rationalist, patriarchal authority, both films reflect anxieties—around sexuality, society, nationalism, cosmopolitanism, and even economics—prominent in 1970s public discourse. To these, Thatcherism would ultimately respond with full and comprehensive—yet still, as we shall see, contradictory—conservative reaction. These films also read the child as presenting a problem of historical risk. A properly historical sensibility—which, both suggest, requires considerable imaginative openness to the esoteric features of the world—is a matter of life and death; both Baxter and Howie die as a result of their failure to correctly read the historical (or transhistorical) forces at work around them (although Howie comes a little closer to doing this than Baxter manages).

Both films are also particularly concerned with the role of institutions: with established institutions of the state and with Protestant Enlightenment tradition coming under attack from neo-paganism on Summerisle and from baroque Catholic mysticism and ambiguous spiritualism in Venice. The former features a ruined church and a revived stone circle (reflecting the real revival of neo-pagan practices[11] in the 1970s), while derelict churches dominate in the latter. Schools also play subtle but critical roles, with the boarding school accident in *Don't Look Now* emphasizing the conflict between John and Laura's adult passions and their responsibilities to their children and Summerisle's corrupted primary school provoking a horrified reaction from Howie.

The films' most notable shared feature, though, is the sheer intensity of the anxiety the missing child provokes before she transforms into an agent of killing. Jessica Gildersleeve has convincingly read *Don't Look Now*'s dominant affect as a dreadful compulsion to anticipate a risk (both to and from the child) that is only ever understood too late, a "dreading forward" taken from "Freud's conceptualisation of anxiety (or *angstbereitschaft*)," with John driven by "desire to paradoxically prevent his daughter's death after it has occurred" (29). Although both films draw on the universally compelling figure of the lost child, they also rely on a specific set of cultural codes and triggers for their full anxious effect and reflect fears of child abuse and abduction (two phenomena, with associated narrative tropes, that would become increasingly prominent in the following decade, as discussed in chapter 4).

Despite this intensity of anxiety over the child, it's worth noting the extent to which this anxiety is a cover or channel for the protagonists' own anxieties about their masculinity and, behind it, their sense of epistemological stability in the world. Howie, in particular, as an ageing virgin, is failing to reproduce the conservative patriarchal order he so values even before he arrives on Summerisle. Though in middle age, these protagonists are still trapped in perverse Bildungsromane, aspirational and mobile yet unable to fully reach adult security and confidence (Howie has never reached them; and Baxter, of course, has them taken away by his daughter's death), leaving the protagonists prone to manipulative, fetishized images of the child-as-future whose recovery appears to promise exactly these things. Cruelly, the objects visually associated with Christine, especially her coat, are used to prey on John's urgent need to restore his own epistemological and affective security, yet they ultimately disclose nothing about the child's death except its contingency and unassimilable alterity.

They are also men who would have been better off killing the child that eventually destroys them, or at least accepting her death. Perhaps one might even have to kill the child—or at least certain versions of her—in order to save her. Yet, willingness to imagine the killing of the child, though a logical consequence of the protagonists' situations, is not presented uncritically. Rather, it functions to give brutal emphasis to the adult drive to locate security beyond social and political change, a compulsion framed and provoked through the child herself as finally unknown and unknowable. The acuteness of these questions and the intensity of their effects signal both the depth of disorientation felt in the United Kingdom in the 1970s and the extent of the risk that the child was perceived to present both toward and from the future she embodied. The films do not endorse violence against children, but they use the willingness to imagine it as a means to force us to take this risk seriously.

Dangerous Youth: Thatcherism between the Child and the Young Man

From the examples explored so far, we can see that certain reference points for Thatcherism's cultural politics emerged long before the first Thatcher government took office in 1979. The violent children of Macaulay, Greene, and Golding established the ghoulish suggestion, initially as a mere subtextual hint, that the child could be such a threat that they might be killed by adults with some degree of legitimacy; and this taboo-defying suggestion would be increasingly exploited, expanded, and rendered explicit in later horror texts, creating a version of the child that would persist throughout the popular culture of the 1980s and beyond (with significant effects for the reception of real crimes by and toward children, as seen in chapter 4).

As we have seen, though, Thatcherism's cultural politics were also driven by the established figure of a dangerous youth—even while they encouraged materialistic ambition and aspiration from young people, especially young men, in ways sometimes perceived as taboo, or at least as constrained in, postwar Britain and under the supposed social-democratic consensus of the 1950s, '60s, and '70s. Even while presenting the postwar and progressive child and youth as images of violent horror, Thatcherism sought to absorb and incorporate aspects of their aggression, materialism, and aspiration into its own vision of a future combining entrepreneurialism, nationalism, and social conservatism.

One way to escape the conflicts and contradictions latent in this project was to frame it as a reversion to an organic capitalist-conservative reality from which the postwar period was an aberration. Margaret Thatcher herself favored dramatically absolutist and moralistic accounts of recent history, with her economics heavily framed by cultural value judgments—she even attributed the alleged failings of Keynesian economics to the Bloomsbury Group's rejection of Victorian values in their private lives (*The Path to Power* 565). These cultural value judgments certainly extended to her views of children and youth. Of course, essentialist views of children as the revealed essence of human nature (an essence to be further manifested in adult society and economics) are liable to satire; and, as we shall see, several literary authors parodied Thatcherism's incorporation of elements it sometimes claimed to abhor in postwar and progressive children and youth, satirizing its pretensions to combine neoliberalism, nationalism, and social conservatism with success and stability and in various ways queering these pretensions or rendering them uncanny.

This literary response often targeted Thatcherism's relationship with the figure of the young man. As a rhetorical and cultural parallel to its economic aim of unleashing wealth through privatizing and deregulating swathes of the British economy, Thatcherism promised to release the ambitious male youth from the stultifying restrictions of the so-called postwar consensus and from the emasculatingly anti-militarist, feminist, and gay Loony Left. In a pervasive trope, Thatcher was the ambitious and indulgent mother; the wets and the postwar hierarchy were the moribund postwar patriarchate to be swept aside. There was an obvious Oedipal dynamic here, recognized at the time (Abse 1989) and subsequently: Thatcher, the desired mother, offered a tantalizing union of id with superego in declaring greed as good. This fantasy had very real political efficacy: not only opponents of Thatcherism but also sympathetic writers of its history, like Thatcher's biographer Charles Moore (2015), agree that Thatcherism's emphasis on materialistic opportunity—and the ambitious young men to whom it appealed—was central to its political success. Both proponents and opponents of Thatcherism asserted that the aspirational, ambitious, creatively destructive young man *was* the future Thatcherism promised;[12] this was a claim widely parodied in both popular and literary culture, from Loadsamoney to Martin Amis's John Self in *Money* (1984). As these parodies suggested, Thatcherism's associations with the creatively destructive male youth (often figured as either childish or as an actual child) threatened to conflict with its claims to conservative morality and social stability.

Literary responses to Thatcherism also emphasized this threat through showing the sanctioned aspirational youth as haunted by his dangerous doppelgängers. These dangerous youth show how their relationship with the anxious political reactions that would condense into Thatcherism is more complicated than their immediate role as signs of social danger and moral delinquency would suggest. They also repeatedly show class and sexuality as attributes of the male youth that troubled the successful channeling of his ambitions and energies into sanctioned, legitimized forms, and they implicate these problems as starting even before his youth, in his childhood. Before turning to those direct responses to the ambivalences and dangers of the Thatcher-Era youth, I want to consider a notorious film (and its source novel) that anticipated their concerns, not least of which the issue of channeling the youth's aspirations and the risks of an attempt to do so by a government: the film, in fact, cited by Margaret Thatcher herself.

A CLOCKWORK ORANGE (1971)

Stanley Kubrick's 1971 film adaptation of Anthony Burgess's 1962 novel *A Clockwork Orange* was widely accused of not only reflecting but also encouraging youth violence (an accusation framed by public concern, growing since the 1950s, over the influence of media on juvenile crime; Krämer xxi–xxii, 103–04), reflecting the source novel's status as "edgier, darker, and more alienating" (Ross 67) than any preexisting major depiction of British youth culture in the twentieth century. Indeed, the film became "such a familiar explanatory framework that [. . .] if no obvious explanation for a brutal crime committed by young people existed, then one might as well try out the idea that it had been 'caused,' one way or another, by *A Clockwork Orange*" (Krämer 107). This notion was sufficiently firmly established that when Margaret Thatcher invoked "the nightmare world of *A Clockwork Orange*"—a full seven years after the film's release and sixteen years after the novel's publication—she could expect its currency and salience to be taken seriously. The discourse around the film's social consequences assumed that children and youth really—or, at least, nearly—were as depicted by it: prone to lasciviously, viciously consuming objects of their desire without social control or moral judgment. The film's early reception showed adult discourse about violent youth becoming more extreme, more willing to imagine targeting children to preempt the violent young man's emergence (Krämer 63–66).

Alex DeLarge echoes *The Destructors*' Trevor in his charismatic leadership of an all-male youth gang (the Droogs), enthusiasm for high culture, and drive for unmediated access to objects of aesthetic and sexual enjoyment. The Droogs inhabit desolate urban spaces, though now the ruins are no longer of Second World War bombsites but rather of the postwar social-democratic future itself (as embodied in the Thamesmead housing estate used by Kubrick as the location for Alex's neighborhood). As with Trevor, Alex's desires are communicated primarily through his gaze—wide-eyed, often directed away from his companions and toward the viewers, a visible sign of an invisible yet materially dangerous imagination—and of a capacity for appreciation. Alex's gaze, grin, and aggressively penetrative physicality claim a right to access beautiful things in a childish, masculinist, and perverse social mobility. This theme (viewed in retrospect) looks forward toward Thatcherite aspiration discourse and its parodies as well as backward toward the Teddy Boys, echoed in the Droogs's neo-Edwardian outfits (Goh 265; Krämer 83), and toward the violence of the skinheads, a subculture with which the film (and novel) had a complicated symbiotic relationship (Ross, 76).

Kubrick's Alex begins the film aged seventeen or eighteen (though Malcolm McDowell, who played him, was actually twenty-eight). As Krämer observes, the Droogs register anxieties over "'teenagers' (a term which had only fairly recently come into widespread use), on their importance as consumers, [. . .] their tastes (especially in music and fashion), their sexual precocity and their delinquency" (63). Alex is still somewhat coded as a child, even though Kubrick aged him relative to the novel's fifteen-year-old: he still lives with his parents and should attend school; his sexual attitudes are juvenile; he delights in dressing up; and he repeatedly appears in bed attended by maternal figures. One Droog, Georgie, accuses Alex of thinking "like a little child."

A succession of institutions attempt to manage Alex's development: the family home on the postwar estate, the (unseen) school, probation service, prison, Ludovico Medical Facility (fig. 2.4), and the hospital. His enforced entry into most of these institutions mirrors his forced entries into the houses of others; in both cases, an entry into protected time and space for perverse "development" is underway. Alex successfully gains illegitimate access to Mr. Alexander's house, "Home," and the house of the Cat Lady—(fig. 2.5), both of which are modernist versions, either architecturally or in their contents, of the English country house; Kubrick suggestively chose a grander setting for Home than the novel's "malenky cottage" suggests (112). After his arrest for crimes committed therein, the authorities gradually assert more control over Alex, eventually via the "Ludovico treatment," which compels a painful, violently nauseous reaction to previous objects of joy, including his beloved Beethoven's Ninth Symphony. Surviving an attempted suicide following torture by a vengeful

Figure 2.4. The postwar institution: the Ludovico Medical Center in *A Clockwork Orange*. From *A Clockwork Orange*, directed by Stanley Kubrick, Polaris Productions/Hawk Films/Warner Bros/Columbia-Warner Distributors, 1971. Screenshot courtesy of Filmgrab.

Figure 2.5. The desired house: the Cat Lady at home in *A Clockwork Orange*. From *A Clockwork Orange*, directed by Stanley Kubrick, Polaris Productions/Hawk Films/Warner Bros/Columbia-Warner Distributors, 1971. Screenshot courtesy of Filmgrab.

Mr. Alexander, Alex eventually enters into an ambiguous partnership with the authoritarian Minister of the Interior, who is invested in displaying Alex as a model of successful transformation and channeling of the young man's dangerous impulses. The film closes with Alex's remark, "I was cured all right," as he slips into a blissful fantasy of sexual exhibitionism. (As Margaret DeRosia observes, Alex imagines his sexual display being watched by a crowd of "Victorian spectators" (63), implying a latent craving for the past that retrospectively provides a nicely ironic echo of Thatcher's Victorian Values.)

This ending uncannily invokes a need for conservative politics, in successfully attacking the bogeyman of the violent young man, to incorporate some of what it claimed to oppose: putting Alex through a second childhood of incarceration, from which his libidinal energies can be gradually revived and redirected into channels the regime can authorize and exploit. The Minister hints at this when he first picks Alex out, recognizing him as "enterprising, aggressive, outgoing, young, bold, vicious," and with a "good job and good salary," he promises a route toward responsible social mobility. Whereas before his arrest Alex violently punishes other

Droogs' suggestions that they should focus on high-value theft, seeing such economically rational crime as a poor substitute for the pleasures of pure destructive consumption, eventually he accepts the economic logic the Minister offers; yet, whether this translation of impulses will prove stable and sustainable remains unknown.

These characteristics are emphasized by the differences between the Kubrick movie and the Burgess source novel. By raising Alex's age, Kubrick made the moral stakes slightly more subtle than they are in the source text, where Alex's younger age makes his actions more obscene but also, importantly, gives greater mental and practical scope for the change and redemption to come later. The way moral choice operates as a thematic concern also differs between Burgess and Kubrick; whereas the novel ends with Alex making a decisive choice about his future, Kubrick's "I was cured alright," a sentiment expressed in conjunction with sexual fantasy, is far more ambivalent. The film's distinctive visual characteristics, and its triangulation between Alex's gaze and the viewer's, constantly emphasizes the attractions of appreciation and consumption in a way that is more visceral than the novel, tempering any sense of moral choice with a participatory susceptibility to give in to forceful desires and drives—this quality of the film was picked up by critics who imagined that even the attraction of the colorful, highly distinctive fashions displayed in it would automatically translate into copycat violence (Krämer 105). Whether or not we sympathize with Alex's predicament, his objects of desire are often literally in our line of sight (and we, the viewer, are often directly in Alex's line of sight—as in the famous extended opening shot—establishing a more erotic dynamic, where the violent threat presented by Alex is mixed with an attraction coerced by the camera). The most significant change between novel and film concerns the former's controversial final chapter (initially omitted from US editions), where Alex appears to make a decisive turn away from violence and toward economic rationalism and social responsibility; above all, his speculative plans about having a child of his own show his ultimate affirmation of reproductive futurism. Kubrick's Alex, however, reconciles to mainstream social order not through a conscience-examining internal reflection, nor through moral choice nor scientific rationalism, but rather—in a brilliant choice on Kubrick's part—via cynical recognition of mutual self-interest with the Minister of the Interior following the failure of a quasi-organicist experiment concerning the relationship between social and physical health (the Ludovico technique is a kind of anti-Theory theory).

Alex is not necessarily easier as a subject for theorizing today. In some respects, he is clearly rather queer; initially, at least, his homosocial, exhibitionist sexuality is cheerfully perverse, rejecting social conformity and reproductive futurism. DeRosia argues that the film's heterosexual encounters "are portrayed as less erotically cathected than, for example, the fight between Alex and his droogs and Billy Boy's gang, or Alex's post-Ludovico beatings. The film's representation of heterosexuality suggests that heterosexual rape, violence, and even consensual sex are really diversions or, more radically, a prelude to or substitute for more meaningful (and homophobically inflected) sadomasochistic encounters between men" (64). Though his queerness is certainly not explicit (and he rejects same-sex advances in prison), Alex is open to identification with a queer version of the death drive; yet, much about him complicates any such reading. His attack on Mr. Alexander—himself somewhat queer-coded, though married to a woman—does not ultimately produce either a moment of ecstatic fulfilment or sustain a continued singular drive but results in trauma, agony, conflict, and forced reintegration. It is also repeated and redirected toward Alex himself, in Alexander's revenge attempt to drive him to suicide—their shared name underlines this repetition, in their doubling of each other. And yet, Alex fails to either actually die or even to permanently lose his mind; if there is a singular drive at work here, it is one that bounces, with comic perversity, between the two men before it is ultimately defeated by a return of, as it were, historical and political process, with all the contingency that the latter, unlike a drive, involves. Alex's suicide attempt fails and only leads to reconciliation with the conservative authorities.

This reconciliation could be read as reflecting Edelman's thesis that the queer death drive is the constitutive other within reproductive futurism itself. Perhaps it is so—though, having failed here to sustain itself in opposition to the dominant (and reproductive) social order, it is far from guaranteed at the end of *A Clockwork Orange* that the queer death drive's absorption into this constitutive function is stable or self-sustaining. In other respects, Kubrick's Alex is the male youth who offers a doppelgänger to Edelman's Child. He is obviously the very opposite of an innocent child providing a secure figure for conservative exploitation, and he is not a completely recognizable queer figure; on the other hand, he is also neither securely *not* a child nor securely *not* queer. Whereas the Child characterized by Edelman depends on embodying a future that is always kept as future—the Child of reproductive futurism can never grow up—Alex is in the process of growing up, indeed is on the very border of adulthood, but has not yet crossed it successfully. And—in Kubrick's, though not in Burgess's, version—he is not yet securely ready for entrance into heterosexual monogamy and his own production of children. Kubrick's Alex is not a blank image for secure adult conservative projection, but neither are his motivations knowable or assimilable to a Freudian, Lacanian, or queer account of his drives. Despite this resistance to theoretical assimilation, Alex does demand—and eventually receives—material and political accommodation. Perhaps this disturbing combination accounts for what DeRosia observes as a surprisingly delayed and reluctant critical engagement with the gendered and sexual dynamics of the film (63).

Kubrick's movie provides an ambiguous warning about simplistic attempts to contain or channel the youth's capacity for creative destruction. It also assumes adult willingness to imagine the killing of this youth (as when Mr. Alexander elicits Alex's suicide attempt) as a remedy to the threat he poses where others, from the probation officer to the prison chaplain, have failed, while the only non-deadly remedy that apparently succeeds is a dubious (or is it pragmatic, even optimistic?) conservative absorption of the youth's aggressive, aspirational energies. An adaptation of Burgess that aged the protagonist slightly away from childhood and into "youth"—while retaining and developing some suggestive associations between this youth and "childness"—*A Clockwork Orange* also underlines the complexity in the relationship between the child, the youth, and the dangers of their imaginations and aspirations.

Dangerous Children and Youth in Literary Responses to Thatcherism

The established cultural repertoire of depictions of dangerous children and youth formed a ready and powerful source on which direct, contemporaneous, and later responses to Thatcherism's period in government could draw. These responses also, of course, developed in line with the peculiarities and particulars of the Thatcherite 1980s and with other developments of the time, from the increasing rise of theory within the academy, to the greater—but highly contested—visibility of queer and LGBTQ+ people in the UK following the decriminalization of homosexuality in 1967, the increase in gay and lesbian activism in the 1970s, and the child-obsessed backlashes of the 1980s. Peter Ackroyd, Doris Lessing, and Alan Hollinghurst—the writers considered next—share a perception of Thatcherism as a project defined by its attempted reversal of postwar and progressive futures. Their responses to this (mostly contemporaneous; one from a later, early 2000s, perspective) invoke the horror child as a recognizable trope, one even evoking—implicitly and sometimes explicitly—the possibility that this child might need to be killed. The deployment of this trope draws upon the horror movie genre and, inter alia, demonstrates the influence of that genre in making the literary descendants of the dangerous British boys and girls we saw in 1950s texts and in *A Clockwork Orange* into more extreme figures. Ackroyd's and Hollinghurst's novels also introduce the figure of the queer child, reflecting their salience for Clause 28–era British conservatism while closely associating the queer child with the horror child. All these authors also explore the relationship between the child and the youth as figures with a fraught but necessarily close relationship; and each of the novels described in the next section include adult attempts, ultimately unsuccessful, to channel the youth's childish energies. The children and youth they depict are often aspirational and entrepreneurial and have conservative objects of desire, but they are deeply perverse in the way they pursue their aspirations.

THE GREAT FIRE OF LONDON (1982) AND HAWKSMOOR (1985)

In his early career in the 1980s, Peter Ackroyd was heavily influenced by the rise of radical theory[13] while he engaged in complex, playful satires that imagined aspects of Thatcher-Era London as haunted by uncanny histories. Ackroyd's debut novel, *The Great Fire of London* (1982), attributed this haunting to a ghostly child. In the novel, filmmaker Spenser Spender plans a new movie adaptation of *Dickens' Little Dorrit*; he secures financing because his plans are perceived as taking a conservative approach to British literary heritage, which is expected to find favor with the Thatcher government (52–53); yet, unusually, Spender seeks to film at a still-occupied London prison that will act as Dickens's Marshalsea. The whole project becomes disturbed by the ghost of Little Dorrit herself—who, despite her fictional status, appears to possess a woman, Audrey, and to haunt a male child abuser, Little Arthur. Little Dorrit subverts all the schemes attempting to capture, theorize, and commoditize her story, proving an unassimilable spectral yet dangerous child. Eventually, Audrey burns down the film set, killing Spender, while the pedophile Arthur leads a prison breakout. Ackroyd uses this ghostly, fictitious, yet materially violent child to signify the chaotic and recalcitrant elements of history that are not readily assimilable to a rationalist neoliberal worldview, even one that promises to protect the essence of history and satisfy the ambitions of entrepreneurial young men.

Ackroyd returned to these themes in 1985 with what would become his most highly regarded novel—one that brings together horror tropes with a queer and psychoanalytic sensibility, and which audaciously mocks Thatcherism's essentialist approach to history and human nature through imagining it as haunted by older, darker, even satanic essentialisms offering alternative channels for childhood desires. *Hawksmoor* is structured as two parallel texts that unify at the ending. One is narrated by architect Nicholas Dyer, a macabre doppelgänger of the real Nicholas Hawksmoor (c. 1661–1736), who recounts his life as it has led from his childhood as a boy orphaned by plague to his 1711 commission to build seven London churches. The other text is a third-person narrative set in the mid-1980s, where a detective called Hawksmoor investigates a series of murders—mostly of children—perpetrated around Dyer's surviving churches. These churches are, in fact, coded embodiments of the gnostic religion into which Dyer was abducted in infancy—after he was abandoned following his parents' deaths in the plague—which recognizes evil and darkness as necessary elements of an unchanging universe, contrasting with the Enlightenment thought promoted by Dyer's rival and former mentor, Christopher Wren, presented in the novel as an ancestor of Thatcherite neoliberal rationalism.

In the 1980s, while detective Hawksmoor investigates the serial murders around Dyer's churches, he faces pressures to use new algorithm-driven technologies, successors to Wren's earlier science of reason and predictability, that promise to anticipate crime and thus secure the future against a London filled with murder, child abuse, delinquency, and homelessness. This is still the urban landscape recognizable from *A Clockwork Orange* and *The Destructors*, while the churches echo *The World My Wilderness* (and, more distantly, *Don't Look Now*). These structures embody the enduring power of the child's ambition: "I cou'd not Weep then but I can build now," says Dyer, recalling the discharge of his parents' bodies into the plague pit (16). In the ambivalent, otherworldly, yet violent threat they pose to children, the often now-derelict churches signal the risk of giving the child access to spaces that are materially rich, superficially sanctioned by authority, yet outside adult or mainstream surveillance. In this, they are very like the grand houses that form a consistent object for the child or youth's desire elsewhere but with the added function—both in their formal Christian existence and in their hidden Manichean coding—of acting as threshold spaces that mediate past and future. They are also institutions, albeit now superficially largely defunct.

Dyer reflects Ackroyd himself as a gay, working-class London boy who became, in the 1980s, celebrated and wealthy through his literary endeavors—which, like Dyer's architectural work, consisted of esoterically synthesizing from the ruins of the past, creating a queer-historicist parallel to Thatcherism's celebration of masculinist aspiration while countering its inherited Enlightenment rationalism and British nationalism. In the latter framework, the future is secured through rational knowledge, an expectation to which the sacrificial murder of children poses a dramatic challenge. These murders are driven, ironically, by Dyer's own childhood ambitions, which lead him to seek a legacy by consecrating each church with a human sacrifice, ideally of a child. These sacrifices are repeated in the 1980s murders and associated, in the novel's subtle synecdoche, with child abduction and child abuse, referenced as contemporary obsessions of 1980s Britain. Both the murderous child (Dyer, in that he is driven by his early childhood experiences) and the murdered child (Dyer's victims) are the means by which an invisible order in the universe is given visibility—in ways that echo, but unacceptably exceed (and thus satirize), the dominant Enlightenment epistemology's demands for visibility and repetition (as in the scientific method).

Critics have recognized the novel's engagement with Freud (Link), Lacan (Gunnarsdóttir Champion), and Derrida (Gunnarsdóttir Champion), whose frameworks are subtly but clearly invoked in the dynamics around childhood ambition, experience of parental death, and destructive creativity with which Ackroyd surrounds his antihero, who himself offers the proto-Freudian recognition that "The Mind in Infancy, like the Body in Embrio, receives impressions that cannot be removed" (14). Beneath *Hawksmoor*'s dazzling, exhibitionist synthesis of theoretical, political, and historical allusion, however, there is an underlying tension between the historically repressed as emerging through dangerously random and obscure motivations and ambitions that confound Enlightenment-neoliberal predictability and, alternatively, as constituting a pattern of repetition that reflects a coherent, if dark and normally hidden, reality. Dyer essentially asserts the second of these in response to his childhood experience of the first, in the forms of the death of his parents and the general chaos of the Plague: "It was as a meer Boy that I was placed into the Extremity of the Human State [. . .] for it was in that fateful year of the Plague that the mildewed Curtain of the World was pulled aside" (14).

There is also a tension between the churches as expressions of an ultimately stable, if uncanny, historical continuity and their roles as spaces of obscure attraction for the child, where apparently legitimate structures disguise ambitions and satisfactions that threaten to complicate the orderly adult world. This tension emerges through the roles of textuality versus materiality in the novel. Margrét Gunnarsdóttir Champion reads *Hawksmoor* as an essentially successful literary incorporation of Derridean *différance*, an "intense effort of imagination to fold virtual space into actual habitations" that pays off handsomely, "whose crucial feature is the embodiment, the materiality, of the word—language as a factor in the building of a real dwelling" (25). In this account, Ackroyd ultimately relieves any tension he initially creates through the novel's ending, where all the textual registers of the novel and its historical reference points collapse into a single reality characterized by essential transhistorical unity, a unity that renders specific historical transitions (like that between postwar and Thatcherite Britain) as ultimately trivial. Here, Dyer's acts of child sacrifice, driven by his childhood aspirations and trauma, effectively collapse the child as subject and object into a single essential figure: a death drive that relieves the tension of an encounter with the Other, finding Edelman's teleological place "of an Imaginary past" where "being and meaning are joined as One" (10). The language of the novel's final encounter explicitly invokes this collapse, in terms that evoke the same Lacanian terminology on which Edelman drew: "And his own Image was sitting beside him, pondering deeply and sighing, and when he put out his hand and touched him he shuddered. But do not say that he touched him, say that they touched him. [. . .] They were face to face [. . .] and who could say where one had ended and the other hand begun?" (216–17).

This conclusion appears when, having pursued his ghostly nemesis, Detective Hawksmoor finally reaches the Church of Little St. Hugh, the only one of the churches in the novel to be wholly fictional, indicating Ackroyd's final attempt to assert textual control over what has been, until now, a mix of material and textual reality; the real dwelling is built on language, as Gunnarsdottir Champion says, but now seemingly *only* on language. (The fictitious church's name alludes to the antisemitic medieval myth of a child-saint murdered by Jews in a ritual sacrifice.) Inside, Hawksmoor has a mystical encounter with his doppelgänger, Dyer, that perhaps signifies his own murder and incorporates him into the novel's series of murders and child sacrifices, whereupon Ackroyd's narrative voice seems to dissolve into a unity with his two protagonists and with some greater transhistorical host:

> [A]nd I must have slept, for all these figures greeted me as if they were in a dream. The light behind them effaced their features [. . .] The dust covered their feet and I could see only the direction of their dance, both backwards and forwards. And when I went among them, they touched fingers and formed a circle around me; and, as we came closer, all the while we moved further apart. Their words were my own but not my own, and I found myself on a winding path of smooth stones. And when I looked back, they were watching one another silently.
>
> And then in my dream I looked down at myself and saw in what rags I stood; and I am a child again, begging on the threshold of eternity. (216–17)

The reference to the "Image" and the emphasis on being "face to face" evokes the Lacanian childhood experience of traumatic splitting from the maternal with which *Hawksmoor* begins, but it is now—mystically rather than theoretically—utterly resolved into a unity behind and beyond history. Killing the child, and killings by the child who has gone through this experience, are but an expression of the desire to return to this. This is, then, another version of the death drive, given a new mystical dimension, where the churches are straightforward recapitulations of the child's experience of loss that express his underlying drive toward epistemological stasis. The killing of the child here transforms a risk in the relationship between past and future into a guarantee of transhistorical continuity.

Insofar as *Hawksmoor* functions as (among other things) a satire on Thatcherite essentialism and on its indulgence of masculine aspiration and entrepreneurialism, it presents an alternative account of historical reality that emphasizes the esoteric, the traumatic, the queer, and the repressed, and it boldly dares to figure these through a fetishized figure for Thatcherism's emphasis on both social mobility and social conservatism: the child. *Hawksmoor* is one of several texts where Thatcherism's attempt to absorb and contain the child's ambitions and aspirational energies is satirized by imagining just how violent, perverse, and queer these energies can become, exceeding any such attempts at containment. The ultimately rather authoritarian, and certainly historically essentialist, ending of *Hawksmoor* does not, however, wholly erase the more difficult, dangerous, and queer dynamics that the novel so powerfully introduces. Despite the author's final turn to a purely textual space, the material yet obscure spaces built by and for the ambitious child and young man recall the possibility of a satisfaction not disclosed to the reader in the all-encompassing way that the ending offers, and which, in belonging to our own material and historical world, might be of more than textual consequence. Their proliferation and grandeur; their epistemological and architectural excess; their persistent, uncanny presence; their roles as sites of encounter that are left obscure to the reader despite the promises of the ending; and the operatic, deeply pleasurable pathos of the language with which Dyer (and Ackroyd) describe them all trouble their apparent role as simple, singular expressions of a powerful death drive. So, too, does their latent role as institutions, holding out the possibility of their ongoing use as spaces of mediation between past and future, as with the ruined—but in child's play revived—churches seen earlier in *The World My Wilderness*. As a response to Thatcherism's contradictions and the centrality of the child-as-future within these, *Hawksmoor*—despite itself—raises the possibility that such a response might be more material than textual and drawn from the very indulgence of the young man's ambition, right from childhood, that Thatcherism promises but ultimately cannot contain.

THE FIFTH CHILD (1988)

Doris Lessing's novel *The Fifth Child* ties together the dangerously inscrutable child and violent youth of postwar fears by satirizing the Thatcherite revival of social conservatism and its rejection of 1960s and '70s progressive movements. Here, the ideal of a middle-class nuclear family with "traditional values" as the answer to "problem children" comes under sustained attack, as Lessing evokes tropes from the horror genre, particularly *Rosemary's Baby* (1968) and *The Omen* (1976), alongside *A Clockwork Orange*-style fears about irrationally violent young men and gangs.

The Fifth Child opens by narrating the relationship of David Lovatt and his wife Harriet, who share a discomfort with a society they perceive as narcissistic, self-indulgent, and disdainful of any healthily reproductive culture (7). Harriet and David earnestly desire a large family and traditional parent roles. Both have liberal, permissive parents of their own, whose examples they are determined to "annul, absolve, cancel out" (18).

Their conservative project is, ironically, itself a youthful rebellion (18), and David's mother and stepfather perceive that their desire for a large number of children shows "the spirit [. . .] of excess" (18). Initially, though, all goes to plan, as Harriet successively gives birth to four children despite the challenges of living against "the spirit of the times, the greedy and selfish sixties" (29) and its manifestations: "Brutal incidents and crimes, once shocking everyone, were now commonplace. Gangs of youths hung around certain cafes and street-ends [. . .] At the end of the road there was a telephone box that had been vandalised so many times the authorities had given up" (29–30). Harriet's fifth child, Ben, is born in 1974 (74–75), his early childhood coinciding with some of the major national crises, referenced in the novel, of the 1970s, frustration with which would ultimately fuel the rise of Thatcherism (74). Ben is all-consuming, demanding far more milk than normal for his age, bruising Harriet's breasts. He is only two months old when Harriet lets slip the direction her imagination has taken: "After all, I don't want to kill the nasty little brute" (67). Her violent impulse responds to the threat she begins, unconsciously at first, to imagine Ben poses to her: "He resisted, he strove, he fought—and then [. . .] closed his jaws over her thumb. Not as an ordinary baby will, in the sucking bite that relieves the pain of teething, or explores the possibilities of a mouth, tongue: she felt her bone bend, and saw his cold triumphant grin. She heard herself say, 'You aren't going to do me in, I won't let you'" (69). There is already a rising suggestion, then, that this child must either kill or be killed. Adults and other children gaze on Ben with "fear" and "horror," but "it was hard to make out what he did think of other people" (70). Ben is obscure in his motivations and pointlessly destructive in his actions, endangering fellow children (71) and killing animals (76). There is a gesture toward the myth of the changeling, and also toward popularized psychoanalytic ideas being confounded, when Ben fails to return Harriet's gaze in a way she considers natural (73). Contrasting with the politics of Hollywood's standard horror-child tropes, here, the unaccountably destructive child seemingly punishes his parents for their attempt to restore a conservative family ideal against the grain of recent history.

Harriet and David's attempt to build a large, nuclear family with traditional values also goes against the grain of increased emphasis on the role of institutions in raising children and giving opportunities to youth, countering such later twentieth-century innovations with an emphasis on the organic nurturing of the future provided by the family home. It is this attempt that makes it particularly shocking when Harriet and David, betraying the ideals they have sought to realize, conclude that Ben must be institutionalized in a specialist facility. Once this conclusion becomes a reality, Harriet shockingly realizes "that Ben was not expected to live long in this institution" (90); the child is, finally, out-of-sight and, gradually, to be killed. However, wracked with guilt, Harriet goes to retrieve him and finds him in appalling conditions; a staff member confirms that Ben was likely to die from the sedatives given to prevent his rages (103). Rescuing Ben, but recognizing the impossibility of raising him normally, Harriet takes the bizarre step of paying a local "gang of unemployed young men" (110) to look after him. In a startling reconfiguration of the usual role of dangerous youth gangs, the conservative adult finds that she needs them to take care of the violent child (110-11). As a teenager, while his disturbing status as alien horror child collapses into the rather more banal template for the dangerous youth, Ben gradually develops into leading his own gang. Eventually, Harriet and David abandon Ben to the gang and "the half-derelict buildings [. . .] of the big cities" (157).

The Fifth Child locates increased adult willingness to contemplate killing the child who threatens to kill within the fraught relationship between 1980s social conservatism and recent progressive pasts. Ben remains fundamentally unassimilable—though not unique: Lessing's narrator notes that "all these schools have a layer, like a sediment, of the uneducable, the unassimilable, the hopeless" (144–45). Does Ben represent some permanent human strain of evil—as Harriet speculates, a "throwback" to some prehistoric race (127)? Or is he merely an expression of historical contingency, of the terrifying randomness of having four "good" children followed by a fifth who turns out very differently? Or perhaps the adults are simply paranoid in the face of an extraordinarily difficult child? Whatever the answers, reactionary conservatism's approach to children emerges as inadequate, as Lessing takes the tropes of the horror child and applies them savagely to Thatcherism's moral hinterland.

The Swimming Pool Library (1988) and *The Line of Beauty* (2004)

Alan Hollinghurst's novels *The Swimming Pool Library* (1988) and *The Line of Beauty* (2004) root Thatcherism's aspirational young man, his dangerous rivals, and his despised queer doppelgänger in a common origin in childhood imagination and ambition. Hollinghurst explores the dissoluble boundaries between sanctioned and feared forms of aspiration, which appears here as both class-driven and materialistic. He also introduces the queer child as a figure of horror for Thatcherite social conservatism, linking them to horror-child tropes. Hollinghurst's protagonists are young gay men with access to conservative elites and who are susceptible both to their pleasures and to those of rival, queer subcultures, for reasons traced to their childhood ambitions. As Will Beckwith, *The Swimming Pool Library*'s protagonist, says, it was "as if from my earliest days my destiny had indeed been charmed" (7–8). Through Will's perverse Bildungsroman and that of *The Line of Beauty*'s Nick Guest, Hollinghurst audaciously draws parallels between Thatcherism and queer subcultures, with both offering to fulfil childhood aspirations that earlier twentieth-century Britain seemingly constrained and both undermining class hierarchies and racialized essentialisms in ways neither they nor the protagonists necessarily intend.

In *The Line of Beauty*, Nick Guest lodges in the home of Gerald Fedden, a government minister, and his wife Rachel—the parents of Nick's university friend Toby, who give Nick access to wealthy society far beyond that available from his own provincial, lower-middle-class parents. Thatcher's role among the Feddens' Thatcherite circle is that of the symbolic mother releasing her sons into pleasures previously restricted by "socialist" postwar values: "The men did something naughty, and got away with it" (62). This oedipal comment comes from a closeted gay character who himself later becomes a successful Thatcherite politician, Paul "Polly" Tompkins, who pursues sex with entrepreneurial "will, opportunism and technique" (62). Having Thatcher as the mother who removes restraint symbolically makes the young man into an indulged child—a trope prevalent in popular culture of the time, as we have seen—and Hollinghurst finds parallels between Thatcher's men "doing something naughty," queer subcultures, and desires and curiosities first established in childhood. These parallels are echoed in such instances as when Nick visits his wealthy boyfriend Wani Ouradi's family and finds that Wani has a young cousin, Little Antoine, whose materialistic energy echoes that of his older cousin: "Little Antoine had a remote-controlled toy car, which Wani was encouraging him to crash [. . .] a bright-red Ferrari with a whiplike antenna. Nick crouched forward [. . .] but the two boys seemed oblivious of him, Wani almost snatching the controls now and then to cause a top-speed collision" (210–11). Antoine's delight is an early form of the drive for unrestrained libidinal pleasure that his cousin, Wani, pursues through his entrepreneurial and sexual careers; and Little Antoine's Ferrari displays pleasure before its integration and containment in an adult order, while betraying a hint that such containment (allegiance to which is especially demanded from an immigrant family like the Ouradis) is far from stable: "The Ferrari smacked into Bertrand's slipper once again [. . .] 'Enough Ferrari for today,' Bertrand said, and gave it back to the child with no fear of being disobeyed. Nick felt abruptly nervous at the thought of crossing Bertrand, and those same naked images of his son melted queasily away" (214). Nick instinctively reads the collision as an uncanny sign of the risks he is himself taking in his relationship with Bertrand's son, imagining Little Antoine's affectionate relationship with Wani as a peculiar parallel to his own (217). This startling co-location of queer desire and material aspiration in shared desires for play, display, and pleasure that originate in childhood hints that the lines between these things are entangled—an entanglement Hollinghurst not only pursues across the boundaries between queerness and homophobic Thatcherism, or those between the white British and immigrants, but also across those between classes, as seen when Nick returns with Gerald to his hometown:

> Some lads, or "louts," roamed about under [. . .] the market hall [that] had been the pride of Nick's childhood [. . .] his private architectural heaven. The moment of accepting it was not by Wren had been as bleak and exciting as puberty. Now he revved round it, the lads looked up [. . .] the achievements of sex and equities and titles and drugs blew out in a long scarf behind him [. . .] pleasures and privileges these boys couldn't imagine and thus beyond their envy [. . .] Gerald sprang out [. . .] torn between his sporty show-off self and a hint of compromised dignity [. . .] in being seen in such a car with a young gay man. (285)

It is not only Gerald who engages in a dubious containment strategy here. Nick suggests the "achievements" his car embodies are beyond the lads' jealousy (though the car itself clearly is not), establishing a mental containment of potential for social disturbance—a disturbance he himself is, in fact, unintentionally carrying out, here and throughout the novel. The containment of pleasures of wealth, spectacle, and beautiful things by social class, education, and capital includes tendencies toward its own destruction, in how noisy displays of their pleasures—a noisiness Thatcherism is ready to indulge—risk the spread of envy, invite voyeurism, and attract emulation that cannot be easily contained. Gerald's comical anxiety to avoid recognizing the affinity between his own exhibitionism and Nick's queerness ironically reflects Nick's own mental containment strategy against the lads here, based as it is on his class mobility and, subtly, on gayness itself as a category that, even in this homophobic society, offers certain privileged, if perpetually compromised, forms of association and access. Such associations, evident in the Feddens' web of quiet codes to hedge their limited tolerance and (literal) accommodation of Nick, are a way of acknowledging that what is openly visible is not all that is there, hence Gerald's ambivalent discomfort in the car; but they also hinge on the paradox of recognizing and thereby neutering the opacity of the sexual, economic, and generational other, the quasi-adoptee that Nick becomes—a function that leaves them on the verge of repressed paranoia, as later events in the novel betray. The fact that not only the Feddens but also Nick himself seems to engage this containment function implies that we might take its problems not only as predicting the inevitable breakdown of socially conservative hypocrisies, but as more fundamentally exposing the attraction of fantasies of greater epistemological and material security than the contingent distinctions of class, education, sexual orientation and age really justify.

The fact that the associations of gayness, certainly as understood by Nick and by most of those around him, are intellectual and aesthetic covers for the fact (betrayed, again, by the car) that they are simultaneously materialistic and, thus, likely not so cleanly beyond the local boys' imagination as Nick tries to imagine. As Urszula Terentowicz-Fotyga points out, Nick believes in his own "right to claim the heritage of the grand mansion" (67) owned by Rachel Fedden's brother—based on his capacity, nurtured in childhood, for aesthetic appreciation—but the security of this claim is pressured on both sides, most obviously by the upper classes who actually own the buildings and things Nick desires but also more subtly by the young working-class and lower-middle-class young men who do not share his education, sensibilities, or sexuality but threaten their own intrusions into elite spaces—like whoever spray-painted the words "CUNTS ENTRANCE" beside the gate to the Feddens' former home (195). Nick's repressed fear here would surely be of a lad like *A Clockwork Orange*'s Alex, the young heterosexual lout as violent as he is passionate for high culture. (Once again, perhaps surprisingly, it is architecture—where aesthetics are bound into material spaces—that provides an object of desire here, the reference to Wren even echoing *The Destructors*.)

Hollinghurst leads his reader, then, toward a subtle skepticism regarding the risk of queer, as well as socially conservative, frameworks of recognition giving us overly reassuring categories within which to contain the imaginative and material ambitions of children and youth. Meanwhile, the hints of repressed connection between Nick's queer penetration of Thatcherite high society and class- and race- or migration-based disruptions of the latter subtly imply that Thatcherism's incorporation of social mobility alongside social conservatism, through indulgence of the ambitious young man, will ultimately prove as unstable as its more open homophobia.

In Hollinghurst's earlier *The Swimming Pool Library*, the protagonist Will's social and sexual adventures—which, like Nick's, cross class and racial lines—are linked to his underlying awareness of class insecurity and its retrospective framing of his childhood self-fashioning: "As a child, on visits to Marden, my grandfather's house, days had been marked by walks along the great beech ride [. . .]feeling decidedly noble and aloof. It was not until years later that I came to understand how recent and synthetic this nobility was—the house itself bought up cheap after the war" (7). The child's infatuation with the house that they believe they deserve, often because of their aesthetic and sensual appreciation for it, is a frequent source of trouble, as we will see again soon in *The Little Stranger*. It registers materialistic aspiration combined with a continuing attachment to organicist, hierarchical assumptions about national identity, race, and class. Louisa Hadley and Elizabeth Ho argue that the organicist heritage associations of the country house in late twentieth-century Britain "perfectly balanced the adventure, freedom, and capitalism of 'enterprise culture'" (12). Hollinghurst, however—like Sarah Waters, as we shall see shortly—imagines this balancing as precarious, at risk of disruption from the child whose appreciation, imagination, and ambition leads them to want to delight in objects and places of material beauty and to seek to possess them outside of authorized channels (a disruption figured, of course, by the disruption to patrilineal inheritance and patriarchal control that queerness threatens). Even a culture that prioritizes organicist and essentialist ideas takes the risk that the child might take these ideas, or at least the objects they value, and pursue them in their own way and in their own time, as we have seen from Macaulay's Barbary and Raoul.

For Hollinghurst, the ultimate consequences of childhood desires and their adult fulfilment tend to be recalcitrant toward adult attempts at containment and even secure recognition. This reality registers, for example, through Will's six-year-old nephew Rupert:

> "I mean," Rupert looked up at me cogitatively, "almost everyone is homosexual, aren't they? Boys, I mean."
> "I sometimes think so," I hedged. [. . .]
> "Am I one?" Rupert asked intently.
> "It's a bit early to say yet, old fellow. But you could be, you know."
> "Goody!" he squealed, banging his heels against the front of the sofa again. "Then I can come and live with you."
> "Would you like that?" I asked, my avuncular rather than my homosexual feelings deeply gratified by this. And really Rupert's cult of the gay, his innocent, optimistic absorption in the subject, delighted me even while its origin and purpose were obscure. (71–72)

Tellingly, the child's enthusiasm to live with his gay uncle coalesces not as any clear aspiration about his own future development but rather as an immediate desire to access the times and spaces his uncle enjoys. The obscurity of Rupert's inner life becomes crucially important when he is an accidental witness to Will's sheltering of his lover, Arthur, after the latter has apparently killed a man. It also registers how queer modes of reading childhood operate as an ambivalent paradox: they allow adults to recognize the obscurity of children; on the other hand, such a practice of recognition and categorization, even as "queer," inevitably at least partially diminishes or sidesteps that obscurity.

Recognizing queerness as an act of making obscure childhood motivations visible takes a dark turn when, at *The Line of Beauty*'s conclusion, Nick is rhetorically transformed into a kind of monstrous child, where his ambition, aspiration, and social mobility are rewritten as a dark and destructive thing, with Thatcherism—in the form of Gerald Fedden—spewing back the aspirational forces it grudgingly allowed to assimilate and the young man it accommodated: "I mean, didn't it strike you as rather odd, a bit queer, attaching yourself to a family like this? [. . .] It's an old homo trick. You can't have a real family, so you attach yourself to someone else's. And I suppose after a while you just couldn't bear it, you must have been very envious I think of everything we have, and coming from your background too perhaps . . .'" (481). Gerald, who is a minister in the Home Office with responsibility for immigration policy, simultaneously evokes Nick as a fake, foreign child and as a child-destroyer—as, in fact, an uncanny child who threatens danger behind the appearance of innocence. The aspirational young man reverts in this narrative to an abject and murderous queer changeling, a horror-child figure with an added queer framing. Nick becomes, retrospectively, a kind of illicit migrant in class and in life, an ironic parallel to his immigrant and second-generation boyfriends, whose status also brings them into actual or potential conflict with Thatcherite values.

Across Hollinghurst, Ackroyd, and Lessing, we see Thatcherism as failing to securely contain the young man's ambitions, even as it promises to indulge them. We also see these ambitions as deriving from childhood, while material objects and spaces appear as objects of desire that, even in their very materiality, attract the child's ambition and the possibility of adult satisfaction, but in ways that refuse strategies of recognition and containment along class, sexual, racial, or nationalist lines.

∼

We have seen how, from the early postwar period, the child, as an embodiment of the future, drew severe anxiety—even producing a willingness, represented with particular force and clarity in literature and film, to imagine that the child might be a killer and might, in turn, need to be killed. We have observed that this perceived threat persisted and evolved while new anxieties about further social changes arose and that this encompassed both teenaged youths and very young children. These tropes became so established that conservative reaction could readily cite them as evidence of a mistaken, perverted future that needed to be revoked and urgently replaced with a healthier relationship with both the national past and the natural order of things. The Thatcher governments eventually gained repeated electoral mandates to do this, promising new opportunities for a new generation of children and youth and seeking to save them from the violent, chaotic, and amoral—or simply ambition-destroying—role models that social democracy and progressive subcultures had supposedly provided. Yet, even as it rendered postwar children and youth as abject images of horror, Thatcherism was nevertheless often suspected of attempting to incorporate the aggressive energies of such (mostly male) youth into its political project, offering social mobility and materialistic aspiration. All of these developments took place within an often fraught traffic between theory, literature, film, and politics. Although early in the period, Donald Winnicott, newly popularized, sought to provide authoritative reassurance on the benefits of correct child-rearing models. The very need for such reassurance affirmed the existence of a risk in the nature of the postwar child-as-future—a risk given vivid and startling articulation by Macaulay, Greene, and Golding. Later, political support for and academic interest in non-normative sexualities, an interest often framed through theories with their roots in psychoanalysis, contributed to turning "theory" into a general target of conservatism.

Assessed retrospectively, much of this material invites theoretically informed—especially psychoanalytic and queer—readings (and it has indeed received such readings, some of them cited previously). Yet, it also challenges such frameworks. Straightforward diagnosis of Trevor in *The Destructors* as the embodiment of a queer death drive—of the sort that we could, as Edelman suggests with different examples, simply choose to embrace—is complicated by how his target is not a heterosexual family but rather another lone, un(re)productive male who seems rather queer himself and wants only to be left alone to enjoy the house Trevor so desires. Many of the protagonists here similarly invite queer theory in, as it were, only to confound it as the basis for a critical reading based on any affirmative recognition. Some of the children and youth here seem to fulfil Bond Stockton's notion of "growing sideways," but the times and spaces they create for themselves either (as with Trevor) involve more consumption than growth, or they appear to fulfil fundamentally conservative visions of life and society (as with Raoul and Barbary, Nick Guest, the demonic Dyer, or even, in a different way, the children in *Lord of the Flies*). Thatcherism's attempt to co-opt and incorporate the child's aspirational and materialistic energies may be naive, but it nevertheless seems to recognize a potential for the object of the child's desires to be, in some respects, conservative. Sometimes this is about a fundamentalist or organicist worldview, but it is also concerned with the material objects and impressive spaces alluringly offered by such a worldview. As we saw, even Alex DeLarge, the most dangerous of postwar youths, has grand houses (and the artwork and people that inhabit them) as a primary object of his desires; and he is ultimately party to an ambiguous accommodation with a conservative political project.

Throughout, the sheer intensity of the child's desire for these spaces and places forms a parallel to the intensity of adult anxieties toward the child and youth. It is partly for this reason that conservatives should ultimately find no more secure comfort than progressives and queer readers from these narratives. The objects celebrated by conservative, hierarchical Britain provoke an excess of desire that—even within Thatcherism's neoliberal attempt to accelerate the timetable of social mobility and fulfilment of individual aspiration—cannot be easily accommodated by any kind of stable adult order, much as it cannot be straightforwardly transversed through interpretative frameworks. Alex DeLarge demonstrates this point from the position of the violent and (at least primarily) heterosexual youth; Nick Guest demonstrates it from that of the queer, subtle, refined, social-climbing young man. The variety and intensity of uses to which the children and youths discussed in this chapter put the spaces and objects they penetrate, take over, and possess, along with the persistent obscurity of their motivations, forces adults to turn from the realm of secure epistemology—whether conservative, progressive, or theoretical—and live in the material, historical realm. This is not a realm that Britain was generally comfortable with in the later twentieth century, as seen in the repeated turns to organicist theories of history, human nature, and the nation (the appeal of which *Hawksmoor*, for example, both satirizes and finally succumbs to).

All these issues speak to a sense of the relationship between past and future as ruptured and in need of restoration and reconfiguration. This sense had cultural salience from the early postwar period through to, and beyond, Thatcherism's attempt to reconfigure the relationship away from postwar social democracy and toward an organicist conservatism and nationalism—which had, in any case, never gone away. Exploring these issues through the dangerous child raises the stakes as high as they can reach. They are also issues for the institutions that attempted not only to accommodate the child and the youth but also, in a more fundamental sense, to mediate between past and future—a project that exists in tension with an organicist view of the world, where such institutions should hardly be required (*Lord of the Flies* being, of course, one attempt to imagine their total absence).

In the final part of this chapter, I turn to an early twenty-first-century novel that looks back on and synthesizes many of these late twentieth-century issues and anxieties while also bringing an uncanny distance to bear upon them. This is Sarah Waters's 2009 novel *The Little Stranger*, which distils and works through many of the themes seen throughout this chapter. These include a willingness from adults—including both characters in the text and potentially its readers—to attribute the source of threats and problems presented by ambitious youth to children and childhood and even to blame their more sinister effects on a very young child, drawing on the tropes of horror cinema in doing so, even to the extent of seeking to blame the child for killing off the future. One of the children so blamed has queer qualities but deprives any progressive associations and thwarts any affirmations.

The Little Stranger also constitutes a sideways, uncanny, retrospective prehistory for Thatcherism's psychocultural dynamics and conflicts in its combination of aspirational social mobility and social conservatism and in its relationship with the postwar period. It not only depicts objects of aspiration—material things and, particularly, a house—as straying outside the legitimated channels through which a socially mobile young man might access them but also as providing a satisfaction that undermines interpretations that regards such objects as merely a substitute, fetish, or cipher for some other drive or aim. This satisfaction emerges as both politically and epistemologically dangerous and as powerfully related to childhood.

Looking Back from Post-Thatcherism: *The Little Stranger* (2009)

By returning to a late 1940s moment preceding, yet closely anticipating, most of the major social-democratic developments of "postwar Britain," Sarah Waters's *The Little Stranger* explores the tensions that later became Thatcherism by imagining them uncannily haunting the time immediately before the postwar developments to which they responded. These tensions play out in the novel's underlying opposition between the grand private house and the postwar public institution—which, for most of the novel, does not yet exist yet anticipatorily haunts the protagonist's consciousness—and in the irony of the narrator's aspirational social mobility functioning alongside his paranoia over the class destabilization represented by the NHS, a combination that emphasizes his proto-Thatcherite orientation. As Emma Parker observes, *The Little Stranger* "exposes the mystification of class oppression, questions the seductive charm of the country house set and stresses the destructive consequences of envy and anger ignited by social inequality" (99); it also reflects "the rising popularity of the country house in the noughties, coupled with the increasing demonisation of the working-class" (100) under New Labour, the heir to (at least elements of) the Thatcherite project. Waters's novel revives an irony that has recurred throughout this chapter: the postwar child wants to possess some material, sexual, or aesthetic object that originates in a deeply conservative form, yet this child's desire nevertheless possesses a genuinely radical—or at least difficult to contain—materialist potential. This theme is literalized in the novel's obsessive focus on material things and their capture by the jealous child who endures within the adult.

Waters's novel presents a spectral child, scapegoated by a creatively destructive protagonist who is consumed by his own childhood desires, adult repressions, and reformulations of those desires. This is Faraday, a doctor in rural Warwickshire, whose career represents a significant social advance from the position of his now-deceased working-class parents. One day, Faraday is called to the local gentry house, where his mother once worked in service and which he vividly recalls visiting as a child for an Empire Day fête (fig. 2.6), when he was entranced by the experience (fig. 2.7). Hundreds Hall is home to the Ayres family, now comprising the glamorous widow Mrs. Ayres; her adult son Roderick, a traumatized war veteran who attempts to keep the estate marginally viable; and her adult daughter, Caroline. Faraday is fascinated by the house's severe decline, contrasting so powerfully with his childhood memory of it; and, initially through providing treatment to the physically and psychologically scarred Roderick, he becomes an increasingly frequent visitor. The Hundreds estate is threatened by its economic incompatibility with postwar social change and by the interest of a local housing developer, who is engaged in building homes for the working and lower-middle classes, in buying its land—a prospect that represents, paradoxically, both a financial salve and a final destruction.

Faraday is soon made aware of a belief in spectral happenings at Hundreds. Although he aggressively opposes such claims, these happenings seem to oddly parallel his own attempts to infiltrate the family by starting a relationship with Caroline Ayres, which intensifies after he engineers for Roderick (who is badly disturbed by apparent encounters with supernatural forces or, alternatively, by war trauma) to be committed, and which he ultimately—but unsuccessfully—attempts to convert into marriage. The specter at Hundreds is repeatedly figured as a ghostly

Figure 2.6. Hundreds Hall in its better days, during Faraday's childhood visit to the fête in the 2018 film adaptation of *The Little Stranger*. From *The Little Stranger*, directed by Lenny Abrahamson, Potboiler Productions/Dark Trick Films/Element Pictures/Film4/Pathé/Twentieth Century Fox, 2018. Screenshot courtesy of Filmgrab.

Figure 2.7. During the fête, the young Faraday turns away from his parents to gaze longingly upon the house. From *The Little Stranger*, directed by Lenny Abrahamson, Potboiler Productions/Dark Trick Films/Element Pictures/Film4/Pathé/Twentieth Century Fox, 2018. Screenshot courtesy of Filmgrab.

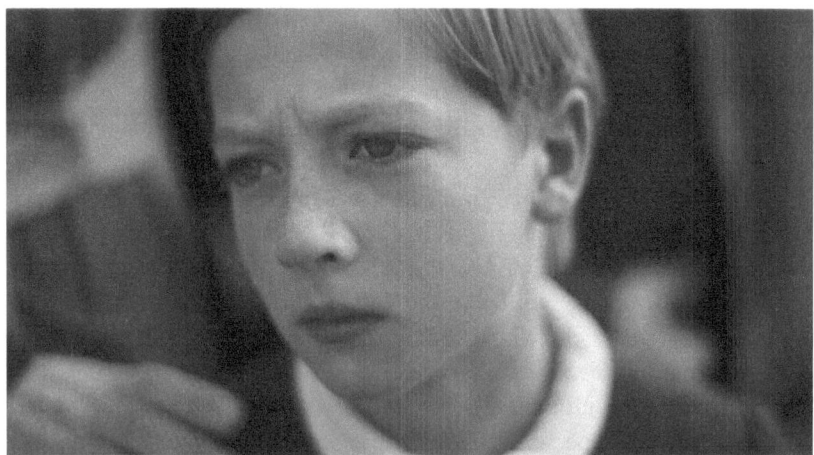

child. Mrs. Ayres identifies it with Susan, her first daughter, who died aged eight—and who was present during Faraday's own childhood visit to Hundreds (1). Yet, if this ghost is a child, it is a violently threatening one. When Mrs. Ayres goes to investigate some strange occurrences, she is locked in the nursery where Susan died. Attempting to escape, Mrs. Ayres cuts herself; she briefly recovers and expresses belief in her daughter's presence, only to hang herself soon afterward. Caroline, too, following a final repudiation of Faraday's attempts to coerce her into marriage, apparently commits suicide by throwing herself off a landing. The novel ends with Faraday, three years later, wandering through the abandoned house, taking physical (if not legal) possession at last.

Waters's novel, which builds on the uncanny role of the grand country house in legitimate and illegitimate claims to inheritance in her earlier *Fingersmith* (2002), is a palimpsest of tropes from the child-horror genre—like grainy photographs (174–75), mysteriously appearing childish writing on walls (298–308), and haunted nursery objects (331–33)—deploying a grammar taken from both horror cinema and literary antecedents like *The Turn of the Screw*. Susan is—apparently—the ghost of Hundreds' lost future, avenging itself on the surviving Ayres family members, who have failed to preserve their inheritance just as they failed to protect the child from mortality. Preserved outside time, she figures the inescapable legacy of the essential value(s) of the Ayreses' class position, unable to tolerate the historical change that has overthrown that position. She is seemingly a killer child, implicated in all the accumulating violence at Hundreds. Yet, there are compelling, if ambivalent, hints that the spectral Susan is a scapegoat concealing another malicious child: Dr. Faraday carries around his own inner child like some malevolent worm burrowing into the walls of Hundreds (something he actually did during his own childhood visit), and he constantly returns to the *Nachträglichkeit* of his childhood intrusion into Hundreds Hall, with its implied continuity in his later attempts to take possession, which only succeed—after a fashion—once the "ghost" has disposed of all the Ayreses. This implication of Faraday as host of the "real" killer-child behind the novel's human and material destruction, though always retained at the level of ambiguous (albeit persistent) subtext, has been widely critically recognized (Parker 106; Boehm 253–54; Germanà 128), and was directly dramatized in the 2018 movie adaptation.

The novel ends suggestively: "If Hundreds Hall is haunted, however, its ghost doesn't show itself to me. For I'll turn, and am disappointed—realising that what I am looking at is only a cracked window-pane, and that the face gazing distortedly from it, baffled and longing, is my own" (499). The film visualizes this self-identification of the "ghost" and directs it toward the child in a more explicit way: as Faraday walks out of Hundreds, he is watched by his child-self standing on the landing (fig. 2.8; fig. 2.9), now noticeably in the position of power on the staircase and in the center of the house that he was seen gazing longingly toward, initially from outside and then from the lowly foot of the staircase, during his original childhood penetration of Hundreds.

Though this cinematic choice effectively emphasizes the preceding story as driven by the pathological effects of male ambition and insecurity, fatally established in early childhood and unintentionally nourished by social change, it is somewhat reductive toward Waters's text. The film reverts somewhat to the crude visual grammar of horror-child cinema, where the source of evil reveals itself as a dangerous child. The emphasis here is less on Faraday's adult malice as arising from his entrapment in a dynamic established in childhood and more on the strength of the child's raging desire as unmediated, un-aged, and unchanging; the root of adult pathology in the child's frustration and refusal of satisfaction is visually replaced by an image of the child—not the adult—satisfied

Figure 2.8. In the final moments of the 2018 film adaptation of *The Little Stranger*, the adult Faraday is watched by his childhood self at the center of Hundreds Hall. From *The Little Stranger*, directed by Lenny Abrahamson, Potboiler Productions/Dark Trick Films/Element Pictures/Film4/Pathé/Twentieth Century Fox, 2018. Screenshot courtesy of Filmgrab.

Figure 2.9. The young Faraday, now elevated to the position of power at the center of the Hall, gazes down on his adult self. From *The Little Stranger*, directed by Lenny Abrahamson, Potboiler Productions/Dark Trick Films/Element Pictures/Film4/Pathé/Twentieth Century Fox, 2018. Screenshot courtesy of Filmgrab.

and dominant at last. The difference is admittedly a subtle one, but still, I think, significant. The boy haunting the adult Faraday, as written by Waters, need not be understood as endogenously malicious—even his childhood vandalism against the Ayreses' property is itself hardly a morally unambiguous gesture in the context of class oppression—but may be understood, rather, as toxically nourished by a history of intergenerational (and unbearable) "aspirational" investment too laden with conflict for any "healthy" development into secure and agentic adulthood. Ironically, in the film adaptation, not only Susan but also Faraday provide horror children as scapegoats for social violence.

Specters of Thatcherism

Waters uses *The Little Stranger*'s early postwar setting as itself an uncanny mirror on the Britain of the later twentieth and early twenty-first century and on that later Britain's use of the postwar period as rhetorical and cultural fetish, reflecting the metafictional approach to history throughout her work (Eve 159–85). The socially mobile yet socially conservative Faraday engages in his own project to kill off one version of the future (the inheritance due to the Ayreses) and replace it with another: a new possession of the grand house justified by his own scientific, aesthetic, and even sexual talents. Faraday is, thus, a figure of proto-Thatcherite social mobility, driven by masculinist and materialistic aspiration—and by his parents' sacrifices for and investments in his potential. He embodies the figure theorized by Serge Leclaire, "the wonderful child [who] is first of all the nostalgic gaze of the mother who made him into an object of extreme magnificence" (2) and who is haunted by the idealized child this excessive investment created.

Faraday's tense combination of covetous admiration, resentment, and social awkwardness toward the Ayreses closely prefigures Thatcherism's own class ambivalences in promoting both social mobility and social conservatism—as does the juxtaposition between Hundreds and the unglamorous but practical new housing estate being constructed in its grounds, gesturing toward the centrality of the working and lower-middle-class family home to postwar politics and, ultimately, toward Thatcherism. (This was famously manifested in the Thatcher government's decision to encourage social housing tenants to buy their homes, which simultaneously appealed to those classes' interests and offered them a vision of upward mobility while moving from an institutionalized and interventionist approach to housing to a symbolic return to organic home-owning family life.) *The Little Stranger*'s use of the house as a supreme object of both aspiration and repressed yet brutal class conflict underlines its sideways satire on Thatcherism as well as its satire on postwar social mobility more broadly; like the house that retrospectively emblematizes the privileged but precariously nouveau riche childhood of Hollinghurst's Will in *The Swimming Pool Library*, Faraday wants to pick up Hundreds for cheap after the war, even if he never openly frames his ambition in such crude terms.

The desired house compounds aesthetic, sexual, gendered, and class elements, established through the novel's primal scene, Faraday's childhood penetration of Hundreds' forbidden interior:

> The parlourmaid [. . .] took me with her, so that I might peep past the green baize curtain that separated the front of the house from the back. I could stand and wait for her there, she said, if I was very good and quiet. [. . .]
>
> I was an obedient child, as a rule. But [. . .] once she had disappeared softly in one direction, I took a few daring steps

in the other. The thrill of it was astonishing. I don't mean the simple thrill of trespass, I mean the thrill of the house itself, which came to me from every surface—from the polish on the floor, the patina on wooden chairs and cabinets, the bevel of a looking-glass, the scroll of a frame. I was drawn to one of the dustless white walls, which had a decorative plaster border, a representation of acorns and leaves [. . .] I did what strikes me now as a dreadful thing: I worked my fingers around one of the acorns and tried to prise it from its setting; and when that failed to release it, I got out my penknife and dug away with that. I didn't do it in a spirit of vandalism. I wasn't a spiteful or destructive boy. It was simply that, in admiring the house, I wanted to possess a piece of it—or rather, as if the admiration itself, which I suspected a more ordinary child would not have felt, entitled me to it. I was like a man, I suppose, wanting a lock of hair from the head of a girl he had suddenly and blindingly become enamoured of. (2–3)

We might wonder whether Faraday's action is really so different from the "spirit of vandalism" in *The Destructors*, where Trevor similarly believes himself to be a special child with special entitlements. This richly layered passage telescopes aesthetic, class, sexual, and gendered desires into a single material object, obtained by an act of determination and obsession. Faraday (echoing Hollinghurst's Nick Guest, but in even more pathological form) believes that his taste and sensibility—in his loaded word, "admiration"—entitle him to possession (with *taste* acting as the equivalent of his *skill* as a doctor, which will later more practically entitle him to an elevated position in the social order; these are qualities that are inherent and therefore associated with their innocently—or violently—direct expressions in childhood). Perhaps, though, this is a mere justifying discourse laid over the "thrill" that comes with the material surfaces the house presents, as hinted by the macabrely gendered and sexualized analogy of the lock of hair.

Although Faraday's taking of the acorn prefigures and imaginatively drives his later social mobility, it is not well-received by the other driver of his childhood ambition, his mother:

My mother found the acorn, of course, eventually. [. . .] When she understood what the queer little thing in her hand was,

> she [. . .] looked at me, with her tearful eyes, as if baffled and ashamed.
> "You ought to know better, a clever lad like you." I expect she said.
> People were always saying things like that to me when I was young. My parents, my uncles, my schoolmasters—all the various adults who interested themselves in my career. The words used to drive me into secret rages, because on the one hand I wanted desperately to live up to my own reputation for cleverness; and on the other it seemed very unfair, that that cleverness, which I had never asked for, could be turned into something with which to cut me down. (3–4)

"I expect she said" betrays that this is *Nachträglichkeit*, an overloaded and condensed memory created through cumulative rehearsal and later experience. The mother's reaction underlines the critical problem of how the aspirational desire to possess more and "better" things can be accommodated within a socially conservative morality, especially when inculcated—as it must be, if the adult is to be truly "driven"—in childhood. Her stifling, shaming attitude enrages Faraday, this Leclaire-style object of adult overinvestment. This also, again, functions as a haunting anticipation of the conflicted and gendered neoliberal conservatism distilled by Thatcherism, where repressed conflicts between materialistic aspiration and social conservatism were always just below the surface.

The later "ghostly" events at Hundreds read not only as the continuation of Faraday's early act of possessive penetration but also as the product of his conflicted attempt to recover his childhood relationship with his mother, whose servile position at the Hall is both repressed and compulsively revisited in Faraday's adult attempts to insert himself into the Ayreses' home. It is the very fact that Faraday's social climbing—in these quietly aggressive attempts at accelerated class mobility—is also consistently destructive that keeps him bound in an agony of desire and loss toward the maternal, as the primal scene with the acorn hints. (After all, the more Faraday penetrates Hundreds Hall, the more he inevitably damages its class integrity, as shown in Caroline's reactions to his attempts to marry her.) When Faraday fails to decisively identify his mother in an old photograph, the moment reflects how class threatens to erase, even as it drives, individualist aspiration:

> I looked more closely at this group. Most of them were older children, but the smallest, still an infant [. . .] had been in the process of wriggling free when the camera shutter had snapped [. . .] Her gaze, as a consequence, was drawn from the camera, and her features were blurred.
>
> Caroline had left her place on the sofa to come and examine the photograph with me [. . .] "Is that your mother, Dr Faraday?"
>
> I said, "I think it might be. Then again—" Just behind the awkward-looking girl, I noticed now, was another servant, also fair haired, and in an identical gown and cap. I laughed, embarrassed. "It might be this one. I'm not sure." (29)

Faraday's rage toward maternal loss and the repressed conflicts involved in his social mobility and masculinist-materialist aspiration are all too readily transferred on to the opaque figure of the lost child, who interrupts his gaze as he searches for his mother.

Bound by his childhood trauma, Faraday's insecurities in his class, gendered, sexual, and professional status are all rooted in the same set of (so to speak) psychic phenomena, which Waters presents in psychoanalytically resonant terms. (Another child who disrupts the Ayreses' chances of restoring their social position, Gillian Baker-Hyde, demonstrates awareness of "neuroses" (92), suggesting that Freudian ideas have become already embedded in popular culture.) Faraday has a latent, jealous attraction to his younger male friend and rival doctor, Graham, while his relationship with Caroline seems like a pathetically narcissistic project, its fundamentally transactional basis disguised only by the intensity of Faraday's desire for the marriage as a route to possession of Hundreds. Faraday's case subtly emphasizes both the role of psychoanalysis for postwar British culture in articulating the danger of childhood experience producing delinquent as well as delayed violence and, conversely, the distinctive British class history for which Freud's and Winnicott's versions of psychoanalysis, with their universalizing diagnostic tendencies, do not comprehensively account.

The Little Stranger, both Freudian novel and ghost story, points to the excess of factors in social violence for which psychoanalytic frameworks—and perhaps theory in general, when distanced from historical and material specificity—cannot comprehensively account and locates that excess firmly in classed, gendered, and spatial history. It is an excess embodied in the acorn prized from the wall, which can be fruitfully read in Freudian terms as an object of both phallic authority and maternal fertility but which must be also read, I suggest, as an actual, material object. The acorn really is a plaster acorn, and Faraday really does want Hundreds Hall, not something else; in fact, Caroline Ayres all-too-obviously provides a rather inadequate substitute object for the Hall that is the real object of Faraday's desire, not vice-versa. The Hall may be an overdetermined signifier, yet it is not merely a fetishistic substitution for something other than its own material presence. It is, of course, massively invested with aesthetic and class ideology, but that investment is so perfectly realized in material form that Faraday needs nothing more than the Hall itself to be satisfied, as the novel's powerfully disturbing ending indicates. We are again in a position where, in Freudian terms, the death drive and the pleasure principle seem to have morphed into something a little stranger than either's original formulation.

Faraday stands, then, in the postwar tradition of creatively destructive children and youth whose desires and motivations demand to be understood in historical and material—and, indeed, materialistic—as well as psychoanalytic and theoretical terms. This child, with their openness to creative transgressions that fulfil a psychic ambition but disrupt social norms, functions here as both genuine embodiment and scapegoat for the material and historical excess that produces violence. We have now, of course, not only access to Freudian terminology to analyze these characteristics but also queer theories. The acorn itself is a "queer little thing," and Faraday's attempt to use a façade of heterosexual marriage to fulfil desires bound up in his oedipal childhood and later homosocial competition with other males is also powerfully queer. Nevertheless, the ambivalence of the "ghost," which persists despite its intensive materialism, and which cannot be quite definitively reconciled to Faraday's self-projection despite strong hints in that direction, also will not reveal itself and become securely identifiable—or even available for theoretical paraphrasing—through being named as queer. Even so, such naming might usefully detach *queer* from contemporary de-facto positivistic usage and return it to *queer* as something that is, indeed, always a little stranger.

THE INTENSIVE MATERIALISM OF *THE LITTLE STRANGER*

Desire for possession of objects and spaces drives this protagonist—and, more subtly, others. After all, the Ayreses are clinging on to Hundreds out of total economic irrationality, driven by motivations so fundamental that they largely remain unspoken (a fact that should calibrate Faraday's more blatant role as a source of obsessive and possessive impulses). The novel's saturating materialism is condensed and (dis)embodied in the poltergeist, a manifestation of aggressive psychic desires so strong as to be capable of disrupting and redistributing material objects—a redistribution given more prosaic form in the nouveau riche Baker-Hydes having taken over the neighboring gentry residence. As a force itself invisible yet saturating the house, attributed explicitly to the ghostly child Susan and implicitly to the aggressive child within Faraday, the poltergeist reflects the ambivalence of claims to possession based either on an organic order (like that taken to underpin the gentry class's traditional status) *or* on individual talent and capacity for aesthetic appreciation (like that claimed by the socially mobile Faraday), with both of these conflicting essentialist claims exposed as subservient to the raw drive for possession that the poltergeist so violently manifests.

When another neighbor, Anne Graham, recalls Susan's death, she suggestively invokes a general, if obscure, power of desire toward material objects to cause real harm: "I went to her seventh birthday party. Her parents had given her a silver ring, with a real diamond in it. Oh, how I coveted that ring! And a few months later she was dead . . ." (35). Dispersed, denuded, and damaged objects here are often memento mori—like the lock of hair to which Faraday compares his stolen acorn—and thus substitute for both the lost child Susan and Faraday's childhood act of penetrative possession. Hundreds' role as a locus for the (unequal) distribution of valuable and pleasurable objects is established from the Empire Day fête of Faraday's childhood visit, where he obtains privileged access to the beautiful things at Hundreds by, ironically, his mother being a servant there. Taken into the kitchen for his "pick of the jellies and 'shapes' that had come back uneaten from the fête," little Faraday is "given a spoon from the family's own drawer—a heavy thing of dulled silver" (1–2). Hundreds distributes objects of value both legitimately (the young Faraday receives a souvenir Empire Day medal from Mrs. Ayres) and illicitly (the acorn, the spoon). In adulthood, Faraday continues to pleasurably recall the Hall's cool marble passages, then filled "with marvellous things" (4–5), mirrored by his internal irritation over the Ayreses' current neglect of their possessions, "the chipped stucco on their walls, and their Turkey carpets worn to the weave" (27). Valuable objects are, of course, not only signifiers of lost pasts but also of aspirational futures, as with Roderick's boyish envy of Faraday's modest car (32).

The Historic House and the Postwar Institution

Faraday's obsession with Hundreds is shadowed by his persistent anxiety about a very different institution: the National Health Service (NHS), the establishment of which is imminent and which promises significant organizational and economic changes for a general practitioner like Faraday, who is deeply pessimistic about this huge innovation. Faraday's anxieties about his own status as a class outsider and unmarried man are at stake in this destabilizing development; he even worries about whether the new NHS will mean he cannot afford to marry (35-36). Britain's landmark postwar institution already functions here as what it would become in popular and political memory: an over-invested national fetish, though depicted here as an object for anxious projections on to an unknown future—an uncanny treatment for the contemporary British reader, for whom the NHS is more likely to be invested with nostalgia.

As the novel's subtle inverted parallel between them suggests, Hundreds is, like the NHS, an institution; it is the local site of a broader and historically integrated institutional system, directed toward control of financial, political, and aesthetic capital.[14] As a gentry estate, Hundreds' history is tied to the long process of land enclosure, while its Empire Day fête shows it connecting the local social order with the prewar imperial state; Caroline sarcastically, but accurately, identifies her mother's function at the fête as a local imitation of Queen Alexandra (64), implicitly and symbolically placing the scene even further back in history than it actually took place—at the Edwardian peak of the British Empire, before not only the Second World War but also the First. If Hundreds is an institution, though, its roles as home and institution are completely intertwined, reflecting the deep conservative organicism that it embodies across the domestic, social, and economic domains. Faraday, of course, does not fit easily into Hundreds as either home or institution—as betrayed, for example, when his social attendance at the small party the Ayreses throw for their neighbors is repeatedly confused with his professional capacity (85). Nor can Faraday, given his class position, ideologically commit to the organicist social vision behind Hundreds' cultural and aesthetic formations, much as he remains trapped in a morbidly envious obsession with exactly those.

The result of Faraday's desiring rage is that Hundreds is gradually denuded before it becomes completely abandoned at the novel's close. Yet, in the deserted house, Faraday disturbingly discovers a perfect site for his belief in access to material and aesthetic goods, and to the times and spaces to enjoy them, as justified by innate sensibility and sensitivity: by an essentialism located, in fact, in the talents and ambitions of the child, which continue to drive the frustrated, aggressive, yet still aspirational young man. Desire is finally satisfied by an empty shell that provides a series of perfect projecting surfaces, affirming the wounded male's ghost-like drive for omniscient possession:

> Hundreds Hall is still unsold. No one has the money or the inclination to take it on. For a while there was talk of the county council making a teacher-training centre of it. [. . .] But the rumours surface, and come to nothing [. . .]
>
> I go out there whenever my busy days will allow. None of the locks has been changed [. . .] Caroline's bedroom continues to fade. Roderick's room, even now, smells faintly of burning . . . Despite all this, the house retains its beauty. In some ways it is handsomer than ever, for without the carpets and the furniture and the clutter of occupation, one appreciates the lines and Georgian symmetries, the lovely shifts between shadow and light, the gentle progression of the rooms. Wandering softly through the twilit spaces, I can even seem to see the house as its architect must have done when it was new, with its plaster detail fresh and unchipped, its surfaces unblemished. In those moments there is no trace of the Ayreses at all. (497–98)

Once again, as in *Hawksmoor*, the desiring child grew into the architect, the total possessor of the time and space he craves and penetrates, through a process of deadly creative destruction.

The final lines balance the "rational view that Hundreds was, in effect, defeated by history" with the "other, odder theory: that Hundreds was consumed by some dark germ, some ravenous shadow-creature, some 'little stranger,' spawned from the troubled unconscious of someone connected with the house itself" (498). The ending implies, in terms that echo psychoanalytic notions but with an uncannily materialist overlay, that this creature is to be identified with Faraday himself: "What I am looking at is only a cracked window-pane, and [. . .] the face gazing distortedly from it, baffled and longing, is my own" (499). Yet there is no indication that Faraday is watched by a more conscious and less baffled childhood self at this point, as the film adaptation has it, concluding by making the adult man almost literally a mere shadow of the boy. Rather, he is engaged in an adult act of material possession, justified and driven by the *Nachträglichkeit* of his childhood visit but shaped and enabled by a historical process and its material detritus, and the haunting of the house by this creep who wanders "softly through the twilit spaces" is conducted by a dangerous adult rather than a deadly child. *The Little Stranger* thus cunningly challenges, even as it invokes, the blame that falls on the horror child of postwar Britain.

The fetishization of the "original" state of Hundreds after its inhabitants have been driven out and killed off hints at the chauvinism and violence behind quasi-romantic visions of the organic and the essential, and although Faraday notes how Hundreds (at least as occupied by the Ayreses) has become a victim of history, he has tempered the risk of historical change for himself: "When the new Health Service arrived I didn't, as I'd feared I would, lose patients; in fact I gained them, probably partly as a result of my connection with the Ayreses [. . .] many people had come across my name in the local papers and seemed to see me as a sort of 'coming man'" (494). Materialistic aspiration, the postwar institution, and nostalgic attachment to an organic and hierarchical past have seemingly reconciled themselves here in a way that provides another sideways comment on the contradictions and conflicts that ultimately produced Thatcherism. Waters's brilliance is in so vividly depicting the psychic and social costs, the underlying violence, of this reconciliation.

The Little Stranger reflects a long cultural history, wherein later twentieth-century Britain has been haunted by visions of violent and dangerous children and youth, and subtly interrogates and reassess this history by both anticipating Thatcherism before its time and, simultaneously, looking back upon its origins in a mix of postwar Britain's aspirations and conservative anxieties. It suggests how the Thatcherite values of aspiration and materialism in the male child are difficult to contain within a socially conservative framework, their reconciliation creating violent and repressive contradictions. The novel, even as it rejects the unequivocal identification of the source of violence with children and childhood, nevertheless characterizes the aftereffects of childhood in terms of risk that we as contemporary readers are subtly encouraged to identify with queerness but which turns out to escape any theoretical categorization, even—or especially—while its material reality is violently evident. If there is a little stranger—or a little queer—behind events at Hundreds, it is never quite securely definable and certainly never contained. The danger consists of its demand for material things and the times and spaces to enjoy them—access to which state, social, and family institutions can either provide or refuse—at extreme psychic cost.

Thatcherism's Demons: Postwar Children and Youth

Throughout this chapter, we have seen the postwar child—in their horrifying, dangerous, and aspirational aspects—register profound questions about the source of security for adult society and its future during a period of recent trauma and profound change. Later in the twentieth century, Thatcherite politics and rhetoric attempted to deploy anxieties about progressive childhoods and the bogeyman of the violent youth to gain support for its own vision of an alternative future based on a combination of organicist and neoliberal notions of reality. Thatcherism also attempted to incorporate elements of the aspirational child and youth in ways that underlined its own contradictions. This has been, then, the collective, cumulative story of imagined children who resist incorporation and containment within a single version of the future. Even as psychoanalytic theories of childhood spread in postwar Britain—and were later rejected by the anti-theories of Thatcherite conservatism—children were suspected of continuing to resist theoretical categorization and definition. The child presents a risk, a known unknown, and it is the depth and intensity of this risk to which an extraordinary body of literature and film during the period has given variously lurid and subtle representation.

Chapter 3

Boy Kings, Queerness, and Radical Nostalgia

Oscillation between openness to imagine killing the child and repressing the impulse is a recurring feature of this book. Whereas in the previous chapter we repeatedly observed the capacity of adults to imagine killing the child in order to erase a danger they were perceived to present or to absorb the dangerous youth into their own project for a revised future, this chapter turns to the repression of that willingness to imagine child-killing and children killing. Though such repression might appear preferable to its opposite, I argue that in the case study explored in this chapter, it also represents an unwillingness to contend with the real difficulties presented by the child-as-future, and this unwillingness is ultimately depoliticizing and ahistoricizing—even (perhaps especially) when displayed in the service of political radicalism. In the context discussed here, such repression emerges as a radical nostalgia, deployed as a tactical counter to conservatism but finally betraying the same underlying desire to turn away from history, its conflicts, and its contingent institutions, toward an organic national reality.

Whereas the previous chapter focused particularly on British conservatism's difficulties with the child-as-future, this chapter explores how radical and queer literature and film could also be prone, in their own ways, to fantasizing the retrieval of an atemporal future from the past—even a queered past. This is less because of any hypocrisy than out of reaction to a genuine and highly material capacity for difference, and for danger, in the child-as-future—one that can be written out to produce a reassuring nostalgia even within an ostensibly radical revision of national heritage and the literary canon. Observing this, I also argue, perhaps counterintuitively, that imagining the child as violently dangerous can be of political and ethical value in that it resists such nostalgia and prevents this difference, the opacity of the absent future that the child makes present, from becoming fetishized or transfigured into an object for reassuring visual recognition rather than risky material accommodation. I make this argument via an example where a dangerous child was erased from the past in an early 1990s queer British film.

As we have seen, Thatcherism celebrated modes of creative destruction that constantly threatened to exceed their own conservative framing and sought to contain this excess by promoting associations between childhood and nostalgia for a reality before and beyond postwar and progressive change. Queerness, a primary object of the Right's phobia, consistently exposed this excess, even acting as its political doppelgänger in literary treatments of Thatcherism like Hollinghurst's, while exposing the contradictions involved in the attempt at containment. This is most acutely revealed when queerness and conservatism battle for control over the child and the institutions educating that child. My case study here is the queer filmmaker Derek Jarman's 1991 movie *Edward II*, based on Christopher Marlowe's 1593 play of the same name. I argue that Jarman's film, explicitly intended as a piece of queer historicist activism, tames the child, transforming Marlowe's boy killer—and boy king—into one who must not kill, within an aesthetically provocative response to the political and cultural battles of the 1980s and early 1990s. Jarman replaces Marlowe's difficult and dangerous child with a messianic queer child who, though mobilized as the creative destroyer of Thatcherite conservatism, ultimately represents an equivalent, if reconfigured, nostalgic essentialism. Jarman's *Edward II* thus emerges as emblematic of how even radical and queer attempts to reclaim the child can absorb the conservative ahistoricity, drive to depoliticize institutions, and resulting fetishizing of the child that they sometimes seek to oppose. This film's relationship with its source text shows both a specifically late twentieth-century British intervention in contests over generational and political temporality and more fundamental and far-reaching issues of reading the child-as-future (a figure of which the boy king is an extreme, and therefore telling, version). The transformation of the child in *Edward II*, understood within the politics of Britain's long Thatcherism, exemplifies broader and continuing difficulties in accommodating the interests of the child-as-future—difficulties that trouble conservatives and progressives alike.

Radicalism, Nostalgia, and Childhood in Thatcher-Era Britain

In the previous chapter, Thatcherism's interest in the child emerged as both ambitious and defensive, haunted by the risk that the aspirational, entrepreneurial child or youth might not contain their aggressive energies within the acceptable channels of capitalist success and conservative nationalism. Against the Left's allegations that her program was undermining social responsibility, Thatcher invoked a "Victorian" alignment between wealth creation and morality and recast the Left as antisocial in their "Loony" fringe of pro-minority movements. Thatcher and her allies also attacked these movements, and their institutional and intellectual underpinnings, through challenges to universities, arts and cultural organizations, and schools. Simultaneously, parts of the British academy were becoming increasingly open to radical theory; by the mid-1980s, the beginnings of queer scholarship were emerging in Britain and attracting substantial conservative opposition, often coalescing into attempts to defund the institutions hosting this scholarship. Thatcher sought to defend the child from the radical humanities, even from theory itself, in an intensified politicization of intellectual life—one revived in the 2010s, as I discuss later[1]—while its particular hostility toward gender and queer theory played out in such controversies as the early 1990s rightwing calls to close down the Centre for the Study of Sexual Dissidence at the University of Sussex, a pioneering early locus for academic queer studies.[2] The fight over the study of sexual dissidence involved then innovative interventions in scholarship on Shakespeare and other major figures of the English literary canon; this was paralleled in queer historical studies with new turns to reevaluate, even to "out," the sexual and gender identities of historical figures—including some who became central to conservative framings of the national heritage—in a trend that accelerated following publication of Alan Bray's pioneering *Homosexuality in Renaissance England* in 1982.

Leftists, social liberals, and progressives fought such cultural battles with a keen sense—shared also by some anti-Thatcherite conservatives[3]—that Thatcherism's claims to close identification with British and English national traditions were less secure than Margaret Thatcher sought to project. Thatcherism was, as already seen, a significant break with then-recent British history's broadly social-democratic consensus, itself closely based on remembering the community of sacrifice created by the Second World War (Kynaston 78–79). Despite Thatcherism's nativist rhetoric, it was influenced ideologically by Friedrich Hayek and the Austrian School of economic thought, rejecting the postwar dominance of Britain's home-grown, globally influential economist, John Maynard Keynes. In this context, leftists and liberals could, and did, invoke and exploit nostalgia against Thatcherite conservatism. Theirs was a nostalgia for the postwar vision of Britain characterized by collective purpose and social solidarity; but it was also, behind this, for a broader and deeper version of a British or English nation not defined exclusively by capitalism, individualism, or the Protestant (in Thatcher's case, Methodist) work ethic. Premodern and neoromantic forms of nationalism could be surprisingly prominent objects of attraction in anti-Thatcherite culture.

Drawing on a tradition going back to Blake and Wordsworth (themselves, incidentally, influential figures in the history of literary representations of childhood) of contesting the relationship between modernity and British nationhood through imagining alternative histories, writers and artists of the 1970s, '80s, and '90s regularly mobilized radical nostalgia against the Right. This often emerged, inter alia, around ecologically minded appreciation for the English landscape—the landscape conservative rhetoric ahistorically associated with an organic and stable national heritage—as seen in the poetry of Blake Morrison; the folk music of Billy Bragg and The Levellers; the fiction of Ian McEwan, Peter Ackroyd, and Jim Crace; and the films of Derek Jarman.

Despite its history-minded nostalgia, the child-as-future emerged at the center of this cultural turn, disrupting the Thatcherite belief that all privileges must be earned and collectively funded benefits curtailed—because the child is the one person who *must* be given something for nothing, yet they are also often regarded as particularly susceptible to the temptations of consumerist materialism, of greed endorsed and indulged. The child was a compelling figure for the leaders of anti-Thatcherite radical nostalgia. (I explore a powerful example of this later in McEwan's *The Child in Time*, perhaps the most comprehensive literary mobilization of these tropes against Thatcherism at its peak.) All these writers and artists saw Thatcherism as engaged in the suppression of alternative traditions within the English and British pasts, and they also consistently posed the child as central to the consequences of this. Yet, for some of them, the child is often associated not only with an organic state of affairs that Thatcherism wishes to deny but also with the queer. Contrary to the usual charge of conservatives, queerness is profoundly natural for all of them—and not only natural but native to the British or English nation, too. In the

1980s, then, queerness emerged as a key discursive site for battles over the nature and status of the child, while romantic nationalism emerged as a site where Thatcherism's underlying contradictions could be teased out, satirized, and challenged, with both emerging alongside an academy that was increasingly intellectually ready to explicitly and provocatively discuss these phenomena.

Derek Jarman

Derek Jarman (1942–1994), probably the most influential queer filmmaker British cinema has yet produced, used his highly lyrical style to engage British postimperial decline against alternative—revenant, uncanny, and queer—Englands, playing provocatively upon the nostalgia suffusing late modern British and English culture and deploying such nostalgia for queer ends and, eventually, against Thatcherite claims to national revival. Jarman's interest in national decline, British society's lurid later twentieth-century collapses into squalor and violence, and potential alternatives drawn from reimagining the past predated Thatcherism's period of governing power but nevertheless tracked its emergence, peak, and endurance after Thatcher's departure from office. In *Jubilee* (1978), a response to Elizabeth II's 1977 Silver Jubilee, Jarman demonstrated his interest in an organic and pastoral English past that was simultaneously queer and yet deliberately contrasted with the youth violence and social dysfunction popularly associated with 1970s Britain; it also showed his willingness to queer the monarchy, the nominally central source of national heritage. Jarman sustained his interests in radical nostalgia, queerness, violence, and the pastoral in *The Last of England* (1987), *War Requiem* (1989), and *The Garden* (1990) as well as *Edward II* (1991).

JARMAN'S *EDWARD II*

Jarman's queer reimagining of Christopher Marlowe's play *Edward II* was produced shortly after Thatcher's downfall but while British public life was still overwhelmingly dominated by her influence (and with her Clause 28 legislation still firmly in force). Jarman's film uses the child-as-future to critique, parody, and reconfigure contests over the future pervading late twentieth-century Britain. I explore this context alongside the film's rather queer relationship with its source material and the killer child therein.

As Bette Talvacchia wrote soon after the movie's release, "Jarman engages the past to structure his own agenda [. . .] here high culture is used as protection against homophobia, and the past is made to join the present to achieve a specific political goal" (112). Jarman's *Edward II*, like its Marlovian source, depicts the downfall, usurpation, and murder of Edward II of England (b. 1284, r. 1307–1327). It concludes with a utopian vision of a queer future, one that—mimicking and aggressively subverting the strategies of reactionary nostalgia—locates the future in a triumphant version of the national past, but one that is queer at its center, with queerness literally enthroned in glory. It is a provocative artistic echo of the academic queer movements that sought to recognize homosexuality within the past, including within British and English histories.

This *Edward II*'s plot begins with its title character succeeding his father as king, whereupon he quickly summons his exiled lover, Piers Gaveston, to return to England. The king's indulgence and collaboration with Gaveston in passion, glamour, and revenge against their enemies quickly scandalizes the court, especially the military leader Mortimer. Edward and Gaveston's shared lifestyle visually contrasts with the somber, militaristic, and business-oriented court, with which King Edward's alienated wife, Queen Isabella, is increasingly aligned; she gradually becomes Mortimer's lover. As the king's enemies mobilize, Gaveston is forced back into exile, only to return once again in a doomed attempt by the queen to regain her husband's favor. Frustrated, Isabella and Mortimer turn the focus of their plotting to the young heir, Prince Edward (the future Edward III). Mortimer, Isabella, and their henchmen begin to capture, torture, and murder the king's allies, including Gaveston himself and the king's other favorite, Spencer. After Gaveston and Spencer's assassinations, King Edward is himself imprisoned and apparently murdered with a red-hot poker; yet, this tragedy is revealed as a nightmare from which the king awakes, as the assassin tosses away his weapon and instead kisses his intended royal victim. Meanwhile, Mortimer and Isabella's new regime suddenly collapses, and we see them imprisoned as the young Prince Edward—a keen but, until now, taciturn observer of events—having put on his mother's earrings and lipstick and listening to Tchaikovsky on his Walkman, walks above the caged heterosexuals while his father is restored in triumph.

Jarman draws upon Marlowe's dramatization of Edward II's erotic relationships with his favorites Gaveston and Spencer, drastically reordering the Marlovian material and giving it a distinctive visual aesthetic that heightens and updates the conflict between the gay king and a homophobic political establishment. Deploying Marlowe's poetry while building on the homoerotic aesthetics of his own previous work (especially *Caravaggio*, 1986), Jarman associates King Edward and Gaveston with playful pleasure and their opponents—led by Mortimer and Isabella—with a puritanical, yet hypocritically perverse, sadomasochistic aesthetic. Jarman also renews Marlowe's (ahistorical) depiction of Gaveston as low-born and, thus, not only a sexual disruptor but also a class disruptor, giving him a distinctive twentieth-century British resonance. This Gaveston (played by Andrew Tiernan) is a young man with a northern accent (reminiscent of Kubrick's Alex), who wears long hair, leather jackets, t-shirts and jeans—a style associated with working-class masculine youth in later twentieth-century Britain. Jarman uses Gaveston and Edward's relationship to imagine a powerful opposition to Thatcherite conservatism and to make an aggressive play on the latter's hypocrisies and repressed contradictions; the film offers political revenge fantasy.

Prince Edward is also an important and disruptive figure in this film (played by Jody Graber, around ten years old at the time). He is a consistent witness to the homophobic violence directed toward the king and his lovers and plays an important role in the euphoric restoration of legitimate rule at the end. Although his roots are drawn from the Marlowe playtext, Jarman very significantly revises the boy's part, not least by giving him a physical and affective closeness to his father that Marlowe refuses and by abandoning the violence with which he ultimately achieves power. (Some of the danger presented by Marlowe's child is, perhaps, transferred in the film onto Gaveston, the viscerally dangerous queer young man.) Jarman, unlike Marlowe, uses the child to imagine a utopian ending, where the son participates in his father's restoration to a transhistorical queer kingship, marked by union with those in his kingdom who are protesting for social and sexual justice. The visual and thematic centrality of the child, as Jarman's film builds to this conclusion, hints that his imagined ideal future could only be achieved, in reality, through children's education and early experience, using their qualities of openness to experience, moral courage, proto-queer playful creativity, and emotional intelligence. This is, thus, a powerful statement against the homophobic logic of Thatcherism and its Clause 28, the protests against which are visually echoed in the film's concluding moments. It is also a provocative claim to the recognition and identification of the queer at the center of English history and British heritage: Edward III grew up, in the history beyond both Marlowe's and Jarman's texts, to become a monarch celebrated for his victories over France during the Hundred Years War and for his cult of Arthurian chivalry.

Edward II is, then, an aggressive "politicization" of a canonical English Renaissance text, as Jarman acknowledged in his book published to accompany the film: "How to make a film of a gay love affair and get it commissioned? Find a dusty old play and violate it . . . Marlowe outs the past—why don't we out the present? That's really the only message the play has. Fuck poetry" (Jarman, *Queer Edward II* epigraph). This would also become an outing of the monarchy, the central continuous national institution of English and British history. (Violating the monarchy, in the course of an impassioned imaginative exploration of later twentieth-century Britain as itself a violence upon the English past, was something Jarman had already achieved once in *Jubilee*.) Jarman's queer mission here has a distinct temporal dynamic, with an ambivalent relationship to the monarchy's own temporality: monarchy manages time by creating a continuity that is essentially atemporal. Marlowe dwells on this point repeatedly, to ironic effect, in his playtext, where Edward II's reign disrupts the smooth patriarchal and monarchical progression of time in catastrophic ways. Monarchy is an institution that, in principle—but not in practice in Marlowe's *Edward II*—protects national continuity against the contingencies of history. In Jarman's film, this mission is disrupted by homophobic violence, only to be restored—in an ironic twist on the source material—through the exalted royal queer prince, the young Edward III, and the queer rescue, resurrection, and restoration of his father.

THE TAMING OF THE CHILD KING: FROM MARLOWE TO JARMAN

The royal child—betrayed, tested, and ultimately restored—is an ancient trope, through which beliefs about political legitimacy and its opposites can be formulated. Royal children who become prematurely sovereign also provide long-established dramatic material (and for Marlowe's early modern audiences, they were a serious and dangerous prospect). A later modern attitude to such tropes was also shaped by the post-Freudian importance placed on early childhood experience (Freud was tellingly prone to use monarchy as a metaphor for the importance of the child in modern culture, coining the phrase "His Majesty the Baby.")[4]

Jarman's Prince Edward acts as a witness of, and ultimately against, the homophobic and patriarchal violence enacted by Mortimer and

Isabella. Prince Edward's function suggests both judgment (children are watching; will you be on the right side of history?) and hope (the child's constant questioning suggests he is already thinking differently about the world around him). In the *Queer Edward II* film companion book, Jarman uses the subheading, "BABIES: WITNESSES FOR THE PROSECUTION" (166). As child witness, Prince Edward/Edward III plays a primary role in defeating Mortimer's murderous coup—literally "plays" because Jarman visually characterizes this defeat as child's play, quite unlike the brutal and sinister violence that Edward III deploys in Marlowe's play, though his childness is critically important in both versions.

This Prince Edward's queerness is key both to his defeat of the heterosexist order and to the restoration of the legitimate monarchy. Jarman reimagines the idea of royal succession, ordinarily an epitome of idealized patriarchal and heterosexual reproduction, as a unity between queer father and queer son. In the final sequence, the young Edward III appears, made up and wearing beautiful jewelry, playing above Edward II's now caged and humiliated persecutors, Isabella (Tilda Swinton) and Mortimer (Nigel Terry). Finally, the child's father appears again, his would-be assassin having, at the last moment, recognized the desire transferred into the murderous penetration he was about to make and drops his poker to kiss the king instead. Through this fantasized moment of erotic and euphoric recognition of the queerness in England's past, Jarman implies, the violence of the British present could be effectively countered. Interestingly, the *Queer Edward II* book includes an alternative ending that has the son, rather than the father, enthroned and intoning the final lines. Implying that this version was filmed (or at least rehearsed) but discarded, Jarman comments that "this would have made a great ending, but did not work, unfortunately" (166). He does not elaborate, but in the final version, the reappearance of the now-messianic father emphasizes the queer child's role here as reconstitutive and redemptive—ushering in an ending of time and even of death—which a closing shot of the new child king enthroned alone might, perhaps, have undermined. Either version of the ending contrasts sharply with that written by Marlowe, which features the child king addressing his father's corpse.

As Alexandra Parsons observes, Jarman foregrounds the queer child in order to attack the conservative *figure* of the child Edelman would later describe as constantly foreclosing politics in the name of a future that is always imminent, never real—a clichéd deployment of the innocent child signaled visually here in the altar boys who appear with the homophobic Bishop as well as through the attempts to entrap and exploit Prince Edward himself. Jarman's movie embeds the child's political role in its case for the historicity of homosexuality; that the queers will eventually triumph is promised by acting out precisely the phenomenon the Clause 28–era Thatcherites most feared: the child being educated into an already-latent queerness. Jarman's film is a brilliant play on conservative fantasies and phobias. It is also a multiplied "play" on recognition itself: the audience is compelled to recognize the presence of the queer in Edward II the king; *Edward II* the play; Edward III the child king; Marlowe, the play's author; and English history and the British establishment.

This also involves recognizing the repressed queerness inherent in Thatcherism's own phobias and performative obsessions—what Hollinghurst memorably named as Thatcherism's "heterosexual queenery" (382). When Mortimer's allies confront Gaveston, the women wear pussybow blouses and carry their hair in large blow-dries, a clear reference to Thatcher's distinctive personal aesthetic, while even the fascistic Mortimer occasionally sports a gorgeous leopard-print gown. Homophobia, here, is hypocritical as well as violent, drawing its rage from repressed desire (as is finally confirmed in King Edward's near-executioner's reversion of violence into sexuality). As Jarman put it: "Marlowe outs the past—why don't we out the present?" To refuse to recognize the queer, to seek to exile it or destroy it, Jarman implies, is stupid; doing this, we risk becoming like Mortimer and Isabella, fools humiliated by a change of future. Outing unifies past and present, which mirrors how the film's ending, in which the plot of the Marlowe play is essentially abandoned by Edward's waking from what turns out to have been only the dream of his murder, stops historical time by cancelling the king's death. A utopian time, Jarman indicates, will arise from recognition of (queer) reality, as affirmed by the now visibly queer child, Edward III, dancing in feminine makeup and jewelry on top of the cage (fig. 3.1) to the tune of the Sugar Plum Fairy—the work of Tchaikovsky, a gay composer and icon of national heritage in his own homeland.

At the film's opening, before the titles, the line "My father is deceased"—which is the opening line of Marlowe's play, but spoken only once there—is repeated twice, referring to Edward I. After the titles, it is repeated a third time by Gaveston while two nude men frolic on a bed behind him. This repetition, framed by queer sex, emphasizes the possibility of time changing; yet it also, ambivalently, emphasizes the possibility of escaping from time completely. Prince Edward, the child-as-future, is

Figure 3.1. By the film's conclusion, the young prince has been transformed into an agent of queer triumph. From *Edward II*, directed by Derek Jarman, Working Title Films/Fine Line Features/Film Movement Classics/BBC Films/British Screen/Palace Pictures, 1991. Screenshot courtesy of Filmgrab.

the primary locus of this hopeful possibility throughout the film, but this possibility is also identified with a certain childness—a kind of innocence, in that it constitutes a rejection of political participation in favor of private play—that is present in the relationship between his father and Gaveston. Thus, when Gaveston confronts Mortimer, he does so swinging, nude, on the throne: an act of childlike play. This confrontation cuts to a shot of Prince Edward playing with his own toys, implying a parallel between them in a gentler, reworked echo of how Marlowe makes his prince a rival to his father's favorites.

Jarman's prince is full of curiosity, innocently open to new and startling discovery (see fig. 3.2); in one scene he encounters a strange circle of nude figures in something resembling a choreographed rugby scrum, ambiguously suggestive of both sexuality and violence (or perhaps violence transformed through play, prefiguring the assassin's erotic transformation of his intended murder). In another scene, this child peers from behind a beef carcass grotesquely hanging in the center of the room, positioned in a visual echo of the throne. Later, he watches his ghastly mother drink blood from the neck of the wounded and tortured Kent. Although the prince curiously questions his father's relationship with Gaveston, eventually he seems to

Figure 3.2. Prince Edward appears initially as a curious and sometimes as a horrified witness to adult misdeeds in Jarman's *Edward II*. From *Edward II*, directed by Derek Jarman, Working Title Films/Fine Line Features/Film Movement Classics/BBC Films/British Screen/Palace Pictures, 1991. Screenshot courtesy of Filmgrab.

thoroughly identify with the queer love in their relationship, and so the violence toward the queer is itself implicitly identified here with violence toward the child, in another tactical move against conservative rhetoric.

Prince Edward is a primary locus through which Jarman presents a passionate affirmation of the potential of play to transform violence and trauma. In a loosely Freudian move, here, adult queers sustain the transformative potential of child's play, enraging and embarrassing the adult social order with their immaturity. This transformative quality is closely aligned with the film's parallel theme of recognition, of outing the queer in past and present; play codes a will to recognize what would otherwise be repressed, providing modes of acknowledgement that "serious" adult society cannot tolerate. Horror films, as Lennard points out, acknowledge this potential in child's play by taking it to extremes, "making childish fun ironically synonymous with adult fear" (133). Although I shall ultimately critique Jarman's strategies as, in some respects, depoliticizing and even repressive of a more dangerously queer child, their realization here is undoubtedly powerful.

All Prince Edward's observations culminate in his decisive choice to refuse to collaborate with his mother and Mortimer, despite their coaxing and coercion, but rather to identify with his father and, ultimately, to celebrate his restoration and the murderous heterosexuals' downfall. His father's final words, "If I live, let me forget myself," are spoken as the camera pans over a crowd of gay rights protesters; while Edward II's death and his son's accession become transfigured into a singular queer permanence, these rulers are identified with the people whose potential for a better future they embody. The child's openness to education and experience and his willingness to play, to puncture the pompous hypocrisies of heterosexual morality—visually identified here with Thatcherism—will be, Jarman suggests, the practical tools for achievement of this progress in reality, for which the queer-monarchical vision serves as utopian inspiration. The film concludes on this triumphantly utopian—yet fantastically nostalgic—trope, with the good king at one with his people: a just sovereign and a sovereign proletariat as a single body, no longer politically or even historically divided. Father and son, past and future, child and adult, replacing heterosexual reproduction with queer eternity in a transformed England. As an expression of desire to escape the realities of political and intergenerational conflict as well as violently opposed visions of the future, this is a powerful yet poignant vision of the political and human pain of 1980s and early 1990s Britain, and it is a moving demand for an alternative national story.

Still, its moral and political limitations are somewhat exposed by exploring how Jarman's utopianism is achieved through a strategically selective use of Marlowe's playtext—and his child. Is this "violated" source really as "dusty" as Jarman claimed, its radicalism only created by aggressive rewriting? Or is there a different and dangerous child there?

Edward III in Marlowe's Play

Marlowe's *Edward II* opens with a son coming into his inheritance: "My father is deceased." Edward I—a masculine, empire-building king, who attempted to unify the island of Great Britain under his rule—had ordered the exile of his son's lover, Gaveston. Now, though, that son is King Edward II, and he has immediately recalled Gaveston, his inheritance thus disrupting the patriarchal and monarchical control over political time that it should guarantee. Even while Edward II appears to consign Edward I to the past, Mortimer[5] affirms that he was "sworn to [Edward II's] father at his death" (1.82). The new accession is politically and temporally conflicting rather than unifying. The next generation, in the form of the child Prince Edward, will become the object of further conflict.

Prince Edward arrives relatively late in the play, but rapidly becomes an important character, and ends as its protagonist and figure of a future continuing beyond the stage. He first appears in a scene immediately following Gaveston's death, arriving with his mother (11.58) to meet his father, who is accompanied by his new favorite, Spencer (Prince Edward will remain, in Marlowe's characterization, a curious parallel and jealous rival to his father's lovers). King Edward proposes that the queen take the prince to France in order to negotiate with the French king, oddly distancing himself from his son both through this instruction and through use of the second-person possessive: "We will employ you and your little son" (11.70). (This line, and the departure for France, are omitted in Jarman's reworking.) The prince's response, his first lines on stage, indicate a—seemingly unmerited—respectful affection for his father and explicitly draw attention to his young age and consequently ambivalent position:

PRINCE: Commit not to my youth things of more weight
Than fits a prince so young as I to hear,
And fear not, lord and father, heaven's great beams
On Atlas' shoulder shall not lie more safe
Than shall your charge committed to my trust. (11.74–78)

The prince announces himself here with exactly the question that will follow him throughout the play and determine its ending: How is his young age to be interpreted in the context of his exercising sovereignty as the representative of—and, eventually, successor to—his father? The prince does indeed accompany Queen Isabella to France; but there—even while King Edward defeats rebel barons at home—she builds an alternative power base that is hostile to her husband.

The prince next appears still in France. Expressing a confidence the audience will likely read as childishly misguided, the prince claims his father "loves me better than a thousand Spencers" (15.7)—a claim belied by the king's actual choices—and threatens to kill Spencer when he is older. (The boy's antagonism toward Spencer is erased by Jarman.) Already, this child is prepared to kill, and if the childish moral simplicity behind his aggression looks merely innocent here, its significance will soon grow. This scene is interrupted by the arrival of Kent and Mortimer (15.35); the latter tells the prince that he is here to "advance your standard" (15.42), an allegiance the prince refuses on the grounds that his father still reigns. However, the prince accompanies his mother and

Mortimer once they return to England's shores with an invasion force (scene 17). Isabella, following their success in battle, names the prince as lord warden of the realm (18.35). The prince shows confusion—or sarcasm—when the adults discuss "Edward," wondering which they are referring to (18.41) and wishing to be reunited with his father (18.70).

As events rapidly move toward King Edward's deposition and establishment of the prince as puppet figurehead for Mortimer and Isabella's new regime, the boy continues to express disquiet, becoming more cognizant of the nature of the coup in which he is an unwilling participant. In scene 21, Mortimer and Isabella continue their attempt to treat Prince Edward as a pawn, while he resists. The battle of wills twice draws attention to the prince's young age: first, when he describes himself as too young to reign (21.92), notably objecting on grounds of youth rather than simply the fact that his father is still alive; and later, when Mortimer loses his temper with the boy: "Why, youngling, 'sdain'st thou so of Mortimer? / Then I will carry thee by force away" (21.110–111). Although the physical violence abuses the child at his weakest, it also sows another seed for Prince Edward's later coup in demonstrating that he will need to counter force with force—and with surprise, with acting *prematurely*, while still an innocent-seeming child.

Ruling in Edward III's name, Mortimer disingenuously claims to be restoring the organic, stable order guaranteed by the monarchy, but this claim depends on deferring the child's authority to rule in his own right—on ignoring, in fact, that this child is already growing up: an ignorance that ultimately costs Mortimer his life. Throughout Prince Edward's appearances, the adults associate his, repeatedly emphasized, youth with an expected passive vulnerability to influence—whether their own or their rivals': "Something he [Kent] whispers in his childish ears" (22.74–76) worries the queen. In scene 23, Mortimer boasts that he commands the child through fear (23.52–53) before the prince enters, having been crowned and proclaimed king though his father lives (23.72–77). When Kent, firmly loyal to Edward II, is brought in as a prisoner, Edward III tries to prevent his execution and attempts to bargain with Mortimer, saying that he will reward him for mercy once he comes of age (23.96–97), but Mortimer refuses to wait patiently for the child's proper growth into the sovereignty he has now been assigned as a puppet. Edward II is finally murdered—and the murderer himself killed in a cover-up. In the final scene, Isabella reports to Mortimer that the new king has received news of his father's death and of their responsibility and has vowed revenge

(25.15–23). Mortimer initially dismisses this given the new king's youth (25.17), but Edward III's coup has clearly been surprisingly well-planned, and the king commands Mortimer's execution, requesting that they "bring his head back presently to me" (25.54). Though Mortimer aggressively rejects the authority of "a paltry boy" (25.57), Edward sends him off to his execution and his mother to imprisonment. In the play's final moments, Mortimer's head is brought in, and the boy king says:

> EDWARD III: Go fetch my father's hearse, where it shall lie,
> And bring my funeral robes. Accursed head,
> Could I have ruled thee then as I do now,
> Thou hadst not hatched this monstrous treachery!
> *[Enter attendants with hearse.]*
> Here comes the hearse. Help me to mourn, my lords.
> Sweet father, here unto thy murdered ghost
> I offer up this wicked traitor's head;
> And let these tears distilling from mine eyes,
> Be witness of my grief and innocency! (25.93–102)

Marlowe portrays Edward III's countercoup and accession as violent and based on a rather naive (and childish?) claim to the restoration of legitimate authority, with the violence ironically enabled by the adult characters' emphasis on Prince Edward/Edward III's status as a child, which they wrongly assume makes him a tabula rasa for manipulation and projection.

Yet, in his father's death, Edward III restores—or rather, creates—the monarchical and patrilineal union with Edward II that was blocked in life by his father's own disinterest and preference for the affections of others. Queer love here is by no means so nicely aligned with the child's interests as Jarman would make it 400 years later—even if Edward III's dominating and shaping of his father's public role, now in its postmortem form, ironically echoes Gaveston's dominance during the late king's life. His final lines promise a rule based on extending violent power into the minds of subjects, sinisterly making the living mind and the decapitated head one and the same, even while he asks the audience (and his father) to witness his own innocence. In a surely disturbing image for the play's audiences from early to late modernity, the child promises that the severed head will be simultaneously memento mori and modus operandi for re-legitimized monarchical rule. His treatment of this bloody relic has been prefigured by repeated imagery of violence toward heads that occurs throughout the play, including Prince Edward's own earlier threat to "have at the proudest Spencer's head" (15.25), an echo that links Edward III's proto-totalitarianism to his jealousy of his father's queer favorites. This child has seemingly absorbed a fetish for destruction of the heads of others from his surroundings: Lancaster demands that Edward II "look to see the throne where you should sit / To float in blood, and at thy wanton head / The glozing head of thy base minion thrown" (1.130–32). Gaveston's execution, as promised early in 1.131–32, is by beheading. Mortimer's own beheading finally fulfils Kent's demand for revenge on the rebels: "let these their heads / Preach upon poles for trespass of their tongues" (1.116–17).

Edward III, following the example called for by his beloved (and by now also beheaded) uncle Kent, situates his rule on the very point of decapitation, where men's heads can be ruled as securely as if they were severed even while they remain conscious: "subjects of the king" without recourse to the death that is "all" (Jarman 166). Watching Edward III's accession-by-execution, the audience perhaps realizes that, like Mortimer, they probably did not read this child in time to protect themselves from such promises. In preparing a written note through which to order Edward II's murder, Mortimer anticipates the child's perceptions and plans to control them, using some ambiguous Latin to instruct the murder while simultaneously disguising the order (23.6–12). However, he has simultaneously failed to "read" the child, and in the failure of his note to have any effect, something ironic and deeply troubling is suggested about the education—in the broadest sense—of this child. Creating a contrast between the preparation of the textual note and the distinctly visual concerns of the young Edward III, the ending shows a telling exchange of gazes between the dead eyes of Mortimer, the witnessing eyes of the prince, and the display of those eyes for the imagined gaze of his dead father and for the audience. Edward III's final lines suggest a prolonged ceremony between the head and the child, which is also a complex and ironic play on recognition itself; this coup d'état ironically underlines the imperative to constantly scrutinize, to read, the child, now turned back by the child upon his adult oppressor. Contemplating Mortimer's head, Edward determines that the nature of his own rule should be best figured as an act of visual recognition, one that disturbingly promises to contain the mental, as well as physical, capacities of others to threaten his rule—quite the contrast to the mass of protestors united with their loving king in Jarman's ending. The accompaniment of the appeal to be "witness of my [. . .] innocency"—that is, to even now read this royal killer as a child—underlines the perversion behind his sudden, if legitimate, entrance into sovereignty. Marlowe's sly implication is that even at the point of this restoration of legitimate (monarchical) time, time is, in fact, as out of joint as ever and that this could not have happened in the same way were it not for the very childness of the new ruler—with his terrifying moral simplicity, his play transformed into real violence in his handling of the severed head. This is a dangerous kid, representing a dangerous future that uncannily and monstrously reworks what the past claimed to be while erasing the actual complexity and contingency of recent events.

As Stephen Guy-Bray observes, Marlowe "calls into question the nature of English kingship itself" (vii) by fundamentally destabilizing the monarchical claim to provide political security through temporal stability, a claim that Marlowe's final scene effectively parodies in the simultaneously violent and childish logic that the young Edward III implements within his gruesome tableau. In Marlowe's early modern context, discontinuous, disruptive rule by someone accumulating power by force of arms or political plotting was often understood as tyranny, in contrast to the assurances of continuity and just rule associated with legitimate monarchy; the deliberate confusion of these modes of rulership by cunning usurpers was a potent and popular dramatic theme (Majumder 136–37). Throughout the play, the monarchical and tyrannical impulses are repeatedly in tension; Edward I's order for Gaveston's exile is voided (or is it?) by his death and his son's succession according to the proper patrilineal and monarchical order; Edward II is the legitimate king but rules with a tyrannical disregard for both his father's wishes and the future's imperatives; Mortimer deposes this rightful king in the name of the new boy king but, in reality, can only rule as a usurper. The disruption of orderly time is ambiguously yet markedly aligned with drives we might characterize today as queer: There is something excessive about Mortimer and Isabella's passion for one another, despite its heterosexuality—and something perverse at its source, in that Isabella ultimately welcomes the murder of her husband by her lover—which itself ironically echoes the deeply antisocial, unproductive passion between Edward II and Mortimer and which renders the removal first of Gaveston and then of King Edward himself as profoundly ironic, the irony eventually confirmed by Isabella and Mortimer's own similar removal from power. The idea of time as ordered around an ultimately atemporal authority in the continuity of kings is compromised and queered from all sides.

We might anticipate that the accession of Edward III, the great epitome of medieval kingship, will end these disruptions. What Marlowe has actually happen, though, is very different when the young Edward III turns the act of usurpation and the violence of execution back against Mortimer in his countercoup. Even though this should be a moment of triumphal restoration of legitimacy, its resolution of the destabilizing factors that have preceded it is hardly convincing. Rutkoski similarly reads the child's role in the ending as indicating the instability of any solutions to the problems of monarchical rule that the play has introduced—though she reads Edward III as weak and vulnerable rather than sinister, a reading countered by both the text and the mise-en-scène of the play's final moments and by, indeed, their historical context. Guy-Bray reads the ending as a "tyrannical continuity" (xxviii) and an "endless loop" (xxvii) and cites Edelman on reproductive futurism in doing so; but this perhaps downplays the extent to which Marlowe has made this a zombie continuity—as Edward III's address to the severed head indicates—its stability dependent on a literally childish view of life and politics, one to which Marlowe allows immediate success but fails to endorse with any explicit gesture toward the famous deeds of Edward III. It also represents a discontinuous change, a coup d'état—at least from the perspective of the child's victims.

Far from ushering in Jarman's utopian time and exalted monarchy, this restoration feels instead like monarchy papering over the queer cracks in its authority with the crude and manic paranoia of the child's play with Mortimer's head—for later modern audiences, a rather *Lord of the Flies*-esque moment—and his disturbing combination of claimed innocence and implicit cynicism. Edward II's disruptive failings are simply ignored by his son, this boy with the terrifying determination of childhood, whose unrequited and unmerited love for his father—which can now, perversely, be safely idealized and falsified following that father's death—echoes the equally perverse passions that brought the previous king to his downfall. Lisa Hopkins suggests that "if we judge him by the devotion to him evinced by his son, Edward II is the best parent in [Marlowe's] plays" (33), but the irony here derives from the fact that the son's devotion is clearly not an accurate reflection of the father's affections.

Marlowe's Edward III kills in the way that he does and with the ambitions that he does because he is a child. This child king, whose childness is constantly emphasized by those around him and even by himself is, tellingly, Marlowe's own deliberate creation to a significant extent: The historical Edward III was born in 1312, acceded in 1327 at the age of fourteen, and deposed Mortimer in 1330. Marlowe massively compresses these events; and, of course, the part is intended to be played by a single actor, who first appears in scene 11, immediately following the final downfall and execution of Gaveston, which in reality took place a few months prior to the prince's birth. The result emphasizes the prince's young age as a constant feature, making his growth from clinging boy to bloody ruler sudden and not particularly natural. In his first appearance, the prince's advice to "commit not to my youth things of more weight / Than fits a prince so young as I to hear" (11.74–75) shows a double-edged precocity of insight that simultaneously notes the prince's youth as a constraint and yet also exposes his understanding of the dangerous world around him. Later, when Mortimer and Isabella attempt to place the prince on the throne, he protests that he is "too young to reign" (21.92) despite the historical Edward III being then in his mid-teens, not necessarily a prohibitively young age for medieval kingship. Becoming frustrated, Mortimer addresses him angrily as "youngling" (21.110). Marlowe consistently made the young Edward III much more of a child than the historical material demanded.

Marlowe's Prince Edward/Edward III has become a figure of increasing interest to queer scholarship on early modern literature, with a growing body of analysis of the child in Marlowe's playtext (and in the production history); Alexandra Parsons, Marie Rutkoski, and Rachel Prusko have drawn attention to his queerness. In her essay "'A Prince So Young as I': Agequeerness and Marlowe's Boy King," Prusko argues:

> Marlowe queers this early modern child by suggesting that he may not be a child at all, but rather an adolescent, thereby deliberately destabilising childhood as an early modern category. His depiction of the character points to the queerness of Edward's status as a royal child, and later as a boy king, an oxymoronic subjectivity that Marlowe underlines and develops through his emphasis on the boy's ambiguous age.
>
> The Prince does not exhibit linear growth: he appears variously as younger and older than the 14-year-old boy who took the throne in 1327. (196)

Although I concur with Prusko's reading of Edward III as ambiguous and "non-normative" (196), in my view, it is neither necessary nor encouraged by the playtext to convert his status from that of a child into an adolescent—a conversion that, though Prusko intends it to underline his ambivalence, risks containing it through applying a category for the "in-between" age. Prusko continues: "Edward's sudden surge to power late in the play is a product of necessary dramatic compression, a device that makes young Edward seem to grow up in an instant, regardless of his numerical age, intensifying Marlowe's queering of the boy. In his early scenes, the prince appears to be much younger than the 14-year-old boy in Hollinshed's *Chronicles*, Marlowe's main source, but Edward's conduct later in the play suggests that he is not a young child" (197). I believe the latter conclusion should be reversed: rather than suggesting that he is not a young child, his conduct at the ending is shocking precisely because he is still a child, drawing upon a child's logic with a ruler's power. Edward may seem to grow up in an instant with his coup; but, in fact, his action is a direct response to how he has seen adults behave around him throughout the play (his reiteration of the imagery, and materiality, of violence against heads seen through the preceding scenes makes this absorption clear). The prematurity of Edward's coming to power is the disturbing factor here, and—in its implied roots in a fantasy of loving union with his father, the union that Jarman unironically makes a reality in 1991—the key source of its dangerous, even deadly, queerness.

This is not, however, a queerness as we might normally recognize it—or, indeed, wish to affirm it. This Edward III is a child who imposes, through violence, a version of reality that is coherent and stable but also violent and blind to moral complexity; this early modern child king thus anticipates a trope we shall see recurring in late modern Britain. We have seen versions of this trope already in Macaulay's Barbary, in Kubrick and Burgess's Alex (at least before his capture), in Ackroyd's Dyer, and elsewhere. If Marlowe's Edward II—and his *Edward II*—have shown that monarchical fantasies of national stability ultimately always contain their own disruption, the desire of the child—Edward III—can, ironically, secure them for longer because of his childish energy, violence, and moral fundamentalism.

So, why did Jarman, working in the Britain of the early 1990s, abandon this dangerous child in his avowedly queer reworking of *Edward II*?

Between Marlowe and Jarman: A Queer Child and a Dangerous Child

Marlowe's Edward III is a child who kills. When Jarman strategically reworks him to create his new queer ending, he loses the much more difficult and dangerous figure presented by Marlowe's child king. Jarman's concern is to out Marlowe's play, to visibly expose it as the queer document it is; ironically, in doing so he misses the real—and really political—nature of this queerly dangerous child. In order to create a utopian restoration-resurrection for Edward II, the succession of his son and the violence required for it (translated by Jarman into a mere game of covering Mortimer and Isabella with flour) are abandoned, with any rupture in time replaced by a restoration of monarchical authority entirely unlike that seen in Marlowe's ending.

This child's coming into authority is no longer, for Jarman, predicated on the adult's death; and monarchy loses its central paradox when the potential for generational conflict, the conflict between living and dead, and the divergence between father and son are all removed. Death forces a negotiation between those who hold authority now (the adults) and the generations who will inherit it—an inheritance that the adults cannot automatically assume will be on their terms. Marlowe's play is a provocative, macabre exposure of just how fragile and contradictory the early modern state, imagined through the lens of its medieval antecedent, could be in attempting to manage this negotiation. Yet, these issues are as relevant for late modern British anxieties as they are for early modern English ones. In abandoning some of the ways in which these themes are realized in Marlowe, Jarman's *Edward II*, for all its compelling queer spectacle, ultimately creates a child for the 1990s who is less difficult, less dangerous, less opaque, less jealous, and perhaps even less queer than in his Marlovian source.

Jarman's aims, and his achievement, should be understood—and valued—in their context. His vision of a triumphant, inclusive, and stable polity, where generational interests harmoniously combine, is obviously, openly, a fantasy; yet, the fantasy carries great affective and moral power as a rebuke to 1980s and 1990s British conservatism, with its relentlessly homophobic deployment of the child as a political weapon. Here, however, the utopian fulfils Bruhm and Hurley's observation that it "is often accompanied by its doppelgänger, nostalgia" (xiii). Although thirty years later it is easy to critique Jarman's passionate nostalgia, it would be obtuse to overlook either how this vision arose directly against the cruel realities of 1980s and early '90s British social conservatism and nationalism—and their moral panics over the child—or how playfully radical its provocation is in adapting a dramatization of national history against the claims of those conservative forces. Nevertheless, this gesture is ultimately, in a fundamental underlying sense, depoliticizing, as it uses one vision of history to fantasize an escape from all history and from politics itself. A queer politics based on achieving such unity through recognition of a permanent queerness in history is also profoundly unrealistic when applied to the child, to whatever extent that child may or may not be recognized as queer, because the child embodies the future's discontinuity from the past and, ironically for Jarman, the capacity to imagine the past as something other than what it "really" was—which are, of course, exactly the attributes Marlowe gives, in forms saturated with irony, to his child-killer king.

If the queer is, as Jarman implies, what has always been there but has been left unacknowledged and repressed, then logically, perhaps, political justice can be achieved through recognition; his film's visual grammar, as I have suggested, certainly heavily implies this. Political representation as the basis for the extension of rights—broadly speaking, Jarman's goal in making his movie—becomes primarily driven by such recognition here, and such recognition of repressed reality is equated with visual attraction to things of beauty, curiosity, and sexual potency. This has a deeply ironic relation to the Marlovian child whom Jarman expunges given that he too, as we have seen, bases the operation of his rule entirely on a kind of recognition, grimly imagined as the child's gaze of, and upon, the dead. His erasure replaces politics with a visual domain, with the demand to recognize that Jarman's film makes so beautifully. This gesture subjugates historical time to utopian images (just as Marlowe's play with the heads is replaced by Jarman's enthroned spectacle), with a resulting turn away from politics as material, institutional, and historical. It is when the child is most spectacularly visible that his materiality and agency are lost, subsumed into a totalizing vision of renewed order—an order no longer institutional but utopian, nostalgic, atemporal. Looking at Jarman's film skeptically, informed by the history of late twentieth-century representations of the child and youth, I am tempted to paraphrase the lines of another violent film's conclusion: this boy has been cured alright.

The adult in authority always has to contend with the child's approaching accession into authority; they can address this either through a process of negotiation, which we might call "politics" or through an act of anticipation, which seeks to foresee the child's movement into adulthood and act to forestall it. Marlowe stages the perverse failure of the latter; Jarman unthinkingly and ironically places his faith in an anticipation that is ultimately a prioritization of identity: the child identifies a better future with the true nature of the past. Ironically, this is exactly the identification that Marlowe's Edward III makes at the end of the play; but there, of course, it is a totalitarian falsification of the past and a renewed threat to the future. All violence could be avoided if only "could I have ruled thee then as I do now," announces this little brute.

The irony Marlowe gives to Edward III's handling of the severed head over his father's dead body speaks, then, of the child's alterity and relationship to the discontinuities of history, even as this child asserts his own terrifying version of nostalgia to be secured through violence. In 1990s Britain, Jarman exorcised this creatively destructive, deadly child. In order to most fully read this late modern gesture, it pays to return to the early modern source.

The Dangerous Child in History and Theory

This peculiar story of the child-killer king being himself, in key senses, killed off in 1991 has implications both for the issue of reading the child in general and for the recent cultural history of children as embodiments of the British future. The case of *Edward II* indicates, above all, that the dangerous child is profoundly difficult for both progressives and conservatives and that radical nostalgia provides a distinctive British field for the resulting battles. Jarman's emphasis on recognizing and retrieving the queer in history is an artistic reflection of an intellectual and political agenda that was influential but still emerging[6] while he made his *Edward II*. In the emphasis he places on recognizing the queer and the child's capacity for queerness, he inadvertently highlights a paradox around which queer theory must always turn: If the queer is that which destabilizes and disrupts categories and restrictive social-familial systems, how can this be adequately represented by any further defined category, including the category of *queer* itself? And how can this be translated to a visual domain without falling into the trap that to see the child is to know the child (or to face the terrifying refusal of such knowledge, as with the exploitatively terrifying children of contemporary and recent horror movies)?

The child underlines this problem because of both the argument—originated by Freud and revived in recent scholarship, including powerfully by Bond Stockton—that *all* children are queer, at least latently some of the time and partly because they do not tend to disclose their disruptive motivations and aspirations within terms that are transparent to adult society or contiguous with its logic—a point that Adam Phillips, for example, makes with particular force. Queer theory that deals with children tends to negotiate around this question of recognition, as I have argued. Queer theory is also open to influence from the theorists' possible desire for a politics that distinguishes the queer from the unequivocally dangerous or violent, particularly when that violence is directed toward achieving socially conservative (or worse) ends. The dynamic between Jarman's and Marlowe's Edward IIIs is an example of this problem; and it is a problem that repeatedly arises in later twentieth-century British narratives of dangerous children and youth, which often emphasize the child's susceptibility to fatally absolutist moralizing even in the middle of their creative destruction of adult society. As we see this play out, we shall also continue to see radical nostalgia—a powerful fetish of the organic and the essential—remain as a major force in British cultural politics around the child.

Twenty-first-century Britain does not, of course, face the possibility of boy kings in the way that medieval and early modern England did. Yet, the timing of children's access to power, and the effects of their accession to it, remains a fraught matter in an era of generational conflict: an era where public life is replete with discourses of childhood naivety and of how that naivety might turn to violent radicalism, potentially in the form of threat to conservative ideas of gender and sexuality—or, conversely, as aggressive readoption of them—and to conservative ideals of the national heritage and stable British values. Adult demands for reassurance from the child in these contexts can paradoxically lead to the child's disappearance, as Jarman has shown in a particular sense and as we shall see in the next chapter.

Chapter 4

Abduction and Abuse

Disappearing Children in the 1980s and 1990s

Child Abuse and the 1980s as Cultural Nachträglichkeit

I should so love to see his face, if you could make his dreams come true, and fix it for him.

—Participant on *Jim'll Fix It*, 1986

Child abuse confronts us with the violence of limits flouted and transgressed. [. . .] In response to this discovery—something which can fairly be called one of the traumas of the 1980s—innocence then returns with all the renewed authority of a value literally and brutally under assault.

—Rose, *The Case of Peter Pan* xi

The last chapter explored the disappearance of a child from a text and his replacement by an alternative. In this chapter I consider child disappearance, both textual and historical, in rather more literal, yet also more expansive, terms to explore how real and fictional cases of child abuse and abduction formed objects of British cultural and political obsession during the 1980s and early 1990s. This obsession reflected, at its core, a project to render the child more knowable and containable for adult perceptions. I observe that this project did real harm to children, while literature provided, and still provides, a site for its culpability to emerge. In the Thatcher-Era 1980s and the post-Thatcher (but still Thatcherite) 1990s, child abuse and abduction became central to British political and media discourse. Some abuse and abduction cases from this period have had a very long afterlife in British political and popular culture and in literature, while some later exposures of abusers in popular culture have retrospectively rewritten aspects of the period. Child abuse and abduction in the UK's 1980s has become something of a Nachträglichkeit of cultural history.

This forms, then, the background to this chapter, where I explore several literary and film responses to these phenomena, examining work from Ian McEwan and Blake Morrison alongside some popular culture of the time and real cases of child abduction and murder during the period. Throughout, I build the argument, cued by the conceit at the center of McEwan's *The Child in Time*, that attempts to protect children from disappearance by making the child ever more visible paradoxically end up "disappearing" the child in their materiality, opacity, and contingency, replacing them instead with an organic and essential child imagined as wholly visible to the adult protector who can resume confidence in the future. Though Jacqueline Rose claimed that "the crisis of child sexual abuse in the 1980s has made it harder and harder to know, when we describe a child and even more our relationship to it, what we are talking about" (xvii), I argue that though this is superficially true in the cases considered here, it covers an underlying project to use child abuse and abduction to restore adult epistemological and political security.

This has a crucial political context where, during and since the 1980s, the supposed risks of child disappearance, abuse, and influence by dangerous minorities have been used to react against social change and to foster and manipulate paranoia. The image of child disappearance is of powerful use for these purposes because it is absolute; the all-encompassing risk to the child is proportionate to their original innocence, and the resulting demand on the adult to recognize and protect the child is sometimes presented as one and the same as recognition of a much broader essential and unchanging reality—much like how, in contemporary rightwing rhetoric, protecting children from harm is presented as dependent on accepting that there are and always have been only two sexes, only two genders.

These dynamics are clarified by their most extreme forms in conspiracist thinking, where imagery of child abuse, trafficking, and disappearance is prominent. This has been powerfully evident in recent years, as in the "save our children" campaigns allied to anti-vaccine and anti-lockdown protests during the COVID-19 era in the UK (Sharma), which alleged organized child abuse by powerful pedophilic elites, connected to the QAnon movement in the United States (McIntyre). The latter conspiracy theory is associated with support for Donald Trump (Smith and Wong), holding that Trump—whose first term's moral outrages are often exemplified, for his opponents, by state abuse of migrant children—is himself engaged in an epic struggle against pedophilic elites. In order to have explanatory power to match its moral significance, a narrative of child abuse and abduction may need, it seems, at least some rewriting; in order for this significance to be made visible, other harms may need to disappear from view. Rightwing rhetoric of child abuse and the conspiracist insinuation of a depth and breadth of elite child abusers of which few ordinary citizens are aware demands political engagement only in terms of revelation and exposure, not of the legitimate negotiation of varying interests or conflicting values.

Mainstream conservative exploitation of this dynamic consolidated in the 1980s, and its more recent revivals echo, as opponents often point out, the Right's rhetorical associations between child abuse and LGBTQ+ minorities that were powerfully established in the 1980s. In particular, the contemporary presentation of transgender rights as a palpable threat to children is a direct echo of rightwing framing of the gay rights agenda in the 1980s, the framing behind Clause 28—as has been argued widely by left-leaning commentators (see, for example, O'Toole; Jones). This is especially the case in characterizations of gender identity as a fantasy-based ideology into which children are indoctrinated (Armitage 14–15, 22–23). In this rhetorical environment, the future and the child are conceived of as absolutist matters of truth versus falsehood, life versus death, and imagining the child's enemy as a gay activist (in the 1980s) or as a trans activist (in the 2010s and '20s) allows the child's interests to be effectively separated from issues of intergenerational or political change. Behind the image of the child, the real child's materiality, ambiguity, and agency all disappear. As I explore further in chapter 6, however, there is a paradox here: the contemporary Right finds itself positioned against the image of the child-as-future rather often, whether in the form of desperately vulnerable refugee children or, for example, Greta Thunberg making demands for the planet to be saved in the name of her own embodiment of the future. One way of deflecting this is to present such children as having been already abused by others—liberal parents, leftwing teachers, etc.—and, thus, to retain the child's figurative, if not practically or individually valid, role as a moral and political absolute. A "real" child must be natural, organic, unindoctrinated: this is the long legacy of the Romantic ideal of the child, combined with the Victorian focus on the child as fundamentally moral but vulnerable.

There are, then, contests over the nature of the child, which may amount to disappearing part or all of an actual child's childness; and political figures have, in any case, an interest in presenting developments they seek to defeat or exploit as amounting to an act of child abuse or destruction. This is because—as per Edelman's starting point in *No Future*—the figure of the child under threat is an imperative that forecloses and avoids acknowledging a future that remains disputed, dangerous, and simply unknown; it avoids the need to take intergenerational change seriously and can even be used to avoid addressing fundamental changes to the human future, such as those presented by climate change. Sheldon argues persuasively that the figure of the redemptive child, even in fictions of dystopian ecological collapse, is used as an evasion of uncertainty, contingency, and excess in historical and biosocial change; as she says, in such fictions "infertility is the conceit, but restoration is the point" (151).

My exploration of 1980s and early 1990s depictions, and retrospective revelations, of child abuse and abduction in this chapter gives an origin story for some of these dynamics in their specific contexts within recent British history and considers a set of literary responses to both the historically immediate and the fundamental issues at stake, including responses that drew on child disappearance and on dangerous children who seemingly must kill or be killed. I explore a range of political and cultural history here, paying close attention to the tragic murder of James Bulger in 1993 and to Blake Morrison's literary, but "non-fiction," response to this, *As If* (1997). I also examine the contemporaneous and retrospective appearances of child abuse in popular culture, the latter particularly via the posthumously notorious Jimmy Savile. I then explore a literary critique and satire of Thatcherism's relationship with endangered children, Ian McEwan's 1987 novel *The Child in Time*, and consider McEwan's subsequent returns to disappearing children, arguing that the trajectory of these returns displays an increasing willingness to imagine the legitimate death of a child in the interests of the security of the adult ethical and social order. This body of material all supports the case that it is, paradoxically, when the child, in a literal or figurative sense, disappears that the child becomes most conceptually visible to adults; and yet, this visibility is achieved through the forced disappearance of aspects of the child that do not fit. If texts like *The Little Stranger* showed the child who is irrepressibly material—seemingly even after death and certainly after childhood—here, we find instead children whose materiality and potential are at serious risk of being killed off in the minds, and possibly even in the real actions and institutions, of adults. Whereas in *Don't Look Now* and *The Wicker Man* a child's disappearance is used to entrap and disorientate adults, here it allows them, perversely, to regain epistemological security. This is achieved and interrogated through a set of visual and conceptual dynamics that have significance, I shall argue, not only for recent British history but also for our theory and practices of reading the child today.

The 1980s, Child Abuse, and Child Abduction

In the 1980s Britain [. . .] saw "the value of children recognised in unprecedented ways" as the very concept of childhood was "redefined" to emphasise "its prerogatives and importance." Bastardy was removed from the law books (1989), and caning outlawed in schools (1982); child abuse entered public consciousness via the sensational Cleveland crisis (where, across six months in 1987, hundreds of children who were suspected victims of sexual abuse, the allegation made against their parents on the basis of an unproven medical diagnosis, were removed from their families, often from bed in midnight or dawn raids, and placed in foster or residential homes); children's rights were publicly debated via the 1985 Victoria Gillick case [. . .] Between them, Cleveland and Gillick provoked radical reforms that altered the status in law of Britain's children.

But in the same year—1989—in which Parliament passed the Children Act [. . .] the numbers of people living on Income Support in the UK had doubled, to nearly 4.5 million, piggybacking another three million dependents, of whom two million were under 16. Four major inquiries into child abuse [. . .] showed the traditional British family to be terminally dysfunctional, children its victims. [. . .] What kind of adult could perpetrate child abuse, we wondered. And, more anxiously, the questions we almost didn't are to ask, What kind

of child could participate in it? What kind of child was its
product? (Chillington Rutter 172–73)

As Chillington Rutter indicates, the 1980s and '90s saw heightened and extended attention to the status of the child, and narratives of child abuse and abduction—primarily from real cases—concentrated this attention into a concern about the very survival of childhood. (It is not coincidental that this is also the period in which the contemporary field of literary and cultural scholarship on children essentially began in the UK.) The conservative reaction against postwar and progressive futures led to a fundamental reconsideration of what childhood is and how it should be protected; this new scholarship was, among other things, a counterreaction to the counterreaction to the postwar child. As Margarida Morgado observes, "child disappearance [. . .] becomes a social, material, and cultural fact interpreted by adults in the contexts of their own needs, anxieties, and fears" (246). In Thatcherite rhetoric, the interests of the child were projected, in theory at least, as an inherent good that should override other interests, as the Children Act of 1989 essentially sought to establish;[1] this was also reflected in, for example, the principles underpinning the establishment of Childline, a national charity supporting at-risk children and youth, in 1986. For liberal and leftwing critics, this was somewhat at odds not only with Thatcherite social policies—which badly failed to ameliorate the material conditions for the most deprived children and their families, as Chillington Rutter notes in the previous extract[2]—but also with its Clause 28 legislation, which prevented supportive discussion of sexual orientation in schools.

Margaret Thatcher reconciled these issues rhetorically by presenting knowledge of non-normative sexuality as an outrageous and dangerous political intrusion on the otherwise organic and apolitical space of childhood; as she notoriously put it, "children who need to be taught to respect traditional moral values are being taught that they have an inalienable right to be gay" ("Speech to the Conservative Party Conference, October 9, 1987"), thus linking supposedly healthy and organic childhood with a general notion of a healthy society and polity. Such intrusion was, at least implicitly, figured as itself a form of child abduction and abuse.[3] This was underpinned by both the violently homophobic association between queerness and pedophilia[4] and by specific cases of child abuse and abduction that generated moral panic in politics and the press, some of which I describe in this chapter. When Ian McEwan depicted, in fictionalized form, a government concerned with "how the nation is to be regenerated by reformed childcare practice" (163), he reflected children's genuine rhetorical and political centrality in Thatcherite politics.

Cases of child abuse and abduction did receive massive public attention in the United Kingdom long before the 1980s, and even the association between these cases and the failures of postwar and progressive society was popularly established before this time—notably in the 1960s "Moors murders,"[5] which are probably modern Britain's most infamous murders of children. Yet, there were genuinely distinctive features of the role of child abuse and child abduction narratives in the public life of 1980s Britain: particularly, the repeated willingness of the prime minister and government to encourage attention to these phenomena as irrefutable evidence of near-catastrophic social decay resulting in threats to and from the young as well as the introduction of new legislation, new policy, and new national and social infrastructure to respond to such threats to children. This intensified political environment produced more open conflicts between politicians, media, theorists, and intellectuals regarding the actual material circumstances of cases of child abuse and abduction. In some instances, these conflicts have either returned and revived in the decades since or have emerged retrospectively through later exposures—some verified, others more contested or outright false—of abuses committed during the period.

These developments took place around real cases with real young victims. The very first case featured on the BBC's program *Crimewatch UK*—which shares narratives and reconstructions of real crimes and encourages viewers to supply tips for the police—in June 1984 was a child abduction and murder: that of sixteen-year-old Colette Aram. Also featured in the same first episode was the abduction of seven-year-old Mark Tildesley, which quickly generated significant media attention.[6] This terrible crime had many of the hallmarks popularly associated with such cases: Mark vanished suddenly and absolutely (at the time of writing, his body has still never been recovered) from a place designed to seductively appeal to children, a fairground, and he was apparently lured into trusting an adult through being gifted money to buy sweets, with a sinister "stooping man" seen by witnesses identified as his likely abductor. The missing boy left an object behind, his treasured bicycle. Both the visual and the narrative impact of the incident on broader society was extensive, and coverage endured for much of the 1980s without results until 1989, when a new enquiry into missing children—Operation Orchid—attributed the murder to an organized pedophile gang. The man ultimately charged with and convicted for Tildesley's killing had an adult male partner, reinforcing the popularly assumed link between male homosexuality and pedophilia. These events consolidated popular fear over child abduction and abuse and repugnance at the figure of the pedophile, which Mark Jones identifies as having become a new focus of major public anxiety in the mid-to-late 1970s (127). These fears were sustained throughout the 1980s, as reflected in the 1987 publication of Ian McEwan's *The Child in Time*—discussed in detail later. The child disappearance that drives events in McEwan's novel is a sudden and absolute one; it takes place in a setting close to the child's home; the child remains permanently unrecovered; and though the case is never solved, there are strong hints toward a pedophile as the culprit. It seems likely, given its extensive and sustained prominence, that McEwan had the Tildesley case in mind.

1980s political and media associations of child abuse and abduction with social decline were also influenced by the long legacy of events from earlier decades: The Thatcherite '80s turned out to be haunted by the legacy of the '60s in an almost literal sense when the Moors Murders gained renewed public attention through the confessions of the two killers in 1987, followed by the discovery of the body of one of their victims, Pauline Reade. These child-killings had already had a well-established cultural prominence even before these developments (as per The Smiths' release of a song inspired by the events, "Suffer the Little Children," in 1984). Associated by several commentators with social and sexual decline from the "permissive society," even to the extent of ignoring "the specificity of the killers in [an] indictment of permissiveness in general" (Jones 116; see also Collins 29), and taking place in postwar housing estates—originally intended to *solve* social problems but often characterized as abject spaces of failed futures, as in *A Clockwork Orange*—the Moors Murders were taken to expose the link between unthinkable crimes against children and the broader failures of postwar, 1960s, and 1970s Britain.

New child murders also joined this grim catalogue in the later 1980s, such as the so-called Babes in the Wood murders in Brighton in 1986. However, one of the most unusual and large-scale instances of child "abduction," the Cleveland scandal, was actually carried out by authorities when, as Chillington Rutter notes, "across six months in 1987, hundreds of children who were suspected victims of sexual abuse, the allegation made against their parents on the basis of an unproven medical diagnosis, were removed from their families, often from bed in midnight or dawn raids, and placed in foster or residential homes" (172–73). In an interview conducted when the initial allegations had not yet been discredited, Margaret Thatcher suggested that child abuse was a reason for communities to keep a closer eye on activity in their own areas because, with child abuse, "you cannot wait for the step of the bobby on the beat for that! Neighbours have to get involved" (April 1987 interview with the *Daily Express*). There is, perhaps, a hint of tension here between the organic values of family and community and the need for institutional protections for children. Later, after the allegations had been discredited, the events were drawn into the class and regional politics of Thatcherism through the suggestion that the families involved had been more readily suspected of abuse due to being working-class and northern, a category of people who had borne many of the costs of the Thatcherite realignment of the British economy. The scandal remained contested for a long period after the initial events, with a 1997 TV documentary, *The Death of Childhood*, controversially claiming that a majority of the initial diagnoses had been accurate; later in the 2000s, some of the now-adult individuals removed from their families sought redress for the trauma caused to them. In the late 1980s, the scandal was a major driver for the introduction of the Children Act (1989), whose legislation was fully implemented in 1991.

The Cleveland scandal's extended aftermath suggests how the heightened, and sometimes distorted, attention to child abuse and abduction in the 1980s could lead to a haunting sense that the demand to fully expose the realities of violence against children had not been properly met. Certainly, this was the case when one of the most prominent entertainment figures of the period, Jimmy Savile, was exposed as a prolific sexual abuser of children in 2012.

Making Child Abuse (In)visible: The Case of Jimmy Savile

When the DJ, TV entertainer, and prominent charitable fundraiser Sir Jimmy Savile was revealed, approximately one year after his death in 2011, to have been one of the most prolific modern British child abusers, the revelations also exposed the terrible inadequacy of protection for children during Savile's lifetime—despite the legislative, political, and social developments in this area. ChildLine founder Esther Rantzen was one of Savile's professional associates. Another was Margaret Thatcher herself, according to whom Savile was "a stunning example of opportunity Britain, a dynamic example of enterprise Britain, and [. . .] of responsible Britain" (qtd. in Davies 49). Regarded as something of an honorary perpetual youth himself (Morley), Savile was thus recognized as an example of the forces (enterprise, opportunity, responsibility) celebrated, promoted, and identified by Thatcherism as imperatives relevant for children's upbringing. These qualities allowed Savile, with the purpose of abusing children, to effectively infiltrate several major British institutions to a truly remarkable extent for an entertainer—albeit, one who was then very prominent. In the late 1980s, the Thatcher government gave Savile "a direct managerial role" (Kirkup and Marshall 5)[7] at the secure psychiatric hospital Broadmoor—an institution with which he had already had a long association, affording him considerable access. Savile was appointed not as a figurehead but as a powerful management figure with extensive influence and "unrestricted access to the hospital" (Kirkup and Marshall 14), seemingly on the basis that his character and achievements, particularly as a noted charitable fundraiser, aligned with the Thatcherite view that entrepreneurial spirit was more effective than institutional process (see Davies 402–06). The grim effect of this, exposed long after the event, was that Savile's crimes themselves became institutional, rather than merely individual, scandals (Boyle 1574).

The Savile revelations exposed a contamination of political, cultural, and medical institutions by a failure of recognition.[8] In 2012–2013, the British media presented the Savile revelations as a kind of double take, a shocking realization of a previous failure of basic recognition; and as the exposures accelerated, the phrase "hiding in plain sight" was used in coverage with increasing frequency, eventually even being used in the official Metropolitan Police/NSPCC report on the scandal (Gray and Watt 6). Despite Savile's media prominence, his visually arresting appearance—as Cadwalladr put it, "the man who dressed like a paedophile was a paedophile"—and how often he publicly remarked on the sexual attractiveness of young women and girls (Boyle 1564, 1572), he was almost never explicitly recognized as an abuser during his lifetime. For at least some people, the monstrous Nachträglichkeit of realizing what Savile had been really gaining via his career prompted a reevaluation of what they, the audience, had been getting out of him—and perhaps, by implication but left unspoken, out of the children he "presented." Savile's career, which so successfully obscured his child abuse, was in significant part based upon *promoting* looking at the child.

The Thatcher-Savile friendship is bleakly ironic in the context of the Thatcher government's vocal concerns over the dangers of predatory individuals sexually corrupting children. We should understand Clause 28, with its notorious reference to "homosexuality" as "a pretended family relationship," as demanding the strategic refusal of recognition, a refusal to see what was visibly there in order to visualize something else: the fetishized innocence of the child. The unspoken, *Turn of the Screw*-esque logic behind Clause 28's response to an imagined homosexual infiltration of education—the assumption that *to know is to be corrupted*—refuses to separate the possibility of knowledge from abuse. Savile, curiously, reversed this refusal of recognition. He constantly made innuendo references to his sexuality and foregrounded its appearance in other ways. Yet, even Margaret Thatcher personally dismissed arguments that an unmarried man, who by his own account preferred promiscuity to sustained relationships, might be inappropriate for a state honor from her socially conservative government. Given this macabre farce, could it be that the desire for recognition of the child did not so much fail with Savile as it was actually fulfilled through what he provided to popular and political culture? Could the imperative to recognize be sometimes dependent, somehow, on a compulsion *not* to recognize, as in Clause 28?

This is a question we are compelled to take seriously when viewing—with hindsight—*Jim'll Fix It*, the television show presented by Savile from 1975 to 1994. The program's conceit saw children writing in to ask "Jim" to "fix it" for them to achieve their aspirations and ambitions. The resulting "fix its" were then performed, either as pre-taped video segments or in the studio, with Savile presiding regally as a kind of desacralized Santa Claus with the mysterious ability to fulfil children's desires, whether bizarre or merely ambitious. In the Christmas 1986 episode, for example, a girl who wished to be mailed to her friend inside a parcel was followed by another who wished to run a clinic for a day, acting as a doctor. The language used by one adult who wrote into the same episode asking that her nephew be taken to "a real life Aladdin's cave" was suggestive: "I should so love to see his face, if you could make his dreams come true, and fix it for him." The anticipation of looking at the child's face was the desire driving the whole show, as any viewing of it now makes clear; its cameras constantly linger on the child's flushed reactions of consumerist, comic, and proud delight, all reflected back by Savile, the child's bizarre middle-aged doppelgänger with his own exaggerated facial expressions.

Vicky Lebeau has described the history of an interest, present since early cinema, in capturing children's faces on camera—delighted, giggling, sometimes crying or wailing. Analyzing this in a tradition of studying the violent gaze of the camera deriving from Laura Mulvey's influential *Visual Pleasure and Narrative Cinema* (1975), Lebeau records how the child on screen codes both apolitical redemption and anxiety about the future, a coding delivered via the camera's close, penetrating, obsessive scrutiny of the child's face. This same overwhelming visual interest in the child's face is underway in *Jim'll Fix It*—perhaps in a visual rebuke to the contemporary discourses of loss of innocence in which Savile himself engaged (Davies 276)—where the camera fixates obsessively on the faces of children reacting with confusion and then delight, identifying, through the expectation it generates, with the ability to manipulate the child's emotions; this manipulation was carried out figuratively by Savile himself, acknowledged winkingly in his huge grins and cod-shock. At first glance, so to speak, this is not the imperative to see the child at risk but, rather, to celebrate the desiring, ambitious, even entrepreneurial child. Yet, just as we can't watch the show "innocently" today, knowing what we know about Savile, so too the very innocence the show performs requires a different, and more skeptical, attention. After all, if the show is about the ambitious child, how can it also be straightforwardly about the innocent child? Is ambition—the desire to be other than one currently is—compatible with innocence? In the show it is, indeed, presented as compatible; and it is precisely in this respect, I suggest, that we find both a subtle violence toward the child and the realization that there *is* a repressed risk from—and, more dangerously, to—the child present here.

Jim'll Fix It clearly aims to confirm adult knowledge of the child, whose desires were typically trivialized and patronized on the show. Many of the fix-its selected concerned young children's ambitions for their own futures: to enter exciting careers, make new discoveries, and perform unusual and extreme feats. Playing these out alongside such "childish" requests as eating lunch on a rollercoaster or getting a biscuit box stuffed with only the child's particular favorite biscuit was trivializing—at least given the format, where even the more profound ambitions were satisfied by a briefly set up "experience" rather than actually advanced in any way. This apparent celebration of childish pleasures was neither the sideways growth theorized by Bond Stockton nor reflective—despite a superficial resemblance—of Adam Phillips's post-Freudian recognition of the child's ability to imagine and act as *other* than just a child while not wishing to *cease* being a child. Rather, the child's role as *merely* a child—whatever the object of their ambition and appetite—was patronizingly affirmed. Bond Stockton notes the irony, relevant here, that while paid labor is generally banned for children in contemporary wealthy societies, it "still is a force, often for pleasure, in the child's imagination ('what will you be when you grow up?'), though sometimes in unimaginable forms, especially if the child is precocious or clever" (*The Queer Child*, 62). The whole goal of *Jim'll Fix It* was to ensure that this imagination, whether grand or foolish, was always imaginable; indeed, it was made directly visible. Here, the camera's gaze—directed and reflected by Savile's exaggerated, mocking facial cues—functions specifically as an anticipation, where the adult knows what is to come much *better* than the child. Thus, one thing certainly being "fixed" here is the potential of the child's wish to disturb the security of adults in any way. As with Clause 28, the possibility that children's development, or even their play, might represent a potential *difference* between past and future is eradicated through a process of recognition—both its extension and its denial.

Savile and the Afterlife of 1980s Child Abuse

The long afterlife of the Savile case—beyond his peak of fame in the 1980s, death in 2011, and exposure in 2012—has been in its own right a remarkable media and (though it seems distasteful to frame it as such) popular-culture phenomenon, with, for example, a major Netflix series in 2022 and an equally prominent BBC dramatization in 2023 both dedicated to the subject. This seems to fulfil James Kincaid's observation that "the media is not so much a source as a friendly satellite bouncing back to us the story of child molesting we often hear, tell ourselves, and find so satisfying that we love even the echoes" (3).

As we have seen, the 1980s were marked by a continued and intensifying public focus on the abuse, abduction, and murder of children. The Right—including the government—repeatedly associated these crimes with the supposedly negative social effects of liberal developments and progressive movements during the preceding decades (and which were still ongoing via their leftwing opponents). In parallel to this, new figures of popular and media hatred like the pedophile; new media forms like *Crimewatch*, which blurred the line between media and law enforcement; and new infrastructure like the Neighborhood Watch, which blurred the line between law enforcement and community action, collectively facilitated a heightened intensity in the demand to identify and recover abused and missing children and the perpetrators of the crimes against them. Yet, even within the decade itself, this intensity, rather than bringing the darkness of depraved adults and deprived children into the light, descended into moral ambiguity and political counterclaim—as seen in the Cleveland scandal—or missed its target completely, as with Savile.

In the immediate period following the 1980s, though, public understanding of issues of child abuse and abduction was both challenged and darkly satisfied by a child murder carried out by other children.

Blake Morrison, *As If* (1997)

> If child-killings are the worst killings, then a child child-killing must be worse than worst [. . .] Those nameless boys had killed not just a child but the idea of childhood.
>
> —Morrison 21

> There's a photograph among my cuttings, a dozen would-be lynchers, young men mostly [. . .] wanting to kill the kids who'd killed the kid, because there's nothing worse than killing a kid.
>
> —Morrison 27

The poet Blake Morrison's *As If* is an extended, imaginative essay on the brutal 1993 murder of two-year-old James Bulger by two older children in Liverpool. These children, aged only ten themselves, were tried as adults in a legal proceeding that Morrison observed first-hand and that received saturation media coverage (Franklin and Petley 149–50). *As If* reflects on the resulting national soul-searching driven by and through often obsessive engagement with the recognition of children as both killers and victim. The aftermath of this has given the case a long presence in British public life and popular memory.

As If begins with a seeming non sequitur, a mini-fiction in the form of a narration of the thirteenth century legend of the Children's Crusade, drawing on Morrison's own vaguely recalled childhood encounter with stories of this semi-historical event (1). In his retelling, the Crusade arises through the special significance assigned to the child as prophetic reflection of the moral failings of the society in which he lives. One such prophetic child gains a huge popular following—mainly comprised of other children but with the support of some adults—while adult institutions react ambivalently to him, caught as they are between embracing the juvenile prophet as a Christ-like arrival (3), following the model their own faith claims to celebrate, and rejecting his message as one of hopelessly unworldly moral oversimplification, proclaimed by a boy of troublingly opaque intentions. The Crusade ends with the prophet murdered by his own followers, in response to this child's failure to live up to the authority of his own innocence (20–21). It is not clear whether the adults' failure was in treating the Children's Crusade with condemnation and indifference or, conversely, in not condemning it hard and early enough.

Back in the early 1990s, John Major, Margaret Thatcher's chosen successor as prime minister, expressed confidence that children had killed and had been killed because society had failed "to condemn a little more, and understand a little less," in his notorious comment on the Bulger case, quoted as an epigraph for Morrison's book and offering a key demand for Morrison to parse. For those who leaned left, Thatcherism itself—the political movement that had reshaped Britain in the preceding decade, which Major sustained with relatively minor modifications[9]—was implicated in the moral failure exemplified by the Bulger murder: by its alleged promotion of selfishness covered by rhetoric of aspiration; its disinterest in societal and psychosocial complexity, to which it preferred moral fundamentalism; and its destruction of the industrial base in the north of England, which turned out to be a rather less than creative destruction, leaving stigmatized regions of socioeconomic decline. For conservative-leaning commentators, though, progressive Britain—and children themselves—were the prime suspects in the killing:

> Features and editorials [. . .] have worried away at the case and, beyond it, at a larger fear: that kids are growing up too quickly, are brutalised and beyond control. [. . .] Some of them use words like "brutes" and "little animals." Some are written by novelists: Anthony Burgess, Martin Amis, William Golding, Alice Thomas Ellis, Piers Paul Read. They scatter the blame at different targets—single mothers, absent fathers, schools, the Church, the Pill, the sixties—but most seem to agree that children, these days, are [. . .] a generation of hoodlums.

> Cherub-faced muggers. Rapists who don't have pubic hair yet. Pre-pubescents with glittering knives. (26)

Most of the sources for the violent child invoked here align with those accused by Thatcherism, particularly the 1960s, with its social and sexual liberation movements and supposed weakening of the nuclear family. Morrison uses quotations from *Lord of the Flies* (25) and *A Clockwork Orange* (233) among the epigraphs opening his chapters and makes the image of Bulger's abduction a dark doppelgänger to a recalled image of postwar hope in "a documentary from 1945, war at an end, a girl and boy walking through bomb-ruins to the brow of a hill, the green future beyond—'the new world is theirs.'" (50) The pernicious offspring of postwar and progressive Britain (or the offspring's offspring) haunted popular imagination into the 1990s, having seemingly managed to outlast the Thatcher government's promises to confront violent youth, restore morality within society, and create a revised future.

Morrison's broader frame of reference emphasizes the traffic between literary children and real (if contested) social phenomena, referring to a huge variety of material from William Blake (51) to *The Wizard of Oz* (50) alongside philosophers of childhood, notably Rousseau (99–100). He also notes children's access to seemingly perverse recent fiction: "A story by [Roald] Dahl called 'The Swan,' involving a child being tied to a railway track, has been advanced as possible inspiration for T&V [Thompson and Venables, killers of James Bulger]. I was brought up to think that books were humanising, civilising, 'better for you' than television. Now I'm not so sure" (141). He also notes that violent film, specifically *Child's Play 3*, was cited as a possible influence on the murder (143).

> At one point in *Child's Play 2* Jenny Agutter appears, famous from *The Railway Children*. In my half-sleep a vast conspiracy is spun, art imitating life, life imitating art. In Roald Dahl's rewrite of *The Railway Children*, adapted for film by Tarantino, the Thompson brothers, waiting for their father to come back from the war, kidnap a small child in a red *Don't Look Now* plastic mac, and tie him to the rails in an attempt to slow down an express train. (154)

In this sequence, Morrison creates a palimpsest of texts about childhood, desire, and violence, recalled as he drifts into sleep; Chucky from *Child's*

Abduction and Abuse | 151

Play 3, a doll who threatens to take the appearance of a child by murdering a child, directly expresses the fear of the child who kills other children (154). Some of this now seems quaint, almost three decades later, but it reminds us that "culture" is often widely and sincerely understood as a serious agent in social problems, albeit in different terms contemporaneously and subsequently. A serious study of the social environment of Liverpool in the early 1990s would consider the massive economic upheaval of the preceding decades, changes to social policy and funding of social services, as well as changes in the family unit; but at the time, the public discourse around James Bulger's murder was as often or more often about, as Morrison reminds us, violent films, sexual awareness, and the effects of divorce.

> As the court's arranged, with most of us sitting behind the boys, it's hard to see their faces, but [. . .] being stared at is bad enough at the best of times, and this is the worst of times. Just because they're murderers [. . .] doesn't make the staring easier to take. Even interrogation is preferable: how can you answer a look? Only with an answering stare, or by turning away. Thompson looks levelly back, Venables down at his lap, and in those postures, before even a word has been spoken, meanings are inferred. (29)

Morrison oscillates between absorption in these gazes and trying to gain some critical distance over their dynamics. He even transfers this gaze toward his own children in a scene that recalls the anxious looking between the older, opaque children and the younger, vulnerable children we saw in *The World My Wilderness*: "On my way to bed I look in at my older son and think: Could he have done what Robert and Jon did? And I look in at my younger and think: if some boys had beckoned, down in Lewisham, would he have gone to them?" (156). The gaze reflects an attempt to secure meaning, to make some invisible essence (at least imaginatively) visible, escaping the mere contingencies of being born into a particular class, a particular family, a particular period, or even just being in the wrong place at the wrong time, as James Bulger was in a Liverpool shopping center. The idea of fiction influencing or even determining reality haunts Morrison: "Fictional precedents for children killing children. *Lord of the Flies*: 'Kill the pig, kill the pig'—and Piggy, too, the one with National Health specs who died like James [Bulger], with a rock in his face [. . .] Films showing children as little devils are now almost a genre—*Rosemary's Baby, The Omen, The Exorcist*" (36). Morrison was not alone in seeking literary and cinematic "precedents" for James Bulger's murder; such comparisons, including to *Lord of the Flies* and to child-horror movies, featured prominently in journalistic coverage of the case (Franklin and Petley 141). Morrison observes an apparently legitimate instance of this when one of the killers is found to have drawn (prior to the murder) a picture, with accompanying narrative, based on his recent viewing of John Carpenter's *Halloween*—which, as Morrison notes (and as I alluded to in chapter 2), "begins with a six-year-old boy committing murder" (238). Yet, if children are allegedly susceptible to acting out the models they find in films or books—exactly the same fear that formed the proximate driver of Clause 28—then the adult is guilty of reproducing literary fictions through their gaze on the real child before them, with texts saturating simple facts to make opaque, invisible, or even absent qualities in the child into tangible and monstrous attributes: "Robert's [. . .] aloneness makes him seem more sinister [. . .] I know little of his life yet, only that he's a fifth child, which makes me think of Doris Lessing's novel, *The Fifth Child*, about a child-ogre, a troll-hoodlum, born into an otherwise perfect family. Some of Lessing's descriptions of her boy-monster might fit how Robert looks in court. Already, there's a feeling against him—a feeling that he doesn't have feelings" (38). The way fiction is used as exegesis for reality here amounts to an evasion of historical contingency, making the unseen reality of the murder knowable (and thereby potentially subject to anticipation, even preemption). Morrison recalls *The Fifth Child* as a supreme example of an essentially, inevitably monstrous child—though, in fact, Lessing's novel has an underlying, ironic awareness of the adult drive to escape the contingencies involved in any child's birth and upbringing. If murder, particularly such an exceptional and morally confounding murder as the killing of a child by other children, could be anticipated by adults, that raises the question of what has gone so wrong that a society and its institutions have singularly failed to do so. The idea that the child murderers, even more than their victim, were in the wrong place at the wrong time (they were playing truant from school), speaks to the failure of institutions—including the school and the family home—to contain children and nourish their futures within appropriate times and spaces. Yet, this is also mirrored—at least for Morrison—by another institutional failure: that of the courts and of the political and media structures pressing upon them. Morrison describes his repugnance at the bloodlust and willful blindness to moral complexity involved in the decisions to try the children as adults and press for heavy sentencing. Here, an invisible imagined (evil) essence is being willed into visible reality, while aspects of reality that do not fit with this essence are rendered invisible; there are multiple forms of child disappearance involved in producing the idea of the child and preserving it from attack (in response to an actual failure to protect a child from deadly harm). The institutional failure of better moral imagination in, sometimes literally, the face of the child echoes the confusion and incapacity of the medieval church in the story of the Children's Crusade; and the alleged failings of the contemporary Church of England, in its supposed liberal reluctance to provide sufficiently robust moral guidance to children, were highlighted in rightwing commentary on the case (Franklin and Petley 140).

Such a willful rejection of complexity assumes that children can reveal a potential for evil that, rather than being the contingent product of multiple circumstances, is simply an essential reality to be contained. The failure of progressive movements, according to this thinking, was to naively refuse such containment, and even books and films—texts for the imagination—were sufficient to thoroughly undermine it. In this schema, the child's imagination becomes less dangerously opaque and indeterminate than simply determined by an act of copying; one striking implication from this is that conservatives perceived violence as on some level genuinely attractive, hence requiring containment and channeling—echoes, again, of *A Clockwork Orange*.

Morrison's anxieties seem to be driven by a sense that the responsibilities involved in parental influence risk becoming unbearable without some kind of epistemological escape (144–45), and this impulse is associated with stories of child abandonment (146), hinting toward repressed awareness of the parent's potential for violence toward the child. Tellingly, but grimly, Morrison notes how images of the abducted child are used to freeze an essential image of childhood such that the image of the disappeared child provides a secure visual representation that the adult risks finding chillingly preferable to the mess and stress of living children: "Those who have lost a child are the only ones not to lose a child [. . .] only the dead kids are immortal, frozen in an ever-smilingness, pretty pages waiting on the imagination." (57–58) Morrison ultimately rejects this perversely alluring dynamic, and his title, *As If*, comes to stand for historical contingency, for the randomness and tragic proximity of alternative futures. It is the fear of this, he implies, that lies behind obsessions over the risks to and from children (including his own). The fear of the child disappearing, abducted before our strangely passive adult eyes, is in part a fear of the knowledge of this contingency. Translated into obsession, it compels us to insistently distinguish between the child and the non-child, even among the children who sit before our eyes, with terrible consequences.

Morrison's account of the Bulger case as a kind of narrative phenomenon, one developed collectively through the national media, is notable for how seriously it takes the interrelationship of fictional and real children. It is curious, in this context, that the Bulger case (as Morrison notes) led to a delay in the release of the movie *The Good Son* (1993), whose narrative focuses on deadly violence between children, to which I shall return shortly. *As If*, like the Savile case, shows the disastrous consequences of a desire to disappear aspects of real children in the name of protecting a potential that it actually destroys.

The Child in Time (1987)

Even before these grim events of the early 1990s, though, the late 1980s had already proved capable of generating a major literary response to fears of child abduction and abuse. Ian McEwan's novel *The Child in Time* (1987) makes the motif of child abduction, alongside themes of child abuse, central to its melancholy satire on Thatcherism—with Margaret Thatcher even appearing here as a coyly implied, albeit unnamed, version of herself.[10] *The Child in Time* portrays a society obsessed with the protection and correct upbringing of the child, defeating postwar and progressive ideas about children, rejecting moral complexity in education, and taking a coldly authoritarian approach to young people abandoned into homelessness and prostitution—"ex-children shuffling to work," in McEwan's pointed phrasing (2). The novel's protagonist is Stephen Lewis, a children's author and the father of a three-year-old daughter, Kate. During a supermarket trip with Stephen, Kate disappears, and despite frantic and extended official and unofficial searching, she is never found.

Stephen, depressed yet obsessive in his quest for the recovery of his daughter, finds that his life starts to lack any other purpose, and his marriage with Kate's mother, Julie, breaks down; Julie moves out to the countryside, adopting a reclusive existence. Stephen's own life is given structure only through his participation on a subcommittee of the Prime Minister's Official Commission on Childcare, an activity officially intended to produce the *Authorized Childcare Handbook*, quotations from which form the epigraphs for each of the novel's chapters and which affirm a value system simultaneously socially conservative, economically utilitarian (121), and nationalist (65). Stephen occasionally visits his friend, Charles Darke, a former publisher and now junior minister in the government, who is a favorite of the prime minister. Darke's older spouse, Thelma, a quantum physicist, enjoys engaging Stephen in theoretical discussion over the relationships between time and space. Suddenly, Darke resigns from the government; he and Thelma move to the countryside, where he undergoes a strange regression to childhood, climbing trees and playing all day. Visiting Julie, Stephen has an odd visionary experience where he sees his parents as a young couple in a pub, before they were married; his parents later confirm to him that this event really did occur, and his mother informs him that it was the day she revealed to his father that she was pregnant with Stephen (172). Julie and Stephen, while attempting to reconcile, sleep together—an echo of *Don't Look Now*'s ambiguous attribution of a redemptive potential in sex for the couple who have lost a child—but, ultimately, their loss remains unbearable, and the couple stay separated. There is, however, an optimistic episode when Stephen helps to rescue a truck driver from a near-fatal road accident in a scene that is suggestive of rebirth (94–96). The novel concludes with Stephen returning to Julie, who is revealed to have become pregnant from their temporary sexual reunion, and with her giving birth. Darke eventually commits suicide; Kate remains missing. The *Authorized Childcare Handbook* is published, but rather than being a true product of the commission's work, it is revealed first to be a predetermined political setup and ultimately as being the writing of Charles Darke himself, who was inspired by his love of Stephen's successful children's book (202–03).

The Child in Time satirically distils left-liberal moral and intellectual disgust with the Thatcher governments, variously indicting their quasi-Darwinian attitude to the economy (90), the ecological damage inflicted by their roadbuilding programs (6–7), their alleged promotion of a coarser popular culture (122–23),[11] and their hypocritical veerings between perverse decadence and sexual prurience. There are riots suggestive of the "race riots" of early 1980s London in the background (18). The postwar Britain all this has replaced is defined, by contrast and in a narrative voice that seems to be Stephen's and McEwan's simultaneously, through the "general principle that on the whole life would get better for more and more people and that it was the responsibility of governments to stage-manage this drama of realised potential, widening possibilities" (23); this is reinforced by Stephen's memories of a childhood that represented significant material progress since his parents' own childhoods earlier in the twentieth century (70). The government depicted here is a more extreme and dystopian version of Britain's real late 1980s governments, generally mapping closely to Thatcherism's real ideological orientations and willingness to tolerate social harm in the service of an essentialist and uncompromising conservatism and economic neoliberalism—though at times the exaggerated parody does move further away from the reality.[12] *The Child in Time* is explicitly oriented from the perspective of a socially progressive postwar generation: still-young people in the '60s and '70s—"the aesthetic and political experimenters, the visionary drug-takers" (22)—who are experiencing disillusionment and political alienation in the 1980s encompassing alienation from their own childhoods and the hopes once invested therein.

McEwan's Britain is, nevertheless, a country obsessed with rebuilding the future through reforming the upbringing and education of children: "There were strong opinions about what constituted a desirable citizenry and what should be done to children to procure one for the future" (4). McEwan relentlessly satirizes the tenacious ignorance behind Thatcherism's "common-sense," authoritarian, socially conservative, and crudely capitalist (22) approach to education, acutely exposing where conservative "realism" actually relies on willed unreality about children. Thatcherism's superficially anti-theoretical stances are exposed as themselves abstract dogma embodied in Lord Parmenter, a Thatcherite figure and the chair of the Sub-Committee On Reading and Writing, on which Stephen sits (5). (The committee member who advocates for the phonetic alphabet [7], a more innovative and theoretically driven approach, is by contrast clearly an anti-Thatcherite concerned with "the sale of State schools, the housing shortage" [17]). The milieu here closely echoes the real late 1980s, with its conservative concerns over the Loony Left's influences on education and the introduction of the first national curriculum for England and Wales in 1988, an innovation explicitly framed by the Thatcher government as an attempt to counter radical and progressive influences (Pierson 132–35).

The echoes of real history are never stronger than in the novel's presentation of child abduction and feared child abuse and of the missing, and therefore all-defining, child around which its events revolve. Descriptions of Kate's disappearance are densely evocative of the tropes central to contemporary narratives of child abduction:

> What else did he buy? Toothpaste, tissues, washing-up liquid [. . .] And who was there when his hand reached for these items? Someone who followed him as he pushed Kate along the stacked aisles, who stood a few paces off when he stopped, who pretended to be interested in a label and then continued when he did? He had been back a thousand times, seen his own hand, a shelf [. . .] and tried to move his eyes, lift them against the weight of time, to find that shrouded figure at the periphery of vision, the one who was always to the side and slightly behind, who, filled with a strange desire, was calculating odds, or simply waiting. (10)

As with the real-life Tildesley and Mehrotra abductions—which Kate's disappearance echoes in becoming a media event (149)—the child disappears within a quotidian environment that is here also a commercial one, thus hinting at the anxieties around children and consumerism; the store manager complains that "supermarkets were the favoured territory of child snatchers" (15). Somewhat unusually among satire on the Thatcher governments, McEwan attacks Thatcherism primarily for its attempts to make children into rationalist economic producers (rather than, as often alleged elsewhere, wild and greedy consumers); but Charles Darke, dominated as he is by his sense of the child within himself and other adults, suggests that this rationalism is merely an aggressive doppelgänger for the childishness of the Thatcherite consumer economy, which does indeed extend to actual children-as-consumers. Bond Stockton observes children's consumerism as produced by historical changes that involved "delaying children's moneyed relations to systematic labor, in the legal workforce, a pause enforced by law" (*The Queer Child*, 222). McEwan imagines an attempt to abolish this pause for actual children and to monstrously replace it with a kind of permanent indulgence for adults—at least those in ideological and personal conformity with Thatcherism's precepts.

Within this environment, the pedophile acts as the semi-imagined "shrouded figure" on the periphery of the gaze, matching the disappearance of his target in his opacity—a presence who must be projected as visible even when he is feared to have escaped observation. Ironically, Stephen later finds himself in the position of being a potential child abductor (147–52) in a hint toward how child abuse within families—as, allegedly, in Cleveland—became one of the popular concerns of the period, in anxious juxtaposition with the more forthright paranoia over the danger of shadowy strangers. *The Child in Time* wholly fulfils Margarida Morgado's observation that "the child lost by parents, the non-existence of children, kidnapped, abducted, and killed children, the absence of children from the family are all related cultural phenomena, also connected to the several theories that warn that childhood is disappearing or that we are witnesses to the 'end of childhood'" (244). The density of meaning invested in child disappearance applies throughout responses to Kate's disappearance, beginning immediately after the event itself:

> Within moments all shopping around him had ceased. Baskets and trolleys were set aside, people were converging and saying Kate's name and somehow, in no time at all, it was generally known that she was three, that she was last seen at the checkout, that she wore green dungarees and carried a green donkey. [. . .] Several people had seen the little girl riding in the trolley. Someone knew the colour of her sweater. The anonymity of the city store turned out to be frail, a thin crust beneath which people observed, judged, remembered. [. . .]
> The lost child was everyone's property. (12)

This closely tracks the media narratives of real child abductions during and after the 1980s,[13] where incidental details of clothes and toys, shared to prompt recognition of the lost child, become part of the event's enduring iconography. There is a hint here that the lost child briefly revives an organic form of community that is otherwise suppressed in the landscape of Thatcherite Britain; the need to find a lost child briefly creates a village out of an anonymous, atomized, commercial space.

The Child in Time not only echoes real child disappearances, but also (like *As If*) literary and film tropes. There are, in particular, multiple echoes of *Don't Look Now*: Kate is wearing a red scarf when she goes missing (8), in an echo of the red-coated child in Roeg's film; toys play a haunting role in signifying the absence—and ghostly presence—of the missing child (126–28); "Julie," Stephen's wife, echoes the name of Julie Christie, who played John's wife Laura in the movie; and in McEwan's novel as in Roeg's film, the couple's attempts to resume sex are central to any possibility of accepting the loss of their daughter (49). These echoes underline the absolute quality of the loss of the child, on which *Don't Look Now* so painfully dwells. Although McEwan, unlike Roeg, does not quite present this challenge as supernatural, the almost implausible absoluteness of Kate's disappearance—and the metaphysical turn Stephen's life takes in its aftermath—make it at least quasi-supernatural, and the effects of the child's loss ultimately generate a literally visionary potential in McEwan's novel just as they did in Roeg's film. In both, too, this challenge is framed specifically through the male protagonist's loss of epistemological and ontological security, including the security of his gendered and sexual roles.

In McEwan's case, this threat to security is also both attributed to and, paradoxically, directed back toward his dystopian version of Thatcherism, the temporal perversity of which is exposed both by the disappearance of the child and by its cancellation of the postwar future. It also registers through a general adult tendency to turn to the child within the adult self to replace the real child's alterity and distinctive interests. Hence, Darke, when still working in publishing, announces: "The greatest of all writers possessed a child-like vision, a simplicity of approach—however complicatedly stated—that made adult genius at one with infancy [. . .] the greatest so-called children's books were precisely those that spoke [. . .] to the forgotten child within the adult" (26). Darke asserts that Stephen's book "is not for children, it's for a child, and that child is you" (28).

Darke's narcissism exemplifies an extreme imagining of the Thatcherite male who channels destructive and "childish" instincts into individualist entrepreneurialism and rightwing politics. This is also true, albeit to a lesser extreme, of Stephen, whose publication of a children's book lends him the characteristics of an entrepreneurial, aspirational yuppie: "Stephen gave up his job, bought a fast car and a cavernous, high-ceilinged flat in South London, and generated a tax bill that two years later made it a virtual necessity to publish his second novel as a children's book too" (30). *The Child in Time* includes multiple ambitious, entrepreneurial, and aspirational men—even the truck driver is proud to recall that he owns his own business, rebuking a teacher who crushed his childhood self-esteem (95). Darke, however, is especially ambitious, his career favored by the prime minister out of "a touch of fondness and desire" (102). This prime minister releases previously repressed materialistic ambitions in the young male (the repression is explicitly blamed on the alternative patriarchy of the postwar, social-democratic establishment, embodied in Stephen's own father); Thatcher, or her lightly coded version in this novel, is the mother who kills off the father to indulge her sons' appetite for pleasurable accumulation. Darke exposes the contradictions in such fantasies and anticipates the ultimate collapse of Thatcherism's attempts to combine a libidinal, oedipal encouragement of masculine aspiration and accumulation with social conservatism and British nationalism (see also Dean, "Spirits of Enterprise," 238–40). When Darke abandons his high-flying career and undergoes his regression to a private second childhood, he comes to embody "childish" ambitions for pleasure that become politically disruptive, mocking Thatcherism's co-option of the male child's energies and appetite for pleasure by following it too closely and too far: "Once a businessman and a politician, now he was a successful pre-pubescent" (106). This theme echoes Bond Stockton's argument, quoted earlier, on the ambivalence of childhood career ambitions and the thin line they tread between productive fantasy, celebrated here in the Thatcherite worldview, and something much less assimilable.

Darke's choice of a much older wife (27)—who views him as her "child" (36, 39)—and his relationship with the prime minister—which his wife considers is characterized by the latter's "desire" for Darke, who "could pass as a young man, a boy" (102)—seem to underline an oedipal tendency that eventually bursts out of its containment. The prime minister herself acknowledges this when she[14] admits to Stephen that "you might think it extraordinary and perverse that I should form an attachment to a young man" (188), and "no doubt you think this all quite ludicrous since he's young enough to be my son" (190). Darke's wife Thelma also acts in an explicitly quasi-maternal capacity toward Stephen when his life is falling apart, reinforcing the sense that he and Darke are close parallels, with Darke as the more extreme of the two; there is a homosocial sideways relationship between these two childhood-obsessed men, which emerges as a masculinist desirous rivalry. Darke himself seems to have an underlying self-awareness, even before his regression, about the ambivalent relationship between childhood and ambition, which he describes in terms that echo Adam Phillips: "For children, childhood is timeless [. . .] Today is what they feel, and when they say 'When I grow up . . .' there's always an edge of disbelief—how could they ever be other than what they are?" (28).

Through his breakdown, Darke's internal sense of childness becomes visible in a way that pointedly contrasts with the disappearance of the real child, Stephen's daughter; both are crises in the visibility of childhood but aimed in opposite directions. Stephen's personal theory that "Kate had been stolen to replace a lost child" (18) and his later paranoia that his wife "had used Kate's disappearance to effect her own [disappearance]"

(134), along with his attempt to take another child as Kate when, in fact, she was merely a substitute misidentified in his trauma (147–52), all hint at the novel's preoccupation with exchanging children—with, as it were, the exchange value of their status, the implications of which are perhaps only partly conscious in McEwan's authorial handling. Ultimately—and somewhat despite its initial, ostensible cues—the novel seems less to reject the replacement of real children by the child within the adult than to reject merely the particular form this takes under Thatcherism.

Stephen's recovery of his own "child within" ultimately merges into the arrival of a new real child, as signaled by his triumphantly boyish ride in the train driver's cab to arrive at Julie's cottage just in time for her to give birth to their second child. Earlier, when Stephen's mother recalls having seen the face of a boy staring in at her and her husband at the pub (176)—occupying the physical place from which, as an adult, Stephen had a parallel vision of his parents at the same moment—the scene directly collapses the adult into the child, visually identifying the child within as the source of essential, atemporal reality (in a less gothic equivalent to the child who appears at the end of the film adaptation of *The Little Stranger*). This is also the moment when Stephen's mother decisively rejects the possibility, which she has been contemplating, of having an abortion (176). This decision, taken on a trip to the countryside, seems to reaffirm an organic reproductive order. At the end of the novel, in the homely, latter-day-Wordsworthian environment of the lonely cottage, the child within Julie collapses into her adult self; the pregnant Julie's "skin had a finer grain, like a child's. What had grown in her was not confined to the womb but was coiled in every cell" (215).

Child-making, as well as healthy forms of child-rearing, is repeatedly associated with a reassuring organic order here, as in Stephen and Julie's post-trauma sexual reunion, the occasion when (as they discover later) a new child is conceived:

> Time was redeemed, time assumed purpose all over again because it was the medium for the fulfilment of desire. [. . .] He wondered, as he had many times before, how anything so good and simple could be permitted, how they were allowed to get away with it [. . .] Not governments, or publicity firms or research departments, but biology, existence, matter itself had dreamed this up for its own pleasure and perpetuity, and

> this was exactly what you were meant to do, it wanted you to like it. (61)

This combines ecological sympathy with natural sexuality as the sources of intimate and social health and the enemy of the complex and the institutional—the enemy too, we might assume, of all theory. Although this is Stephen's perspective, the powerful and detailed musings seem to be affirmed by the author—tellingly, this moment does result in a successful pregnancy, McEwan using his prerogative over plot to convey moral meaning—and although, immediately after this charged moment, the memory of the lost child disrupts the mood (62), the retrospective knowledge of the creation of a new child seems to endorse the euphoric simplicity attributed to the couple's intimacy.

This is tied to McEwan's attraction to a kind of organicist and atemporal essentialism where the recovered child within the self comes to be a startlingly effective replacement for the missing real child and eventually does, literally, replace that real child. Stephen's mental recovery of his childhood parallels Julie's pregnancy. Jacqueline Rose draws a distinction between the "persistence" of childhood "as something which we [adults] endlessly rework in our attempt to build an image of our own history" and the "reductive idea of a regression to childhood" (12); though McEwan is interested in the former, it seems to ultimately transform into the latter through motifs of regression, recovery, and rebirth. Rose is interested in how childhood's persistence within adults, as a "reworking," is a function of the actual alterity of that childhood; *The Child in Time* is, among other things, an extended fantasy of overcoming that alterity, even to the point where the child can witness his parents making the decision to bring him into the world.

This is an oceanic vision, dissolving any distance between subject and other. Through the child retrieved or created in a neoromantic rurality, the adult can hope "to fill the present and be filled by it to the point where identity fade[s] to nothing" (McEwan 103): a permanent present that is, clearly, ahistorical and atemporal, absolving the subject of their anxious responsibilities through submission to a totality, a pastoral death drive. When Stephen discusses the nature of time with Darke's wife, Thelma, she links "the indivisibility of the entire universe" with "the infinite, unchanging time of childhood" (118). After Darke's suicide, Thelma expands on his understanding of childhood, with which McEwan seems sympathetic: "He [Darke] wanted the security of childhood, the powerlessness, the obedience, and also the freedom that goes with it, freedom from money, decisions, plans, demands. [. . .] Childhood to him was timelessness, he talked about it as though it were a mystical state" (202). In practice, this unchanging infinity is associated, neoromantically, with the rural as the site of healthy living, natural childhood, and contentment. Ultimately, the decisions of multiple characters to move to or at least visit the countryside all accordingly produce some kind of moral resolution—even if, in Darke's case, a grim one. Even Stephen's rescue of the truck driver after his crash, with its imagery suggestive of a birth, is occasioned by the rural isolation in which the two men find themselves, in contrast to the failure of the urban emergency response early in the novel.

Reinforcing McEwan's sympathy toward an organicist sensibility, he gives a very sympathetic depiction of a radical theorist arguing to the committee that children's reading should be delayed because it interrupts and disrupts the child's organic appreciation of the world. Although the committee perceives this argument as a bizarre, esoteric intervention, it is treated sympathetically by both Stephen and the narration. The view being advocated is presented in Edenic terms: "It is in effect, Mr Chairman, nothing less than a banishment from the Garden, for its effects are lifelong. Premature literacy makes for adults in whom an unforced, intelligent empathy with the natural world [. . .] is stunted; adults for whom the apprehension of the unity of creation will remain a difficult, elusive concept [. . .] whereas this apprehension is a gift to us in childhood" (74). Pondering this, Stephen reflects on how almost every theory on child-rearing has also had its opposite advocated, reciting a list of examples, with the implication being that over-theorizing is ultimately futile (76–77) and that the only morally adequate response is some form of surrender to the natural order of things. The organic vision of childhood and its retrievability for the adult—provided they have sufficient access to organic spaces and knowledge—escapes the contingency involved in the child's life as an inherently temporary and unstable period, as in the traumatizing fact that, as Stephen recognizes, "there were many paths that Kate might have gone down, countless ways in which she might have changed in two and a half years and [. . .] he knew nothing about any of them" (152).

My somewhat harshly critical reading of this novel should not overlook its importance as a meditation on political violence toward children and childhood, nor should it diminish its richness as an imaginative exploration of fraught relationships between the disappearing (and retrieved) child and adult perceptions of time and history. A more generous reading would note how McEwan puts the over-invested child—including the child within the egotistical masculine self—into their place as one among many children who eventually turn into adults and whose function, even in their parents' world, is never quite as definitive or central as it seems (44, 56). The treatment of Stephen and Julie's eventual meeting of minds over the acceptance of Kate's disappearance—their move, in Freudian terms, from melancholia into mourning—is poignantly handled and makes clear that the retrieval of the lost child through the arrival of another is partial, incomplete, and ambivalent (217). McEwan also shows a genuine appreciation for the child's capacity for imaginative satisfaction—which emerges, for example, in a memory of Kate building a sandcastle with her parents and being determined to stay there (104), evoking Adam Phillips's arguments on such play's resilience toward adult notions of development through lack and trauma. The novel's function as political satire is pointed, yet it is also poignant. In the opening pages, McEwan uses a framing device where Stephen sees Kate in the face of a beggar girl, who suggests he might have a perverted interest in her; he sees the same girl again ten months later—seemingly dead, though he does not recognize this at first (193)—a reminder of how childhood prematurely vanishes far more often along class lines rather than through pedophilic abduction. This girl dies on the same day as Darke, two instances of adults both perversely identified with children and allowed to die.

However, the strain of depoliticization and organicism works throughout the novel to form its most apparent alternative to the inhumane version of Thatcherism that McEwan clearly deplores. The ending offers epistemological security (and a recovered child) to the male protagonist in a way that optimistically reverses the ending of *Don't Look Now*. In this novel, Thatcherism's moral failure is not so much its essentialism about childhood—as the reproductive center of all meaning, a role that Edelman prompts us to regard critically whether in rightwing or ostensibly progressive forms—as it is its unnatural and inadequate version of that essentialism. Rather than Thatcherism exposing a polymorphous perversity in the child's appetites and ambitions that it attempts and ultimately fails to co-opt, it seems to be ultimately merely a perversion to be rejected in favor of an alternative reality of natural childhood, retrieved through return to the organic rather than established through historical and political agency. Such agency, with its inherent potential for perversity in both origins and effects, is the potential of real children, acknowledged but ultimately erased—disappeared—by this novel, despite its textual richness. This erasure appears as the traumatic abduction that stimulates the crises of the novel but which ultimately becomes a morally useful, even necessary, killing-off of the child. In his later work, McEwan repeats the gesture with reduced ambiguity.

The Good Son (1993)

Following the success of *The Child in Time*, Ian McEwan was invited by Twentieth Century Fox to write a screenplay on a childhood theme. After a somewhat complicated development history, including the engagement of major child-star Macaulay Culkin to play the lead and a cancellation of the UK release due to the Bulger murder, *The Good Son* was the result. Although this is an American rather than British film, it is worth consideration for its place among McEwan's depictions of dangerous and endangered children.

When the movie opens, twelve-year-old American boy Mark Evans has recently suffered the death of his mother, Janice. Before traveling abroad on business, Mark's father delivers him to his Uncle Wallace and Aunt Susan's house in Maine for the winter. Mark is reintroduced after ten years to his cousins Connie and Henry; he seems to see his Aunt Susan as an oedipal substitution for his own deceased mother, given their visible resemblance and his need for restorative order after the bereavement. Susan and Wallace carry the burden of their own bereavement; their third child, Richard, died in an accident some time earlier. As Mark and Henry play together, Henry shows a strong destructive tendency that is initially trivial but rapidly accelerates into serious violence when he throws a dummy off a highway bridge, causing a massive accident in the traffic underneath; he seems to be planning to kill his sister. Mark is profoundly disturbed by his cousin's behavior, but Henry manipulates him against discussing it with his aunt and uncle. Mark does, however, eventually warn Susan after Henry takes Connie ice skating and deliberately steers her on to thin ice; Connie ends up in a coma. Although Susan is initially disbelieving, she becomes suspicious of Henry's behavior and even discovers signs that he may have killed his younger brother, Richard. As Susan and Mark develop their oedipal affection, Henry, enraged at his isolation, implies that he might kill his mother. Susan asks Henry if he killed Richard, to which her son responds, "What if I did?" and flees his horrified mother. Susan chases him to the edge of a cliff, where Henry pushes her almost over the edge and picks up a rock to drop on her—but at the last moment, Mark tackles him. During the struggle, Susan manages to pull herself up and grab hold of the boys as they roll over the edge. With only enough strength to save one of the children, Susan releases Henry. She pulls Mark up, and together they gaze down at Henry's body bleeding into the ocean.

The Good Son was unsurprisingly controversial in its explicit and unrelenting depiction of a child so malevolent that he kills and ultimately must be killed. Henry was played by Macaulay Culkin, then at the height of his fame from *Home Alone* (1990), where he famously portrayed a child who deploys playful violence in the interests of defending his family's home. Much of the uncanny effect of *The Good Son* undoubtedly comes from its playing against the audience's associations for this child actor, in a shift from the "good" child whose capacity for creative violence is morally sanctioned to one whose destructive energy is both perverse and deadly serious. Both films visually invest in repeated close-ups of Culkin's young face as he delights in the successes of his plans.

The Good Son invokes the heritage of dangerous, creepy children on page and screen; the brother and sister echo the two children of *The Turn of the Screw* (and *The Innocents*), while the close-ups on Culkin's perverse smile echo the devilish child at the ending of *The Omen* (1976). It differs from the Jamesian tradition in that any ambiguity over the child is replaced by clear evil, and *The Turn of the Screw*'s ambiguity over whether the children's alleged malevolence has an adult source—in either the dead servants or in the governess's own paranoia—is entirely absent; but this evil is presented in a far more naturalistic form than that offered by Damien and the horror-child tradition of Hollywood cinema. Unsurprisingly, reviewers found the result disturbing: according to Roger Ebert, "a creepy, unpleasant experience, made all the worse because it stars children too young to understand the horrible things we see them doing."

The Good Son is unusual in how it takes tropes from the children of horror cinema but places them in a setting that is both more realistic than either supernatural horror or the quasi-supernatural realm of slasher movies dedicated to the violence of male youths and yet is actually *less* morally ambiguous than many such movies; it is less ambiguous even than Lessing's *The Fifth Child*, which was published in between the publication of *The Child in Time* and the release of *The Good Son*. A Freudian dynamic, usually a source of ambiguity and of moral—as well as narrative—tension is introduced here between Mark and his aunt; but this finally operates, oddly, as a source of redemption and security, retrieving a vision of childhood as perfect unity between boy and (substitute) mother, albeit one achieved only by raising the camera's gaze above the small dead boy lying in the waves.

The Good Son's most striking characteristic is its willingness to present two children in unequivocally Manichean terms and, thus, to both require and absolve the adult in making a choice—fatal for one child—between them. *The Good Son* departs sharply from the British political framing of *The Child in Time*, moving to a North American context that is—given that the action takes place primarily in a slightly isolated suburban home and a peaceful surrounding community, with almost no visible external influences—rather generalized;[15] Henry's malevolence seems to be truly inherent, or to come as a perverse random element that might appear in any typical family unit, rather than being historically, socially, or politically specific.

The Good Son affirms the validity of making a choice between good and bad children—a theme that emerges again two decades later as the principal concern of McEwan's novel *The Children Act*. The film's most startling image bluntly encapsulates its willingness to imagine a choice between good and bad children (and, behind them, good and bad versions of childhood) as quite legitimately resulting in the violent death of one child. The camera's willingness to linger on the boy's body bleeding out into the ocean is, to me, one of the most shocking scenes found anywhere in the material explored in this book. Recalling the echoes between *Don't Look Now* and *The Child in Time*, here, Henry's blood mixing with the water reads visually like a morally fundamentalist response to all the ambiguous, watery deaths of children in that famous film of child-focused trauma and adult ambivalence. The anxiety over the disappearing child, haunting the adult imagination, is replaced by a willingness to gaze on the broken and bloodied body of the "bad" boy.

The Children Act (2014)

In McEwan's 2014 novel, named for the Children Act of 1989, Fiona Maye is a judge for the High Court of Justice specializing in family law who is experienced in handling extremely complex cases. Her case history has included one involving the separation of conjoined twins—a choice between saving one child or the other—that has privately left her traumatized. Fiona is herself childless. As the novel opens, Fiona's husband, Jack, informs her that he wishes to indulge in an affair, blaming their lack of sexual intimacy. Their subsequent argument is interrupted by an urgent call about a teenager with leukemia who, as a Jehovah's Witness, is refusing blood transfusion. This boy, Adam Henry, is only three months away from his eighteenth birthday—and, thus, from the legal right to make decisions over his treatment. Fiona decides to visit Adam in order to help her determine whether he is competent to refuse treatment (the rights of children to do so being framed by the legal concept of Gillick competence).[16] Adam turns out to be an intellectually lively and morally sensitive young man. Back in court, however, Fiona rules that Adam is not competent to refuse the treatment; she allows the hospital to transfuse him against his will and that of his parents. Months later, Fiona starts to receive letters from Adam, informing her that he is now grateful to have had the treatment; out of professional probity, Fiona does not respond. Adam secretly follows and confronts her, announcing that he has abandoned his parents and wants to live with Fiona. Disturbed, Fiona firmly refuses to indulge this, and arranges for his safe return to his parents. As Adam prepares to depart, she goes to kiss him on the cheek, but they kiss on the lips; Fiona is horrified, but the transgression goes unwitnessed by others. Later, Fiona receives a new letter from Adam, who has returned to his faith; he describes her in satanic terms. Fiona is eventually told that Adam has died after his leukemia returned and he—now a legal adult—refused treatment. Breaking down, Fiona describes the sequence of events to her husband, and they recommit to their love and marriage: a new healing in the aftermath of a child's death, echoing that which concludes McEwan's earlier novel.

Adam Henry embodies the contingency of the child and the child's desires, their extreme vulnerability to social and family influence uncomfortably juxtaposed with the need to recognize and make space for the child's potential for agency (the danger presented by the latter emerges clearly in Adam's sexual approach to Fiona). The novel asserts the need to give the child time and space to grow—recognizing the opacity, and difficulty, of his ambitions for the adult world—but in fairly conservative terms; Fiona effectively has to safeguard these things against the boy's will. *The Children Act* testifies to the ambiguity and contingency behind the child's agency, and to the arbitrariness of the legal barriers between childhood and adulthood, but finally seems to affirm the need for wise judges—and perhaps wise adults in general—whose troubles are ultimately resolved through the child dying. Adam's death is simultaneous with Fiona reviving her marriage, replacing the child's future with adult satisfaction in a fashion that recalls the conclusion of *The Child in Time*. Ultimately, it seems to be for the best that this troubled and troubling child dies, leaving the adult to find consolation even in his disturbing memory.

McEwan's Children

Ian McEwan produced, as a sustained strand within his career, a powerful set of imaginative responses to child abduction, abuse, and killing, enduring for much of the period from Thatcherism to Brexit. These emerged within the context of growing concern over such phenomena: concerns that solidified and gained prominence in the 1980s, had a particularly acute and fraught public moment with the Bulger murder, and have remained a constant focus of public and media attention in the UK ever since. *The Child in Time*, via McEwan's satirical and dystopic projections, is an extraordinarily productive literary placing of these concerns within Thatcherism's broader ideological project. It captures, perhaps more directly than any other text considered in this book, the anxiety and moral disgust of the progressive classes in the face of the 1980s destruction of the postwar future. McEwan is acutely sensitive to the ambiguities and contradictions of the neoliberal break in futures that Thatcherism introduced and uses the figure of the disappearing child effectively to code their repressed severity.

Ultimately, however, these ambiguities are resolved through a renewed moral confidence, which emerges as an adult confidence in abandoning problem children—whether in the form of missing real children or chaotic children resurfacing within the adult—and restoring the moral status of the child, childhood, and reproduction as sources of organic innocence, stripped of ambiguity and restored as the simple transmission of good values. In this, McEwan wholly fulfills, incidentally, Edelman's sense of reproductive futurism as a force for political restriction and reflects his argument that this futurism could appear as strongly in ostensibly progressive forms as in conservative ones. McEwan's concerns with restoring adult confidence in the face of problematic children becomes noticeably depoliticized in his subsequent work, despite the acuity of *The Child in Time*'s satire.

So, too, the threat of adult abduction and abuse, so powerfully and expansively—yet also subtly—imagined in *The Child in Time*, recedes before the dangerous child in his later work: the danger in *The Good Son* comes entirely from within the child; and in *The Children Act* Adam himself effectively (but unsuccessfully) requests for Fiona to abduct him from his parental environment, and he is a source of sexual threat to her more than vice-versa. Even in *The Child in Time*, the cost of making the child abductor a spectral presence, available for paranoia and projection but little more, is that he ultimately becomes a metaphysical, more than materially deadly, figure. For all that *The Child in Time* is concerned with the perversities in adults' relationships with children—including the children they themselves once were—the decision to make Kate's abductor into an abstract force, a signifier of the damage done to the child-as-future by the governing ideology in particular and by paranoid over-theorizing of children in general, strips the novel of the chance to engage with the issues of "what kind of adult could perpetrate child abuse" and "what kind of child was its product" (Chillington Rutter 173). Only a few years after the publication of *The Child in Time*, the Bulger murder prompted the further question of how to understand children as the perpetrators of abduction and abuse of other children. By finally using the idea of adult violence toward the child more as an (albeit very effective) metaphor for political and structural violence, while the intimate realm of the adult's relationship with the child is either redeemed (in Stephen) or killed off (in Darke), *The Child in Time* has less to say to such issues than it might. Nevertheless, McEwan's texts show the persistence and virulence of the idea of disappearing children and disappearing childhoods as a source of both intimate and political anxiety for adults. They repeatedly present the frantic intensity of the adult's need to know the child in visual terms; all three of the McEwan texts feature adults gazing intensely into the face of the child they fear they are in some sense losing or have already lost, searching for an answer to their own epistemological insecurity.

Conclusions: Child Abuse and Cultural Nachträglichkeit

The material explored in this chapter has borne out Jacqueline Rose's contention, quoted in the opening, that public prominence of child abuse could "fairly be called one of the traumas of the 1980s" and that the consequence is that "innocence then returns with all the renewed authority of a value literally and brutally under assault" (xi). We have also seen that child abuse and abduction narratives from the 1980s and early 1990s have had a long and influential afterlife, sometimes becoming instances of cultural Nachträglichkeit through their later reiteration and revision, whether in the continuing influence of the Bulger murders on how crimes by and against children are understood or in the retrospective reinterpretation of Jimmy Savile's influence over important British institutions through the belated knowledge of his child abuse. Not only the sustained power of child abuse and abduction events to provoke political and public responses but also the growing relevance of more conspiratorial narratives of elite child abuse and trafficking indicate the grim continued relevance of these phenomena in the late 2010s and early 2020s.

The texts explored in this chapter all suggest—either explicitly or through the readings I have advanced here—that the concern with child abuse and abduction is closely tied to a broader desire to make the child knowable, visible, and containable. The tendencies this desire produces evade any less comfortable account of the child's own aspirations. Thatcherism's break with postwar and progressive notions of the future and its combination of co-opting the (particularly male) child's ambitions with a paranoia toward violent youth aligned with this desire and gave it special coherence in the 1980s and early 1990s, as we have seen. At the same time, the turn to discourses of child abuse and abduction—and of serious danger toward and from children more generally—raises the stakes behind political change, making the future not a matter of political negotiation, policy planning, or exchange of ideas but one of moral absolutism, life or death, and upholding or breaking the ultimate taboo. Child abduction narratives are particularly salient for this purpose because they combine presumed abuse with certain disappearance. Disappearing children raise the stakes when deployed in political rhetoric, and when used by literary authors, they allow those authors to show how the stakes have already been raised in ways beyond the terminology of conventional political and historical discourse. Several of these texts, especially *The Child in Time*, expose these contradictions and thereby anticipate the eventual breakup of Thatcherism's alliance between neoliberalism and social conservatism; the high-stakes nature of the deaths, disappearances, and abuses of children that convey this anticipation also indicate why that breakup has taken the form of such violence toward the future in the era of Brexit. This is discussed in the next chapter.

Chapter 5

Children of Nowhere

Migration and Haunted Futures in Ishiguro's *A Pale View of Hills*

Citizens against the World

Niki, the name we finally gave my younger daughter, is [. . .] a compromise I reached with her father. For paradoxically it was he who wanted to give her a Japanese name, and I—perhaps out of some selfish desire not to be reminded of the past—insisted on an English one. He finally agreed to Niki, thinking it had some vague echo of the East about it. [. . .] Keiko, unlike Niki, was pure Japanese, and more than one newspaper was quick to pick up on this fact. The English are fond of their idea that our race has an instinct for suicide, as if further explanations are unnecessary; for that was all they reported, that she was Japanese and that she had hung herself in her room.

—*A Pale View* 9–10

We applaud success. We want people to get on. But we also value something else: the spirit of citizenship. [. . .] If you believe you're a citizen of the world, you're a citizen of nowhere.

—Prime Minister Theresa May, "Speech to the Conservative Party Conference, October 5, 2016"

In 1982, the debut novel from a writer who would go on to become probably the most celebrated British author of the early twenty-first century[1] opened with the death of a child.[2] This child's death is blamed on migration and transnationality, implicated here as simultaneously geographic and temporal transgressions.

Prime Minister Theresa May's speech, quoted in the epigraph, addressed a temporal rupture in British politics—the Brexit vote of June 2016—by diagnosing a geographic transgression in the alleged tendency of Britain's cultural and economic elite toward greater identification with other elites beyond the nation than with the national community itself and in their resulting acceptance of historically high levels of immigration. May advocated for reestablishing a supposedly lost generational and geographic unity, based on recognizing an organic reality in the national community—with both "young black men" and "white working-class boys" cited as potential beneficiaries, despite the generational divisions evident in the Brexit vote and the racialized nature of its popular framings.

This was, despite a forward-looking gloss, antihistorical insofar as it sought to cancel one future and curtail generational change; and it was anti-institutional insofar as it sought to replace both plural institutions—which overlap and qualify the power of the nation-state—and competing political constituencies with a unified national community that the organizations of the state properly exist to serve. The ruptures this agenda sought to heal were in significant part the eventual consequences of policy decisions taken in the early 1980s, when Ishiguro wrote *A Pale View of Hills*; it brought the political consequences of those decisions to a forced stop and an urgent reconfiguration after almost four decades of dominance.

A Pale View, written during the period when those 1980s policies were in the first stages of their implementation, provides a compelling, uncannily anticipatory, literary frame for understanding why Thatcherism's imagined future for Britain eventually turned into the fractured borders of Brexit—and why this was a matter of the child who embodies the future and who attracts profound, even deadly, threat. Although later Ishiguro novels, especially *The Buried Giant* (2015), have been recognized as thematically anticipatory of Brexit (Shaw 92–93; R. Robinson 1084–85), I am making a claim here with a much longer scope: that in subtly recognizing Thatcherism's contradictions, especially regarding the future it attempted to create via the child, *A Pale View* anticipates their explosive fragility. It particularly recognizes how these contradictions were both geographic and temporal in the combination of the rejection of postwar consensus, openness to globalization, more aggressive support for American hegemony, renewed nationalism, and hostility to migration, especially non-white immigration. The migrant or second-generation child, a figure at the foreground in both this and the subsequent chapter, is an overinvested figure for this geographical-temporary nexus, located here somewhere in between the UK, Japan, and the USA. This figure also sustains and intensifies themes and concerns already established in the preceding chapters, especially the fraught role of institutions in accommodating and mediating the child-as-future, and this child is ultimately resistant to all theoretical capture that claims any kind of total recognition or absorption into any particular signification. As before, this resistance is imaginatively associated by adults with a risk of death both emerging from and directed toward the child.

A migrant or transnational child always threatens to become a citizen of the world, a citizen of nowhere, haunting Britain's confused attitudes toward cosmopolitanism, migration, and race in its post-Empire and increasingly neoliberal era from the early 1980s to the mid-2010s. These confusions and contradictions influenced Brexit, but they also persist within it. Despite hostility to migration and transnational institutions featuring heavily in motivations for the vote, leading Brexiteers nevertheless sought to make Britain more open to trade with regions of the world beyond the EU, especially North America and parts of Asia—the maximally neoliberal version of Brexit being known as the "Singapore on Thames" vision (Wolf). East Asia has also played a notable role in Britain's negotiation of its post-Empire future, especially in relation to the status of Hong Kong; though openness to immigration from Hongkongers with British National Overseas passports was a rare, relatively liberal development of the post-Brexit British migration regime, in the early 1980s the prospect of immigration to the UK from Hongkongers avoiding Chinese rule was an object of significant concern and hostility from the Thatcher government. Japan, meanwhile, a onetime Second World War enemy, had become at this time an apparent capitalist success story, contrasting with the underperforming UK. In these contexts, a racialized child haunts the prospects of neoliberalism and globalization, and an ethnically Japanese child—whether "pure" or mixed-race—has a complex place within these dynamics, a complexity Ishiguro exploits to maximum uncanny effect in *A Pale View*. As with the British tabloids' association between "pure Japanese" ethnicity and suicide, in this novel "race" accompanies death as means of keeping the generationally and geographically mobile child grounded, framed, and territorially and epistemologically secured for the comfort of adults.

Between Futures and Fractured Borders

A Pale View opens in early 1980s Britain[3] in a home counties village, where the elderly Etsuko reflects on the death of one of her daughters, Keiko, and the current lifestyle of another, Niki. These reflections lead her to recall life in Nagasaki soon after the Second World War and her friendship then with a young mother, Sachiko, and Sachiko's daughter Mariko. The 1980s narrative returns at intervals but with persistent intrusions from this earlier period. Etsuko's biography between the two periods is never properly explained, and this gap generates some highly charged ambiguities, including over the circumstances of Keiko's birth. There is also a third, albeit apparently only fantasized, period in play that is frequently imagined, invoked, and overloaded with significance; it is set in the postwar United States. This novel combines two themes dominant throughout Ishiguro's oeuvre: internationalism, transnationalism, and postwar, postcolonial globalization (the role of which in Ishiguro has been influentially discussed by Rebecca Walkowitz, Emily Horton, and Alexander M. Bain, among many others); and the ethics of memory (which has also been extensively analyzed; e.g., Teo's *Kazuo Ishiguro and Memory*; Petry, *Narratives of Identity and Memory: The Novels of Kazuo Ishiguro*).

All the novel's temporalities are simultaneously geographically identified—1950s Nagasaki, 1980s England, imagined postwar America—and the unexplained relationship between them is simultaneously an unexplained migration. The unanswered question of how Etsuko arrived in England equally applies both temporally and geographically. The reader might, initially, assume that Etsuko's recollections of early 1950s Japan will answer this question. They do not. Or, at least, as Henry James—one of Ishiguro's influences—had his narrator put it when introducing his own ghostly children, "the story *won't* tell [. . .] not in any literal vulgar way" (118). Etsuko herself is an unreliable narrator, her unreliability reflecting a trauma conveyed in slender glimpses of decimated futures and dead children.

The novel's early 1980s setting is a subtly unstable place and time, despite the banal security of the English home counties location, described by Niki as an affluent residential simulacrum of the "real" countryside (47). The very quietude of Etsuko's current surroundings ironically encourages her to retrieve disturbing memories of Nagasaki in the early 1950s.[4] Not only the aging Etsuko is reaching back, though; her daughter Niki and one of Niki's friends are trying to retrieve and relive Etsuko's migration vicariously, as though it might resolve something in their own sense of where 1980s Britain sits within national, transnational, and generational histories. Disputes over how to secure and enjoy the future result in competing attempts to retrieve and rewrite the past, while the earlier period of Etsuko's life offers an uncanny, darkly ironic model for the "moving on" after the death of others that Etsuko finds herself experiencing again in the 1980s. Her earlier experiences offer a model of mourning for a loss of certainty and authenticity and for a lost child or, rather, for an expanding number of lost children, the boundaries between each of them becoming decreasingly stable as the novel proceeds, who form the "traumatic voltage," in Caroline Bennett's phrasing, running throughout the narrative's "two sets of mother-and-child" and "intergenerational conflict" (86).

Etsuko's narrative uncannily shifts between the ruptures of the British 1980s and the human and ideological losses—apparently so much more severe—of mid-century Japan. These somewhat unlikely parallels challenge any complacent reduction of the violence and trauma they involve to ethnonational difference or to the safety of a past that will remain safely past, and they operate throughout the novel: the tensions between Etsuko's social conservatism and Niki's lifestyle (94), with the latter's rejection of conventional family values and Thatcherite social aspiration, echo the crises over education and young people that earlier surround Etsuko's father-in-law, Ogata. The ruined legacy of Ogata's educational and institutional career has a parodically banal parallel in the ineffectiveness of Niki's childhood piano teacher (50–52)—another failed educational project, unmourned by the child to whom it was directed (51). As often in Ishiguro, the tragicomical banality produced by an unlikely comparison does not dissipate the force of the more politically serious catastrophe but, rather, makes its implications disturbingly lacking in secure limits.

These counterintuitive equivalences between Thatcher-Era Britain and postwar Japan most obviously challenge Britain's Second World War exceptionalist mythology and, implicitly, its role in Thatcherism's rhetorical politics, which combined such British exceptionalism with celebration of the aspirational example of the United States. Collapsing the British 1980s into early 1950s Japan, Ishiguro subtly but fundamentally undermines the temporal limits of a "postwar" period, making Thatcherism's forceful ending of the British postwar social-democratic trajectory less a successful closure than a compulsive rewriting of the past. It is not the only compulsive rewriting of the postwar going on here, though: Niki's friend, planning her poem about Etsuko (whom she has never met), is engaged in a smaller-scale yet similarly intellectually aggressive version of the same rewriting. In a supreme irony, here, the risky historical and generational change represented by the child is projected by the child back on to the parent via an act of writing about generational and geographic alterity—one that ostensibly celebrates but actually contains and guards against that alterity, much as we might expect a parent or an authoritarian educator to do when patronizing a child.

The United States plays a peculiar part in these dynamics. None of the novel's events take place there, but the USA becomes Sachiko's object for the projection of her aspirations for the future. In one of the novel's most striking moves, it gradually—then, eventually, suddenly—becomes apparent that Sachiko may be herself wholly or partly a projection of Etsuko's. Etsuko, however, has ended up in the United Kingdom, not the United States; and other than references to her British husband, there is little explanation of why or how this migration came about. The unexplained geographic movement intersects with the novel's temporal ruptures, and America acts as a lost future in the middle of this migration, known only through projection and repression—a future repeatedly associated with the feared loss of a child, as Etsuko implies to Sachiko:

> "I understand your concern, Etsuko. But really, [. . .] I've heard so much about America, it won't be like an entirely foreign country. [. . .]"
> "Actually," I said, "it was Mariko I had in mind. What will become of her?"
> "Mariko? Oh, she'll be fine. You know how children are. They find it so much easier to settle into new surroundings, don't they?" (43–44)

"Mariko will be fine in America, why won't you believe that? It's a better place for a child to grow up. And she'll have far more opportunities there, life's much better for a woman in America [. . .] She could become a business girl, a film actress even. America's like that, Etsuko, so many things are possible. Frank says I could become a business woman too." (46)

"Out there, she could do all kinds of things with her life. She could become a business girl. [. . .] All these things are much easier in America, Etsuko [. . .] What can she look forward to here?" (170)

"America" thus becomes not only an object for projecting aspirations for the child's future but also, gradually, an analogue for the child-as-future herself in the adult narrator's mind. To doubt "America," as Etsuko does, is to lose faith in the postwar child—or at least in one's confidence in both knowing "how children are" and in the future itself as possibility and potential. Britain, by contrast, seems to be where one ends up when one no longer has confidence either in how (or what) children are or the future they embody.

The final quotation here comes shortly before the novel's key twist, a "small but explosively significant slippage" (Bennett 84): the moment when Etsuko, finding Mariko after she ran off, begins speaking as though *she* is both the child's mother and the one planning the move to the United States, shockingly implying perhaps that Sachiko may have been, throughout, partly or wholly Etsuko's self-projection. This is also the moment at which Etsuko-Sachiko seems to be about to kill the child. The act of killing is—literally—"tied up" in the proposed migration:

"In any case," I went on, "if you don't like it over there, we can always come back."

This time she looked up at me questioningly.

"Yes, I promise," I said. "If you don't like it over there, we'll come straight back. But we have to try it and see if we like it there. I'm sure we will."

The little girl was watching me closely. "Why are you holding that?" she asked.

"This? It just caught around my sandal, that's all."

"Why are you holding it?"

"I told you. It caught around my foot. What's wrong with you?" I gave a short laugh. "Why are you looking at me like that? I'm not going to hurt you." (173)

The child, embodiment of the future, risks becomes being a mere deadweight dragging the adult back toward the past: most immediately to the Japanese imperialism and militarism under which—as Ogata's prewar and wartime pedagogy emphasizes—the child's role is to reproduce the racial essence, the same sacrificial essence that the British media later assume endures in the suicidal Keiko. That essence has become, of course, associated with a destructive sacrifice on an unprecedented (and atomic) scale that failed to gain the promised victory or national renewal; the only future available to join is that offered by the former enemy and now occupying, quasi-colonial power, the USA.

Yet, if the child, either in her very inscrutability and insecurity under the adult gaze or in her recently valorized embodiment of racial essence irrevocably disturbs the postwar retrieval of creation from destruction, then the adult's alternative is to kill the child; and here, "America" names the future the child is to be killed for, as Mariko seems perhaps to have intuited in her uncanny final appearance. Yet, the only named "child" whom the novel securely identifies as deceased is Keiko, who died neither in nor for the United States or Japan but in the UK, apparently in the early 1980s (and who may or may not have been the child with whom Etsuko is apparently pregnant during the Nagasaki narrative).[5] The aspirational future projected onto the USA, in which the child can transparently substitute for the adult's own ambitions—"She could become a business girl [. . .] I could become a business woman too"—becomes a phantom on the novel's geographic and temporal horizon, neither Japanese past nor British future but somehow implicated in all the ruptures into which both fall. Chu-chueh Cheng claims that "in Etsuko's elliptical account [America] reconciles the past she shares and the past she buries. It masks the English 'other' she has become and the Japanese self from which she has become estranged" (234). This spectral USA, fantasy of a future that never was and the powerfully desired destination of a migration that didn't quite make it, is just part of the series of attempts by characters—and, behind them, whole societies and polities—in this novel to mediate between past and future by investing in the child as a security, a guarantee, for their relationship. Other such attempts are carried out here by educational institutions.

Institutions, America, and Education

Whereas the fantasy of America drives Sachiko's hopes for the future after the war—which are not Sachiko's alone but seemingly also the repressed wishes of Etsuko herself—before the war, the movement between past and future is mediated through institutions like that represented by Ogata, Etsuko's father-in-law. He makes it clear that this was their (and his) role when arguing with his son, who complains:

> "But then I remember [. . .] being taught all about how Japan was created by the gods, for instance. How we as a nation were divine and supreme. We had to memorize the text book word for word.[6] Some things aren't such a loss, perhaps."
>
> "But, Jiro, things aren't as simple as that. You clearly don't understand how such things worked. [. . .] We devoted ourselves to ensuring that proper qualities were handed down, that children grew up with the correct attitude to their country, to their fellows. There was a spirit in Japan once, it bound us all together." (66)

Later, in confronting his critic, Shigeo Matsuda, Ogata returns to his theme: "'We may have lost the war,' Ogata-San interrupted, 'but that's no reason to ape the ways of the enemy. We lost the war because we didn't have enough guns and tanks, not because our people were cowardly, not because our society was shallow. [. . .] We cared deeply for the country and worked hard to ensure the correct values were preserved and handed on'" (147). Ogata's lost educational institutions are strange parallels to the America of Sachiko's (and Etsuko's) imagination; the latter provokes a prospective anxiety about the child's future that mirrors the retrospective anxiety directed by Shigeo Matsuda and by Ogata's own son, Jiro, toward the institutions that prepared Japanese youth for genocidal warfare through inculcating belief in racial and imperial destiny. In both cases, an unsettling fear that the process of preparing the child for the future might turn into killing that future is powerfully present, as it is in Mrs. Fujiwara's atavistic fear that a pregnant mother walking in the cemetery will transmit her morbid surroundings into her unborn child's gestation (25). The constant surrounding imagery of children's deaths subliminally raises the stakes; though it is slightly more subtle, the backdrop of child murders in Nagasaki operates in a similar way to the killings in the background of *Don't Look Now* and *Hawksmoor*. In both cases, too, there is some ambivalence between the educational institution as a historical entity and practical organization—the contingent product of policy and material needs for the child's future—and as transmitter of some deeper "spirit" binding things together—whether that is the "spirit" of individualist aspiration or imperial, racial destiny. This tension between the institution as historical entity and as incubator of an essentialism (the cemetery that, in Mrs. Fujiwara's mind, nourishes the fetus) is subtly significant for *A Pale View*'s imagining of 1980s Britain's own historical and geographical disorientation.

Like America as the fantasy object of forward movement, the educational institutions that Ogata once built to mediate between past and future—and, in a geographic parallel to this temporal function, to drive expansion of the Japanese empire—haunt the novel's "real" future, the British 1980s. Here, they are only bathetic, ironic, and even embarrassing echoes, as in the irritatingly mediocre piano teacher, Mrs. Walters—who, despite her banality, prompts Etsuko to lie about Keiko's death, linking her with the repressed violence against children in the earlier narrative—and in Niki's lifestyle in London, with its suggestions of student life even though she is not studying anything (51), which is ironically framed by an echo of earlier aspirations: "You see, I had great plans for you once" (51).

Both Ogata's nationalist-imperialist educational institutions and Sachiko/Etsuko's vision of America have been lost and strangely mirror each other in that loss; they are incongruously matched, rather like Mrs. Walters's equation of Chopin and Tchaikovsky (50). These earlier objects of future-making in Ishiguro's narrative have, in fact, been lost in *Britain*, specifically 1980s Britain: a time that neither successfully revives the past nor kills off its ghosts, as Keiko's death shows, and a place that neither fulfils the fantasies of future aspiration nor allows release from them. There is irony in how early 1980s Britain is read here through memories and fantasies of Japan and the United States, given that both were significantly more economically successful during this period than the United Kingdom,[7] the latter still dealing with the traumatic humiliations of the 1970s; these rival countries' presence here thus subtly emphasizes the impression of this Britain as stagnant and stalled, a condition that extends to Etsuko's own circumstances. Whereas Ogata saw his institutions as reproducing Japan's natural destiny, in an educational parallel to the biological fertility mediated and managed through the patriarchal and domestic order—reflecting his obsession with the proper relations of husbands, wives, and children (65–66)—Etsuko's house and village are, as Niki points out, surrounded by a kind of suburbanized faux English pastoral, the quietude of which grimly reflects Etsuko's denuded household, with one child dead and the other semi-estranged.

A Pale View of Thatcherism: 1980s Britain and Its Doppelgängers

Early Thatcher-Era Britain is more present in *A Pale View* than initial appearances suggest. Etsuko's home counties life (which early reviewers of the novel read primarily[8] as a frame for an authentically "Japanese" work by an essentially Japanese author)[9] seems to exist in eerily apolitical isolation; there are no references to economic or industrial challenges or to a female prime minister. In a novel where racial nationalism, patriarchal conservatism, and conflicts over migration all feature prominently, *A Pale View* makes no explicit reference to Thatcherite nationalism or hostility to immigration. Yet, the ghosts of prewar Japanese educational institutions and of a fantasized aspirational postwar America function here in part as proxies and fetish objects for the early 1980s conflicted shift in British futures, where Thatcherism,[10] as we have seen, attempted to replace the social-democratic future of "consensus" politics, which had allegedly led to paralyzing industrial strife, violent social and racial division, and inexorable postimperial decline (mitigated only, and controversially, by entrance into the European Communities).[11] It sought to replace these things with a neoliberal economy—viewed as more productive, more open to global trade—a reinvigorated capitalist work ethic, and a celebration of materialistic aspiration. Framed by this ending to postwar Britain's future-building project, Ishiguro's novel returns to the immediate postwar period—albeit, uncannily, in another country and one on the losing, rather than winning, side of the Second World War (a loss accelerated by the atomic bombings of Tokyo and of Nagasaki). As with Thatcherism itself, which simultaneously sought to initiate a new future of released entrepreneurial energy and to retrieve a "Victorian" past, it is uncertain whether we—and Britain—are moving forward or backward in *A Pale View*.

Thatcherism's conflicted temporality was accompanied by the repressed contradictions of its rhetorical geography. It was explicitly a project of nationalist revival,[12] underpinned by considerable xenophobia, manifested in Thatcher's aggressive attitude to Britain's rights in Europe (Geddes; George) and in her government's hostility to immigration, especially non-white immigration (Dixon 173). Yet, Thatcherism's emphasis on personal aspiration, and the potential for free markets to fulfil that aspiration, was explicitly inspired by an idea of postwar American prosperity, which postwar Britain had never enjoyed to the same extent; Margaret

Thatcher made regular rhetorical recourse to America's Reagan-Era example. The United States' role in *A Pale View*, as the future that goes missing between the 1950s and 1980s narratives, absorbs additional irony in this context, suggesting that Thatcherism's idea of America-as-future is a spectral fantasy that it doesn't authentically possess even *as fantasy*, given how it already has a powerful presence between two housewives in early 1950s Nagasaki. The latter subtly implicates Thatcherism's Americanophilia as ironically naive in underestimating the potential conflict between Americanization and nationalism that is so evident in the Nagasaki narrative.

Japan's role also becomes ironic here: as an East Asian immigrant, Etsuko belongs to a category of migrants that Margaret Thatcher argued needed urgent restriction due to their supposed immutable otherness to the British, a difference she regarded as greater than that of white non-British immigrants.[13] Yet, Etsuko's Japanese origins complicate and ironize this status—both because her own memories of Japan include a powerful, if ambivalent, role for the American dream on which Thatcherism drew and because by the 1980s Japan had become, certainly by comparison to the struggling UK, a capitalist success story (Brown, 367–69). This points to a crucial but suppressed contradiction within Thatcherism's combination of free-market, globalizing capitalism with rhetorical nationalism and xenophobia—the combination that would eventually be stretched to breaking point, over three decades later, in Brexit. These fractures are already evident, if suppressed, in *A Pale View*, where the uncanny relationships between postwar Japan, postwar America, and early 1980s Britain hint at the ruptures latent within this Britain (in forms subtler and yet more fundamental than more obvious political framing might achieve).

If Japan is, for Etsuko, the ghost of the past, America is the ghost of a future that has been bypassed, but it is also the ghost of a dream that refuses to die. It is for the sake of Britain's future, the object of Thatcherism's dreams—the contradictions of which the specters of Japan and America expose—that the child must also die, at least if that child threatens to be a citizen of nowhere.

Killing the Child

A Pale View is full of children and youth for whose deaths adults bear degrees of responsibility, including Keiko, Etsuko's "pure Japanese" daughter who has committed suicide; Mariko, who perceives Etsuko as threatening her (it is unclear whether Mariko ultimately survives or not); the baby in Tokyo whom Mariko allegedly witnessed being murdered by its mother during the war (74–75); the children murdered around Nagasaki by an unknown serial killer (100); and the young men inspired by Ogata's racial-nationalist educational program who die in the war, one of whom may be Mrs. Fujiwara's son Suichi (150). Any systematic list of children killed in this novel is, however, uncertain and incomplete because the identities of these children are unstable; they merge and multiply: the serial killer on the plot's margins functions as an invisible adhesion and framing figure for this potentially endless multiplication of child-killing, as do Mariko's recurring visions of the child-killing woman she once saw (74–75) and Etsuko's recurring dream about a child being killed (55, 96).

Within the novel, this multiplication reinforces the difficulty for adults in rescuing the child and securing the future they represent, or at least assimilating their memory into a secure order of signification. (In fact, the whole novel could be read as the slow disintegration of Etsuko's attempted assimilation of the dead Keiko's image.) The dead child becomes the signifier of an epistemological lack; but even as signifier, it is never secure, refusing to be fetishized into the pathos of moral symbolism. (Although the child, as a multiplying and shifting figure across time and space, connects Etsuko's personal loss with the catastrophes of war, imperialism, and atomic bombing, it does not *reconcile* these very differently scaled losses; it is a connection without consolation, made within the void of the child's absence.) This epistemological lack is made absolute through its (dis)embodiment in the remembered or imagined dead child.

Nevertheless, the child's death in this novel also, disturbingly, often seems to promise the adult's liberation. The child who embodies the future paradoxically comes to represent the past—which the adult may wish to sustain but, alternatively, might seek to escape. These conflicting imperatives are related to the collapse of an imperialist racial utopianism, as voiced by Ogata in his apologetics for his prewar educational program (66, 147), where the child, if properly brought up, guarantees the continuation of the past while also more fully realizing the essential racial value operating teleologically behind that past. In the early 1950s, however, Ogata's ideology has few other remaining apologists—with the possible, and telling, exception of Etsuko herself (149). The pragmatic Mrs. Fujiwara voices the straightforward alternative of embracing the child-as-future; though one of her sons has died, the other "still has all his life ahead of him" (151). However, the child-as-future is still potentially at risk from the revenant past; Mrs. Fujiwara fears for the "pregnant girl and her husband spending their Sundays thinking about the dead [. . .] they should be thinking about the future [. . .] that's no way to bring a child into the world, visiting the cemetery every week" (25).

A similar ambivalence is at work in Sachiko. Her careerist and materialistic aspirations for her daughter in America are clearly her own projection; and that Etsuko shares at least some of these aspirations is indicated, for example, in the detail—typical of how Ishiguro conceals pathos within banality[14]—that she desires an American-style washing machine (152). This shared aspiration becomes potentially deadly for the child when Etsuko starts to speak for—or through, or as—Sachiko and is recognized by Mariko as a threat (172–73).

Although the novel never reaches the American object of this putative child sacrifice, Etsuko's England is not free of either real or imagined child deaths; indeed, Etsuko considers that her migration to this country has killed one of her daughters. Her England is marked by futures—and children—either lost (Keiko) or stalled (Niki). Etsuko's own future, despite the multiple temporal and spatial journeys she has made during the course of her life, also appears to be stalled; the descriptions of her home life and environs repeatedly associate it with stifled movement. Niki—though her life also appears stalled to her mother—unconsciously resists this with her physical restlessness (9, 47) and by reminding her mother of her earlier migration, insisting on its positive value (176).

The stillness of Etsuko's home and its environs suggests time and space drained of significance and potential mobility, an impression given a disturbing edge by its parallel in the comfort she locates in the image of her dead daughter. If not for the American future, it is now for the English "calm and quietness" (47) of Etsuko's home that the child might be killed. This killing even becomes banal here, for as Etsuko says, musing on her mental image of the dead Keiko, "it is possible to develop an intimacy with the most disturbing of things" (54). A different, uglier version of this banality comes with the parallel between Mariko, shortly to be threatened with death, and the kittens her mother tries to force her to drown before their departure for America. (The banality of killing and its connection to slippage between human and nonhuman status is a theme that Ishiguro would return to throughout his work, most prominently in *Never Let Me Go* [2005].) In *A Pale View*, child-killing is both a material reality and a symbol of what adults will attempt in order to secure their own future, even if an essentially empty future is the only one available.

This capacity for violence toward the future—and the child—is uncannily repeated across countries and periods, only to find a "home" in Etsuko's house in early 1980s Britain; but it is a house haunted by the ghosts of other times and places that trouble its claims to historical exceptionalism and future aspiration.

Are There Such Things as Schools in America? Children, Institutions, and the Future

Just as *A Pale View* is in important respects "about" early Thatcherite Britain, despite the subtlety with which the novel engages its political context, it is also subtly yet profoundly concerned with institutions. Sometimes this concern is apparent by their absence: Mariko is not going to school in Nagasaki (16), though Sachiko says she did attend school before the war (45), and Sachiko notes defensively that "there are such things as schools in America" (44). Ogata's career was an institution-building one, later accused of complicity in indoctrinating children, with deadly results: "In your day," Shigeo Matsuda asserts, "children in Japan were taught terrible things. [. . .] And that's why the country was plunged into the most evil disaster" (147). The idea of children as vulnerably absorptive of their own education reemerges—albeit in an ironically banal version—in the 1980s narrative, as Niki and Etsuko bicker over the legacy of Niki's childhood piano tuition, where Etsuko asserts, "I doubt if you would have forgotten everything. Nothing you learn at that age is totally lost." (52) This comment, apparently mundane in its immediate context, uncannily echoes the earlier fears that children exposed to totalitarian ideology and modern mass destruction will be indelibly marked, unable to recover—the fear that *they* will be the child forever gestating inside the cemetery. This fear mirrors, and merges with, the view of the child as bearer of ineradicable racial essence. One of the novel's most disturbing images for this, an image on which many others hang—so to speak—is the mother Mariko apparently saw drowning a child during the war:

> "You see, Etsuko, she turned around and smiled at Mariko. I knew something was wrong and Mariko must have done too because she stopped running. At first I thought the woman was blind, she had that kind of look, her eyes didn't seem to actually see anything. Well, she brought her arms out of the

> canal and showed us what she'd been holding under the water. It was a baby." [. . .]
>
> "[Mariko] saw everything? She saw the baby?"
>
> "Yes [. . .] She didn't start talking about it until a month or so later. We were sleeping in this old building then. I woke up in the night and saw Mariko sitting up, staring at the doorway. [. . .] I asked Mariko what was wrong and she said a woman had been standing there watching us [. . .] Mariko said it was the one we'd seen that morning." (74–75)

This scene, which draws heavily on the dynamics and visual tropes of horror movies, establishes an obsessive gaze toward the child—and toward that child's gaze—that persists throughout the novel and provokes a significant question for its concern with institutions: If the educational institution seeks to build a future and to manage the relationship between the future and the past, on what basis can adults have confidence in the capacity of the child to use their education correctly?

The scene begins with looking at a woman who has chosen not to see[15] what she is doing or whose gaze is focused on some other mental image away from the child's material body that she is destroying. Ironically, though, her "blindness" instigates a mutual, rapidly accelerating paranoia in the gaze between mother (Sachiko) and child (Mariko), with the murderous woman now a permanent image mediating between them. In a remarkable metastasis of paranoia and violence, the child who has seen terrible things—and who apparently cannot stop seeing them—provokes an obsessive gaze from the adult back toward the child: a gaze that becomes, in turn, the justified object of the child's fear ("a woman had been standing there watching us"), as it is when Mariko eventually perceives Etsuko-Sachiko as a murderous threat. The child, embodiment of the future, comes to signify the inescapable hold of the violent past and, recalling that violence, reminds the adult of killing the child as a potential solution to the temporal paralysis she now represents. The child who kills the future becomes a future that can reasonably be killed. Yet, to do this, the adult must willfully refuse to see the child's materiality even when their gaze on the child's body and face is at its most obsessive.

One reason that Mariko is not—at least so far as the text discloses—ultimately killed is that she turns the adult's paranoid gaze back upon her, anticipating the threat she represents: "Why are you looking at me like that? I'm not going to hurt you," (173) Etsuko tells Mariko just before, "without taking her eyes from me," (173) the child runs away. This turning of the adult's gaze on the child back on to the adult has a subtle parallel in Ogata's postwar shaming by younger men, where the gaze—and the profound bio-historical anxiety generating it—becomes itself a matter of and for institutions and their roles in making the future through the child. The destruction of the child whom the adult recognizes as having gone irretrievably "wrong"—a destruction Matsuda attributes to the prewar authorities, which Etsuko-Sachiko seems to threaten for Mariko—is an alternative to granting the confidence in their future that would merit their access to a future-building institution like a school;[16] Etsuko's obsession with Mariko's access to schools precedes her eventual, apparent attempt to murder her.

Ogata's pedagogy was based on promulgating an essential ethnonational reality that the child is trained to reveal and embody (66). Clearly, there is a possible ambivalence here (exposed by Japan's defeat in the war) over whether this is, indeed, a reality being revealed or merely an ideology being indoctrinated, with unsettling implications for adults. If the "Japanese race" actually is inherently oriented toward violence, whether through genocidal imperialism or (as Keiko's case is taken to suggest) through suicide, then the child figures its inescapable reproduction. If, however, such violence is a matter of pedagogical indoctrination (of the type of which Matsuda accuses Ogata) or traumatic exposure (as with Mariko witnessing the child-killing woman in Tokyo), then it might be equally irremediable while additionally making individual adult responsibility unbearable. Ishiguro disconcertingly dissolves any secure distinction between racial and psychological essentialism;[17] his adult characters' obsessions expose this dissolution, and their gaze on the child embodies it. He finds the perfect trope for this in how the traumatic witnessing of the atomic bombing—a bombing defended on the basis that it ended a war Japan would otherwise have continued in the name of its racial destiny[18]—allows the association of this trauma with psychological and racial essentialism simultaneously. Ishiguro may have been influenced by powerful twentieth-century associations between atomic and nuclear bombing and the destruction of the child and their innocence in examples from visual culture like the notorious "Daisy Girl" of the 1964 American presidential election,[19] with its close-up on the girl's eye registering the sight of the bomb, or the images of children maimed by the bombings of Japan themselves less than a decade before Ishiguro's own birth in Nagasaki. (The "Daisy Girl" ad showing the entire world disappearing into the child's eye at the moment of atomic destruction provides a foundational example of how obsession with the child's gaze conveys an ever more expansive, and at least potentially paranoid, association between child psychology and geopolitical destruction in twentieth-century popular culture.)[20]

Educational institutions constitute sites where the adult gaze on children's minds and bodies can be practically managed, securely contained, and properly channeled whether the object and purpose of that gaze—the child and the future, respectively—are understood in psychological, racial, or liberal terms. Such institutions are intrinsically concerned with monitoring the child and their development. (Ishiguro would repeatedly return to this theme, most fully through the peculiar boarding school, Hailsham, in *Never Let Me Go*.) Educational institutions in *A Pale View* are poised on the ideological and rhetorical margin between revealed essentialism and deliberative, historically contingent education (or indoctrination). These institutions are—however profoundly essentialist in their ethos—necessarily, in some respects, pragmatic, based on created structures and deliberative work rather than revealed truths. When Ogata is challenged over his record, he reacts not by defending his ideology but rather by first indignantly asserting the sustained hard work and commitment he devoted to his career.[21] When Etsuko anxiously queries Mariko's future after the proposed migration to America, Sachiko's assertion that "there are such things as schools in America" (44) misses the point (perhaps deliberately) but also highlights the tension between the ideological and pragmatic functions of schools as institutions. What Etsuko is really concerned about is, of course, not merely the existence of available schools but the place of education within a racial integrity from which it would be harmful to draw the child apart—to make her, as it were, a citizen of nowhere. Sachiko's naive—or passive-aggressive—answer draws attention to how, in contrast, on one level a school is always a school: whether in Japan or the USA, a school serves the function of temporarily relieving parents of their responsibility and monitoring the child while preparing them for adult society. Rather like Niki's later failure to attend university, Etsuko and Mariko's tense debate over schools gives the impression that the child's participation in an institution could serve an important function in managing the adults' obsessions over their children and suspicions of their alterity.

The imagined American school is not, however, merely projected as a pragmatic entity, but it is associated with Sachiko's American dream of personal aspiration and opportunity, of an "America" as inherently and organically itself as Ogata imagined the "spirit" of Japan to be. The modern educational institution nurturing individual aspiration is, at least in Sachiko's imagining, no less essentialist than the imperial educational institutions Ogata formerly led. This has subtle yet provocative resonance with how the Thatcherite version of reality—prioritizing neoliberal economics, social conservatism, and nationalism—was presented as natural, and thus permanent and essentially unchanging, and as countering and cancelling the postwar and social democratic idea of historical process. Thatcherism, even alongside its identification with an American-inspired future of unleashed entrepreneurial energy, also claimed, as we have seen, to be a reversion to a past British moment. This was sometimes a Victorian one, in Margaret Thatcher's rhetoric, but beyond that it was actually a permanent and natural state; in a famous quotation attributed to Thatcher,[22] "the facts of life are Conservative." Once this reversion to the past and revelation of essential reality was completed, there need be no more history in any meaningful sense other than for the continued accumulation and expansion of assets and power for a stable set of values and a triumphantly organic nation-state.[23] The echo of this in Ogata's ideals and educational program is unmistakable. Thatcherism's conviction of "the facts of life" profoundly affected the attitudes of the Thatcher governments toward institutions suspected of seeking to inculcate something other than such facts. These governments abolished some institutions—like local government bodies and publicly owned companies (Vinen 196–200)—and reduced the autonomy of others, recasting them as more exponents of revealed and quasi-natural reality than as historical entities with agency, deliberative policy, and political contingency. Institutions that held on to some autonomy, including universities and some arts organizations, were attacked and undermined.

In *A Pale View*, the only opposing institution, of sorts, to Thatcherite dominance in the 1980s narrative is Niki's quasi-commune, where a vaguely New Age–esque subculture sets itself as an alternative to Thatcherism's combination of neoliberal economics and conservative nationalism as well as to Etsuko's own social conservatism. Niki's friendship group is seemingly prone to romanticizing and thus misconstruing history; Horton suggests that they also engage in orientalism, as Niki "reduces postwar Nagasaki to a poignant poem or postcard image, and simultaneously exoticises Etsuko's pain to inspire her companions' curiosity" (31). Despite these dubious tendencies, Niki's circle of friends and their quasi-institution is, however bathetically and incoherently, an attempt at both a pragmatic and a deliberative response to the circumstances of the time—one opposed to Thatcherism's version of domestic and historical reality.

More substantial institutions that seek to make the future require adults to give something away for, potentially, nothing (the kind of moral economy of which Margaret Thatcher definitely did not approve).[24] They require the adult to take a risk on the child, recognizing a potential or latent but not yet revealed or transparent value in them, in order to secure the future—a kind of risk-taking, or "investment," that is at the center of late modern capitalism as it is in modern conceptions of childhood. *A Pale View* provides a highly disturbing imagining of the risk of this faith in the child failing, a risk that manifests in the adult's paranoid gaze and actual violence toward the child. It also locates how globalization, migration, and the conditions of a postwar, (largely) post-Empire country intensify adult perceptions of this risk in ways that drive toward paranoia. Ishiguro's novel also convincingly, and crucially, presents this dynamic between adult society and the child as sustained across both neoliberal narratives of childhood—as in the aspirational projection of how Mariko could grow up to achieve great things if she reaches America—and in the alternative modern essentialisms of race and nation. The roles of the USA and Japan jointly create an anamorphosis: an indirect, even distorted, sideways look at early 1980s Britain, and particularly Thatcherism's combination of neoliberal and ethnonationalist narratives, that ultimately reveals the terms on which both invest the child. In the language of Theresa May, who began her political life as a Thatcherite, it was for entrepreneurial "getting on" *and* for being a citizen of somewhere: that is, of an imagined Britain.

In this context, *A Pale View*'s psychoanalytically charged narrative landscape—what Bennett calls its "cornucopia of repressive symptoms such as splitting, dissociation, rationalisation and projection" (88)—underpins its political resonance. In *The Interpretation of Dreams*, Freud argued that dreams (prominent in this novel) fulfil wishes by refusing the necessity of choosing between incompatible opposites; this willed refusal can carry over into waking and even public life, but—Freud noted—the resulting inevitable collision will produce trauma. In *A Pale View*, the child is the object of a similar repression, and the novel subtly implicates Thatcherism as a project that offered its own wish-fulfilment based on incompatible aims, with the child as its object for a willed future but also as the target of the paranoia generated by its repressed contradictions. Against this, institutions—even despite the essentialist ideologies they often serve—open the possibility, even unwillingly and against their own ideological conceits, of historical contingency and the resulting need for political and material choices, accepting the future as unknown rather than predetermined. It is emerging institutions of this character that Ogata, who spent his career trying to convert educational institutions into mere transparent conveyers of an essential and permanent reality, confronts to his horror in postwar Japan (146–48). This is also the character that threatens the long-term endurance of Thatcherism and anticipates its eventual collapse under these contradictions, the collapse that would come with Brexit, characterized by Theresa May (and many others) as a reaction against the citizens of nowhere. The novel's depiction of neoliberal and ethnonationalist essentialisms as competing yet aligned, and of migration as a crucial site for their enmeshed overinvestments, is also at heart of its striking anticipatory qualities.

After *A Pale View*: British Institutions and Knowing the Child

The underlying tension over the roles of institutions in *A Pale View* raises the question of the proper conditions for the child's access to institutional time and space in the name of the future and of the value(s) for which an investment in the child-as-future might be risked. In 1980s Britain, these were not abstract questions but, rather, central issues for public policy, and they remain so today. Thatcher and her ministers, as seen already, took educational institutions as critical to their attempts to curtail and replace the postwar future.

Ishiguro's subtly radical insistence on the basic, even banal, unknowability of the child and his critique of adults' transformation of that alterity into the pathos and predictability of fetish or horror have profound historical resonances. *A Pale View* positions the unknowability of the child-as-future—and especially the migrant child, or migrant's child—as a central fault line for a Thatcher-Era Britain caught between the aspirational fantasy of "America" and the racial-nationalist past signified by Japan, depicting a Britain repressing the historical and contingent questions over its own future that this polarized framing evokes. The conflicts over Niki's lifestyle and Keiko's death imagine this repression breaking apart into a generational conflict, one suggesting the (at best ambivalently realized) promise of resolution that can only be achieved through an intensive filial reconciliation rather than a historical process.

This intensity emerges in *A Pale View* alongside a demand for visual recognition and reassurance, for the transformation of the inscrutable child into something intimate and familiar, a transparent alternative to the risk of accepting an unknown future. This imperative has political parallels in Thatcherite demands for recognition and protection of an essential childhood innocence against absorption into perverse versions of the future—demands mobilized around anxiety over the institutional conditions to which children are given access, as seen earlier in relation to Clause 28. It is remarkable how perceptively and intensively Ishiguro's *A Pale View*, though published early in the decade of Thatcher's governments, registers these issues and their underlying paranoia in its own uncanny fashion. It does so partly by drawing upon a postwar British tradition (explored in chapter 2) of visual obsession with children as figures of horror and violence and by uncannily reworking—and disrupting without repudiating—the tropes offered by this tradition. If the child is the object both of adult demands for recognition and of an underlying paranoia that they might not be recognizable *at all*, the same paradox also applies to this Britain, which fails to know its future even at the moment it, under Thatcherite leadership, appears most confidently to identify that future. Yet, Ishiguro's insistence on the alterity of the child is not merely powerful as historical allegory but also for its fundamental portrayal of the adult need for intergenerational reassurance and the violence this provokes when thwarted, frustrated, or—indeed—fulfilled.

Children of Nowhere

A Pale View exposes Thatcherism's contradictions and anticipates their explosive potential: the potential we have seen realized in Brexit. The migrant child here maps historical, generational, and geographical changes, whether on the grand international scale of the rifts and reconfigurations brought about by the end of the Second World War—which included not only Japan's defeat and occupation but also, to a significant extent, the fracturing and decolonization of the British Empire—or on the minute interpersonal scale of the intimate gazes between mother and daughter—which position the child's body and face as being as epistemologically opaque as they are materially unavoidable. *A Pale View* also shows educational institutions as a critical crisis point for the link between the individual child-as-future and confidence in the future on a much vaster scale. The epistemological crises provoked by the child are represented here through conflicts and contradictions between the visual, narrative, and material domains. These conflicts are not easily resolvable, nor is the child easily retrievable to adult knowledge through any kind of easy theorizing or reassuring framing, whatever its particular political orientation.

Recalling my opening quotation from Theresa May's Brexit-agenda-setting speech of 2016—with its notorious attack on "citizens of nowhere"—that polished, tactically positioned piece of political rhetoric may seem at first very distant from the child-killing, future-killing themes and scenes found in Ishiguro. Yet, in the *intensity* of identification with the organic nation that May demanded and the uncompromising terms in which that demand was made—precisely because it was presented as the necessary recognition of an essential reality, not a point of political negotiation[25]—there is an echo of the demands that thread through *A Pale View* and its subtle characterization of the British position of the early 1980s.

Mariko, the putative migrant child in *A Pale View*, remains inscrutable to Etsuko yet, nevertheless, has a powerfully material presence, as the dreamlike clarity of particular objects (rope, lantern, swing, the child's body itself) in the novel's various scenes of her death suggests (and which is heightened by the contrasting opacity of the "real" narrative significance of these scenes). This novel uses the figure of the migrant child to suggest how fiction can reassert the radical difficulty of the child in general for the adult through its literary resources of opacity, ambivalence, slippage, and contradiction. The proximity of migrant children and mobile youth to both imagined and very real violence continues as the subject of my next chapter.

Chapter 6

Migrant Children and Mobile Youth in Twenty-First Century British Fiction

The migrant child, as *A Pale View of Hills* shows, condenses and intensifies the paranoia British politics and culture of the late twentieth and early twenty-first centuries directed toward the child-as-future, giving that child's otherness and opacity an additional channel in which to register and a figure on which to adhere.

We shall find that the claims and qualities of the migrant child are negotiated through the visual domain, with visibility and transparency key to the presumption of innocence and capacity for assimilation to an authentic, secure Britain. Yet, the migrant child possesses—even by the bare fact of coming from elsewhere—an opacity of intention, experience, and imagination that disturbs the adult who seeks a guarantee of the future in their face. As we shall see, just as Etsuko made the image of her child comfortingly familiar only after said child's death, so too the visual dynamics of the migrant child find innocence ultimately in death; the living child is more difficult. The very racialized otherness that the migrant child's affectively powerful image makes visible is used against its innocence, especially when the child is suspected of actually being a young adult—a category that is inseparably close to the period of childhood yet ideologically and legally divorced from it with brutal consequences.

British media hostility toward migration often focuses on migrant access to the protection of institutions and to material assets and objects, framing such access as fundamentally illegitimate and a sign of the non-innocence of the migrants concerned (Musolff 251-56). Although children, as vulnerable dependents, have some of the strongest claims to such protection and assets, they also attract some of the greatest paranoia and boundary-policing for precisely this reason.

Here, I explore both migrant children and mobile youth as prominent figures and ambiguous agents in the UK's recent contests over its futures, for the conflicts between neoliberalism and nationalism that Brexit—a political phenomenon overwhelmingly driven by hostility to immigration—exposed and for how we might read the politics of the child when the child-as-future is no longer securely the irrefusable, universal figure of reproductive futurism. This will involve considering multiple fictional children and youth who help to account for the willingness of early twenty-first-century Britain to imagine killing the migrant child.

Mobile Youth and Migrant Children on the Road to Brexit

Brexit was a political phenomenon driven by public hostility toward migration and transnational institutions and directed toward mobile youth as its emblematic victims. As observed earlier, within the Brexiteer rhetorical framework, young and mobile British people are repeatedly presented as naive cosmopolitans, enablers of globalized migration, while young males appear as some of the most dangerous migrants—particularly economically mobile, young, male Eastern Europeans (Veličković 71–103) and Muslims (Cherry, " 'I'd Rather My Brother' " 270–71). Aspirational young male migrants consistently attract particularly hostile attitudes. Such hostility, though, has also turned on younger children—and to an obsession with isolating the "genuine" child from young adults.

Thatcherism's contradictory legacy in leading Britain into the European Single Market—with its associated free movement—while promoting hostility to immigration eventually erupted when intra-EU migration became increasingly politically salient following the EU's 2004 expansion to incorporate ten new member states, with further expansion taking place in 2007. In the UK, which saw significant migration from some of these acceding states (Evans and Mellon 77–78) "attitudes toward the EU were increasingly 'fused' with concerns about immigration" (77), and young male migrants from Eastern Europe became an increasingly prominent bogeyman, popularly associated with criminality (Stansfield and Stone 595–96).

The political prominence of Eastern European migration in the 2000s and 2010s UK was also a product of policy decisions from the Blair governments, which (particularly in their earlier years) took an affirmative position toward globalization, multiculturalism, and the EU. This aligned with Blair's belief in internationalist interventionism,[1] most controversially implemented in 2003 alongside the US in Iraq. This internationalism did not, however, mean that Blair's Britain ever approached "open borders," despite hyperbole from opponents. Irregular migration was a constant target of rightwing media, who pushed the perception that young men seeking to cross the Channel were illegitimate asylum seekers; and so, in order to appear "tough" even while affirming internationalist and humanitarian values, Blairite Home Secretaries asserted the need to make transparent judgments over the motives and status of those claiming asylum (Mulvey 443–44), including distinguishing between young adults and children and between refugees and economic migrants. These demands for transparent categorization of migrants often rhetorically merged with post-9/11 fears, especially about young Muslim men, and they continue today despite often limited meaningful distinction (Oberman) between migration to seek safety and to seek economic security or advancement[2]—with the latter consistently framed in paranoid terms despite the celebration of entrepreneurialism and aspiration that Thatcherism initiated and Blairism sustained.

When the Conservatives returned to office in 2010 (first as part of a coalition), Prime Minister David Cameron pledged to drastically reduce immigration from outside the EU (D. Robinson 74). Despite Cameron's rhetorical continuation of Blairite internationalism, the UK had never accepted relatively large-scale migration as a routine element of its twenty-first-century existence, and Cameron promised to reduce annual net migration to under 100,000 people (Trilling). Cameron's Home Secretary, Theresa May, sustained a relentless focus on marginalized migrants (Griffiths and Yeo 530–31) while expanding reductionist policies into previously accepted groups—notably international students, who were targeted precisely because of suspicions that, as aspirational young people, they might seek to build careers in the UK. When May became the first post-referendum prime minister, she was primed to interpret the result as a rejection of unrestrained neoliberalism, cosmopolitanism, and migration, all targets of her "citizens of nowhere" speech discussed in the previous chapter, which aligned with the conservative theorist David Goodhart's call for return toward an authentic national Somewhere against a cosmopolitan, transnational Nowhere.

This version of Brexit prevailed politically, despite Remainer attempts to invoke the future of opportunity and mobility offered to young people through EU membership or at least in continued participation in the

Single Market—arguments reflected in the strong correlation between younger age and support for Remain (Goulard). Voters born after 1980 had spent most or all of their lives with norms shaped by expanded intra-European mobility, whereas the dominant tendency in older generations was to regard this as an aberration from norms rooted in national borders (Helm). Broader discontent with the country's post-Brexit direction would be a significant factor in the 2017 general election, with its alleged "youthquake" (see Sturgis and Jennings)—a win for the Conservatives that, nevertheless, fatally damaged May's premiership—while Conservative politics of the later 2010s and early 2020s would be widely regarded (even by some younger Conservatives) as gerontocratic in protecting the assets of older generations over the interests of younger adults (see Oxley). Brexit broke any hierarchy of interests that claimed, even rhetorically, to put the young first; and, in reordering the Thatcherite alliance of neoliberalism and nationalism, May emphasized that economic interests needed to serve national and social cohesion (Marlow-Stevens and Hayton 877–78), reformulating "One Nation" Toryism for the Brexit Era (Atkins and Gaffney 298–99), which, in practice, meant rejecting free movement. This emphasis would be further extended under May's successor, Boris Johnson, whose electoral success in capturing many seats in the former "Red Wall" of core Labour Party support was credibly attributed to an agenda combining an anti-cosmopolitan hostility to free movement and "uncontrolled" migration, with an emphasis on national and social cohesion and reinvigorating the post-Brexit NHS (Cutts et al. 10).

Across this period, then, generational mobility—both geographic and political—has intersected with migration as a political issue, material reality, and aspirational possibility. This context is powerfully reflected in a Brexit-Era novel of mobile youth between Britain and Europe.

Brexit and Mobile Youth: David Szalay, *All That Man Is* (2016)

David Szalay's *All That Man Is* (2016), published a few months before the Brexit referendum, captures the ambiguous, resented position of youth within the context of free movement available to EU citizens. Szalay's novel is a series of loosely interconnected episodes involving young men's travel around the EU's marginal Nowheres of transnational modernity: railway stations, motorway service stations, half-built hotels, and speculative real-estate developments. These episodes offer a bittersweet reworking of the classic European Bildungsroman based on the masculine self (and sexual) development through travel. Although Szalay's tone and framing are bathetic and ironic, the characters' experiences—which include a French university-dropout, whose holiday leads him into a joint sexual arrangement with a British mother and daughter, and a twenty-something Hungarian, one of those young Eastern European men so negatively stereotyped in Britain, visiting London as a sex worker's bodyguard—all ultimately offer some encounter with unexpected dimensions of life, implying that even marginal, unloved bits of transnational time and space are of real, if unpredictable and opaque, value for those who enjoy rights to move within and around them.

There are repeated associations between this mobility and the speculative investments that the free movements of capital and people within the EU facilitates, in how Szalay's young male characters often spend their time within the marginal spaces that these speculations have produced. As in the queer parodies of Thatcherite Britain discussed earlier, here too the sanctioned entrepreneurial potential of young men is, in part, cover for a less quantifiable, less predictable, and less ideologically and practically safe proliferation of opportunities. In the first episode, teenagers Simon and Ferdinand are on a gap year before their A-Levels, traveling between Berlin and Vienna via Prague, when their mildly homoerotic relationship is interrupted by sexual offers from their female host (which one of them takes up). The humiliations and unfulfilled aspirations at stake here associate transnational mobility (and institutionalized rights to enjoy that mobility) with the frustrations involved in gendered and sexual development into adulthood. The developmental value of migration and mobility is not transparent for Szalay—and it often emerges in ironic, banal, and underappreciated forms—but it is all the more real for it.

This lack of transparency, however, attracts hostility. In Szalay's panorama of 2010s travel within and between Britain and Europe, it becomes increasingly apparent that public attitudes to young male ambition, creativity, and—above all—mobility have become skeptical, even paranoid. Thatcherism's vision of the aspirational, entrepreneurial youth—a vision that underpinned the UK's participation in the European Single Market and, thus, in free movement within the EU—is now constrained everywhere by hostile anxiety toward the perceived loss of the authentic created by transnational mobility. With its fast food shops, chain coffee places, and generic pubs, London feels flat and unassimilable to Balázs, the young Hungarian guarding a sex worker and her pimp in Szalay's third chapter;

this transnational London, where Balázs immediately notices "the number of non-white people in the street" (112), appears to him (ironically, given the nature of his own presence there) as just as much a globalized Nowhere as anti-metropolitan Brexiteers would assert. In Szalay's Europe, repeated failures of mutual understandings of and suspicions about the intentions of others show mobility provoking a reactionary fetishization of authenticity that accelerates resentment of migrants—even from those who are mobile youths themselves.

All That Man Is, written just prior to the referendum's outcome, has become an important Brexit anticipatory fiction. As Kristian Shaw argues in *Brexlit*, literature provides a way to "read Brexit backwards" (2), whether over a relatively extended historical scope (as with my reading of *A Pale View of Hills* in the previous chapter) or one focused on the years immediately preceding the referendum (as with *All That Man Is*). This should not imply a teleological approach, of course, and the specific attention Szalay pays to the contingent, the chaotic, the bathetic, and the banal in the British-European infrastructure of cultural and physical mobilities itself discourages any such framing. Through the backstories of its Eastern European characters, Szalay's novel draws attention to European free movement as a recent, post–Cold War phenomenon and, therefore, to migration and borders as themselves contingent institutional and historical phenomena. Furthermore, spatial borders intersect, Szalay implies, with generational ones and vice-versa. The connections Szalay draws between hostility to migration and generational mobility gesture toward a broader conflict between neoliberalism and reactionary demands for epistemological, territorial, and generational security: a conflict once, perhaps, contained by the sanctioned and legitimated aspirational, entrepreneurial male youth but no longer—and least of all when this youth is also a migrant.

The 2010s Migrant Crisis and the Deaths of Children

In Britain's decades-long journey toward Brexit, some very recent history played a crucial part, especially the mid-2010s "European Migrant Crisis," when conflict in several countries, particularly Syria and Libya, led to an increase in refugees migrating into Europe, including via the Mediterranean, where thousands of deaths at sea occurred. Images of children were central to media reception of this crisis; after two-year-old Syrian Alan

Kurdi died in September 2015, a widely reproduced photograph of his body lying on a beach provoked promises of safe channels for refugees from European leaders. Prime Minister David Cameron declared that he "felt deeply moved by the sight of that young boy [. . .] Britain is a moral nation and we will fulfil our moral responsibilities" (Dathan, "Aylan Kurdi"). In August 2016, the image of five-year-old Omran Daqneesh, sitting in an ambulance in Aleppo covered in dust and blood from a head wound, was similarly reproduced across international media. Sitting alone as though already being exhibited, he embodied the awful vulnerability of children in war; as Vicky Lebeau (136) observes, in such usages, the child's body becomes both an aestheticization of pain and an imperative for saving action. Yet, the image through which the demand is made—and through which affect is both generated and contained—becomes itself a precondition for action: the child must be made visible in a particular way, confirming abject vulnerability and utter innocence, if they are to be permitted to cross the nation's affective and territorial borders, excusing rather than exercising their status as a migrant. Affect, and a demand for action, arises from the refugee child's image but is channeled via a rhetorical adoption that restores the borders the migrant child has fractured. Here, an affirmative national identity permits the expansion of affect while the child's supposedly universally legible demand for that affect permits the expansion of national identity in a kind of neo-imperialist internationalism. This operation depends on the child being utterly passive, vulnerable, and abandoned and ends by restoring the coherence of national and territorial identity, resolving a potentially disturbing border fracture. Echoing Jacqueline Rose's remark of 1980s political rhetoric that "often 'Englishness' and childhood innocence appear as mutually reinforcing terms" (xii), we see this alignment reiterated even via the migrant child. Rosen and Crafter argue in "Media Representations of Separated Child Migrants" that:

> The conflation of childhood with vulnerability and separated child migrants with victimhood, even when framed in humanitarian terms, is troubling, and not only because these ascriptions cannot fully capture the complexity of any real human being. Treating children as innocent victims, and purporting to work in their "best interests," has typically worked against their interests, status, and well-being [. . .] It turns upon narratives of individual suffering [. . .] which can deflect attention from the

political and economic roots of contemporary migratory flows. Further, it reduces questions of responsibility and support to the good will of a rescuer, who can easily withdraw support. (76)

This seems very much like Edelman's thesis of the Child's role, translated into a context of transnational humanitarian crisis. It is only the child, *as* child, who is recognized as deserving rescue. The reassurance Cameron carefully telegraphed was that (implicitly, unlike an adult refugee) there's nothing to fear about the child—no private intentions, just a passive, vulnerable body under the adult's gaze.

This political and media treatment of the migrant child reflects broader discourses and visual cultures around the vulnerable child of international disaster, who is traditionally captured at a distance from audiences in the UK, Europe, or North America. Bond Stockton has theorized this as "kid orientalism," where a Western audience recovers the innocent child it perceives as having lost "at home" in visions of struggle in Global South countries: "Children-quite-experienced-in-peril are, without their knowing it, restoring our public's stubborn longing for innocent children who need our protections" ("The Queer Child Now and its Paradoxical Global Effects," 509), as in the genre of documentary filmmaking about "third world" children, where depictions of "children imperiled [. . .] are for many viewers relocating the 'Western'-style innocent child to foreign soil, where it can strangely be rediscovered" ("The Queer Child Now," 514). However, she suggests that "these documentaries mostly guarantee that their viewers will get blocked at the level of the face—by children's faces—and at the level of visual images in general" ("The Queer Child Now," 509):

> A glossy reproduction of a glassy stare, in high definition; lassitude with "resilience" [. . .] Completely strange to say, each child's face—its most personal, most tender signifier—makes me not see the child I am viewing. [. . .] This grim tautology meets and defeats my gaze at every turn, making me try [. . .] to do an impossible visual manoeuvre [. . .] to slip behind its face, to see *around* what the signifier's showing me. And not telling me. Stashed behind each image [. . .] a growing dormancy. ("The Queer Child Now," 516–17).

Here, the very completeness of the image of the child's face, in its affirmation of innocence-through-experience, inevitably leads to a kind of paranoia in the viewer who cannot help but know that the perfect affective image must be blanking out the dynamism, complexity, or simple opacity of their internal responses to those experiences (the "growing dormancy" "stashed behind each image"). As Sheldon writes of *The Turn of the Screw*, that foundational—and, incidentally, highly visual—novella of the child and paranoia, "persistent acts of interpretation" from the adult can "call the face into being as the trace of obscured interior depths waiting to be deciphered," but when these depths are unavailable, resistant to transparency, "the child's face thus brings out the affective dimensions of hermeneutic indeterminacy. The task of managing innocence—contaminated by questioning, forbidding examination—generates a quest that can only spoil what it seeks to verify" (9-10). We can't help but know that something is hidden by the image of innocence, and the more the latter's affective-political role is asserted, the more we know this (just as the pervasive fundamentalism of reproductive futurism, also transmitted via the child's image, drove Edelman to propose embrace of the queer death drive that it conceals).

We might flatteringly suppose that this reaction constitutes healthy critical skepticism against reductive coercion. However, in migration contexts, the same instinct has a rightwing variant that might give us pause because the effect of the migrant child is *not* all that we might have assumed when reading David Cameron's reaction to his image at, as it were, face value. (It's noticeable that Bond Stockton's analysis of kid orientalism doesn't significantly consider what happens when the innocent child rediscovered on foreign soil moves from that soil to "ours" as migrant or refuge.) The very universalism of the vulnerable migrant child's claim on receiving countries quickly becomes a problem, especially when it happens at scale; between 2012 and 2022, over two million children made a first-time application for asylum within the European Union and EFTA (Eurostat). The very prevalence of migrant and refugee children underlines rightwing fears based on a horror of large-scale migration, consistently presented in the language of invasion, swamping, etc. The combination of the mundanity of children being migrants with the exceptional, overriding, and universalist nature of their claim on rights to protection is perfectly set to inflame such fears. We shall see *His House*, a film I discuss later, repurpose a popular rightwing trope about adult migrants who illegitimately carry a child as a means to gain rights to escape and remain in safety; after all, how can one operate a system that sharply bifurcates the rights of adults and children in migration and not fear such a scenario?

There are several twenty-first-century phenomena that register reaction *against* acceptance of the migrant child, including explicit statements to this effect, policy decisions that de facto militate against it, associations between "foreign" children and threat, and attempts to distinguish between the child and the young adult that treat a legalistic distinction as an ethically and materially absolute one and that harm children and young people as a result. All of these are ways of registering and legitimating fear of the migrant child, opening the possibility of passively or even actively deploying violence against them.

Although the immediate reaction to Alan Kurdi's image largely combined sympathy and horror across the political spectrum, even in that close aftermath, far-right figures began to claim that Kurdi's parents bore some responsibility for his death, thus implicitly undermining the right of refugees to protection by suggesting that their migrations were undertaken by choice rather than necessity (Dathan, "UKIP Candidate Sparks Outrage") and that additional barriers to migration might protect rather than harm child refugees. As Breslow points out in the US context, the evocation of the innocent child in migration discourse is often "simultaneously mobilised to criminalise those very children's parents" (136). These events occurred in a context of significant attention to Islamist terrorism, as ISIL reached the peak of its power during the mid-2010s, committing several terrorist attacks in Europe, including some carried out by recent migrants. This accelerated already-strong political and public Islamophobia, which in the UK gained one legitimated political outlet through concerns about the radicalization of children in schools, notably in the so-called Trojan Horse Affair, where several schools in Birmingham were accused of an organized plot to indoctrinate children into extreme beliefs.

Framed by these contexts, the mid-2010s "Migrant Crisis" had significant effects on politics across Europe, North America, and beyond, including acting as a key influence on Brexit and on support for Donald Trump in the US. When, as a presidential candidate, Trump declared that he would "look Syrian children in the face" and deny them entry (Revesz), he directly acknowledged the storied moral imperative and affective impulse bound in the image of the suffering child even while refusing it. This reflects a Right that has found the imagery of universalist reproductive futurism—of the type Blair promulgated and with which Trump's 2016 opponent, Hillary Clinton, was associated—increasingly difficult to sustain alongside increasing twenty-first-century shocks to neoliberal globalization and American hegemony. Although Trump was obviously an American rather than British leader, there was (and remains) significant ideological, rhetorical, and tactical traffic between the US Right under his dominance and its British counterparts. Hence, when Trump further broke taboos by later mandating the separation of undocumented migrant children from their parents when apprehended at the USA's southern border, British far-right figure Nigel Farage explicitly praised the policy and urged Trump to sustain it (Williams). Reaction against the universal and absolute claims of the migrant child was often more subtle than this, however, arising—for example—among the unacknowledged consequences of policy decisions like Theresa May's removal of British support for search-and-rescue missions in the Mediterranean (Travis) despite the arguments of campaigners that this amounted to allowing children, as well as adults, to drown at sea.

Probably the largest-scale reaction against the migrant child in the British context, however, has emerged through claims that children seeking refuge in the UK are not children at all but, rather, young adults. The impulse to break the taboo against denying the child refuge thus emerges inter alia through a media and political obsession with verifying the age of young male migrants—with proving that apparent or claimed children are not, in fact, really children and thus can be legitimately imprisoned, deported, denied care, etc. These dynamics in British political, media, and public discourse on migration are not new—they stretch back at least into the rightwing panics over cross-Channel migration under the Blair governments—but they accelerated during the 2010s and into the early 2020s.

In October 2016, only shortly after the massive reaction to Alan Kurdi's image, British tabloids published photographs of individuals supposedly brought under the Dubs Amendment (legislation for transfer of unaccompanied child refugees) who allegedly—in the intrusive photographs they displayed for the reader—looked like adults, not children. The same gesture has been regularly repeated in the British media since then despite expert counterattack (Coram) and has been particularly directed toward refugees and migrants crossing the Channel from France, with calls for X-rays and dental examinations to show who among the claimed children is not, in fact, a child (Rosen and Crafter 73–74)—to expose who carries, as in *Don't Look Now*, the knife of adult threat behind the morally compelling appearance of childhood (Ibrahim 9).

If imagining the death of the child or wishing violence upon the child is taboo even for some of the most prominent anti-migrant voices, hostility to the male youth takes the opposite position. Young men are perceived as physically and economically able, as not vulnerable, as potentially physically and sexually violent, and as susceptible to dangerous radicalization. *All That Man Is* captures the quotidian, quietly insistent hostility this can produce toward mobile male youth—even those privileged by access to the mobilities available to British and European citizens—but this hostility is significantly more explicit and vigorous when directed toward more heavily marginalized and racialized young male migrants. Peter Cherry, in *Muslim Masculinities in Literature and Film* (2021), notes how the protests against Salman Rushdie's novel *The Satanic Verses* following its publication in 1988 "gave birth to the now-familiar stereotype of the British Muslim male as a 'third column' who defines himself against the so-called values of secularism and individualism said to define Britain" (45). The Muslim migrant youth who claims the rights of a refugee child sustains, for the rightwing media, an even more intensely suspected version of this figure. As Cherry points out, these figures have a heritage in British political and media prominence that significantly predates 9/11 and the War on Terror and have attracted literary representations, as in Hanif Kureishi's Bildungsroman *The Black Album* (1995), which portrays young British Muslim men caught between materialistic and Thatcherite aspirations, Islamism, and other conflicting forms of political and social radicalism, all of them in part defensive strategies against racism and hostility to migrant and second-generation young men.

As Kureishi's juxtapositions highlight, migrant and mobile youth are not treated with suspicion only when perceived as potential forces of religious extremism but also when associated with qualities of aspiration, entrepreneurialism, and materialism that elsewhere have been celebrated under neoliberal politics. A very common trope in British media reporting on migration—one especially, though not exclusively, targeted toward young male migrants—involves refugees, asylum seekers, and irregular migrants apparently possessing objects such as mobile phones, designer clothing, or even cars—all of which are presented, in this reporting, as luxury goods even if they would not necessarily be considered such in other contexts (Stein). The point of such reporting is to allege that those who possess such things cannot be vulnerable (an argument both inaccurate on its own terms and often incoherent in its targets), but it betrays a deeper fear of socioeconomic agency among migrants. To have possessions is to have agency, which is why, bleakly, the washed-up corpse of a child—a signifier of an already-vulnerable human who no longer even possesses their own body as an object—attracts a sympathy often refused to the living migrant youth. Here, the headlines rhetorically wondering where migrant youths obtained their possessions (or the funds to purchase them) cover a concern less about the source of those goods than about their implications for the future. The uncertain yet visible implications of these consumer goods becomes a proxy for the unreadable intentions of young migrants themselves.

We can see, then, a public discourse over migrant children and mobile youth characterized by a paranoid alternation between the refugee child as image of innocence and their doppelgänger, the migrant youth who merely *appears* to be a child. We can see, too, the function of material objects, alongside faces and bodies, for the projection of this paranoia. The prominence and pervasiveness of these themes in British public discourse constitutes an essential background for the alternative migration narratives produced as literature and film during the first decades of the UK's twenty-first century.

Remi Weekes, *His House* (2020)

The 2020 British horror movie *His House*, directed by Remi Weekes, reflects asylum seekers' experiences in the 2010s UK by audaciously deploying horror tropes as the most appropriate cinematic language for the trauma and cruelty embedded in their lives by state hostility. Weekes makes a ghostly migrant child the source of unbearable responsibilities and complex status jeopardy under the border politics of twenty-first-century Britain—a child offering adults perverse hope for securing their own futures before returning as a chaotically, violently haunting signifier.

His House opens with a brief sequence showing two adult refugees (later named as Bol and Rial) fleeing from South Sudan with their young daughter, Nyagak. On an overcrowded boat, they make a dangerous crossing of a stormy English Channel; though Bol and Rial survive, the child is lost. Months later, Bol and Rial are finally granted probational asylum in Britain; the Home Office provides them with poor-quality housing on the edge of London. As reviewer Clarisse Loughrey observed, the film "crystallises the UK's 'hostile environment' toward immigrants and brings it to gnawing, icy life"—the "hostile environment" was a policy objective explicitly defined by Theresa May as Home Secretary in 2012, which subsequently "mutated to refer to generalised state-led marginalisation of immigrants" (Griffiths and Yeo 521). Though they experience hostility from both locals and Home Office staff, Bol tries to assimilate, adopting elements of British culture, whereas Rial is keen to retain visible signs of their roots in South Sudan, creating tensions.

The couple begins to experience strange phenomena in their new home, seeing visions of their dead daughter and other figures. Rial identifies the unwelcome presence as a "night witch" whom, she believes, has followed them on their journey; if they repay the debt associated with this migration—the nature of which is not immediately apparent—Rial suggests, the witch will return Nyagak to them. Bol burns everything they brought with them and later, in desperation at the continued haunting, tears apart the house looking for the witch, which jeopardizes the couple's security when their Home Office caseworker becomes aware of the damage. Bol successfully summons the night witch, who tells him he has stolen a life that was not his to take. Rial finds herself, seemingly in a vision, back in a South Sudanese warzone. As she and Bol desperately seek to escape, they find a bus transporting refugees to safety—but reserved for children and adults accompanying them. Desperate, Bol sees Nyagak—a random child—in the crowd, and abducts her, falsely claiming she is their daughter. The couple escape, leaving Nyagak's real mother running behind the bus, before the vision returns to Nyagak's drowning. Here, the child's death has seemingly followed, with bleakly perverse irony, from the unique priority status attributed to child refugees, starting the sequence of events that led to Nyagek's drowning in the channel. Bol decides to repay the debt to the witch, and Nyagak reappears. Rial, however, chooses to save Bol instead of accepting this alternate reality by slitting the witch's throat. Later, the caseworker returns to inspect the house and finds it has been repaired; Bol and Rial tell him they want to remain there.

His House offers a horrific, ironic, and elegiac view of the migrant child's centrality to the imagination and reality of migration crisis and to the failures of British politics, society, and institutions to accommodate it. The demand the child places on the adults—even when she seems to offer their physical or spiritual salvation, as Nyagak does directly for Bol and Rial—is always ultimately too much for adults to bear, even as it arises from unrealistic separation of the protection of the vulnerable child from the contexts in which adults live and die (a separation literalized through the child's haunting absence here). As in *A Pale View of Hills*, the ghostly child, for whose death the adults feel an irreconcilably ambiguous yet inescapable responsibility, figures the opacity at the center of any traumatic migration and the futures destroyed and exchanged in the journey. The child's unquiet ghost here also underlines the failures of her "parents" (particularly Rial) to make progress with their lives in the UK through assimilation (despite Bol's efforts to do so); this child is both an unbearable moral demand and a sign of a trauma located elsewhere that cannot be readily erased into the "innocence" required of deserving migrants. The presence of the caseworker, and the risk represented by the damaged home, is a reminder that Bol and Rial hold only provisional status and so must continually demonstrate their unthreatening innocence if they are to avoid deportation. The persistent, endangering presence of the ghostly child—a child whose possession by Bol and Rial constituted a lie—is a sign of the couple's lack of security and authenticity in their new environment. This lack is interpreted as lack of innocence by the skeptical, hostile Home Office staff, who are willing to accommodate them only as meek, childlike, grateful, and blank figures, not as humans with agency (which could only be read as threatening and illegitimate) or complex experiences. This acrid compound of traumas and tropes wreathes Bol and Rial, their house, and their place within British migration politics.

There are multiple overlapping ironies in the dynamics around the dead migrant child here. On the one hand, had Nyagak survived, her status as child could have made Bol and Rial's claim on the UK's protection stronger. On the other hand, the child's absence makes the adults' assimilation potentially simpler, a matter of changing their own practices rather than dealing with (as Etsuko does in *A Pale View*) the raising of a child between national and ethnic identities; children, as signifiers and embodied demands for the generational transference of assets and identities, threaten to make it impossible to imagine assimilation as zero-sum, turning it into a matter of riskily speculative investment in the future rather than straightforward affirmation of a present status. As in *A Pale View*, it is ironically the specter of the child that reminds mobile adults where they have come from—ethnically, geographically, and historically—of the indelibility of their migration. The violence that the child's memory, via the night witch, does to the house highlights the material jeopardy this child poses to the future as Bol and Rial struggle to negotiate the racist and resentful routes grudgingly offered to them to secure their future in the UK; this is in ironic contrast to the hopes they once vested in this child's role within the moral economy of migration.

His House, even from its title, registers the house as a key symbolic and material space and economic asset in British culture, and it thus acts as a signifier of these refugees' claim on the nation. (Strikingly, popular anti-migrant sentiments in the UK are often articulated through the house—via allegories of home invasion, squatting, etc.—as metaphor for the country and its state resources [Musolff 251–52].) A Home Office staff member openly expresses their resentment at Bol and Rial for being allocated such a home, access to which, in this case, is granted and controlled by the state through a state institution—which itself uses the loaded name "Home Office," here given the double significance of control over both the home granted to Bol and Rial and over the British home*land*. Here, the institution functions only to monitor for signs of danger in the migrants, to look for pretexts to deprive them of the access begrudgingly provided. Bol and Rial's home is pointedly, painfully unhomelike and inorganic, reflecting the hostility toward their own alien status in Britain.

In the film's unusual ending, the adults ultimately have to accept the child's death, even refusing the opportunity to reverse her death (in this sense, Bol and Rial kill the child twice over). Yet, here, this imperative affirms the inescapable reality of violent borders, refusing to allow the child's recuperated image to be a moral escape route from that reality (even though she has given Bol and Rial a practical escape). The alternative final vision of the lost girl—in another revision of the *Don't Look Now* scenario, though initially seeming to threaten the life of her "father"—finally allows him and his wife to move on with their lives together. Final acceptance of the child's death underlies the need to see the migrant child not as a unique innocent but as part of a broader continuing history of migration for survival and future aspirations; to see clearly, Bol and Rial must surrender (as Etsuko never does) their attachment to the image of the child that haunts the politics of migration in which they are so traumatically and tragically immersed.

Killing Children in the Countryside: Migration and Organicism in Two 2010s British Novels

If the migrant child simultaneously connotes the most inescapable of Britain's international responsibilities and the encroaching danger of the world beyond the nation's borders, the essence of "native" nationalism is often portrayed by a long Romantic-inflected tradition—one with, as already seen in McEwan, a substantial continuing presence in late twentieth-century fiction—as rural and anti-metropolitan. The non-cosmopolitan small town or village is the supreme Somewhere for the British conservatives of the twentieth and early twenty-first centuries: "For we all hailed from such villages but lately, and rightly do they remain the repository of our national pride," as the neoromantic fascist of *All Among the Barley* ahistorically puts it (162). In the previous chapter, we saw one 1980s English home counties village used as an unlikely site for the ghosts of children haunting Etsuko's migration history. I turn next to two 2010s British novels that use English villages, at earlier periods of history, as sites of violence against migrant adults and children in the name of the native child and their embodiment of the environment as a supposed site of organic harmony. These are Jim Crace's *Harvest* (2013) and Melissa Harrison's *All Among the Barley* (2018); here, the English village's traces of the precapitalist, feudal order, as well as its later related fetishization as a site of national authenticity, makes it dangerous territory for the child-as-future in times of migration and generational change. Simultaneously, the use of earlier settings to depict migrant crises where the child is at stake allows both authors to cast a sideways look, another anamorphosis, on such crises in their own period, covering the years immediately before and after the Brexit vote, respectively.

Jim Crace, *Harvest* (2013)

Harvest describes events in an English village, related by narrator Walter Thirsk, during an unspecified but seemingly late medieval moment within the centuries-long process of *enclosure*: a central component in the early rise of capitalism in England, where common farmland, within villages owned by a lord of the manor, was divided and "enclosed" into private commercial estates, displacing many former inhabitants. The novel's deliberate lack of chronological precision both draws attention to historical process rather than chronological moment and produces an uncanny kind of atemporality, ironically stripped of the nostalgic essentialism that usually attends it and unusually combined with a surfeit of material specificity. Crace locates these phenomena within a community with anxieties catastrophically inflamed by immigration, precarity, and a threat to the child.

Harvest's villagers are bringing in crops at summer's end. Theirs is a modest and isolated village, unusually even lacking a church. Its solitude is interrupted by the arrival of some strangers—a husband and wife and adult son—at the village's edge, who establish a makeshift home and lay a hearth (1), which the villagers begrudgingly recognize as traditionally conferring a right to remain. Following the burning of the manor stables during a night of revelry, suspicion readily falls upon the recent arrivals. After a confrontation, the two male strangers are arrested by Master Kent (the manorial owner) and placed in the pillory.

Kent reveals to the villagers his plans to replace their common lands with enclosed fields for sheep, to produce wool, which he presents as promising greater economic security (40–41). He has hired a chart-maker, nicknamed Mr. Quill, to remap the landscape. During harvest festivities, a young girl, Lizzie Carr, is selected to be the village's Gleaning Queen (67); soon afterward, the older stranger is discovered to have died in the pillory. The events are interrupted by the arrival of Master Kent's cousin, Edmund Jordan, who has identified his own legal claim on the now potentially lucrative land; Jordan seeks a more ambitious enclosure scheme and to fund construction of a church. When Kent's horse is found slain, Jordan declares that the person responsible will be hanged. The villagers implicate the migrant woman, who remains at large, while Mr. Quill befriends the younger male stranger still in the pillory. He learns that the migrant family had to leave their own village when it was enclosed, leaving its community economically unviable.

The girl Lizzie Carr and two women villagers are beaten by Jordan's men and coerced to confess to witchcraft. They implicate and scapegoat Mr. Quill, an educated cosmopolitan migrant, as influencing their actions. Jordan's groom taunts them, claiming their young daughter will be burned alive; someone attacks and disfigures him. Fearing Jordan's revenge, all the villagers flee their homes, leaving only Walter behind. Jordan indicates his satisfaction at the villagers having thus cleared the land for him, and Walter is instructed to monitor the manor while Jordan and Kent depart temporarily to carry out business. Walter releases the younger migrant man from the pillory, and the next morning finds that the migrant couple have wrecked everything in the manor house and disappeared. Walter discovers Quill's body; it is unclear who is responsible for his death. Walter sets fire to the manor house himself and leaves the ruined village, beginning his own uncertain migration.

There are some obvious analogies here to British preoccupations of the 2010s: migration, as dangerous and received with paranoid hostility; authenticity and community;[3] and economic and generational change. Through *Harvest*'s combination of reference to a centuries-long economic phenomenon and refusal of historical specificity, Crace implicitly locates those conditions of the 2010s within a much longer history, drawing on a tradition of Marxist analysis of the English rural economy as represented in Raymond Williams's *The Country and the City* (1973). Crace implies that anti-cosmopolitan politics fundamentally derive from class injustice; the migrant woman is even blamed (139) for the change of land use to sheep farming—a change imposed by the elite, for which she can only be the scapegoat and of which she is, in fact, a direct victim. Crace is also alert, however, to specific manifestations of the resulting organicist politics that run deep within English and British politics:

> And it makes sense in such a distant place as this, where there is little wealth and all our labours are spent putting a single meal in front of us each day, to be protective of our modest world [. . .] though we are only the oxen to [Master Kent's] halter, it is allowed for us to be possessive of this ground and the common rights that are attached to it despite our lack of muniments. And it is reasonable, I think, to take offence at a ruling—made in a distant place—which gives the right of settlement and cedes a portion of our share to any vagrants who might succeed in putting up four vulgar walls [. . .] It's true, of course, that some of us arrived this way ourselves, and not so long ago. I count myself amongst those aliens. But times have changed [. . .] We're growing old and faltering [. . .] Why should we share with strangers? (17–19)

This passage is a remarkable reflection of the attitudes and anxieties that would converge into Brexit. *Harvest* belongs to the body of *BrexLit*, defined by Kristian Shaw to include 2010s fiction that is "prescient" toward Brexit (96) as well as work that reflects on it after the fact. There is a clear analogy in the passage for how the political rhetoric of the British Right associates distant and non-organic institutions with allegedly unjustified migrant rights, which are in turn associated with a lack of material and legal security among the hostile "native" population. Brexiteer themes including a sense of ephemeral but important rights of "native" people being trammeled; distant and unaccountable institutions; an unrealistically welcoming approach to migrants; and even generational problems, an ageing population, and a falling birthrate all feature here.

The conflict between organicism and migration—associated here with mobility, economic change, and general unpredictability, exposing the contingency behind historical circumstances—runs throughout the novel. Crace seems to attribute paranoid organicism to the material contingency of the village environment, with the harvest of the title encapsulating its alternations between abundance and scarcity. The moral ambiguity of Master Kent, the apparently benevolent landowner whose rule collapses through a mix of complacency and complicity, shows the weakness of the allegedly organic social order, which can now only be sustained—in the face of an economic transition that permeates the village at first slowly, then very suddenly—through willful blindness, nostalgia, fantasy, and relentless hostility to outsiders. There are, of course, multiple migrants in the novel who receive such hostility, including Mr. Quill, Edmund Jordan, and Walter himself. The narrator recalls his arrival in the village as a young economic migrant, "not a product of these commons but a visitor who's stayed" (64), who also becomes obsessed with the land's abundance and fecundity, which translates into his own sexual and reproductive ambitions: "When first I came to these vicinities I thought I'd discovered not quite paradise, but at least a fruitful opportunity—some honest freedom [. . .] Some fertile soil! I'd never known such giving land and sky. [. . .] I'd found a treasury [. . .] And then I set my eyes on Cecily and saw a chance to build a future here" (63).

Consumer objects are extreme rarities, and thus objects of overinvestment and obsession, in the village (a woman's shawl is at the center of the events that lead rapidly to the village's depopulation). Crace's style involves a highly intensive yet ambivalent materialism that emphasizes the sensory dimension of this context, with the obsession directed toward these objects implicated in moral harm without transferring onto the objects themselves in any kind of gothic essentialism. The enthralling qualities of such objects—for adults who experience them from positions of scarcity and voyeuristic, unfulfillable desire—are linked to childhood play (the social flexibility of which is indicated by Lizzie Carr being crowned Gleaning Queen) rather than the child's presumed embodiment of a future where stable continuity is valued over mobility without traces of desire for the latter ever quite disappearing. (That paradox is clear in Walter's own position of ambivalent belonging within the village and his recurring attraction to resuming the migration and mobility experienced in his youth.) The transformative potential of material goods speaks to a repressed, profoundly inorganic potential in the child-as-future, a connection that appears in the seizure of the girl Lizzie Carr: "This girl, bedecked beyond her station in a valuable cloth and mustardy with flowers, like a fairy child, was far too young and tame to fit the description of the savage woman they'd only recently been informed about [. . .] But she was baffling. And her clothing was suspicious. [. . .] The meaning of those shawls and sashes [. . .] would reveal itself in time no doubt, and after thorough questioning, beginning with this mystifying child" (140). It is the child's class and moral ambiguity, her appearance as another kind of outsider, that leads to her victimization by Jordan's men, and this arises from her visible possession of objects beyond those deemed legitimate for her age and social position. In reality, she has these objects because of her ritual role as the chosen Gleaning Queen, the essence of this role being to embody and thereby tame an unknown, dangerously unpredictable future "like a fairy child"—a representation of dependency on (and aesthetic containment strategy for) unpredictable nature in the harvest. When Jordan's men threaten to burn Lizzie as a witch, they seek to destroy a figure of limited but ambiguous power; for the villagers, though, the threatened killing of the child risks destroying any remaining security over the future. The child sits alongside the migrants as the target of threats and violence, the alignment emphasized by similar use of objects: the migrant woman's possession of a shawl from a superior class marks her as criminally suspicious (27) in the same way that Jordan's men regard Lizzie Carr's attire.

As Gleaning Queen, Lizzie is also a parodic or uncanny version of institutional order—one that locates such order in the organic world of nature and the harvest and thus, in principle, is divorced from more human institutions. This reflects the villagers' faith in "common rights [. . .] despite our lack of muniments" (18)—though they are less content about customary "rights" when those are exercised by the migrant family (1). This child, in balancing the claims of the institutional and the organic within the village order as a "queen" who embodies the alluring but cruelly contingent fecundity of the land the villagers only precariously possess, represents a balance that the migrants are taken to disturb in how they base their claim in purely institutional terms (via the rights attendant on setting up a hearth) without an organic connection to the community (though actually they turn out to have all too much in common with the doomed village). It is, appropriately, the violent threat to this child—who comes from an established village family, though she is actually selected as queen by an outsider, Mr. Quill—that destroys the village's future.

This destruction is also enabled by the fact that village's own institutions, and its relationship with any institutionalized judicial or political order, are extremely weak. This is symbolized by its (historically improbable and therefore uncanny) absence of a church, whose crucial functions, particularly for pre-Reformation and precapitalist England, were mediating relationships between past and future and between generations (see Duffy, especially "Death and Memory" 327–37). The pillory, described as "our village cross" (127) is an ironic, grim stand-in for the institutional role that a church should properly perform—just as the martyrdom of one migrant man on the pillory and the near-resurrection of the other after his release from this "cross" underline the village's crimes and, ironically, their apparent lack of access to redemption. Master Jordan uses the village's status as outside formal institutions against it (112). Though Crace does present the village as something of a genuinely organic environment, in the proximity of the human lives there to nature, the ambivalent and ultimately weak role of institutions in managing this relationship underpins the gaps in material and epistemological security that generate violence toward migrants, particularly when refracted through the intensifying image of the "native" child—herself cast as akin to a "fairy child," hinting at even a native child's suppressed potential as parallel to the otherness of outsiders, which is to be contained through ritual and symbol. (Lizzie's role here is thus somewhat opposite, incidentally, to that of Rowan in *The Wicker Man*: a child figure of nativist faith in organic fecundity who entices the mobile outsider's sympathy and moral obligation, only to entrap him on her community's behalf.)

This potential is also signaled through the villagers' materialism and, particularly, their attitude to the rare commodity goods that come within their view. They have a paranoid focus on the migrants' access to material objects as well as to a space within the village; this is initially focused on the shawl worn by the migrant woman, allegedly too luxurious for her to own legitimately (27). There is a connection to how such obsessive envy can operate across classes, too, in how Master Kent, in an attempt at humane protection of the migrant woman, claims that the shawl in fact belonged to his late wife. The parallel with British attitudes to contemporary migrants, with constant paranoia over their "benefits" and distinguishing between refugees and economic migrants, is clear.

Much of *Harvest*'s political power derives simultaneously from the force of these parallels and from how Crace places them within a longer and deeper set of historical processes that are felt intimately, materially, and through relationships with figures who act as objects of fear and desire simultaneously—most prominently here, the migrant woman (whom several villagers, including Walter, treat as a sexual target) and the native child as Gleaning Queen. Migration, material insecurity and materialistic aspirations, violence toward the child, ambivalent relationships with institutions, and an overwhelming attachment to organicist narratives of social order—even in the face of their clear inadequacy—are at the heart of this. If Crace encourages us to take a very long view in understanding Britain's (and particularly England's) contemporary political predicaments and moral failures, threats toward and fetishizations of the child-as-future act as the opposite to this, creating a moment of violent intensity through which the uncertainty of the future can be destroyed, but only at the cost of a much broader historical destruction. Crace sustains a sense of melancholic and elegiac sympathy with his characters even while unsentimentally depicting their terrible complicity; although his unnamed village is an isolated, insular, and hostile society, it is not an enraptured and enthralled gothic milieu as found, for example, on the Summerisle of *The Wicker Man*, and the child at the center of its celebrations is another victim rather than a trap.

MELISSA HARRISON, *ALL AMONG THE BARLEY* (2018)

Melissa Harrison's *All Among the Barley*—one of the few texts discussed here whose publication postdates the Brexit referendum—signals to three periods in modern British history. One is the 2010s period of its publication; another is where the novel's frame narrative ends, in the 1980s; and almost all its events take place in the early 1930s. As one of the late 2010s' most celebrated British ecological writers, Harrison is highly engaged (and in a more nuanced and historically sophisticated way than some on the anti-Brexit liberal left) with the ideological and historical context of the Brexit Era (Harrison, interview by Bedford), and this informs *All Among the Barley*, where the associated conflicts are fought through a living child and a vulnerable, and later dead, migrant child.

Living on her family's farm in a southern English village, fourteen-year-old Edie Mather is imaginative, lonely, willful, and innocent. Despite her family's hard-laboring economic precarity, Edie has a deep appreciation and curiosity for the natural environment. Observing her older sister—married with a baby, exhausted, and depressed—Edie senses how adulthood jeopardizes such enjoyment. Their mother, Ada, is stoic but oppressed by their economically strained, alcoholic father, George Mather. George leases their land from the absent but financially uncompromising rentier and landowner Lord Lyttleton, against whom he drunkenly rants during the village's harvest celebration (173). In historical terms, the Mathers' ancestors would have prospered after enclosure as tenant farmers of a large estate, unlike the displaced of *Harvest*, but now they are pressured by a new phase of modern capitalism. (Though traces of feudal infrastructure, in a village clustered around a now-unoccupied manor house, still remain even in the 1930s, they have not yet reached the terminal postwar decline we saw depicted in *The Little Stranger*.) Edie has a series of awkward sexual encounters with a local boy (181) that reinforce her apprehension at her options for adulthood; yet, she starts to believe that the women in her family possess powers of witchcraft, in contrast to their surface-level limitations, and that she herself has inherited these.

Constance FitzAllen arrives into this tense situation. Constance, an urbane middle-class woman, is obsessed with traditional rural life, which she is researching for a magazine associated with a political movement. Constance attaches herself to the Mathers, developing a bond with Edie that is hinted to derive from their shared gender nonconformity and passions for nature and craft—and from Edie's naivety: there is a subtly disturbing sense of grooming about the relationship. Despite her occasionally patronizing enthusiasms and ambiguous motivations, Constance mostly wins the family's acceptance; George's employee, John Hurlock remains skeptical.

A neighboring farm lies derelict—an inspiring wilderness for Edie and a disturbing sign of the fate awaiting farmers who fail to adapt to changing economic circumstances. The abandoned farmhouse has been occupied by a transient family; curious, Edie spies on them and is seen by their young child.

It is gradually revealed that Constance represents a fascist organization (the Order of English Yeomanry) that fetishizes authentic rural life as the moral alternative to "international financiers" (115), code for an antisemitic worldview. Constance holds a meeting at the village pub to encourage locals to join the organization. Here, she is confronted by John, who reveals Constance's responsibility for evicting the migrant family:

> "[F]or no reason that I can see other than that they were Jews—them being to her mind responsible for everything that's wrong with the world these days. [. . .] I was at a union meeting three days ago in Corwelby where all the talk was of a family called Adler not long arrived from our direction, the

father carrying a girl by the name of Esther, four years old and no more than a bag of skin and bones. She were dead." (302)

The meeting descends into fighting. In the chaos, Edie unexpectedly discovers her own image answering back to the image of the dead migrant child John has invoked: "there on the floor was a discarded magazine, trampled by boots, an image of my face smiling idiotically out at me from the crumpled page" (305). It is the magazine carrying Constance's stories about the Mathers. Edie reflects that the image "was both me and not me, and I thought about the possibility that hundreds of people might have seen it—had seen it already. It had been stolen from me, my own image pressed into the service of something I hadn't consented to" (306). Edie has the uncanny experience of seeing herself as the image of the Child, framed and isolated from herself; lying discarded and prone, it is a grim doppelgänger of the image of the dead child that John has just conjured. This is the fetishized image of the child as discussed by theorists; but, unusually, we see the actual child depicted returning the gaze upon it. What happens next reflects, albeit ambivalently, the agency of the child in the face—their own face, framed—of the Child.

The same night, a fire destroys the Mathers' farmhouse. Though George (who disappears) is himself suspected of starting the blaze, Edie believes it was created from her own anger, in a kind of magical transference, and she tells others about this (320–21). The novel ends with a sudden return into the framing point of recollection from which Edie—unbeknownst to the reader until now—has been speaking. She has been recounting her story from the 1980s, where she lives inside a mental institution, in which she has been confined ever since the 1930s events—her insistence that she caused the fire seemingly the proximate trigger for her incarceration (321). However, she is now facing the prospects of this institution's closure and being transferred back into the village under the Thatcher government's "care in the community" program (a real policy that sought to reduce institutionalization of the mentally ill). Edie shows little understanding of how drastically her village will have changed.

Here, an intensified nationalism arrives into the 1930s home and village—ironically via a metropolitan outsider—as a response to economic disruption, to the anxious contingency of depending simultaneously on the land's fertility and on a changing surrounding economic order (the same combination, in an earlier iteration, driving disaster in *Harvest*). Constance's organicist and racialized nationalism is both nostalgic and utopian—echoing some Brexit-Era versions prevailing alongside the novel's publication—based on affirming and protecting the reproduction of a national essence beyond history, politics, and social change. As she claims in print of the Mathers, "there is a purity of purpose to their labours; for it is not enrichment they seek, nor government assistance, but the simple perpetuation of their own kind" (163). Her organicist reproductive vision imagines escape from both capitalism and the welfare state and that such escape can only be secured by confronting the malign, inauthentic instability she identifies with the migrant family, with mobility and cosmopolitanism in general, with citizens of Nowhere, and with Jews. Constance's agenda reflects real 1930s movements that sought to promote English rural life as the source of social health and national authenticity, as famously captured in H. V. Morton's *In Search of England* (1927), directly referenced in *All Among the Barley* (260; see also, Cunningham 228–37). Her concerns simultaneously resonate with the Brexit Era of the novel's composition and publication, notably her relentless fetishization of authentic lifestyles and her hostility toward metropolitan cosmopolitanism (Harrison 162–63), where "none of it seems quite real compared to life here" (134). Constance has been seeking the road to Somewhere.

Nevertheless, Constance proposes to reserve both herself and Edie from full or permanent participation in the "real life" of rurality, perhaps betraying a broader ambiguity in the characters' relationships with mobility and the consumer economy that simultaneously holds the Mathers in place and holds out the prospect of—generational, economic, and geographic—movement. Consumer goods, in particular, act as alluring transgressions of the unforgiving economic "authenticity" within which the Mathers live. Constance targets the middleman for the Mathers' eggs, as he is Jewish, and finds an alternative gentile buyer, as though this would remove the contingency and vulnerability built into their place in the market (and world). For Edie, clothes are ambivalently exciting goods that signify the generational and gendered transition to adulthood (126–27), while motor cars signal the world of modernity, luxury, and mobility beyond rural precarity (173, 258). Edie, for all that she loves the locality, is attracted to mobility; she wanders whenever and wherever she can, and when she is unexpectedly given a lift by a wealthy young Cambridge student, touring the area in his "smart blue motor-car" (258), she suddenly (though unsuccessfully, 262) asks the glamorous youth to take him away with her (262).

Mobility, then, is a powerful, if always fraught, object of desire here, even for some who seem to revere unchanging stability in rural England; and the ability to migrate is powerfully aligned with classed and gendered prospects. Lord Lyttleton himself has moved away from the village, making money in London while extracting rent from his tenant farmers; George Mather's resentment of the absent landowner—defined for him by another automotive symbol of mobility, his "damned Rolls Royce" (173)—seems, tellingly, to align with his antisemitism. Mobility and migration are also aligned with the possibilities of generational and socioeconomic change, and Constance wraps her offer to take Edie to live in London—an almost unthinkable migration—into a "feeling Ada would like to spare you marriage if she could" (196), a possibility of generational and geographic escape—albeit one confined to select individuals who are, as Constance queerly codes it, "like me" (197).

Constance's hypocrisy perhaps indicates a genuine insight: that migration and mobility—at least in their aspirational rather than coerced forms—paradoxically require some material, epistemological, and institutional security, some roots in place, rather as Lord Lyttleton's mobile lifestyle and entrepreneurial activities are secured by his rentier base in his ancestral manor (simultaneously both an economic unit and an institution). Institutional security for people like the Mathers (though even more for people like the Adlers) is weak, however, so Constance (with her own rather more bourgeois insecurities) tries to find it for them in fetishizing a racialized belief in an organic rural safe haven that is secure from the contingencies and chaos of 1930s capitalism, which she projects onto the abject figure of the Jew. At the novel's end, Edie's forthcoming exile from the institution that has sheltered her—however dubious the original grounds for her institutionalization—underlines the codependence of personal, epistemological, and material security.

In these contexts, the (actual or potential) migrant child becomes an overinvested figure. Constance's offer of a chance to migrate to London is, perversely, made to Edie only because she embodies the innocent quasi-wild child of neoromantic myth on the cover of the rightwing magazine, a perverse double to the abject migrant (and Jewish) child whose death Constance regards as acceptable collateral. John's implicit question, on announcing this child's death, continued to surround images of dead migrant and refugee children in the 2010s: What kind of political project—or society—allows a child to die for the sake of its imagined ethnic, economic, and territorial security? What is so valuable that its protection weighs more than the child's life?

In our own times, these questions lead to compulsive gazing on the migrant child's image. In this novel, though, we see the migrant child's own gaze through that of another child, Edie herself:

> That's when I saw them, sitting in the shade [. . .] a woman Mother's age in a dark dress and headscarf, and a little girl no more than four years old, lying on a rush mattress with her head turned towards me and gazing at me with deep-shadowed and strangely fervent eyes. I froze in the doorway, but then I saw that the woman was sleeping, her head resting on the tree's gnarled trunk. Letting out my breath, I looked back at the child, and although she smiled a little—I'm sure she did, I'm sure to this day that she smiled at me—she did not blink or look away. (189)

This mutual gaze embodies the simultaneous humanity and opacity of the migrant child. Constance's reaction to the episode is chilling:

> "You spied on them! How perfectly thrilling."
> "I didn't mean to. They were asleep. Well, the lady was—outside, under a tree."
> "Ah yes, indolent to a fault. I wonder where the menfolk were. I've a good mind to write to Cecil Lyttleton, you know. It's no way to be bringing up a child."
> [. . .] I thought of the glittering eyes of the girl staring at me from the bed. [. . .]
> "But they aren't doing any harm, are they?"
> "Edie, they simply don't fit in here—quite apart from the fact that they're living scot-free on Lyttleton land, while your father and everyone else pays rent. [. . .] They're Jews, Edie. And we don't need any more of them in Elmbourne—the egg merchant Blum and his wife are bad enough." (198–99)

Echoing rightwing rhetoric of the 2010s, Constance grotesquely dresses her hostility toward migrants—a hostility that soon causes the child's death—as concern for the child's welfare. She also identifies the migrants, supposed economic parasites, with elite control of international capitalism, echoing twenty-first-century British racism and exposing its debts to earlier twentieth-century antisemitism in its paradoxical assertion of shared interests between marginalized migrants and powerful international elites (as in the idea that humane approaches to migration are the product of an elite conspiracy). Theorist of antisemitism Zygmunt Bauman argued that this paradoxical claim underpinned how "doing something about the Jews was [. . .] an effort to fight the world's contingency, opacity, uncontrollability [. . .] ambivalence" (151–52), a characterization true of Constance's motivations. As her rhetoric shows, antisemitism and anti-cosmopolitanism are also ways to fantasize escape from historical change under capitalist modernity, seeking a return to an organic, unchanging stability—even if it is one that Constance hypocritically sees as allowing her and Edie a basis upon which to remain personally mobile.

Both Constance and Edie are, in different ways, products of their own awareness of being "different," even while Constance affirms and Edie is unwittingly co-opted to represent the essential value of the native, the authentic. Edie's fantasy of being a witch via her female bloodline is her way of conceptualizing her difference. Constance understands it differently:

> "But Connie, what about 'Englishmen and Englishwomen living in harmony with the land'? What about 'the perpetuation of our native kind,' and all that?
>
> "Oh, rot [. . .] town life can be dreadfully enervating, it's true. But do you really want to spend your whole life in the same place, among the same people, doing the same things year in and year out, until you die? [. . .] Only—I have a feeling Ada would spare you marriage if she could. [. . .] Because . . . because you're like me, Edie. And I want to help."
>
> "Am I?"
>
> She linked her arm through mine and squeezed, and I could feel the hot flank of her body through the silk blouse she wore.
>
> "*Yes*, darling. You are." (196–97)

Constance's queerness—seen here operating behind her combination of affirming national authenticity in rural life while somehow reserving herself (and, putatively, Edie) from its restrictions—seems to fulfil Edelman's argument that queerness acts as constitutive within conservative reproductive futurism; disturbingly, though, Constance simultaneously reserves her own queerness for this function and splits and renders it abject in her fevered projections of diseased cosmopolitanism. Edelman's argument is also borne out in how Constance's absolute moral distinction between Edie and the dead Jewish girl attempts to establish a reproductive futurism on her own macabre terms. Constance is no less queer because of her fascism; noticeably, however else she attempts to fit in with the Mathers' lives, she is utterly unwilling to accept a conservatively gendered role for herself, even temporarily. She thus underlines my contention earlier that the queer as a recognizable figure, identified through critical practices based on recognition and potentially on affirmation, is not necessarily a politically adequate or ethical imperative, nor is it inevitably a source of danger to conservative essentialisms.

It is the child herself, however, who constitutes the real threat and alternative both to reproductive futurism and to nascent fascism here in her curiosity and openness to the world, as shown in her encounters with Constance; with the mobile youth on his driving trip; with the migrant child, even if they only interact via a mutual gaze; and, above all, in her reluctance to be subsumed into a restrictive social position or fixed image, including the literal image on the magazine. Ironically, Edie's belief in a lineage of female witchcraft is her own defensive, internal attempt to channel her waywardness into a knowable, essentialized, and quasi-organic form based on bloodline and mythologized sex difference. This is also a way to concretize the danger she presents to the available adult social orders (including Constance's queer alternative) and to attribute spectacular power to it, evidenced in her claiming the fire as her own act of creative destruction. It is telling that this attempt to spectacularly dramatize her own impulses, while seeking escape from the more mundanely difficult choices they present in a period of historical transition and potentially deadly ideological and generational conflict, results only in disaster.

This turn to creative destruction is, however, a reflection of the poor options available for the kind of place—geographic, social, or institutional—that might be available to accommodate such a child as Edie. Beyond the locations of the family farm, the village, and the projected presence of London, a few institutions exist on the margins of the novel. Edie has already left school at age thirteen; she misses the access to books but is aware of her failure to make friends there (18). The village church functions as an institution that upholds the national and imperial order

(144) and yet is behind the times and cannot match the liveliness of the pub (298). The Order of English Yeomanry, for which Edie becomes unwitting mascot, is itself an attempt to create a new kind of institution. Any institution as a historical and political entity, however, has at least a latent tension with the notion of an organic, harmonious, authentic form of society. This conflict makes an uncanny return in the 1980s at the novel's end, when the aged and unworldly Edie faces the closure of the institution that has sheltered and incarcerated her—but which seems to have ironically foreclosed any "developmental" purpose for the child it took in—and a forced return to a supposedly more normal life in the community, though the reader is aware that historical change will have transformed that community out of all recognition. *All Among the Barley*'s disturbing frame narrative captures, then, the uneasy relationships between institutions providing protected times and spaces, the belief in an organic and authentic British (or English) society, and the politics of historical change—all through a narrator effectively arrested in her childhood.

There is something horrific and uncanny yet moving in how the apparent voice of a child narrator finally collapses into that of a very old woman, the child's apparent ingenuity revealed to be a product of trauma and socially engineered mental incapacity. This also works against the expectations of the Romantic Bildungsroman (a genre with which *All Among the Barley* toys), where the child possessed of unusual imaginative gifts and given an equally unusual, if initially traumatic, entrance to the wider world might expect to nevertheless eventually succeed within that world. No such future is to be Edie's. This ending is also a moment of historical collapse; through the uncanny endurance of this child's voice, later-twentieth-century—and, implicitly, twenty-first-century—British history emerges here as stilted by the traumas of the past: both the 1930s and centuries-long conditions of precarity and institutional insecurity during England and Britain's development as a capitalist and imperial power that would be fundamentally reconfigured by the Second World War and the ideological and generational conflicts that preceded and followed it. The neoromantic celebration of the child's innocence and imaginative openness, for which we might have expected a partial final celebration, becomes instead something terrible. It is both a return of history and a sudden realization of being stuck in time as a monstrous injustice, with no desirable nostalgia to be recovered. It is also a backhanded testament to the power of the child to disturb and confound. This child's potential for mobility, in every and any sense, led to her future being entirely killed off; she haunts a forgotten corner of 1980s Britain.

Migrant Children and British Institutions in Ishiguro

In the previous chapter, we saw Ishiguro's first novel explore some undercurrents in early Thatcher-Era Britain's hostility to migration as anticipating the later collapse of its alliance between neoliberalism and nationalism. There, the migrant child, as a feared source and vulnerable object of adult violence arising from the resulting paranoia, came to signify an epistemological gap that in some sense *is* the opacity of migration itself, its untranslatable intersection of the generational and geographical.[4] When this reality combines with the opacity of the child-as-future under the adult gaze, the overinvestment can provoke severe anxiety—and can even be fatal, if the hints of *A Pale View* and other texts discussed here are to be taken seriously.

Ishiguro has continued to return regularly throughout his career to migrant children and mobile youth, most explicitly in *When We Were Orphans* (2000). Here, I read it alongside Ishiguro's *Never Let Me Go* (2005), which I argue also contains a significant, if subtler, engagement with the same theme. Just as *A Pale View of Hills* anticipated the repressed conflicts and contradictions in Thatcherism, so *Orphans* undertook a similarly bleakly astute sideways look at Blairite affirmations of globalization and liberal interventionism, while *Never Let Me Go* provides an uncanny alternative history of later-twentieth-century Britain. Children and youth are central in these novels, as are the institutions that give them time and space to develop, but only in terms that prove horrendously compromised by paranoid essentialism and intergenerational violence.

WHEN WE WERE ORPHANS (2000)

Christopher Banks's childhood is spent in the early twentieth-century Shanghai International Settlement, and it is characterized by powerful affection for his mother and close friendship with the Japanese boy next door, Akira. A family friend, "Uncle" Philip, tells Christopher that he is a child who especially represents internationalism and hope for a peaceful future world (though Christopher's play with Akira obsessively references their different national identities). In a utopian exaltation that illustrates why this novel has so often been read through the lens of post-Cold War, pre-9/11 liberal internationalism, Philip declares: "I think it would be no bad thing if boys like you all grew up with a little bit of everything [. . .] one day, all these conflicts will end, and it won't be because of great statesmen or churches or organisations [. . .] It'll be because people have changed. They'll be like you, Puffin" (76). Banks's childhood is traumatically disrupted, however, when first his father, a businessman, and later his political-activist mother successively disappear, apparently abducted. Banks is sent to England, where he attends boarding school and later becomes a successful private detective. Though he is pursued by a woman, Sarah Hemmings (who was also orphaned as a child), Banks never marries; he does, however, adopt an orphaned girl named Jennifer. Pressure from prominent figures, who emphasize his combination of detective skills with his personal connection with Shanghai, leads to Banks returning there in 1937 on a mission to recover his parents but also—by means never clarified—to avert a growing catastrophe of global significance. This mission is entirely wrapped up in Banks's childhood experience—his memories of it and the meanings others project onto it—though it requires him to leave behind an actual child, Jennifer.

Banks reaches a Shanghai that is deteriorating as conflict between Japanese and Chinese nationalist forces rages just beyond the International Settlement. Demanding of local officials that searching for his parents take priority over such concerns, Banks travels into the warzone to reach a house where he believes his parents may be held. His hold on reality, however, appears increasingly frail as he makes dubious identifications of his supposed childhood home, though the building is completely different, and of a Japanese businessman (166) and later a soldier (249) as his childhood friend Akira, though these identifications are contradictory and the soldier's reactions strongly suggest a misrecognition.

Banks's mission, overloaded by his delusional merging of international conflict with the need to recover his parents, fails decisively. He does, however, rediscover Philip, who reveals what he claims to be the truth about Banks's childhood experiences in a *Great Expectations*-esque backstory: Christopher's mother's activism against the opium trade, in which the company employing her husband was engaged, led to her becoming a problem for powerful people. As a result, Mr. Banks ran away with a new mistress while Mrs. Banks was enslaved to warlord Wang Ku and coerced into becoming his concubine in return for the young Christopher's safety and continued financial support. Philip was complicit in the kidnapping. The novel's final section shifts to 1958 in Hong Kong, where Banks reunites with a woman he believes to be his mother, though she does not recognize him and responds only ambiguously to him. Christopher returns to England and the now-adult Jennifer—who is recovering from her own troubles, having previously attempted suicide (307).

Orphans was published at a high point of Western interventionism and globalization under American hegemony: after the Soviet Union's fall but before 9/11, the War on Terror, and the rise of China as rival superpower. *Orphans*' return to an earlier twentieth-century period of colonialism (and an International Settlement) in crisis has been read as an uncanny refraction of the period of the novel's production, its historical turn proving an ironic anticipation of that period's underlying fault lines (see Bain; Dean, "Ishiguro and the Abandoned Child"). From an early 2010s perspective, we could read the novel as a millennial anticipation of the crises in Western hegemony and liberal internationalism; the rise of renewed multipolar, Great Power conflicts that would succeed the period of relatively, apparently stable Western hegemony in the late 1990s; the ever-more-paranoid politics of hostility to migration; and the renewed nationalisms and nativisms associated with these developments. In his study of cosmopolitanism in Ishiguro, Ivan Stacy reads *Orphans* as a point of transition (1070–71), when Ishiguro's willingness to allow his characters—often with, as in *A Pale View*, traumatic but ambiguous complicities in international disasters—to find consolation in cosmopolitanism underwent a more skeptical turn.

Banks's return to Shanghai, and the rhetorical demands that prompt it, reflect a demand for ethical interventionism made through the image of the abandoned, vulnerable refugee child—who Banks himself once was, albeit in a privileged form. Though Banks's childhood migrations are sometimes presented by characters as central to the global condition, this is ultimately a dubious mix of paranoia and conspiracism directed toward Banks by others and self-aggrandizement in Banks's own mind. Even the central conspiracy "revealed" by Philip, which seems to thoroughly account for Banks's childhood and explain its hidden significance, has been critically recognized as far from securely reliable (Ringrose 173, 177). Perhaps the hidden fear behind all the contradictory projections onto Banks, including from himself, is that his childhood was *not* in fact all that significant. Lack of secure representational significance in Banks's world, as in ours, can have drastic implications, for the political reception of tragic images of migrant children like Alan Kurdi is haunted by the unacknowledged knowledge of all the children who are *not* seen and accorded no particular significance. *Orphans* hints at this by presenting migrant children of vastly bifurcated significance, from Banks's ward, Jennifer, to the refugee children on Shanghai's streets who become indistinguishable from mere objects, as when Banks travels to his supposed childhood home:

> The pavements were filled with huddled figures [. . .] of every age—I could see babies asleep in mothers' arms—and their belongings were all around them; ragged bundles [. . .] mostly Chinese, but as we came towards the end of the street, I saw clusters of European children [. . .] when once I thought we had run over a sleeping form, and glanced back in alarm, my companion merely murmured: "Don't worry. Probably just some old bundle." (182–83)

Orphans is concerned with the distinctions between human and non-human status and with how these map onto distinctions of race and nation, child and adult. Here, human status intersects with both migration and generational status, from the utopian vision of a globalized, cosmopolitan future that Philip projects on to the young Banks to the darker implication behind Colonel Chamberlain's words when tasked with bringing this now quasi-refugee child "back" to a homeland he has never previously visited: "Shanghai's not a bad place. But [. . .] you've had about as much as you need. Much more, you'll be turning into a Chinaman [. . .] you're going to England. You're going home" (28).

The risk of racialized alterity metastasizing within the self is presented as a geographic risk—a danger of living "abroad"—but also a generational one and never more so than when it begins in early childhood (as seen already in *A Pale View*). This perceived risk relies first on the idea that the child has some kind of inescapable ethnic inheritance—an assumption that here preys on the young Christopher and Akira—and secondly on the idea that he is, nevertheless, in crucial respects blank, susceptible to environment and influence. *Orphans* raises the implications of a situation where the abandoned child betrays suggestions of being not merely unhomed but also *unheimliche*, perhaps showing some uncanny sign of an interior life that cannot be made transparent or have its motivations neatly sifted: hence, the fear of several older British people, starting with Chamberlain, that Banks's interior life might be irretrievably "othered" by his Shanghai childhood. In adulthood, Banks is pressured by their demands that he demonstrate both his Britishness and his special connection to Shanghai, allowing the latter to be reassuringly formulated within a heroic colonial narrative.

Banks cannot be wholly and securely the "blank" refugee child for the receiving state to project a flattering image of its humanitarianism because he is associated with a place of colonial mythmaking, the International Settlement, where brutal exploitation (particularly through the opium trade) and the collusion of rival colonial powers against the Chinese are transformed into high claims to civilization. The territory's name captures such a claim, of course, suggesting "settlement" as outpost of marginal, defensive white European civilization—one dangerously proximate to the "dark places of the earth," to borrow a phrase from Conrad's *Heart of Darkness* (1899), an important intertext for *Orphans*. This dangerous proximity—which perhaps implies that a child from such a place is always perilously close to the borders of innocence—is powerfully evident in the adult Banks's dialogue with Canon Moorly, which follows a heated debate over the recent German invasion of the Rhineland:

> "But on the question of how the balance of power might be maintained, how we can contain the violent conflict of aspirations in Europe, on such things I'm afraid I have no large theory as such."
>
> "No theory? Perhaps not [. . .] But you do have, shall we say, a special relationship to what is, in truth, the source of all our current anxieties [. . .] You know better than anyone the eye of the storm is to be found not in Europe at all, but in the Far East. In Shanghai, to be exact."
>
> "Shanghai," I said lamely. "Yes, I suppose . . . I suppose there are some problems in that city."
>
> "Problems indeed. And what was once just a local problem has been allowed to fester and grow. To spread its poison over the years ever further across the world, right through our civilisation. But I hardly need remind *you* of this." (138)

Even as Moorly insists Banks knows what he is referencing, neither he nor the reader is likely to be clear about this. Perhaps Moorly is referring to the opium trade; yet, this is not quite a perfect fit with his words and their context from the preceding scene. Our inability to securely place Moorly's reference point actually heightens our attention to its characteristics: this malevolent agency is foreign, powerful, migrating, an existential risk to "our civilization," dangerously unrecognized by the societies it threatens. If Moorly attributes special knowledge of this threat to Banks, the implications make Banks a rather less than wholly innocent migrant—despite his life in Shanghai and subsequent migration taking place during early childhood.

This is also despite the adult Banks being the product of British institutions, particularly his boarding school, and participating in elite London institutions through his adult career. Though Banks has apparently undergone a successful Bildung and seems to be on the cusp of fulfilling the aspirations of youthful ambition as he excels in his career and receives romantic interest, others obsessively interpret his character through his early childhood. The simultaneous insistence on the importance of Banks's childhood and ambivalence over the source of his adult agency makes Banks embody the conflict between the innocent refugee child and the mobile young man; the latter (despite his white British ethnicity) must be transformed through colonial heroism to counter the latent, abject, and foreign legacy of the darkness at the border of his childhood. Banks, the former migrant child, is to be fully absorbed into Britishness by becoming, symbolically, his own rescuer (or what current popular discourse might call his own white savior). The complex, chaotic, and opaque histories in which Banks's life is embedded are thus reduced to this imperative, where the child within Banks's adult self becomes the mirror image of what it is called upon to attack: an original source of colonial heroism to conquer the source of global evil located in a childhood poised at the border between these Manichean forces, a border found in Shanghai.

In presenting a narrative of hidden global influence coming from a single sinister but opaque source, Moorly's ambiguous conspiracy theory about Shanghai as the source of global evil imitates the terminology, paranoid logic, and imagery of antisemitism while having uncannily drifted from the latter's usual target (the obsession with Shanghai is not obviously compatible with an anti-Jewish mythos). Moorly's language also echoes earlier comments from Sir Cecil Medhurst, who similarly uses imagery that suggests antisemitism without being quite securely confined to it:

"We'll do what we can. Organise, confer. Get the greatest men from the greatest nations to put their heads together and talk. But there'll always be evil lurking around the corner for us.

> Oh yes! They're busy, even now, even as we speak, busy conspiring to put civilisation to the torch. [. . .] The evil ones are much too cunning for your ordinary decent citizen. They'll run rings around him, corrupt him, turn him against his fellows. I see it, I see it all the time now and it will grow worse. That's why we'll need to rely more than ever on the likes of you, my young friend. The few on our side every bit as clever as they are. Who'll spot their game quickly, destroy the fungus before it takes hold and spreads." (43–44)

The "spread" of these wicked citizens of Nowhere against ordinary decent citizens is a paranoid, antisemitically tinged vision of cosmopolitanism and internationalism—what twenty-first-century rightwing conspiracists call *globalism*. This displacement of the formal and rhetorical tropes of antisemitism is underpinned by the novel's 1930s context and interest in morally ambivalent international institutions (the scale of which ranges here from Mrs. Banks's home, to the corporation employing her husband, to the League of Nations itself). Sir Cecil is himself an internationalist who helped build the League (42); yet, after a drink he descends into this rambling paranoia. Like Constance's more explicit version in *All Among the Barley*, these displaced antisemitic formulae reduce international crises to the deliberate malevolence of a single source, as the variants on the heart-of-darkness trope that recur throughout *Orphans* imply (136–38). Any savior in this narrative would be necessarily an individual with privileged insight into this real source of dark global power. Yet, the constant assertions that Banks must know more than he is letting on hint at the potentially disturbing implications of this proximity: If he has the insights they are claiming, what could his failure to acknowledge them imply about his intentions or about the full nature of his childhood experiences and allegiances?

The paranoid image that runs, barely acknowledged yet clearly implicated, behind all this is of the migrant child and mobile youth representing a potential threat to Britain's self-image as a nation-state transforming its colonial inheritance into leadership of a civilized, globalized world, not least through effective interventions against malevolent threats (a transformation in which Blair-Era Britain was engaged at the time of the novel's composition). If the threat is really so serious as Moorly and Medhurst indicate, and if Banks's relationship is as close to it as they propose, and if Banks turns out *not* to be a reliably British defender against this threat, the implication of necessary violence toward him—demanded, ultimately, by his childhood migration, when the little citizen of Nowhere crossed the border and falsely appeared to assimilate, not least through his access to institutions—becomes clear.

This accords the figure of the migrant child overwhelming significance. Yet, *When We Were Orphans*, as its past-tense title suggests in invoking an orphan state as implicitly resolved and assimilated, is also concerned with the fact that such significance itself is a form of epistemological and ideological reassurance—whether in utopian and internationalist or paranoid and racist versions—though one consistently based on dubious assumptions. The risk behind this significance, in turn, is one of moral and epistemological threat in its absence: What if, instead, the migrant child is simply abandoned, their death casually accepted, as with the refugees/bundles at the side of the road as Banks drives nightmarishly through Shanghai toward the (possibly false) consolation of retrieving his childhood home? This, surely, is an unspeakable yet present possibility behind the rhetorical and signifying cage in which Banks's mobility is trapped, the unbearable possibility of *no* particular signifying relationship within the world, or at least none of much consequence.

As the slippage between refugee children and "bundles" suggests, material objects act as proxies and projections for the affirmation of signifying power and repressed doubt over its permanence and efficacy. Banks himself tellingly absorbs this attitude, showing anxiety when the orphaned Jennifer is casual about the significance of objects lost on her migration from Canada:

> I received one day a letter from the shipping company apologising for the loss of the trunk at sea and offering compensation. When I told Jennifer of this, she first simply stared. Then she gave a light laugh and said:
> "Well in that case [. . .] I will just have to go on an enormous spending spree. [. . .] After all, they were just *things*. When you've lost your mother and your father, you can't care so much about *things*, can you?" (131–32)

Banks finds Jennifer's lack of attachment to her things as signifiers of her already-past childhood, her parents, and her place of origin disturbing, despite her reasonable argument that bereavement should reduce rather than intensify her investment in them. The opacity this detachment introduces—making her migration narrative less transparent, less secure in its significance and its implications about the child's motivations—embodies the refusal to signify that Banks unconsciously recognizes others' (like Moorly) fear in him, and he thus understands it as a threat. Here, the fear of migration as producing empty, flattened, globalized realities intersects with the fear of the migrant as a dangerously unknowable threat; for the anxious Western adult subject whose attitudes Banks has internalized, lack of knowledge of the other results either in hostility and paranoia or in the assertion that there is simply nothing of moral or human significance there—an assertion central to the next Ishiguro novel I explore.

Banks is ultimately a supreme version of the impossibility of the migrant child, whose very role as redeeming both his supposed essential Britishness *and* his function as an object of interventionist internationalism only ends in failure in the face of impossible expectations, historically reflecting how millennial neoliberal, internationalist optimism already contained the seeds of its severe disruptions, which would emerge only slightly further into the twenty-first century. The overwhelming and irrational demands for Banks to demonstrate his meaning, his significance, as a one-time migrant child shows the fear of ambiguity and opacity that those around him can only translate into reading him as either heroic or malevolent. As Ishiguro would go on to explore, these paranoid dynamics do not exclusively arise in contexts explicitly concerned with migration; rather, migration intensifies and legitimates broader generational fears and anxieties about children.

Never Let Me Go (2005)

Ishiguro's *Never Let Me Go* is a powerful meditation on the intersections between generational status, age, and the possibility of mobility in life and the world told through children conceived in order to be killed.

Kathy H., a "carer," narrates the novel from the late 1990s. She reminisces about her childhood at Hailsham, a residential educational institution seemingly housed in a former country house. Hailsham provided a rounded education, encouraging its children to produce artworks and mimic the outside economy of production, trade, and consumption; some of the students' art is collected by a patron of the institution, known only as Madame. Kathy has close friendships with fellow students Tommy, a somewhat isolated boy, and the more socially ambitious Ruth. Although the Guardians (as Hailsham's teachers are known) tightly control students' access to information about their place in the world, one guardian, Miss Lucy, breaks ranks to tell them they are clones created to donate organs to the non-clone population and will thus inevitably die young—no older than their early thirties. These children are reproductions reared for slaughter. After leaving Hailsham, Ruth, Tommy, and Kathy are sent to another facility, known as the Cottages, where they are left to temporarily explore the outside world while awaiting initiation of their donations. They become aware of a rumor that a couple can have their donations deferred if they are demonstrably in love, a privilege said to be reserved for Hailsham alumni. Tommy speculates that Madame collected their artworks to accordingly determine which couples were truly in love (173).

In the final section, Ruth's health is seriously damaged by her organ donations; Kathy has become her carer. Ruth provides Madame's home address to Kathy and Tommy, urging them to seek a deferral shortly before she makes her second donation and "completes" (a euphemism for death). Kathy becomes Tommy's carer, and they form an intimate relationship; they decide to visit Madame's house to see if they can indeed gain a deferral, taking Tommy's artwork as proof of their capacity to love. They find Madame living with Miss Emily, Hailsham's former Head Guardian. The two women reveal that Hailsham was an attempt to provide a humane education and some protected time and space for the children before their adult fates, while the artwork harvested there was intended to prove to mainstream society that they were real human beings with souls. This endeavor eventually failed, and Hailsham and similar institutions were replaced with farm-like rearing facilities. Deferrals were only ever a myth. The novel ends with Kathy driving home after Tommy's completion.

The rise and fall of Hailsham forms an uncanny parallel to Britain's real late twentieth-century history.[5] Hailsham is established as a progressive (if compromised) institution early in the second half of the twentieth-century, while its decline (approximately between the mid-1980s and early 1990s) uncannily mirrors Thatcherism's real rolling-back of postwar and progressive institutions. As Miss Emily tells Kathy and Tommy: "There was a certain climate and now it's gone [. . .] It just so happens that you grew up at a certain point in this process" (261). In *Never Let Me Go*'s uncanny alternative twentieth-century Britain, fully acknowledging the clones' humanity would be politically disruptive, potentially risking their evading the purposes for which they were created or at least pursuing personal goals and mixing with the "normal" population with unpredictable outcomes. Hailsham, it becomes retrospectively clear, was a liberal attempt to increase the clones' capacity for social interaction and encourage them to pursue individual aspirations, but only within the strictly limited, complicit framework of eventual acquiescence to the fate that marks them from childhood, indeed from conception. A macabre project to protect childhood innocence while eliciting (limited) youthful aspiration and creativity is the core of Hailsham's carefully constructed program. Despite the limited liberal-humanist nature of Hailsham's political purpose, though, even this proves to be too much, and the institution is abandoned in favor of the dark organicism of the human farm—ironically termed a "government home" (260)—where presumably any such development is discouraged if not outright impossible, keeping the newer generations of clones frozen out of Bildung in a perverse and abject doppelgänger to the fetishized state of childhood innocence.

Hailsham tries to locate the clones' rights to basic human status by establishing their proximity to (while never wholly attaining) the organic value assumed inherent in the non-clone population—demonstrated, neoromantically, through the production of artwork. Yet, it is also an institution that changes the students' senses of self as well as their relationships to each other and to the surrounding society by giving them access to protected time and space, material objects, and a program to guide their use of that access. There is, thus, a structural conflict between the organic and the artificial or institutional running throughout Hailsham, betrayed in a hectic surveillance suggesting underlying anxiety that the students' embodiment of humanity can never quite be secure, partly for the ironic reason that the institution itself is generating their supposed demonstrations of human essence—their artworks—through deliberate institutional policy rather than organically. For all Hailsham's complicity and constraints, its provision of time and space to the clones—its creation and protection of a childhood for them—does have unpredictable effects of real ethical (if not, in the final instance, political) consequence. Kathy's access, via the "sales" held at Hailsham, to a cassette tape with the novel's eponymous fictional song on it, which prompts her fantasies of an impossible reproduction and the later apparent recovery of the tape while Ruth searches for her "possible" (a stranger from whom she suspects she could have been cloned) indicates how this is true (see also Dean, "Violent Authenticity" 143–44).

Never Let Me Go's society is obsessed with authenticity and originality as projected sources of stability, of the guarantee that the future will be like the past—literally, in removing risks of death for the "normal" population and thereby gerontocratically extending the lives of the old. This belief in originality reduces the self to the child and the child to the circumstances of their (re)production. A general ideological organicism is reflected by almost all the novel's events taking place either in the countryside or at the seaside, far from urban or industrial sites; this is an England where London might as well not exist, but rural counties have an outsize presence in the clones' imaginations.

This organicism is, of course, a biopolitical process, dependent on technologically controlled reproduction. Rebekah Sheldon argues that in dystopian fictions, such technologized reproduction often produces a renewed reproductive futurism that fetishizes ideals of the natural, the organic, and the lineal, abstracting from the messiness, excess, and abundance of reproduction outside these fetishes—an abundance typically blamed in other dystopian fictions, though not in *Never Let Me Go*, for the destructive event(s) on which the narrative is predicated. (Suggestively, Sheldon even frames this as a kind of enclosure, in a line of inheritance from the agricultural enclosure of rural Britain during the rise of modern capitalism [152].) *Never Let Me Go* is, indeed, somewhat unusual among dystopian fictions in depicting a deeply perverse future where the underlying dystopian turn in the backstory occurred not with an event of destruction but, rather, with a discovery of creation in the science of human cloning and its incorporation into population management; it is such a discovery of miraculous creation that more usually ends and redeems the dystopia, but Ishiguro makes it the origin and necessary predicate for his Britain's macabre condition. Destruction, meanwhile, is not originary here but constant and incorporated into the continuation of the organicist—if not, in fact, actually organic—and nativist reproductive order. "In the form of biotechnological enclosures—focussed on life to produce profit regardless of the cost to the living substance that provides the means of production—somatic capitalism finds itself facing two equally pressing problems: it must not only control distribution in the form of management but also get as close as possible to replicating life-itself and enclosing it through patent law" (Sheldon 152). This characterization works remarkably well—if with important twists—when applied to *Never Let Me Go*, where an organicist model of reproduction is achieved through highly *in*organic control over life itself under conditions of tight management. It would not be an excessive stretch to frame this as a kind of *migration control* regime in that it functions to bring what might be wayward and divergent into a bordered order where what is reproduced is what is already known (cloning, of course, being the most perfect version of this order). A crucial twist here, though, is that this controlled channel of protected reproduction is directed not toward producing the child-as-future but, rather, toward the biological maintenance of the original, native, adult population; the energy that capitalist growth seeks to ride in the aspirational youth is redirected toward participation in the process of dismantling, deconstructing, and integrating the new generation into the bodies of the old, into the *country* of the old, as the culmination of their *Bildung*. This is reproductive futurism minus the child.

Although *Never Let Me Go* has generated a significant body of critical analysis since its publication, which has parsed the significance of the clones as a second-class, exploited population serving the "normal" classes (see, for example, Black; Robbins; Rollins), it is only more recently that criticism has started to explore the significance of those normal classes also constituting a "native" population—specifically a "native British" population—being served by these exploited others, whose deaths are regarded as acceptable. This is an all-too-salient framework through which to read the novel given the Brexit-Era invigoration of nativism and anti-immigration politics; it also seems to me a necessary framework, given how suggestively the novel tracks real late twentieth-century history. Thomas Docherty argues that *Never Let Me Go*'s clones exist in "the position of unwelcome immigrants [. . .] for they present a threat to the existing conformities" (125). The clones raise the issue "of migration, miscegenation [. . .] and the question of authority and social control. These replicants are migrants, presented as being individuals who may be able to assimilate and integrate, but who are all the more threatening precisely because of that fact" (126). I agree that the parallel between the clones and those whose migration status accords them less secure rights than those held by "native" British citizens is central to the ethical and political significance of *Never Let Me Go* and to its uncanny reflection on childhood and youth in recent British history.

It might seem perverse to read *Never Let Me Go* in relation to migration since the characters never leave Britain, and possibly not even England—although Kathy's driving around and the trips the clones take together, though geographically modest, are invested with considerable significance. The clones are presumably created and born in Britain and believe themselves identical to preexisting British citizens, so they are virtually "original" citizens themselves and, thus, potentially as assimilable as any outsider class could be. (With grotesque irony, they will ultimately be successfully assimilated *right into the bodies* of native/original citizens.) Yet, as Docherty points out, assimilation—however much the rhetoric of contemporary migration politics demands it—can be an uncanny thing, likely to produce paranoia over the hidden other within the innocent migrant just as contemporary British media push fear of the hidden migrant youth within the apparently innocent refugee child. As in the world of visual art to which *Never Let Me Go* makes such extensive reference—and as Walter Benjamin famously theorized—although nothing is more identical to an original than a copy, simultaneously, nothing is *less* original than a copy, and the difference in value between the two is enormous, even absolute. Much as some Brexiteers high-handedly dismissed cosmopolitan, multiracial—and young—urban life as a vacant neoliberal Nowhere needing a renewed subjugation to an authentically British-English Somewhere, so too the nativist order in *Never Let Me Go* demands that the young clones are regarded as flat, insubstantial copies, vacant of authentic human nature, with exchange value but without essential value.

As a reviewer asked shortly after the novel's release, "if you were scheduled to have your organs plucked out any day now, but in the meantime were permitted to wander around the British countryside pretty much as you chose, wouldn't you decide at some point, 'This is a really bad deal, and I'm moving to France?'" (qtd. in Black 791). (Did European free movement ever exist in *Never Let Me Go*'s world, we might wonder.) Of course, the merit of this query depends on whether France or anywhere else treats clones any better, and *Never Let Me Go* simply doesn't disclose this. The question does seem, inter alia, to recognize both how specifically British the novel's setting is and how migration is conspicuously present by its absence, even as conceivable possibility. The fact that Kathy, Tommy, and Ruth do not consider attempting to migrate, even when they possibly have the greatest imperative to do so, perversely draws attention to the moral logic of migration itself, of the fundamental justice in young people attempting to do what they can to survive and lead an agentic life; the borders inculcated in these clones' minds from childhood prevent them from imagining this. The beached boat that the three contemplate on their last trip together (220) materializes this irony. Nevertheless, the clones' adherence to the borders within which they were raised does not provide them with any moral or practical reward. Instead, they are the ultimate citizens of Nowhere, their lives regarded as lacking any native or authentic substance. (Hailsham, of course, tries and fails to counter the latter belief.) In these projected qualities, the clones resemble Brexiteer charges against the cosmopolitan, the young, and the mobile.

Kathy's geographic mobility (within England), as she drives for her work, is associated with aspiration; being a carer seems to be the only skilled career open to the clones, and it partly answers the maternal instincts that drove her earlier fantasy aspirations for the future, as seen in her use of the "Never Let Me Go" song. However, this is obviously a constricted mobility, both temporally and spatially, that can no more become a migration beyond national borders than it can fulfil adult aspirations beyond Kathy's thirties; tragically, Kathy is only free to move around so much because her mobility is ultimately meaningless. Just as the novel functions as a grim parody of a classical Bildungsroman, the youth mobility it depicts is similarly a brutally denuded version of aspirational geographical and generational mobility, the phenomena that became so fraught in Britain between Thatcherism and Brexit.

As Miss Emily reveals to Kathy and Tommy at their final, revelatory encounter with her and Madame: "However uncomfortable people were about your existence, their overwhelming concern was that their own children, their spouses, their parents, their friends, did not die from cancer, motor neurone disease, heart disease. So for a long time you were kept in the shadows, and people did their best not to think about you. And if they did, they tried to convince themselves you weren't really like us. That you were less than human, so it didn't matter" (258). Although this is framed in terms of human status and lack thereof, it is also possible to read it as equally about native status and its absence: a matter of who is and is not "our own" or even "like us" at all. Contemporary immigration politics sometimes makes little meaningful distinction between human status and native status but rather tends, as Lyndsey Stonebridge puts it, to make "passports not people [. . .] the real bearers of human rights and human dignity" (5). *Never Let Me Go* emphasizes a parallel between generational mobility (or lack thereof) and human status, with the clones constituting a generation sacrificed to save the generations that have produced them.[6]

The liberal generational transaction that holds that adults should make sacrifices for the child-as-future—the basic presumption behind reproductive futurism—is utterly reversed here, with Hailsham's maintenance of childhood innocence and artificial development of personal aspirations covering for the underlying acceptance of the reversal. Nevertheless, even this grim parody of Bildung is conducted sincerely and has its own material reality. The fact that the Britain of *Never Let Me Go* feels the need to terminate it shows the latent, even if utterly complicit and compromised, risk presented by the institution that accommodates this: the risk of sideways growth, to use Bond Stockton's terminology, that it presents. Indeed, the clones' key relationships in the novel *are* all lateral, deprived as they are of parents or the potential for children.

As a residential institution, Hailsham has features in common with the other homes and institutions obsessed over by the children and youth we've seen throughout this study—and we should note its status as a repurposed country house, a variation on such houses in *A Clockwork Orange*, *The Little Stranger*, and elsewhere. Like those houses, Hailsham conveys material assets—and the times and spaces in which to use them—to children and youth, and it becomes an overinvested object of desire as a result, as Kathy's nostalgic obsession with it throughout her narrative and the special class status it supposedly grants to its alumni emphasize. One of *Never Let Me Go*'s many deep ironies, however, is that the ambitions and aspirations the children develop in and through Hailsham are generally marked by their mundanity and modesty—and yet, even these must be killed off. Given that *Never Let Me Go* was published over a decade before Brexit, it seems strikingly anticipatory (like *Orphans* before it) in reading deep generational and epistemological conflict—conflict so profound it justifies and requires violence toward the child—into its uncanny reworking of recent British history.

Hailsham is also somewhat like the houses and institutions seen earlier as objects of desire for children and youth in that, as a former country house and now a British boarding school, its associations are fundamentally conservative. Like any fantasy of an organic origin—the fantasy that entirely governs the Britain of *Never Let Me Go* and justifies its violent injustices—Hailsham's presence functions as a source of stability, which is why Kathy so compulsively returns to it in memory and conversation and why it is imagined to act as the basis for a "deferral" of the future; it is a past that is always available for recourse against the material problems caused by historical and personal change. The Hailsham students even consider themselves, seemingly not entirely incorrectly, to be a privileged group within the broader clone population. Kathy's constant recourse to Hailsham—in memory, narrative, and her impulses while traveling through England—and her comparative disinterest in the circumstances of that broader population constitute her own version of the impulses embraced by the normals, who—as Miss Emily explains—prioritize "their own" people and shut out the troubling signs of humanity from those on the other side of the internal, invisible border between the two populations. Yet, if the need for material stability (achieved, for these children, via the institution that gives them protected time and space) drives the parallel need for epistemological, ethical, and political stability—which is overwhelmingly delivered here, as in the real twenty-first-century UK, in highly conservative, essentialist, and often inhumane forms—that does not mean that an imperative for material stability is, in itself, conservative. On the contrary, access to such material stability provides the space, literally, for imagination and for the child's ambitions and relationships to run and play, as Ishiguro depicts with taut elegiac beauty. When this is provided on essentialist and organicist terms, though, even a conditional extension of access—such as Hailsham provides—implies the possibility of disrupting those terms through visibly exposing their contradictions. The fear of this possibility both reflects and provokes an obsessive drive for epistemological stability that turns ever more openly into, to borrow a phrase, a death drive that is directed against children, but perhaps not in forms queer theory or, indeed, many of our existing frameworks imagined: a death drive where futurism no longer inheres in the reproductive image of the child but, rather, in the adult's consuming body, ever more stabilized against its own mortality and against the uncanny alterity of clones who are themselves children and youth.

Conclusions: Migrant Children and Mobile Youth

The migrant child has become a figure before which the claims of internationalist neoliberalism, close cousin of reproductive futurism, come to die. As Bond Stockton's analysis of imagery of children in the Global South, as presented for consumption in the Global North, shows, no matter how vigorously an image of the child as vulnerable innocence is delineated and circulated, audiences will always suspect that something lies beyond and behind the frame. The migrant child paradoxically clarifies the broader reality that the child-as-future's persistent opacity often attracts adult violence in frustrating the adult's search for guarantees of the future through the child's innocence. Ironically, it is the dead child whose image can mostly fully provide that innocence and that guarantee; often, the dead child is ultimately the only acceptable migrant child; and the UK, like many countries, is practically prepared to accept the deaths of migrant children in the interests of maintaining its borders, having demonstrated an increased willingness to do so in the early twenty-first century.

The particular framing of the guarantee about the future being sought in these circumstances is subject to change. *Never Let Me Go* brilliantly shows the alignment between nativism and a broader kind of originalism that ultimately reduces to the adult human subject itself, in the subject's foreknowledge and fear of death. All demands for epistemological stability, Ishiguro implies—including those demands concerned with the British nation's position in the postwar, postcolonial world, as foreshadowed in *Orphans*—ultimately derive from the materiality of the mortal body and of the objects with which and through which it lives, a claim imagined in *Never Let Me Go* through the final assimilation of these internal migrants, these uncanny near-human and non-citizen-Brits, into the bodies of the original and native population. Even without such an uncanny parallel history, migrant children and mobile youth remind adult British society of its status as material and contingent—and thus subject to historical change, at a national level, and to death, at the level of the individual subject—because, in some sense, to migrate is to put the material ahead of the epistemological, to physically traverse borders that are imagined as fundamental and organic. It is always an unwelcome reminder, just as Kathy and Tommy's polite reminder of their humanity and request for refuge, for temporary asylum from their fate, is ultimately unwelcome. It suggests that, to take an image from *Orphans*, the disposable "bundle" may in fact be a child: a child whose privacy and agency, figured by their prior existence beyond national or other borders, haunts demands for their assimilation.

Material objects and their relation to personhood are of critical importance here, as the texts explored in this chapter so often emphasize, reflecting a reality where visible ownership of possessions is enough to provoke paranoid and aggressive headlines about migrant youth in early twenty-first-century Britain. As we have seen in earlier chapters, attempts to take possession of objects of value often constitute class transgression, driven by the curiosity of the child and/or the aggression of the youth; this transgression is dramatically magnified when undertaken by migrants, for whom *lack* of possession is presumed to be a necessary sign for innocence. This emphasizes that the Thatcherite (and broader neoliberal) celebration of material aspiration and entrepreneurialism is only acceptable within tightly defined channels—channels that attempt to deliver epistemological security but are continually breached by the realities of migration, generational change, and the opacity and creativity of children and youth, and all these breaches are mutually reinforcing. The fact that Kathy's possession of a random object (her tape) generates a chain of imaginative reproduction registers the power of objects in these respects, while the failure of Tommy's artwork to achieve a deferral shows the determination of a conservative reproductive order to put limits on their potential. Paradoxically, Kathy's overinvestment in the tape and Jennifer's underinvestment in the mementoes of her parents in *Orphans* demonstrate the same situation, despite the former facing a refusal of her own significance and the latter facing an anxious adult's demand to signify; both are required to defer to the established adult order in ways that reassuringly overcome the adults' death (for Kathy) or fear of death (for Jennifer).

The flexibility of significance betrayed by children's use and reuse of objects is a doppelgänger of the child's own state: their combination of opaque, uncertain potential and irrefutable materiality. (It is no wonder the Fort/Da game features so strongly in Freud's *Beyond the Pleasure Principle*, as it offers an object-based scene for reassuringly, seemingly secure interpretation within a work provoked by the gaps in and threats to such security.) *His House* imagined this combination of opacity and materiality returning even after the migrant child's death, wrecking the assimilation of her death into her "parents'" attempts to assimilate into the UK and figuring the unbearable nature of a paranoid system's demands for guarantees of future security from the refugees it grudgingly allows to settle. Mobile youth, of course, intensify this combination of materiality and opacity further as recent children starting to depart childhood and realize their potential. The mobile youth lives at the intersection between geographic and generational mobility—including in very literal senses, given the different relationship with travel and national borders normalized for those young Britons who grew up with free movement inside the EU—attracting the hostility seen in *All That Man Is*.

Both youth and childhood are themselves phenomena that depend on time and space, wholly or partly provided and protected by formal institutions. Such provision (from an institution that will normally be in, or govern, a fixed place) is not inherently opposed to migration or mobility. Rather, the latter may rely on it, just as the migrants in *Harvest* do, but anti-migration sentiment tends to turn, as in most of the texts discussed here, to an organicism that is hostile to institutions and to the institutionalization of rights. It is a paradox that the right and ability to be geographically and generationally mobile (and materially aspirational) depends on such institutionalized rights and on a meaningful connection with an institutionally protected home—a point Ishiguro makes to devastatingly ironic effect with the role of Hailsham in *Never Let Me Go*.

These observations have significant implications for how theory reads the child, too. First, they demonstrate that the child of reproductive futurism is now always, and increasingly, hedged by other kinds of children that threaten the presentation of blank innocence; they also demonstrate that the migrant child makes both reproductive futurism and (neo)liberal internationalism fraught and frail—now often openly opposed by the Right, certainly in migration contexts and often also in relation to generational change. Furthermore, the possession and use of material objects by migrant children and mobile youth implies, in some of the texts I have explored here, the possibility of a satisfaction that is creative but not in reproductively secure ways or forms that are transparent to the adult author. This challenges both the child of Freud's Fort/Da game and the Freud of the death drive located firmly beyond the pleasure principle. Jennifer's treatment of the objects lost in her migration in *Orphans*—objects to which she denies essential significance as substitutes for absent parents yet not the possibilities of providing satisfaction—is just one example of both these frameworks being frustrated in an episode of the migrant child's creative destruction of adult fetishes and securities. Such children challenge any interpretative framework that depends on recognition—that is, on substituting the child's opacity and materiality for a securely knowable signification under the adult's gaze.

Never Let Me Go provides a vision of abundance of objects and bodies—reproduced with the total security offered by cloning, yet of persistently uncertain potential in their reuse—that troubles all ideas of essential authenticity, including those that are nationalist and organicist but also, as Sheldon's work allows us to see, those based on ecological anxiety and associated defensiveness. The diverse range of organicist ideologies at work in the early twenty-first century challenges a world where the child always comes with uncertainty attached, and this is never more so than when crossing a border. It is a British tragedy that this country has generated such particularly powerful case studies to illustrate the point.

Conclusions and Speculations
Reading the Child-as-Future in the Twenty-First Century

We have observed and explored a remarkable series of children killing and being killed across British fiction, film, culture, and political rhetoric from Thatcherism's postwar hinterlands to Brexit's aftermath. The breadth and intensity of this material demonstrates both its significance for studies of recent British cultural and literary history and the relevance of these British cases for expanding, contextualizing, and challenging theoretical and critical accounts of the child in contemporary fictions and histories. I have tried to show how the (mostly) fictional children explored here reveal a strain of anxiety within recent British history, the severity of which other kinds of text cannot as fully describe, and an epistemological dimension of historical crisis that only the child can fully embody. Scenes and themes of deadly violence directed toward and arising from children—so taboo and yet, as we have seen, so pervasive—illustrate that politically, morally, and epistemologically fundamental issues are at stake in the role of the child-as-future in the United Kingdom's late twentieth and early twenty-first centuries.

These case studies have combined close attention to the specific concerns and anxieties of recent British history with depictions of the frustration of *any* secure or comprehensive interpretative framework that risks making the child-as-future prematurely safe for adults. They are salutary cases, then, in the context of the turn against unequivocal embrace of the child-as-future and the old conventions of reproductive futurism, especially from aggressive and increasingly paranoid conservative political projects reacting to the reduction in Western stability since the turn of the millennium, which have powerfully affected the UK as a key ancillary to

American hegemony and as a nation-state with its own challenges from a postcolonial, post-Empire world, including migration "crisis" and generational conflict—to all of which Brexit has given a particular framing and catalyst.

It is within these contexts that I have read the opacity and alterity—an activity whose ethical value derives from its verging on paradox—of the children considered here, with their provocative (and sometimes dangerously productive) recalcitrance to the adult gaze provoking an implicit or explicit perception of threat that arrives to justify, or even necessitate, the killing of these children. Such threats are both central and common to aspects of late twentieth and early twenty-first century cultural material like horror movies. However, those movies are typically formulated precisely around the thrill of violent taboo-breaking; the significance and reception of dangerous children in the texts considered here are typically more fraught and ambivalent (though my reading of children in McEwan, for example, gives an example of how there may well be an underlying drive toward morally simple destruction underneath the apparent complexity). The theme of child-killing as a repressed fantasy of resolving social and historical complexity and redeeming the future from its terrifying opacity runs throughout many of these texts—even if it only rarely receives the kind of explicit endorsement one might expect in a Hollywood horror movie.

I have argued that this fantasy is closely bound up in other forms of desire for historical stability, even for escape from history altogether, in relation to the UK's revisions of its own national narratives within and around the period from the rise of Thatcherism to Brexit. In the previous chapter, migrant children and mobile youth became central to exposing the intergenerational conflict and anxiety that is such a feature of 2010s British politics (echoing earlier versions of that anxiety, as seen in chapter 2) and the will for and belief in an organic, ahistorical essence for society and the state, which I've argued is a consistent feature of British political culture and rhetoric in this period. I have also advanced the specific argument that narratives of killing the child-as-future in this period sometimes reflect or anticipate the disintegration of Thatcherism's alliance between neoliberalism and nationalism, a disintegration that emerged explicitly in the aftermath of the 2016 Brexit vote. The disintegration is not, of course, total—neoliberalism and nationalism remain often mutually supportive—but Brexit did produce a recognizable reordering and reconfiguration in their relationship and in the associated hierarchy of political priorities and their narrative framings. The consistent underlying drive behind both the Thatcher Era alliance of neoliberalism and nationalism and its Brexit Era disintegration has been the will to find national political and epistemological security in a postwar (and later post–Cold War), postcolonial, post-Empire context.

These phenomena are not wholly unique to the UK: in the 2010s, intergenerational conflict and an ambivalent attitude toward the child-as-future became prominent features of political culture in the Global North and beyond in ways that demand that we revise Edelman's assumptions about the political function of the child made in the early 2000s. Nor is the UK unique in its tendencies toward organicism and essentialism; these are, after all, broad categories that can be defined by nationality, ethnicity, or ideology, with variations in every country and territory.

The British Case

There are, nevertheless, a few features of the British context for killing the child-as-future that have, I think, persuasively emerged as distinctive. British cultural ambivalence toward neoliberalism was evident from Thatcherism's strained attempts to incorporate entrepreneurialism and aggressive masculinist aspiration, associated with the male youth, into a sanctioned and celebrated narrative, despite how these features could appear as danger signs both before that phenomenon (in paranoia about aggressive youth from the 1950s to the 1970s and beyond) and afterward (particularly in the figure of the migrant youth). All this suggests a divide between neoliberalism and organicist nationalism that has been especially and persistently fraught in the British case, even during the period of the strongest attempt to unite these phenomena: the 1980s. The way this divide functions is somewhat different to how this might play out, for example, in the USA, where individual aspiration—including as pursued via migration—is a more established and long-embedded feature of (at least some powerful versions of) mainstream nationalist rhetoric, albeit one fraught with underlying contradictions and hedged by historical and ongoing traumas. When Edelman speaks, reflecting on the American 1990s and early 2000s, of the child-as-future's centrality to a dominant neoliberal politics, it is with a confidence that the British case could never quite have merited. The odd role of postwar America as a projected fantasy for migration, bathetically exchanged for 1980s Britain, in Ishiguro's *A Pale View of Hills* correctly recognizes the ambivalence even within Thatcherite attraction to American dream-style aspiration and its associated rhetoric of the child as entrepreneurial future-maker.

The will for an organicist version of reality (and of the nation) is markedly intense and noticeably in conflict with neoliberal imperatives throughout many of the texts explored here. The exact object of British conservative organicism is rather vague and ironically flexible; it could be the rural village that raises a child, as fascistically and fetishistically celebrated by Constance in *All Among the Barley*, harking back to the precapitalist feudal communities already under threat in *Harvest*. Yet, if such a village functions as a fantasy of the real, authentic, deep England, in the 1980s it is available to Etsuko only as an overly tidy suburban dormitory. British organicism could equally be located in the great houses of Lord Summerisle's castle, Hundreds Hall, the modernist country houses in *A Clockwork Orange*, or the repurposed country estate of Hailsham. Yet, all these places have only ever been accessible on restrictive terms—as shown by various characters' violent obsessions with accessing, preserving, or enjoying them—and they almost exclusively feature here primarily as reused and revived fantasies of what they once were, always already historically split from their original natures. An organicist national identity could be found in the aesthetics of monarchy—as in the queer, nostalgic, utopian fantasy of Jarman's *Edward II*—but how could such an admittedly seductive aesthetic vision ever be translated into anything approaching material or political reality? On the evidence of the material here, British organicism is powerful, yet it is disparate and vague in its objects, none of which offer it an unequivocal, universally recognizable, or wholly cohesive vessel. Importantly, though, this vagueness does *not* reduce the intensity of the desiring drive for organicism. No object of desire is stronger than that which is both overinvested (cathected, in Freudian terminology) and readily substituted. As we have seen, this is true across both explicitly conservative and nominally radically progressive responses to the child-as-future that turn to an organic essence in which to place them or for which to sacrifice them.

This organicism can be read historically as a defensive reaction to a British nation-state that—if we accept the arguments of David Edgerton—is a rather recent and unsteady creation, its contemporary version suffused with nostalgia for its brief period of coherence between the Second World War and integration into Europe in the mid-1970s. We could be much more temporally ambitious and reach back to the enclosure driving the events in *Harvest* to observe the role of the rise of early modern capitalism (and, later, industrial capitalism) in establishing the countryside—with its connotations of the natural and the organic, later centered by Romantic movements—as a site of nostalgia for lost harmony. Certainly, the British Empire (which has a subtly significant background presence in some texts considered here, as with the Empire Day fête in *The Little Stranger*) has been, as Peter Mitchell has argued it is within contemporary British politics and culture, associated with the promotion of tropes and projected sites of essential Britishness or Englishness, not least in reaction to its legacies returning to haunt the country in the form of migration. Recognizing the deep, pervasive history of the Empire combined with the continuing global reach of the English language—and, paradoxically, with the UK as former but not current global hegemon—emphasizes and exposes the unique anxieties involved in Britain's contemporary historical position. *Our House* showed the centrality of the child's status to colonial legacies "coming home" and encountering this position in the context of bleak migration conditions, which are only likely to further deteriorate in an era of continuing climate change and increasing revival of multipolar warfare. We have seen the child accordingly emerge as a risk to contemporary British border nationalism and its underlying organicism as the living subject and awkward object who threatens to jeopardize any perfect vision of the organic island nation (the vision that Golding so uncompromisingly skewered through the violent children of *Lord of the Flies*).

Institutions

I have repeatedly contrasted the quest for organic realities to which to reduce the child-as-future with the institutions that manage access to times and spaces where the child might find objects and ideas of desire, potentially in ways that thwart organicist teleology and remain obscure to adult scrutiny. I have argued that this can apply even where institutions ostensibly subscribe to organicist or other conservative ideologies because institutions are the material realization of the need to create rather than merely beget the future and, thus, at least incipiently or latently threaten to confound any political project that claims to rely purely on the organic.

We have repeatedly seen institutions, through giving (and sometimes denying) the child access, expose the risk that the child-as-future is taken to present. They give this child material space and time to develop and so attract adult paranoia as a result; the fact that even Hailsham's liberal patron, Madame, has a viscerally paranoid reaction to the students whom she is helping the institution protect (35) and has a further strange reaction when she spies on Kathy's use of her private time and space is telling here. The value of institutions is not that they are benevolent (Hailsham certainly is not) nor that they guarantee the child's healthy or correct development (many do not) but that, insofar as they function as institutions, they do so in historical, political, and material terms rather than as mere authentic expressions of an organic reality. In giving space to the child-as-future, acknowledging that they materially embody a future that does not yet exist—that is hauntingly both present and absent at once—institutions clarify the risk presented by this child. It is not coincidental, therefore, that in rightwing organicism and nationalism, hostility toward institutions (*as* institutions) and anxiety over who has access to them and on what terms are often combined with hostility toward the child-as-future, the child as embodied generational and historical change. The institutions also—often ironically, given their ostensible programs of control over the child's development—expose not only the historicity but also the materialism of the child's desires: a materialism that presents political and practical choices for adults and that is not easily resolved through any all-encompassing interpretative framework, whether conservative, progressive, or even queer.

Insofar as institutions accommodating the child-as-future have to give something to this child on the basis of recognizing a potential that can never be wholly secure, they latently threaten the logics of both neoliberalism (with its reliance on transparent identification of value) and (ethno)nationalism—which, as with Ogata in *A Pale View*, seeks to recognize and incubate a preexisting essential spirit or quality in the nation's children. *Never Let Me Go* provides a parable of how the resulting frantic search for an "original" essence as the basis for the child's institutional access and institutionalized rights becomes a fraught, paranoid, and ultimately unacceptable activity in an uncanny late twentieth-century Britain governed by fetishes of authenticity, the organic, and the native. This reflects the broader conflict between demands for visual, visible transparency and the opaque materiality of the child that we have observed frequently throughout this book, and which we saw even as resulting in the child's abduction being imagined as a route to redemption of either the child within the adult or the adult's organic reproductive potential in the work of authors like Ackroyd and McEwan.

Reading the Child: Queerness, Conservatism, Materialism

These dynamics have, as I have suggested, profound implications for our theoretical frameworks and critical practices for reading the child. I have emphasized throughout my dispute of Edelman's demand that the child must be read either as the figurative opposite to the queer death drive or, alternatively, as an embrace of it, as the child who grows up queer. My approach is closer to Bond Stockton's emphasis on the child's sideways growth: a kind of growth that children recognized as in some sense queer particularly reveal but that actually inheres in children in general. However, though this notion of lateral growth acknowledges the strangeness of the child, it does not necessarily fully capture their danger, their presentation of a historical *risk*. Whether we are speaking of the young Edward III handling the severed heads of his enemies and planning his future rule through their example or of Alex DeLarge proclaiming, "I was cured all right" as he faces reconciliation with a governing order for which he lately provided a bogeyman, the children and youth we have seen here tend to disrupt the passage of time from past to future in ways that, though they may well begin and develop in a sideways fashion, are neither to be held steady within that lateral position nor to be readily assimilated into mainstream or teleological history. These children promise that the future will indeed be very different to the past, their raising of the stakes confirmed by the possibility of violent death as either an alternative to or a fulfilment of this promise. Though many of the children described here are arguably queer in multiple ways, sometimes the objects of their desire or visions of the future are conservative, fundamentalist, or essentialist (Barbary in *The World My Wilderness* being only one example). The historical risk presented by such children should not be tempered by implied or explicit association with progressive—let alone utopian—politics. To do so would be, as with conservative discourses of childhood innocence, to make the politics and ethics of the child much easier in our adult discourse than they are in material reality. Any adherence to theoretical categorization—including the category of *queer*—risks becoming based on practices of selective recognition, where the recognition effectively creates a conceptual hierarchy for rhetorical affirmation. Categorization risks distracting from the child's intensive materiality and materialism, which have been such consistent features of the children explored here.

Still, it is clear that queerness nevertheless provides a framing and terminology for how the danger of the child-as-future is both articulated by and subject to attempts at containment, as currently renewed moral panics so forcefully show.[1] These panics are typically predicated on upholding a childhood innocence that translates to adult indifference, ultimately lacking any substantive meaning attributed to the child's ambitions and desires. On one level, this is an attempt to revive the old project of reproductive futurism. However, it is notable how the image of the innocent child has become, really, the thinnest of excuses; as the politics of migration show, the practical demands of actually protecting children on a universal basis are too overwhelming, and too contrary to the rest of a contemporary conservative agenda, for the Right to sustain. The child of this renewed 2010s to 2020s rightwing moral panic is even more abstracted and even less material than the 1990s to 2000s child of reproductive futurism discussed by Edelman. The Right's discourse of childhood has become an almost purely abstract fetish of the organic and essentialist, which can barely be articulated or envisioned with any depth, lest it start to fall victim to the complexity or dynamism of a living thing. Far from being on the road to Somewhere, contemporary rightwing politics make the child as flat and insubstantial as any imagined citizen of Nowhere. This means that whatever evasions and omissions queer terminology allows, they nevertheless do not prevent queer theory from being used to identify some of the material risks in the child-as-future that so haunt the contemporary Right.

There are broader implications for our critical practices of reading the child—and reading in general—here than just those directly related to queer theory. In a period of debate over the ethics and value of symptomatic versus surface reading as the dominant critical practice of the literary studies academy in the early twenty-first century (Best and Marcus), reading the children we have explored here demands an ethical practice that is neither wholly symptomatic nor wholly surface-based. The child-as-future affirms interior reality and its consequentiality but in ways that refuse full symptomatic reading. They do not, however, allow us to avoid dealing with their implications—we can no more remain on the surface than we can treat the child as the transparent object of our gaze. Rather, we have to take a somewhat critically humiliated approach (not dissimilar to that recently advocated by Thom Dancer in his *Critical Modesty*), making space for the presence of what we cannot securely interpret and assimilate. (Psychoanalytic reading practices, of course, have long grappled with the problem of interpreting opaque motivations without simply eliminating their opacity.) This critical approach has a political parallel in how these children demand institutional access without providing epistemological security (the dilemma seen at the heart *of Never Let Me Go*, for example). Accepting the child's resistance to total visibility and assimilation underlines the need for their material accommodation.

The scenes and themes of child-killing we have seen throughout this book remind us that to neglect the child's materiality is to underestimate the risk they present; the problem of the opacity of the future they embody is a much more serious problem precisely because they *do*, paradoxically, materially embody it. Think of the decisive (yet itself ambiguous and opaque) moment in *A Pale View*, where Etsuko approaches the runaway child Mariko with soothing comments about how the future will all work out even while she is seemingly closing in on the little girl with a rope. Through evoking the fantasy of a future full of aspirational possibility, Etsuko hopes to put the child off her guard; yet, she does not herself actually believe in such dreams but prefers the security of destroying the vulnerable girl before her (and preempting, incidentally, her migration). Material objects in the texts we have explored emphasize both the intensity of the child's desires for material things and for the times and spaces in which to enjoy them as well as the tendency of those objects to frustrate categorical definition and control. Such objects are liable to go awry and astray from both their physical and their signifying positions; little Christine Baxter chases the ball that leads her to her death, while Kathy H. seeks out the tape on which she based her fantasy of a different future and, improbably, even finds it again. Material objects may be invested by fantasy objects of desire (as with the little piece of Hundreds Hall that the young Faraday violently prizes from the wall), but this does not mean that the objects themselves are ever purely conceptual or reducible to theoretical categorization. In this, they reflect the children who pursue them, for whom they often act as uncanny traces.

It might seem paradoxical to see a material object—a tangible, empirically accessible thing that you can, if permitted, pick up, buy, use, etc.—as emphasizing the child's opacity, but the texts and children explored here have demonstrated how it can become so. *Don't Look Now*, for example, taught us to separate the object from our predetermined image of the child if we are to not repeat John Baxter's fatal misrecognition of "Christine's" red coat. In psychoanalytic terms, this implies that objects are not purely reconstitutive or inevitably substitutive for a loss or lack, just as the object sought by Baxter was not to repair the loss of his daughter as he hoped. Contrary to Freud's analysis of the Fort/Da game, produced as preparation for his theory of the death drive, the child's play with an object and desire for its possession does not prove to be simply and exclusively a substitution for the absence or loss of a parent. It is the refusal of such a reconstitutive status for the death of her parents that Jennifer, too, provides in *When We Were Orphans*, catalyzing the crisis in Christopher Banks's relationship to his own childhood, caught as it is between oedipal (oriented toward the mother) and sideways/queer (oriented toward Akira) models. Faraday in *The Little Stranger* is also caught in his oedipal dynamic, and Sarah Waters's novel is full of signals that the objects over which he obsesses are at least partly substitutions for his loss—but, as I have argued, Hundreds Hall is ultimately more satisfying than this dynamic accounts for, and the child-ghosts of the past are also more scapegoats than straightforward causes for the violence generated by Faraday pursuing satisfaction in the hall.

It might seem initially strange to suggest that materialistic aspirations toward particular objects are politically dangerous within the neoliberal consumerism of the later twentieth and early twenty-first centuries; yet, we have now seen many (at least, literary) examples of this being so. Partly, this points to relatively stable neoliberal practices requiring stability of inheritance, exchange, and mobility—a stability that is, in practice, constantly strained by sociopolitical and psychosocial realities and generational change, producing paradoxical situations like conservative politics that claim to value entrepreneurial mobility and masculine ambition but cast young migrant men as supreme figures of fearful hate. If neoliberalism encourages materialistic aspiration, it also depends on a belief in fundamental transparency of value—of human, physical, and financial capital—that is disrupted at source, as it were, by the use and reuse of objects by the clone children of *Never Let Me Go*. Virtually all the texts explored in this book underline how children and youth always tend toward disruption of transparent and ahistorical notions of value.

Beyond this, the satisfaction these children and youth achieve from the objects they seek and sometimes gain has, I suggest, an underlying radicalism of sorts. This is indicated in how this satisfaction challenges the frameworks offered by psychoanalytic and queer theories, which overwhelmingly tend toward substitutive models of understanding objects of desire. Obviously, these models have power and utility, and I have made use of them here. Yet, they also hand power back to the analyst or interpreter who understands the supposedly real dynamic behind the object of desire, a dynamic that is conceptual and schematic (and, therefore, orderly), and thus ultimately tends toward transparency. Seeking such transparency brings psychoanalytic and queer theorists closer in line with the conservative adults they tend to critique, struggling to accept that the child-as-future embodies a future that is not and cannot be fully visible to them yet cannot be escaped and must be accommodated—unless, of course, they kill the child and destroy the future. Accepting that objects can be satisfying without this satisfaction being transparent for reading from the outside refuses this extension of adult power.

Does all this mean adults can do nothing to seek to establish any secure and peaceful political order that is not constantly being destroyed by generational change? They surely can. In fact, the child-as-future's resistance of full and transparent visibility demands, I suggest, a material politics based on accommodation and democratic acceptance of the child's—and, by extension, all people's—alterity: their resistance to assimilation into a single and unchanging order of things. The cost of doing this, though, would be surrendering the desired guarantee about the future that adults so vigorously seek from the child. They would have to give something for, potentially, nothing. They would have to make a riskier investment than Thatcherite entrepreneurialism demanded and, rather than taking back control as Brexit promised, accept loss of control. This is an action that has proved difficult for mainstream politics and public discourse in the UK to accept. In recent history, regularly repeated panics over the "undeserving" receiving publicly funded support—above all, when those "undeserving" are migrants—underline the alien quality of such a notion. Ironically, even governments during this period that have claimed to celebrate entrepreneurial creativity—the creation of new value and new potential where its origins were unlikely or obscure—are unwilling to surrender their fetishes for guarantees of reproductive value. They are, curiously, in a sense less enlightened than the regime at the close of *A Clockwork Orange*, where, recognizing the Ludovico technique's failure, the minister hopes that giving Alex sufficient access to good things—the things he has so vocally and consequentially desired—might be sufficient to give both him and the public a different future. It is curious that the "nightmare world of *A Clockwork Orange*" feared by Margaret Thatcher ultimately includes one of the most optimistic and pragmatic gestures toward the British future of any text explored here. Whether the future will live up to this optimism is (especially in Kubrick's adaptation) undisclosed, but that is exactly the point: a humane and non-essentialist politics would have to take the risk.

Notes

Chapter 1

1. This is discussed further in chapter 2.
2. This occurred on January 31, 2020.
3. As one pro-Remain campaign group argued in May 2019: "Thanks to free movement, a British kid fresh out of college with poor grades has the same right to seek a job in Madrid or Milan as a Premier League superstar" (Lythgoe).
4. See Savage for a history of the development of "youth" as an object of adult anxiety in the first half of the twentieth century.
5. Bond Stockton is specifically referring to the "gay child" here, but part of her argument is that gay children illuminate aspects of the condition of childhood in general.
6. For a contemporary British example of this usage, see Mullan.
7. Cawood attests to (while critiquing) how the "winter of discontent," widely regarded as having a decisive influence on the 1979 election, became "a synonym for the failure of postwar democracy."
8. For an example of an anti-Brexit argument on this, see Wolf; a more extended argument that Remainer, pro-migration, and cosmopolitan values had proven fundamentally destructive is given in Goodhart.
9. On the complex relationships between Brexit and Thatcherism, see Jessop; Willetts; MacLeavy and Jones.
10. Of course, this is not to suggest that educational institutions necessarily do not reflect the ideological and political priorities of their surrounding society. Yet, even institutions that lack autonomy must have some degree of separation from society in general in order to serve a defined and specific purpose, even if that purpose is ultimately to serve the surrounding society or governing regime.
11. See, for example, Lacan's discussion of jouissance (264, 269).
12. The ambiguity is sufficient that the psychoanalytical literary theorist Josh Cohen, in his analysis of the Freud text, describes the game as a straightforward example of the death drive rather than as a contrast to it (107).

13. Another aspect of this context is the devolution of the United Kingdom, developed through the increased autonomy of Scotland, Wales, and Northern Ireland in the late twentieth-century (particularly following reforms implemented by the Blair government) and the possibility of either further devolution or the secession of Scotland (a possibility narrowly defeated in a 2014 referendum, but which remains a live political issue).

Chapter 2

1. As expounded in the opening chapter of Thatcher's memoir, *The Path to Power*.

2. Margaret Thatcher's taste in literature was primarily for well-established classics, and she had limited interest in film. See Moore Vol. 1, 31–32.

3. The band members give varying accounts about how much the song was intended as anti-Thatcher protest, but it was certainly a piece of absurdist provocation.

4. This description arises in Bond Stockton's discussion of the 2005 film *Charlie and the Chocolate Factory*.

5. The theme of postwar social optimism fading even while the bombsites remain raw perhaps reflects the fall of the Attlee government.

6. In *The Innocents*, Miles physically hurts Miss Giddens—and seems even at risk of strangling her at one point—and uses sexually threatening language toward her, such as referring to her as a "hussy"; all of these are innovations not in the Henry James source material. The suspected sexual history between Miles and Quint is also made more explicit. See Frayling 81–82.

7. My reading here emphasizes how the film demands acceptance of the apparent true nature of the world, underlined by the threat of violence. However, it could also be read as encouraging an acceptance of the otherness involved in death and in the historical fact of loss, humiliating the subject's (particularly the authoritative adult male's) pretensions to epistemological completeness.

8. As Hughes notes (62, 66), Summerisle's neo-paganism is actually a Victorian mishmash of traditions mostly from outside Scotland, making this Scottish isle very British.

9. The couple's cosmopolitan orientation is suggested by the actors' different American and British accents.

10. The decline of Protestant Christianity in the UK during the second half of the twentieth century is a somewhat under-explored framework for the period. For an overview of the issues and an argument for their centrality, see Bradley.

11. This focused on the "Stonehenge Free Festival," which began in 1972, a major countercultural and neo-pagan event.

12. For my previous discussions of this point, see Dean, "Spirits of Enterprise" 232–34; and "Thatcher's Young Men and the End of the Party" 231–50.

13. His engagement with theory is evident in his work of New Criticism, *Notes for a New Culture* (1976).

14. On the significance of country houses within the development of British capitalism, see Raymond Williams's classic, *The Country and the City*.

Chapter 3

1. This renewed hostility toward the supposed influence of theory and academic radicalism on children and youth has emerged particularly in conflicts over the rights of transgender and non-binary youth, with queer theorist Judith Butler becoming an emblematic target for "gender-critical" activists who oppose the extension and/or existence of these rights. I return briefly to this context at the opening of chapter 5.

2. There is a brief account of the controversy surrounding the center in Sinfield, "Playing the System."

3. For an example of a near-contemporaneous Tory argument against Thatcherism's claims over British cultural heritage, see Gilmour.

4. Freud uses this phrase in his 1914 essay, "On Narcissism."

5. This is the junior of the two Mortimers in the play.

6. As noted previously, Alan Bray's *Homosexuality in Renaissance England* (1982) was influential in establishing the intellectual and political imperative to recover the queer dimensions of early modern English history, but this remained a relatively marginalized and controversial interest throughout the 1980s.

Chapter 4

1. The Children Act of 1989 required, as its opening clause, that "When a court determines any question with respect to (a) the upbringing of a child; or (b) the administration of a child's property or the application of any income arising from it, the child's welfare shall be the court's paramount consideration."

2. Oppenheim and Lister observe: "In 1992–3 [approximately two years after the end of Margaret Thatcher's premiership] there were 4.3 million children living in poverty—a third of all children—compared to 1.4 million (10 percent) in 1979 [the year Thatcher's premiership began]" (127).

3. As I have previously argued; see Dean, "The Disappearing Child in Thatcherism and Theory."

4. On how this association functioned in the debates over Section 28, see Gillen 78.

5. These were a series of murders of children aged between ten and seventeen carried out between 1963 and 1965. The idea that these killings were the results of the postwar "permissive society" was advanced by the novelist Pamela

Hansford Johnson in her book published soon after the trial, which she witnessed: *On Iniquity* (1967). Ian Field discusses the context for this further, including the link between the reception of the murders and literary representations of troublesome youth in postwar Britain, in his thesis (150–59).

    6. For a journalistic account of Mark Tildesley's murder, see Oliver and Smith, *Lambs to the Slaughter*.

    7. There is a detailed account of the nature and context of this role in Kirkup and Marshall (43–49).

    8. The posthumous Savile revelations prompted the Metropolitan Police to investigate, in 2014–2016, false allegations of historic child abuse and child murder against a series of prominent figures in 1980s Britain, including Leon Brittan, Margaret Thatcher's Home Secretary, and her predecessor as Prime Minister, Sir Edward Heath. The allegations were later found to be wholly untrue, but they did echo more well-founded exposures of abusers—including Savile and another popular family entertainer, Rolf Harris—and they also drew renewed attention to the unsolved abduction of eight-year-old Vishal Mehrotra in 1981, with it being revealed for the first time in 2015 that police investigations had indicated a possible link with the pedophile gang responsible for the murder of Mark Tildesley.

    9. On the relationship between the Major premiership and Thatcherism, see Leonard, "John Major—'Thatcherism with a Human Face'" in his *A Century of Premiers*.

    10. There are several hints that the prime minister of the novel is a version of Thatcher (beyond the fact that the government's program in the novel is clearly an exaggerated parody of Thatcherism), one of which being that the stated age of McEwan's prime minister, sixty-five (79), is close to Thatcher's at the time he was writing (she was sixty-two in 1987).

    11. At one point in the novel, Stephen recalls his family members watching a show that seems to recall Jimmy Savile's programme *Jim'll Fix It*, where they "had once been a part of [. . .] a studio audience and had had the time of their lives. Each of them brought away a medallion showing a profile of their host, wreathed in laurel like an emperor, and on the obverse, a pair of hands firmly clasped in friendship" (123). Although this show does not appear to be targeted toward children, the medallions echo the famous *Jim'll Fix It* practice of giving medals to children featured on the show.

    12. McEwan's government is implied to have lowered the school leaving age (23), which was never part of the real Thatcher governments' agenda; in fact, the 1980s trend was in the opposite direction. See Bolton 10.

    13. An example is the disappearance of Madeleine McCann, a British child, in Portugal in 2007, where details of Madeleine's distinctive eye, clothing, and toy were all widely shared as part of the saturated coverage of the case at the time (and repeatedly after).

14. I am using female pronouns for the prime minister on the basis of my reading of her as a version of Margaret Thatcher, though it is important to note that McEwan himself avoids doing so.

15. Of course, this is not to imply that the choice of location belonged to McEwan, and my comments here should be contextualized with the understanding that his would have been just one of several creative inputs into the film.

16. *Gillick competence* is a concept in the law of England and Wales used to determine whether a child under the age of sixteen is competent to consent to medical treatment. Competence is based on when the child is considered to have sufficient maturity to fully understand the treatment concerned.

Chapter 5

1. Ishiguro was knighted in 2018, having been awarded with the Order of the British Empire (OBE) in 1989. Japan awarded him the Order of the Rising Sun in 2018, following his receipt of the Nobel Prize for Literature in 2017.

2. The description of Keiko as a "child" here primarily refers to her being viewed entirely from her mother's perspective, in ways that connect and elide her with other children in the novel.

3. This is assuming that the novel's frame narrative takes place roughly during the period when it was written, which seems like a reasonable assumption given the ages of Etsuko and her children relative to the earlier period set in Japan.

4. While the precise timeframe of the Nagasaki narrative is unclear, Etsuko implies that it takes place contemporaneously with the Korean War (June 1950–July 1953), though even this is vague, as Etsuko says merely that "there was fighting in Korea" (11). She notes that the reconstruction of Nagasaki was underway (11). I, therefore, refer to this narrative as taking place in the early 1950s, though this does not fully reflect the textual ambiguity.

5. There are suggestions during the novel that Keiko is this child, and she is explicitly referred to as Jiro's daughter (90), but it is never absolutely certain that the deceased adult daughter and the child gestating in the womb in the Nagasaki narrative are one and the same, reflecting the novel's web of ambiguities and identity slippages around children, parents, births, and deaths.

6. Ogata is, indeed, seemingly only able to conceive of learning as indoctrination, as he betrays when he asks his son, "What is this? Something you read somewhere? [. . .] Did you read that in your newspaper?" (66). When accusing Shigeo Matsuda, he remarks, "I suspect Shigeo never even stopped to consider what he was doing. I think he wrote that article with a pen in one hand and his books about communism in the other" (60). He is the most outspoken essentialist in the novel and consistently, explicitly downplays individual agency and responsibility.

7. During the 1980s, the Japanese "economic miracle" largely continued unabated, with Japan becoming the world's second-largest economy after the USA (excluding the Soviet Union). Although, like Britain, the USA had experienced economic problems throughout the 1970s and into the early 1980s, the effects were less severe than in Britain.

8. For a discussion of this tendency in Ishiguro's early reception, see Karni 321.

9. See Walkowitz 1053–54 for an example of a reading that engages with and contests Ishiguro's reception by essentializing critics.

10. It is worth noting that in 1982 Thatcherism was still in its early and insecure phase, with a weak economy and high unemployment rate. Thatcher's victory in the Falklands War, defeat of the miner's strike of 1984–1985, and the economic boom of the later 1980s were all still to come.

11. For an overview of Thatcherism's complicated relationship with the European project, see Vinen 230–48.

12. See Vinen 149–53 on how the Falklands cemented Thatcherism's narrative of national revival.

13. For an overview of the Thatcher's government's immigration policies and the influence of Margaret Thatcher's personal views on East Asian immigration, see Partos (chapter 4).

14. As Sloane observes, for Ishiguro "moments of genuine gravity" are "often banal" (4).

15. Seeing things that may not be there—and failing to see things that are—are important and loaded motifs in *A Pale View of Hills*. Shigeo Matsuda accuses Ogata of teaching children themselves "not to see" (147).

16. Of course, in Matsuda's case, Ogata's questioning of the value of his education is retrospective.

17. In this context, "psychological essentialism" indicates an assumption that certain traumas irrevocably damage their subject's agency and autonomy.

18. The argument that the atomic bombings prevented an ultimately more deadly extended war has been a principal justification used for the attacks on Hiroshima and Nagasaki since they were undertaken. A detailed overview, which takes into account the role of racial stereotyping in how Japan's actions were interpreted by the Allies, is in Takaki, *Hiroshima: Why America Dropped the Atomic Bomb* (1995).

19. This advert used the motif of a girl plucking a daisy, set against a nuclear countdown, to register the terror of a nuclear attack, particularly through the camera's deep dive into the girl's eye.

20. On "Daisy Girl," see also Sheldon 14.

21. This would be echoed in Mr. Stevens's self-defensive rhetoric in *The Remains of The Day*; commitment to *form* (in every sense) replaces critical attention to content, which is assumed to be given and immutable.

22. It is unclear whether Thatcher actually used these words. Their origin may be a Conservative Party policy statement of 1976, "The Right Approach," which included the line, "Once again, the facts of life have turned out to be Tory" (16).

23. This way of thinking among the Anglophone Right in the 1980s and 1990s would famously have its most influential explication in Francis Fukuyama's *The End of History and the Last Man* (1992).

24. Margaret Thatcher was fond of delivering her revisionist reading of the parable of the Good Samaritan, based on Luke 10:30–37, arguing that "No-one would remember the good Samaritan if he'd only had good intentions; he had money as well" (1980 interview for *Weekend World*).

25. Ironically, the Brexit "deal" May negotiated with the European Union eventually failed precisely because a majority of Brexiteers within her own party sought to pursue Brexit as recognition of a settled reality of an independent nation rather than as a negotiation with the European Union.

Chapter 6

1. This position was most famously articulated in Blair's 1999 Chicago Speech.

2. Accordingly, and in order to avoid any implicit moral distinction, I do not treat *migrant* and *refugee* as mutually exclusive terms here.

3. In the early 2010s, Prime Minister David Cameron set out a vision of a "Big Society," where services previously provided by the state would be increasingly provided by local, voluntary, and charitable organizations, in rhetoric that positioned an organicist version of society and community over an institutionalized one. The Big Society initiative's critics charged that it was merely a weak cover for the austerity policies pursued by Cameron's government. The fetishization of organic community reemerged in the Brexit Era of the second half of the 2010s, but—in a partial reorientation—it was repositioned primarily against transnationality and migration rather than against the welfare state.

4. The ethics of translation and its impossibility is critically recognized as a major theme in both Ishiguro's work and its reception. See, for example, Walkowitz, "Unimaginable Largeness."

5. For a fuller argument on this point, see my article: Dean, "They Built a Whole Lot Like That in the Fifties and Sixties."

6. The exact population economy of *Never Let Me Go*'s Britain is left opaque; it is possible that the clones may also be donating organs for "normal" citizens of their own age or younger. As vulnerability to disease generally increases with age, though, it is likely that the donations overwhelmingly service the older population. The only "normals" closely depicted in the novel are all older than the clones themselves, while the latter are the only children or young people to

appear, emphasizing the impression of gerontocratic exploitation. (The 2010 film adaptation followed the novel's cues by filling street backgrounds, when the clones visit seaside towns, with elderly people.)

Conclusions and Speculations

1. At the time of writing, the moral panic over transgender rights, particularly in relation to children, continues to intensify. They have also extended to more explicitly encompass attacks on broader LGBTQ+ rights, especially as applied to children, with any exposure of children to LGBTQ+-themed culture or education presented as abuse or indoctrination. See Strudwick.

Works Cited

Abbasi, Kamran. "The Olympics and the National Health Service: A Definition of Health." *Journal of the Royal Society of Medicine*, vol. 105, no. 8, Aug. 2012, p. 321.
Abse, Leo. *Margaret, Daughter of Beatrice*. Jonathan Cape, 1989.
Ackroyd, Peter. *The Great Fire of London*. Penguin, 1982.
———. *Hawksmoor*. Penguin, 1985.
———. *Notes for a New Culture: An Essay on Modernism*. Barnes and Noble, 1976.
Alyeksyeyeva, I. O. "Defining Snowflake in British Post-Brexit and US Post-election Public Discourse." *Science and Education a New Dimension*, vol. 39, no. 143, 2017, pp. 7–10.
Amis, Martin. *Money: A Suicide Note*. Penguin, 2000. Originally published 1984.
Anderson, Benedict. *Imagined Communities: Reflections on the Origin and Spread of Nationalism*. Rev. ed., Verso Books, 1983/2006.
Ariès, Philipp. *Centuries of Childhood: A Social History of Family Life*. Translated by Robert Baldrick, Vintage, 1965.
Armitage, Luke. "Explaining Backlash to Trans and Non-binary Genders in the Context of UK Gender Recognition Act Reform." *Journal of the International Network for Sexual Ethics and Politics*, special issue, vol. 8, 2020, pp. 11–35, https://doi.org/10.3224/insep.si2020.02.
Atkins, Judi, and John Gaffney. "Narrative, Persona and Performance: The Case of Theresa May 2016–2017." *The British Journal of Politics and International Relations*, vol. 22, no. 2, 2020, pp. 293–308, https://doi.org/10.1177/1369148 120910985.
Bain, Alexander M. "International Settlements: Ishiguro, Shanghai, Humanitarianism." *NOVEL: A Forum on Fiction*, vol. 40, no. 3, summer 2007, pp. 240–64.
Barnett, Anthony. *The Lure of Greatness: England's Brexit and America's Trump*. Unbound Publishing, 2017.
Bauman, Zygmunt. "Allosemitism: Premodern, Modern, Postmodern." *Modernity, Culture, and "the Jew,"* edited by Bryan Cheyette and Laura Marcus, Polity Press, 1998.

Bennett, Caroline. "'Cemeteries Are No Places for Young People': Children and Trauma in the Early Novels of Kazuo Ishiguro." *Kazuo Ishiguro: New Critical Visions of the Novels*, edited by Sebastian Gores and Barry Lewis, Palgrave, 2011.

Best, Stephen, and Sharon Marcus. "Surface Reading: An Introduction." *Representations*, vol. 108, no. 1, 2009, pp. 1–21.

Black, Shameem. "Ishiguro's Inhuman Aesthetics." *Modern Fiction Studies*, vol. 55, no. 4, winter 2009, pp. 785–807.

Boehm, Katharina. "Historiography and the Material Imagination in the Novels of Sarah Waters." *Studies in the Novel*, vol. 43, no. 2, 2011, pp. 237–57

Bolton, Paul. "Education: Historical Statistics." House of Commons Library, 27 Nov. 2012, https://researchbriefings.files.parliament.uk/documents/SN04252/SN04252.pdf. Accessed 23 Jan. 2022.

Bond Stockton, Kathryn. "The Queer Child Now and Its Paradoxical Global Effects." *GLQ: A Journal of Lesbian and Gay Studies*, vol. 22 no. 4, 2016, pp. 505–539. https://doi.org/10.1215/10642684-3603186

———. *The Queer Child, or Growing Sideways in the Twentieth Century*. Duke UP, 2009.

Boyle, Karen. "Hiding in Plain Sight: Gender, Sexism and Press Coverage of the Jimmy Savile Case." *Journalism Studies*, vol. 19, no. 11, pp. 1562–78, 2018, https://doi.org/10.1080/1461670X.2017.1282832.

Bradley, Ian. "The Strange Death of Protestant Britain." *The Tablet*, 13 Dec. 2017, https://www.thetablet.co.uk/features/2/11857/the-strange-death-of-protestant-britain-the-near-loss-of-religious-sensibilities.

Bray, Alan. *Homosexuality in Renaissance England*. Columbia UP, 1982.

Breslow, Jacob. *Ambivalent Childhoods: Speculative Futures and the Psychic Life of the Child*. U of Minnesota P, 2021.

Bristow, Jennie. "Post-Brexit Boomer Blaming: The Contradictions of Generational Grievance." *The Sociological Review*, vol. 69, no. 4, Jan. 2020, pp. 759–74, https://doi.org/10.1177/0038026119899882.

Brown, Kenneth D. "Conservative Government, British Decline and Japanese Success, 1979–1990." *Contemporary British History*, vol. 25, no. 3, July 2011, pp. 365–85, https://doi.org/10.1080/13619462.2011.597549.

Bruhm, Steven. "The Global Village of the Damned: A Counter-Narrative for the Post-War Child." *Narrative*, Volume 24, Number 2, May 2016, pp. 156-173 DOI: https://doi.org/10.1353/nar.2016.0013

Bruhm, Steven, and Natasha Hurley, editors. *Curiouser: On the Queerness of Children*, U of Minnesota P, 2004.

Burgess, Anthony. *A Clockwork Orange*. Penguin, 2000. Originally published 1962.

Cadwalladr, Carole. "Jimmy Savile by the man who knew him best." *The Guardian*, 13 July 2014, https://www.theguardian.com/media/2014/jul/13/jimmy-savile-man-who-knew-him-best-dan-davies-in-plain-sight

Campbell, Colin. "Beatniks, Moral Crusaders, Delinquent Teenagers and Hippies: Accounting for the Counterculture." *The Permissive Society and Its Enemies: Sixties British Culture*, edited by Marcus Collins, Rivers Oram Press, 2007.

Cawood, Ian. Review of "Crisis? What Crisis? The Callaghan Government and the British 'Winter of Discontent,'" by John Shepherd. *Reviews in History*, Jan. 2015, https://reviews.history.ac.uk/review/1711.

Cheng, Chu-chueh. "Cosmopolitan Alterity: America as the Mutual Alien of Britain and Japan in Kazuo Ishiguro's Novels." *The Journal of Commonwealth Literature*, vol. 45, no. 2, 2010, pp. 227–44, https://doi.org/10.1177/0021989410366892.

Cherry, Peter. " 'I'd Rather My Brother Was a Bomber than a Homo': British Muslim Masculinities and Homonationalism in Sally El Hosaini's *My Brother the Devil*." *The Journal of Commonwealth Literature*, vol. 53, no. 2, 2018, pp. 270–83.

———. *Muslim Masculinities in Literature and Film: Transcultural Identity and Migration in Britain*. I. B. Tauris, 2022.

"The Children Act 1989." *Legislation.gov.uk*. https://www.legislation.gov.uk/ukpga/1989/41/section/1/enacted. Accessed 22 Jan. 2022.

"Children in Migration—Asylum Applicants." *Eurostat*, 29 Apr. 2022, https://ec.europa.eu/eurostat/statistics-explained/index.php?title=Children_in_migration_-_asylum_applicants#Development_from_2012_to_2022.

A Clockwork Orange. Directed by Stanley Kubrick, Polaris Productions/Hawk Films, 1971.

Cohen, Josh. *How to Read Freud*. Granta, 2005.

Collins, Marcus. "The Permissive Society and Its Enemies." Introduction. *The Permissive Society and Its Enemies: Sixties British Culture*, edited by Marcus Collins, Rivers Oram Press, 2007.

Conservative Central Office. *The Right Approach*. 1976, https://www.margaretthatcher.org/document/109439.

Coram Children's Legal Centre. *Migrant Children's Project Factsheet: The Age Assessment Process*, Mar. 2017, https://www.childrenslegalcentre.com/wp-content/uploads/2017/03/Age-assessment-process.march_.2017.pdf. Accessed 28 Nov. 2021.

Cousin, Geraldine. *Playing for Time: Stories of Lost Children, Ghosts and the Endangered Present in Contemporary Theatre*. Manchester University Press, 2007.

Crace, Jim. *Harvest*. Picador, 2013.

Cunningham, Valentine. *British Writers of the Thirties*. Oxford UP, 1989.

Cutts, David, et al. "Brexit, the 2019 General Election and the Realignment of British Politics." *The Political Quarterly*, vol. 91, no. 1, 2020, pp. 7–23, https://doi.org/10.1111/1467-923X.12815.

" 'Daisy' Ad (1964): Preserved from 35mm in the Tony Schwartz Collection." *YouTube*, uploaded by Library of Congress, 7 Sept. 2016, https://www.youtube.com/watch?v=riDypP1KfOU. Accessed 25 June 2020.

Dancer, Thom. *Critical Modesty in Contemporary Fiction*. Oxford UP, 2021.

Dathan, Matt. "Aylan Kurdi: David Cameron Says He Felt 'Deeply Moved' by Images of Dead Syrian Boy but Gives No Details of Plans to Take in More Refugees." *The Independent*, 3 Sept. 2015, http://www.independent.co.uk/news/uk/politics/aylan-kurdi-david-cameron-says-he-felt-deeply-movedby-images-of-dead-syrian-boy-but-gives-no-10484641.html.

———. "UKIP Candidate Sparks Outrage after Blaming Aylan Kurdi's 'Greedy' Parents for His Death." *The Independent*, 4 Sept. 2015, https://www.independent.co.uk/news/uk/politics/ukip-candidate-sparks-outrage-after-blaming-aylan-kurdi-s-greedy-parents-for-his-death-10484911.html.

Davies, Dan. *In Plain Sight: The Life and Lies of Jimmy Savile*. Quercus, 2014.

Dean, Dominic. "Children Return to US Presidential Campaigns: But Are They Political Weapons or Horror Movie Tricks?" *The Conversation*, 19 Aug. 2016, https://theconversation.com/children-return-to-us-presidential-campaigns-but-are-they-political-weapons-or-horror-movie-tricks-63466.

———. "Ishiguro and the Abandoned Child: The Parody of International Crisis and Representation in *When We Were Orphans*." *The Journal of Commonwealth Literature*, vol. 56, no. 1, 2018, pp. 150–67, https://doi.org/10.1177/0021989418787230.

———. "Spirits of Enterprise: The Disappearing Child in Thatcherism and Theory." *Literature and History*, vol. 26, no. 2, Nov. 2017, pp. 231–50, https://doi.org/10.1177/0306197317724668.

———. "Thatcher's Young Men and the End of the Party." *Thatcherism in the 21st Century: The Social and Cultural Legacy*, Palgrave Macmillan, 2020.

———. "'They Built a Whole Lot Like That in the Fifties and Sixties': Ishiguro and the Ghosts of English Institutions." *Textual Practice*, vol. 36, no. 10, 2021, pp. 1731–52, https://doi.org/10.1080/0950236X.2021.1970011.

———. "Violent Authenticity: The Politics of Objects and Images in Ishiguro." *Textual Practice*, vol. 35, no. 1, 2019, pp. 129–51, https://doi.org/10.1080/0950236X.2019.1651762.

The Death of Childhood. Created by Tim Tate and Narinder Minhas. Interesting Film Company/Diverse Productions for Channel 4, 1997.

DeRosia, Margaret. "An Erotics of Violence: Masculinity and (Homo)sexuality in Stanley Kubrick's *A Clockwork Orange*." *Stanley Kubrick's A Clockwork Orange (Cambridge Film Handbooks)*, edited by Stuart McDougal, Cambridge UP, 2003, pp. 61–84, https://doi.org/10.1017/CBO9780511615306.004.

Dixon, David. "Thatcher's People: The British Nationality Act 1981." *Journal of Law and Society*, vol. 10, no. 2, winter 1983, pp. 161–80

Docherty, Thomas. *Complicity: Criticism between Collaboration and Commitment*. Rowman and Littlefield, 2016.

Don't Look Now. Directed by Nicholas Roeg, Casey Productions/Eldorado Films, 1973.

Duffy, Eamon. *The Stripping of the Altars: Traditional Religion in England c.1400–1580*. Yale UP, 1992.

Dufresne, Todd. *Tales from the Freudian Crypt: The Death Drive in Text and Context*. Stanford UP, 2000.

Eaglestone, Robert. "Cruel Nostalgia and the Memory of the Second World War." *Brexit and Literature: Critical and Cultural Responses*, edited by Robert Eaglestone, Routledge, 2018.

Eatwell, Roger, and Matthew Goodwin. *National Populism: The Revolt Against Liberal Democracy*. Pelican, 2018.

Ebert, Roger. Review of *The Good Son*. *Chicago Sun Times*, 24 Sept. 1993, https://www.rogerebert.com/reviews/the-good-son-1993.

Edelman, Lee. *No Future: Queer Theory and the Death Drive*. Duke UP, 2004.

Edgerton, David. *The Rise and Fall of the British Nation: A Twentieth-Century History*. Penguin, 2019.

Edward II. Directed by Derek Jarman, Working Title, 1991.

Evans, Geoffrey, and Jonathan Mellon. "Immigration, Euroscepticism, and the Rise and Fall of UKIP." *Party Politics*, vol. 25, no. 1, 2019, pp. 76–87.

Eve, Martin Paul. *Literature Against Criticism: University English and Contemporary Fiction in Conflict*. Open Book Publishers, 2016.

Field, Ian. *The Moors Murders: The Media, Cultural Representations of Ian Brady, Myra Hindley, and the English Landscape, c. 1965–1967*. 2016. U of Manchester, PhD dissertation. https://www.academia.edu/43047696/The_Moors_Murders_The_Media_Cultural_Representations_of_Ian_Brady_Myra_Hindley_and_the_English_Landscape_c_1965_1967.

Franklin, Bob, and Julian Petley. "Killing the Age of Innocence: Newspaper Reporting of the Death of James Bulger." *Thatcher's Children? Politics, Childhood and Society in the 1980s and 1990s*, edited by Jane Pilcher and Stephen Wagg, Routledge, 1996, pp. 115–35.

Frayling, Christopher. *BFI Film Classics: The Innocents*. Palgrave Macmillan, 2013.

Freud, Sigmund. *Beyond the Pleasure Principle*. Translated and edited by James Strachey. Norton, 1989.

———. *The Interpretation of Dreams*. Translated by James Strachey, Avon Books, 1998.

———. "On Narcissism." *Collected Papers*. Edited by Joan Riviere and James Strachey, vol. 4, Basic Books, 1959, pp. 48–49.

Fukuyama, Francis. *The End of History and the Last Man*. Hamish Hamilton, 1992.

Geddes, Andrew. *Britain and the European Union (The European Union Series)*. Palgrave, 2013.

George, Stephen. *An Awkward Partner: Britain in the European Community*. 3rd ed., Oxford UP, 1998.

Germanà, Monica. "The Death of the Lady: Haunted Garments and (Re-)possession in *The Little Stranger.*" *Sarah Waters: Contemporary Critical Perspectives*, edited by Kaye Mitchell, Bloomsbury, 2013.
Gildersleeve, Jessica. *Don't Look Now*. Auteur, 2017.
Gillan, Audrey. "Section 28 Gone . . . But Not Forgotten." *The Guardian*, 17 November 2003, https://www.theguardian.com/politics/2003/nov/17/uk.gayrights.
Gillen, Martina. "The Policy of Promotion: The Clash of Rights in Sex Education Law." *Northern Ireland Legal Review*, vol. 53, no. 1, spring 2002, https://doi.org/10.53386/nilq.v53i1.683.
Gilmour, Ian. *Dancing with Dogma: Britain under Thatcherism*. Simon and Schuster, 1992.
Goh, Robbie B. H. " 'Clockwork' Language Reconsidered: Iconicity and Narrative in Anthony Burgess's *A Clockwork Orange.*" *Journal of Narrative Theory*, vol. 30, no. 2, 2000, pp. 263–80.
Golding, William. *Lord of the Flies*. Faber and Faber, 1958.
Goodhart, David. *The Road to Somewhere: The New Tribes Shaping British Politics*. Penguin, 2017.
The Good Son. Directed by Joseph Ruben, Twentieth Century Fox, 1993.
Goodwin, Matthew, and Caitlin Milazzo. "Taking Back Control? Investigating the Role of Immigration in the 2016 Vote for Brexit." *The British Journal of Politics and International Relations*, vol. 19, no. 3, 2017, pp. 450–64.
Goulard, Hortense. "Britain's Youth Voted Remain." *Politico*, 24 June 2016, https://www.politico.eu/article/britains-youth-voted-remain-leave-eu-brexit-referendum-stats/.
Gray, David, and Peter Watt. *Giving Victims a Voice: Joint Report into Sexual Allegations Made Against Jimmy Savile*. NSPCC/MPS, Jan. 2013, https://www.nspcc.org.uk/globalassets/documents/research-reports/yewtree-report-giving-victims-voice-jimmy-savile.pdf.
Greene, Graham. "The Destructors (1954)." *Grahame Greene: Twenty-One Stories*. Vintage, 2009.
Griessler, Christina. "The UK's Discourse on the 'Migrant Crisis' in Summer 2015." *The Migrant Crisis: European Perspectives and National Discourses*, edited by Melani Barlai et al., Lit Verlag, 2017.
Griffiths, Melanie, and Colin Yeo. "The UK's Hostile Environment: Deputising Immigration Control." *Critical Social Policy*, vol. 41, no. 4, Nov. 2021, pp. 521–44, https://doi.org/10.1177/0261018320980653.
Gunnarsdóttir Champion, Margrét. "In the Beginning was the (Written) Word: Peter Ackroyd's *Hawksmoor* as a Myth of Creation." *Orbis Litterarum*, vol. 63, no. 1, 2008, pp. 22–45.
Guy-Bray, Stephen. Introduction. *Edward II*, by Christopher Marlowe, edited by Martin Wiggins and Robert Lindsay, Methuen, 2014, pp. vii–xxviii.
Hadley, Louisa, and Elizabeth Ho. " 'The Lady's Not for Turning': New Cultural Perspectives on Thatcher and Thatcherism." Introduction. *Thatcher and*

After: Margaret Thatcher and Her Afterlife in Contemporary Culture, edited by Louisa Hadley and Elizabeth Ho. Palgrave Macmillan, 2010.

Hansford Johnson, Pamela. *On Iniquity: Some Personal Reflections Arising Out of the Moors Murder Trial*. Charles Scribner's Sons, 1967.

Hatherley, Owen. *The Ministry of Nostalgia*. Verso, 2016.

Harrison, Melissa. *All Among the Barley*. Bloomsbury, 2018.

———. "Melissa Harrison on Nostalgia, Responsibility and the Future of the Countryside." Interview by Joe Bedford, 30 Aug. 2022. https://joebedford.co.uk/melissa-harrison/. Accessed 28 Jan. 2023.

Helm, Toby. "Immigration is Lowest Concern on Young Voters' Brexit List." *The Guardian*, 22 Jan. 2017, https://www.theguardian.com/uk-news/2017/jan/21/immigration-lowest-priority-young-people-brexit-poll.

Higonnet, Anne. *Pictures of Innocence: The History and Crisis of Ideal Childhood*. Thames and Hudson, 1998.

His House. Directed by Remi Weekes, Netflix, 2020.

Hollinghurst, Alan. *The Line of Beauty*. Picador, 2004.

———. *The Swimming Pool Library*. Vintage, 1988.

Hopkins, Lisa. *Christopher Marlowe: A Literary Life*. Palgrave, 2000.

Horton, Emily. "Diaspora, Trauma, Spectrality and World Literary Writing in *A Pale View of Hills*." *Kazuo Ishiguro: Twenty-First Century Perspectives*, edited by Kristian Shaw and Peter Sloane, Manchester UP, 2023.

Hughes, William. "'A Strange Kind of Evil': Superficial Paganism and False Ecology in *The Wicker Man*." *EcoGothic*, edited by Andrew Smith and William Hughes, Manchester UP, 2013.

Iakhnis, Evgeniia, et al. "Populist Referendum: Was 'Brexit' an Expression of Nativist and Anti-elitist Sentiment?" *Research and Politics*, vol. 5, no. 2, April–June 2018, pp. 1–7, https://doi.org/10.1177/2053168018773964.

Ibrahim, Yasmin. "The Child Refugee in Calais: From Invisibility to the 'Suspect Figure.'" *International Journal of Humanitarian Action*, vol. 5, no. 19, 2020, pp. 1–12, https://doi.org/10.1186/s41018-020-00087-z.

The Innocents. Directed by Jack Clayton, Achilles Film Productions/Twentieth Century Fox, 1961.

"Institution, N." *Oxford English Dictionary Online*, Oxford UP, June 2020, www.oed.com/view/Entry/97110. Accessed 18 June 2020.

The Iron Lady. Directed by Phyllida Lloyd, 20th Century Fox, 2011.

Ishiguro, Kazuo. *An Artist of the Floating World*. Faber and Faber, 1986.

———. *Never Let Me Go*. Faber and Faber, 2005.

———. *A Pale View of Hills*. Faber and Faber, 1982.

———. *The Remains of the Day*. Faber and Faber, 1989.

———. *When We Were Orphans*. Faber and Faber, 2000.

James, Henry. "The Turn of the Screw." *The Turn of the Screw and Other Stories*. Oxford UP, 1992.

Jarman, Derek. *Queer Edward II*. BFI Publishing, 1991.

———. *Queer Edward II*. British Film Institute, 1991.
Jessop, Bon. "The Organic Crisis of the British State: Putting Brexit in Its Place." *Globalizations*, vol. 14, no. 1, 2017, pp. 133–41, https://doi.org/10.1080/14747731.2016.1228783.
"*Jim'll Fix It* Christmas special." *Jim'll Fix It*, created by Jimmy Savile and Bill Coton, BBC, 24 December 1986.
Jones, Mark. "Down the Rabbit Hole: Permissiveness and Paedophilia in the 1960s." *The Permissive Society and Its Enemies: Sixties British Culture*, edited by Marcus Collins, Rivers Oram Press, 2007.
Jones, Owen. "Anti-trans Zealots, Know This: History Will Judge You." *The Guardian*, 15 Dec. 2017, https://www.theguardian.com/commentisfree/2017/dec/15/trans-backlash-anti-gay-zealotry-section-28-homophobia.
Joseph, Keith. Note from Sir Keith Joseph to Margaret Thatcher recommending Patricia Morgan's "Delinquent Fantasies." Mar. 1978. Churchill Archive Centre, Margaret Thatcher Foundation. https://www.margaretthatcher.org/document/111830. Accessed 3 July 2021.
Karni, Rebecca. "Made in Translation: Language, 'Japaneseness,' 'Englishness,' and 'Global Culture' in Ishiguro." *Comparative Literature Studies* vol. 52, no. 2, 2015, pp. 318–48.
Kettle, Martin. "How the Reformation Sowed the Seeds of Brexit." *The Guardian*, 27 Oct. 2017, https://www.theguardian.com/commentisfree/2017/oct/27/protestantism-wane-reformation-brexit-martin-luther.
Kincaid, James. *Erotic Innocence: The Culture of Child Molesting*. Duke UP, 1998.
Kirkup, Bill, and Paul Marshall. *Jimmy Savile Investigation: Broadmoor Hospital*. West London Mental Health NHS Trust and the Department of Health, June 2014, https://assets.publishing.service.gov.uk/government/uploads/system/uploads/attachment_data/file/323458/Broadmoor_report.pdf. Accessed 24 Sept. 2023.
Krämer, Peter. *A Clockwork Orange (Controversies)*. Palgrave Macmillan, 2011.
Kuhn, Reinhard. *Corruption in Paradise: The Child in Western Literature*. Brown UP, 1983.
Kureishi, Hanif. *The Black Album*. Faber and Faber, 1995.
Kverndokk, Kyrre. "Talking about Your Generation: 'Our Children' as a Trope in Climate Change Discourse." *Ethnologia Europaea*, vol. 50, no. 1, 2020, pp. 145–58, https://doi.org/10.16995/ee.974.
Kynaston, David. *Austerity Britain 1945–51*. Bloomsbury, 2007.
Lacan, Jacques. *The Seminar of Jacques Lacan: Book II The Ego in Freud's Theory and in the Technique of Psychoanalysis 1954–1955*. Translated by Sylvana Tomaselli, Norton, 1991.
Lebeau, Vicky. *Childhood and Cinema*. Reaktion, 2008.
Leclaire, Serge. *A Child is Being Killed: On Primary Narcissism and the Death Drive*. Translated by Marie-Claude Hays. Stanford UP, 1998.
Lennard, Dominic. *Bad Seeds and Holy Terrors: The Child Villains of Horror Film*. SUNY Press, 2014.

Leonard, Dick. *A Century of Premiers: Salisbury to Blair*. Palgrave Macmillan, 2004.

Lessing, Doris. *The Fifth Child*. Flamingo, 2001.

Link, Alex. "'The Capitol of Darknesse': Gothic Spatialities in the London of Peter Ackroyd's *Hawksmoor*." *Contemporary Literature*, vol. 45, no. 3, 2004, pp. 516–37.

The Little Stranger. Directed by Lenny Abrahamson, Potboiler Productions/Dark Trick Films/Element Pictures/Film 4/Pathé/Twentieth Century Fox, 2018.

"Local Government Act 1988." *Legislation.gov.uk*. http://www.legislation.gov.uk/ukpga/1988/9/contents. Accessed 26 June 2019.

Lockley-Scott, Anna. "Towards a Critique of Fundamental British Values: The Case of the Classroom." *Journal of Beliefs and Values*, vol. 40, no. 3, 2019, pp. 354–67, https://doi.org/10.1080/13617672.2019.1613083.

Loughrey, Clarisse. "*His House* Review: In This Refugee Story, the Haunted House Finds a New Dimension of Intimacy." *The Independent*, 29 Oct. 2020, https://www.independent.co.uk/arts-entertainment/films/reviews/his-house-review-netflix-horror-film-cast-director-refugee-b1371001.html.

Lovelock, Julian. *From Morality to Mayhem: The Rise and Fall of the English School Story*. Lutterworth Press, 2018.

Luckhurst, Roger. *Corridors: Passages of Modernity*. Reaktion, 2019.

Lythgoe, Luke. "Quitting EU Will Make Us Less Free—So Vote on May 23." *InFacts*, 13 May 2019, https://infacts.org/quitting-eu-will-make-us-less-free-so-vote-on-may-23/.

Macaulay, Rose. *The World My Wilderness*. Virago, 2018.

MacLeavy, J., and M. Jones. "Brexit as Britain in Decline and Its Crises (Revisited)." *The Political Quarterly*, vol. 92, 2021, pp. 444–52, https://doi.org/10.1111/1467923X.13039.

Majumder, Doyeeta. *Tyranny and Usurpation: The New Prince and Lawmaking Violence in Early Modern Drama*. Liverpool UP, 2019.

Marlowe, Christopher. *Edward II*, edited by Martin Wiggins and Robert Lindsay. Methuen, 2014.

Marlow-Stevens, Samuel, and Richard Hayton. "A Rhetorical Political Analysis of Theresa May's Statecraft on Brexit." *Parliamentary Affairs*, vol. 74, no. 4, Oct. 2021, pp. 871–89, https://doi.org/10.1093/pa/gsaa014.

May, Theresa. Speech to the Conservative Party Conference. "Theresa May's Keynote Speech at Tory Conference in Full." *The Independent*, 5 Oct. 2016, https://www.independent.co.uk/news/uk/politics/theresa-may-speech-tory-conference-2016-in-full-transcript-a7346171.html.

McEwan, Ian. *The Children Act*. Vintage, 2014.

———. *The Child in Time*. Vintage, 2001.

McIntyre, Niamh. "QAnon Conspiracy Theory Gaining Ground in the UK, Analysis Shows." *The Guardian*, 18 Sept. 2020, https://www.theguardian.com/us-news/2020/sep/18/qanon-conspiracy-theory-gaining-ground-in-uk-analysis-shows.

Meek, James. *Dreams of Leaving and Remaining*. Verso, 2019.
Mitchell, Peter. *Imperial Nostalgia: How the British Conquered Themselves*. Manchester UP, 2021.
Moore, Charles. *Margaret Thatcher The Authorised Biography Volume One: Not For Turning*. Penguin, 2013.
———. *Margaret Thatcher: The Authorised Biography Volume Two: All That She Wants*. Allen Lane, 2015.
Morgado, Margarida. "A Loss Beyond Imagining: Child Disappearance in Fiction." *The Yearbook of English Studies*, vol. 32, 2002, pp. 244–59.
Morgan, Patricia. *Delinquent Fantasies*. Temple Smith, 1978.
Morley, Paul. ". . . Pete Tong." *The Guardian*, 28 May 2020, https://www.theguardian.com/music/2010/may/28/pete-tong.
Morrison, Blake. *As If*. Granta, 1997.
Morrison, James. "Re-framing Free Movement in the Countdown to Brexit? Shifting UK Press Portrayals of EU Migrants in the Wake of the Referendum." *The British Journal of Politics and International Relations*, vol. 21, no. 3, 2019, pp. 594–611.
Mullan, Phil. *Creative Destruction: How to Start an Economic Renaissance*. Policy Press, 2017.
Mullen, Antony, Stephen Farrall, and David Jeffery, editors. *Thatcherism in the 21st Century: The Social and Cultural Legacy*. Palgrave Macmillan, 2020.
Mulvey, Gareth. "When Policy Creates Politics: The Problematizing of Immigration and the Consequences for Refugee Integration in the UK." *Journal of Refugee Studies*, vol. 23, no. 4, Dec. 2010, pp. 437–62, https://doi.org/10.1093/jrs/feq045.
Musolff, Andreas. "The Scenario of (Im-)migrants as Scroungers and/or Parasites in British Media Discourses." *Representing Poverty and Precarity in a Postcolonial World*, edited by Marion Gymnich, Barbara Schmidt-Haberkamp, and Klaus P. Schneider, Brill, 2021, https://doi.org/10.1163/9789004466395_016.
Nicholas, Lucy, and Sal Clark. "Leave Those Kids Alone: On the Uses and Abuses and Feminist Queer Potential of Non-binary and Genderqueer." Special issue of *Journal of the International Network for Sexual Ethics and Politics*, vol. 8, 2020, pp. 36–55, https://doi.org/10.3224/insep.si2020.03.
Norris, Pippa. *Cultural Backlash: Trump, Brexit, and Authoritarian Populism*. Cambridge UP, 2019.
Oberman, Kieran. "Refugees and Economic Migrants: A Morally Spurious Distinction." *The Critique*, 6 Jan. 2016, http://www.thecritique.com/articles/refugees-economic-migrants-a-morally-spurious-distinction-2/.
Oliver, David. "Health Tourism, Immigration, and the NHS." *British Medical Journal*, vol. 361, 2018, https://doi.org/10.1136/bmj.k2536.
Oliver, Ted, and Ramsay Smith. *Lambs to the Slaughter*. Sphere, 1993.

Oppenheim, Carey, and Ruth Lister. "The Politics of Child Poverty 1979–1995." *Thatcher's Children? Politics, Childhood and Society in the 1980s and 1990s*, edited by Jane Pilcher and Stephen Wagg, Routledge, 1996, pp. 115–35.

O'Rourke, Kevin. *A Short History of Brexit: From Brentry to Backstop*. Pelican, 2019.

O'Toole, Michelle. "I'm a Trans Woman Who Grew Up under Section 28—I Worry It Could Make a Comeback." *The Independent*, 11 May 2020, https://inews.co.uk/opinion/im-a-trans-woman-who-grew-up-under-section-28-i-worry-it-could-make-a-comeback-425234.

Oxley, John. "The Conservatives Can't Rely on Older Voters Forever." *The New Statesman*, 26 Aug. 2022, https://www.newstatesman.com/comment/2022/08/conservatives-cant-rely-older-voters-forever.

Parker, Emma. "The Country House Revisited: Sarah Waters' *The Little Stranger*." *Sarah Waters: Contemporary Critical Perspectives*, edited by Kaye Mitchell, Bloomsbury, 2013.

Parsons, Alexandra. "History, Activism, and the Queer Child in Derek Jarman's *Queer Edward II* (1991)." *Shakespeare Bulletin*, vol. 32, no. 3, 2014, pp. 413–28, https://doi.org/10.1353/shb.2014.0040.

Partos, Rebecca. *The Making of the Conservative Party's Immigration Policy*. Routledge, 2019.

Patient, Richard. "The Business Elite Need to Get Their Heads around the Second Glorious Revolution." *Brexitcentral*, 3 Feb. 2017, https://brexitcentral.com/business-elite-second-glorious-revolution/.

Petry, Mike. *Narratives of Identity and Memory: The Novels of Kazuo Ishiguro*. Peter Lang, 1999.

Phillips, Adam. *The Beast in the Nursery*. Faber and Faber, 1998.

Pierson, Chris. "The New Governance of Education: The Conservatives and Education 1988–1997." *Oxford Review of Education*, vol. 24, no. 1, 1998, pp. 131–42.

Pong, Beryl. "The Archaeology of Postwar Childhood in Rose Macaulay's *The World My Wilderness*." *Journal of Modern Literature*, vol. 37, no. 3, 2014, pp. 92–110.

Powell, Tom. "Jon Venables' New Identity 'Exposed' in Social Media Posts—as Investigation is Launched." *Evening Standard*, 5 Dec. 2017, https://www.standard.co.uk/news/crime/probe-launched-into-social-media-posts-which-may-identify-james-bulger-killer-jon-venables-a3710211.html.

Prusko, Rachel. "'A Prince So Young as I': Agequeerness and Marlowe's Boy King." *Queering Childhood in Early Modern English Drama and Culture*, edited by Jennifer Higginbotham and Mark Albert Johnston, Palgrave Macmillan, 2018, https://doi.org/10.1007/978-3-319-72769-1_9.

Revesz, Rachael. "Donald Trump: I Will Look Syrian Kids in the Face and Say 'Go Home.'" *The Independent*, 9 Feb. 2016, https://www.independent.co.uk/

news/world/americas/us-politics/donald-trump-i-will-look-syrian-kids-in-the-face-and-say-go-home-a6863876.html.

Riley, Charlotte Lydia. *Imperial Island: A History of Empire in Modern Britain*. Bodley Head, 2023.

Ringrose, Christopher. "'In the end it has to Shatter: The Ironic Doubleness of Kazuo Ishiguro's *When We Were Orphans*." *Kazuo Ishiguro: New Critical Visions of the Novels*, edited by Sebastian Groes and Barry Lewis, Palgrave, 2011.

Robbins, Bruce. "Cruelty Is Bad: Banality and Proximity in *Never Let Me Go*." *NOVEL: A Forum on Fiction*, vol. 40, no. 3, 2007, pp. 289–302.

Robinson, David. "Migration Policy under the Coalition Government." *People Place and Policy Online*, vol. 7, 2013, pp. 73–81, https://doi.org/10.3351/ppp.0007.0002.0004.

Robinson, Richard. "'Many Strange Tongues' in the Fenlands: *The Buried Giant* as Brexit Allegory?" *English Studies*, vol. 103, no. 7, 2022, pp. 1083–102, https://doi.org/10.1080/0013838X.2022.2150941.

Rodger, James. "Woman Who Revealed James Bulger Killer Jon Venables' Identity Spared Jail." *Birmingham Live*, 23 Jan. 2020, https://www.birminghammail.co.uk/news/uk-news/woman-who-revealed-james-bulger-17622287.

Rollins, Mark. "Caring Is a Gift: Gift Exchange and Commodification in Ishiguro's *Never Let Me Go*." *CEA Critic*, vol. 77, no. 3, 2015, pp. 350–56.

Rose, Jacqueline. *The Case of Peter Pan, or the Impossibility of Children's Fiction*. Rev. ed., Macmillan, 1994.

Rosen, Rachel, and Sarah Crafter. "Media Representations of Separated Child Migrants." *Migration and Society*, vol. 1, no. 1, 2018, pp. 66–81, https://doi.org/10.3167/arms.2018.010107.

Ross, Stephen. *Youth Culture and the Post-War British Novel: From Teddy Boys to Trainspotting*. Bloomsbury, 2019.

Royle, Nicholas. *The Uncanny*. Manchester UP, 2003.

Rozsa, Matthew. "Why the Moral Panic over 'Grooming' is So Effective at Manipulating the Right-Wing Mind." *Salon*, 30 Jan. 2023, https://www.salon.com/2023/01/30/why-the-moral-panic-over-grooming-is-so-effective-at-manipulating-the-right-wing-mind/.

Rutkoski, Marie. "Breeching the Boy in Marlowe's *Edward II*." *Studies in English Literature, 1500–1900*, vol. 46, no. 2, 2006, pp. 281–304.

Rutter, Carol Chillington. *Shakespeare and Child's Play: Performing Lost Boys on Stage and Screen*. Routledge, 2007.

Samuel, Raphael. "Mrs. Thatcher's Return to Victorian Values." *Proceedings of the British Academy*, vol. 78, pp. 9–29, https://www.thebritishacademy.ac.uk/documents/4021/78p009.pdf. Accessed 18 Jan. 2021.

Savage, Jon. *Teenage: The Creation of Youth 1875–1945*. Pimlico, 2008.

Schumpeter, J. A. *Capitalism, Socialism, and Democracy*. 5th ed., Routledge, 1976.

"Section 28." LGBT Plus History Month web resource, https://lgbtplushistory-month.co.uk/wp-content/uploads/2020/02/1384014531S28Background.pdf. PDF download. Accessed 26 June 2020.

Sehmer, Alexander. "Refugee Crisis: Former Ukip Candidate Peter Bucklitsch Apologises for 'Mistaken' Tweet about Aylan Kudri's Death." *The Independent*, 5 Sept. 2015. https://www.independent.co.uk/news/uk/home-news/refugee-crisis-former-ukip-candidate-peter-bucklitsch-apologises-for-mistaken-tweet-about-aylan-kurdi-s-death-10488020.html.

Shapira, Michal. *The War Inside: Psychoanalysis, Total War, and the Making of the Democratic Self in Postwar Britain*. Cambridge UP, 2013.

Sharma, Ruchira. "How a Desire to 'Save Our Children' Took People Down the Rabbit Hole into the QAnon Delusion." *The Independent*, 11 Sept. 2020. https://inews.co.uk/news/long-reads/qanon-uk-conspiracy-theory-save-our-children-march-explained-642000.

Shaw, Kristian. *BrexLit: British Literature and the European Project*. Bloomsbury, 2021.

Sheldon, Rebekah. *The Child to Come: Life After the Human Catastrophe*. U of Minnesota P, 2016.

Sinfield, Alan. *Literature, Politics and Culture in Postwar Britain*. 3rd ed., Continuum, 2011.

———. "Playing the System: The Sussex MA, and an Anxiety." *The Radical Teacher*, no. 45, 1994, pp. 20–22. www.jstor.org/stable/20709802.

Sloane, Peter. *Kazuo Ishiguro's Gestural Poetics*. Bloomsbury, 2021.

Smith, David, and Julia Carrie Wong. "Trump Tacitly Endorses Baseless QAnon Conspiracy Theory Linked to Violence." *The Guardian*, 20 Aug. 2020, https://www.theguardian.com/us-news/2020/aug/19/trump-qanon-praise-conspiracy-theory-believers.

"Spitting Image 1987 Election Special." *Spitting Image*, created by Peter Fluck, Roger Law and Martin Lambie-Nairn, Spitting Image Productions for Central Television, 11 June 1987.

Stacy, Ivan. "The Boatman's Tale: *The Buried Giant* and Cosmopolitanism in Crisis." *English Studies*, vol. 103, no. 7, 2022, pp. 1065–82, https://doi.org/10.1080/0013838X.2022.2146284.

Stansfield, Richard, and Brenna Stone. "Threat Perceptions of Migrants in Britain and Support for Policy." *Sociological Perspectives*, vol. 61, no. 4, Aug. 2018, pp. 592–609, https://doi.org/10.1177/0731121417753369.

Steedman, Carolyn. *Strange Dislocations: Childhood and the Idea of Human Interiority 1780–1930*. Harvard UP, 1998.

Stein, Tania. "Migrant or Refugee—Does the Label Even Matter?" *Global Social Challenges*, 24 Apr. 2018, https://sites.manchester.ac.uk/global-social-challenges/2018/04/24/migrant-or-refugee-does-the-label-even-matter/.

Stonebridge, Lyndsey. *Placeless People: Writings, Rights, and Refugees*. Oxford UP, 2018.
Stratton, Jon. "The Language of Leaving: Brexit, the Second World War and Cultural Trauma." *Journal for Cultural Research*, vol. 23, no. 3, 2019, pp. 225–51, https://doi.org/10.1080/14797585.2019.1633073.
Strudwick, Patrick. "'Groomer': How the Dangerous New Anti-LGBT Slur from America is Taking Hold in Britain." *Inews*, 26 Apr. 2022, https://inews.co.uk/news/long-reads/groomer-new-lgbt-slur-incite-hatred-spark-violence-1585179.
Sturgis, Patrick, and Will Jennings. "Was There a 'Youthquake' in the 2017 General Election?" *Electoral Studies*, vol. 64, 2020, https://doi.org/10.1016/j.electstud.2019.102065.
Szalay, David. *All That Man Is*. Vintage, 2016.
Takaki, Ronald. *Hiroshima: Why America Dropped the Atomic Bomb*. Little, Brown and Company, 1995.
Talvacchia, Bette. "Historical Phallicy: Derek Jarman's 'Edward II.'" *Oxford Art Journal*, vol. 16, no. 1, 1993, pp. 112–28. www.jstor.org/stable/1360540.
Teo, Yugin. *Kazuo Ishiguro and Memory*. Palgrave Macmillan, 2014.
Terentowicz-Fotyga, Urszula. *Dreams, Nightmares and Empty Signifiers: The English Country House in the Contemporary Novel*. Peter Lang, 2015.
Thatcher, Margaret. Interview with the Daily Express, 22 Apr. 1987. Thatcher Archive, Margaret Thatcher Foundation. https://www.margaretthatcher.org/document/106610. Accessed 8 Apr. 2024.
———. *The Path to Power*. HarperCollins, 1995.
———. Speech to the Conservative Party Conference, 9 Oct. 1987. Thatcher Archive, Margaret Thatcher Foundation, https://www.margaretthatcher.org/document/106941. Accessed 24 Jan. 2021.
———. Speech to the Conservative Party Conference, 13 Oct. 1978. Thatcher Archive, Margaret Thatcher Foundation, https://www.margaretthatcher.org/document/103764. Accessed 3 July 2021.
———. "TV Interview for London Weekend Television *Weekend World*." Interview by Brian Walden, 6 Jan. 1980. Thatcher Archive, Margaret Thatcher Foundation, https://www.margaretthatcher.org/document/104210. Accessed 25 June 2020.
Travis, Alan. "UK Axes Support for Mediterranean Migrant Rescue Operation." *The Guardian*, 27 Oct. 2014, https://www.theguardian.com/politics/2014/oct/27/uk-mediterranean-migrant-rescue-plan.
Trilling, Daniel. "10 Years On, David Cameron's Toxic Net Migration Pledge Still Haunts the UK." *The Guardian*, 14 Jan. 2020, https://www.theguardian.com/commentisfree/2020/jan/14/david-cameron-toxic-migration-pledge-decade.
Veličković, Vedrana. *Eastern Europeans in Contemporary Literature and Culture: Imagining New Europe*. Palgrave Macmillan, 2019.
Village of the Damned. Directed by Wolf Rilla, Metro-Goldwyn-Mayer, 1960.
Vinen, Richard. *Thatcher's Britain: The Politics and Social Upheaval of the 1980s*. Simon and Schuster, 2009.

Walkowitz, Rebecca. "Ishiguro's Floating Worlds." *English Literary History*, vol. 68, no. 4, 2001, pp. 1049–76.

———. "Unimaginable Largeness: Kazuo Ishiguro, Translation, and the New World Literature." *Novel: A Forum on Fiction*, vol. 40, 2007, pp. 216–39, https://doi.org/10.1215/ddnov.040030216.

Waters, Sarah. *The Little Stranger*. Virago, 2009.

The Wicker Man. Directed by Robin Hardy, British Lion Films, 1973.

Willetts, David. "Thatcherism and Brexit as Political Projects." *The Political Quarterly*, vol. 92, 2021, pp. 428–35, https://doi.org/10.1111/1467-923X.13033.

Williams, Raymond. *The Country and the City*. Spokesman Books, 2011.

Williams, Sophie. "Nigel Farage Sparks Furious Backlash for Attacking 'Screaming Media' over US Child Migrant Separation." *Evening Standard*, 21 June 2018, https://www.standard.co.uk/news/world/nigel-farage-sparks-furious-backlash-for-attacking-screaming-media-over-us-child-migrant-separation-a3868226.html.

Wolf, Martin. "The Brexit Delusion of Creating 'Singapore on Thames.'" *The Financial Times*, 7 Feb. 2019, https://www.ft.com/content/a70274ea-2ab9-11e9-88a4-c32129756dd8.

Wroe, Nicholas. "Living Memories." *The Guardian*, 19 Feb. 2005, https://www.theguardian.com/books/2005/feb/19/fiction.kazuoishiguro.

Index

Ackroyd, Peter, 3, 18, 48, 75–81, 89, 91, 105, 112, 129, 181, 255
All Among the Barley, 20, 37, 213, 219–227, 234, 252
All That Man Is, 200–202, 208, 246
Amis, Martin, 69, 149
Antisemitism, 79, 220–226, 233–234
A Pale View of Hills, 5, 20, 37, 173–195, 197, 202, 210–211, 228, 230–231, 252, 254, 257
Architecture, 45, 50–53, 70–71, 77–78, 81, 85, 87, 98–99, 103, 105–106, 142, 200–201, 209, 252
As If, 19, 138, 148–154

Benjamin, Walter, 241
Beyond the Pleasure Principle, 22, 26, 26n12, 58, 246–247, 258
Bildungsroman, 14, 67, 84, 201, 208, 227, 242
The Black Album, 208
Blair, Tony (Prime Minister of the United Kingdom), 21, 35, 198–199, 199n1, 206–207, 228, 234, 262
Bond Stockton, Kathryn, 2, 4, 7–8, 7n5, 21, 23, 25, 28–31, 47, 53, 53n4, 90, 132, 146–147, 157, 160, 204–205, 243–244, 255
Brexit, 1, 3, 5–18, 34–37, 40, 46, 64, 171, 174–175, 184, 193–194, 195,

198–202, 206, 213, 215, 219, 222, 240, 243, 250
British Empire, 35–36, 54–55, 93, 103–104, 175, 192, 194, 250–253
British nationalism, 5–6, 8–12, 14–16, 34–37, 89, 155, 183–184, 192–195, 198–203, 205–215, 219, 221–227, 233–234, 236, 240–242, 244–245, 247, 249–254, 259
Bulger, James, 19, 138, 148–154, 165, 169–171
Burgess, Anthony, 18, 69–70, 73, 75, 149–150

Cameron, David (Prime Minister), 199, 203–205, 214n3
Carpenter, John, 60, 152
Cars and driving, 84–85, 222–223, 237, 240
Children Act 1989, 42–43, 139–140, 140n1, 143, 167
Child abduction, 19, 24, 43, 62–64, 66, 77–78, 135–143, 144n8, 147–165, 169–171, 205, 210–211, 254–255
Child abuse, 12–13, 19, 24, 43, 66, 76–78, 123, 135–154, 144n8, 156–157, 169–171
The Children Act, 19, 167–170

The Child in Time, 19–20, 37, 45, 112, 136, 138, 142, 154–167, 169–170, 171
Children: children being killed, 54–56, 60, 83, 141–142, 148–154, 165–169, 179–181, 185–189, 202–203, 206, 208–212, 220–221, 223–224, 226, 231, 246; children killing/as killers, 50, 54–56, 62–64, 71, 75–80, 82–83, 95, 106, 113, 122–125, 127, 129–133, 148–154, 165–169; children as migrants, 20, 205–207, 209–212, 217, 220–224, 228–236, 244–247; children as queer, 4, 28–29, 74, 88–89, 90, 92, 128–131, 225, 255; Ghostly children, 95–96, 209–212; "horror children," 3–4, 18, 29–30, 37, 40, 48–49, 51, 55, 57, 59–67, 76, 81–84, 89, 92, 95–97, 106, 120, 132, 151–152, 166, 188, 194, 209–212, 250
Children's fiction, 14, 54–55, 150, 155, 159
Children's Crusade, 148–149, 153
Child's Play movies, 150–151
Christianity, 50, 64–66, 77–78
Churches, 50, 52, 61, 65–66, 77–81, 213–214, 218, 226–227
Church of England, 149, 153
"Citizens of Nowhere," 173, 175, 184, 190, 193–195, 199, 222, 234–235, 241, 256
City of London (original urban core of London; financial district), 44–46, 50
Class (socioeconomic class) 27, 33, 36, 41, 44, 46–47, 49, 53, 60, 65, 69–70, 72–73, 78, 80–81, 84–90, 92–104, 115, 143, 151, 164, 174, 215, 217–218, 220, 223, 240–241, 243, 245
Clause 28, 42–43, 76, 113, 115, 118, 137, 140, 140n4, 145, 147, 152, 194

Clayton, Jack, 59–60
Cleveland scandal, 139, 142–143, 148, 157
A Clockwork Orange (novel by Anthony Burgess), 18, 39, 42, 69–71, 73, 75–77, 81, 86, 129, 149–150, 153
A Clockwork Orange (film by Stanley Kubrick), 18, 39, 42, 45–46, 48, 65, 69–77, 81, 86, 142, 153, 243, 252, 259
Cold War, 23, 49, 59, 202, 229, 251
Conspiracy theories, 37, 136–138, 224–225, 230–235
Consumerism/materialism, 4, 8, 18, 41, 44–48, 53, 65, 68–70, 72–73, 76, 84–87, 89–90, 98–106, 112, 145, 157–160, 180, 183, 186, 208, 218–219, 245, 247, 251–252, 257–258
Conservative Party, 15, 31, 42–45, 39, 43–44, 140, 173–175, 183, 191
Countryside (rural England and Britain), 3, 36, 61–64, 93, 161–163, 182, 212–228, 239, 252
Covid-19 pandemic, 37, 137
Crace, Jim, 3, 20, 37, 112, 213–221, 246, 252–253
"Creative destruction," 1–3, 7–9, 40, 44, 53–58, 69, 75, 78, 93, 102, 105, 110, 132–133, 149, 159, 180, 226, 247
Crime, 43–45, 56, 67, 69–73, 77, 82, 141–142, 144, 147–154, 171, 218
Crimewatch UK, 141–142, 147
Culkin, Macaulay, 165–166

Dahl, Roald, 14, 150
"Daisy Girl," 189–190
Death drive/death instinct, 21–22, 24–28, 26n12, 30, 32, 53–56, 58, 74, 79–81, 90, 102, 162, 205, 244, 247, 255, 258
Derrida, Jaques, 21, 78–79

The Destructors, 18, 52–58, 67, 90
Don't Look Now, 61–67, 77, 139, 150, 155, 158, 164, 167, 181, 207, 212, 257
Doppelgängers, 40, 69, 74, 77–80, 83, 110, 145, 150, 157, 183, 209, 221, 238, 246

Edelman, Lee, 4, 5, 21–31, 33, 39, 53–54, 56, 74, 79, 90, 117, 127, 138, 164, 169, 204–205, 225–226, 251, 255–256
Edgerton, David, 11, 252
Edward II (film), 19, 23, 29, 110–133, 252
Edward II (play), 19, 29, 33, 110–133, 255
Edward I (King of England), 118, 121
Edward II (King of England), 114–127, 129
Edward III (King of England), 29, 33, 114–133, 255
Elizabeth II (Queen of the United Kingdom and the Commonwealth Realms, 1926-2022) 15, 113
Enclosure (of common lands), 104, 213–215, 220, 239, 253
"End of history," 23, 25, 35
Enfield, Harry, 45, 47
English Reformation, 10, 218
Entrepreneurialism, 18, 37, 44, 68, 76–77, 80, 84–85, 111, 144, 146, 159, 183, 191–192, 199, 201–202, 208, 223, 245, 251–252, 258–259
Essentialism, 12, 14–17, 20, 30, 42, 56–57, 64, 68, 77, 80–81, 84, 87, 103, 105, 110, 151–153, 156, 162–164, 180–182, 181n6, 187–193, 212–213, 216–217, 222, 226, 228, 238, 244, 250–256, 260
European Union (or predecessor European Communities), 6, 9–15, 35, 64, 175, 183, 198–202, 205, 246

Family units, 21–22, 41–44, 49–50, 52–53, 71, 81–85, 88–89, 93, 98, 139, 142–143, 145, 150–152, 166–168, 177, 214, 217, 219–222, 228–229
Farage, Nigel, 207
The Fifth Child, 18, 48, 75, 81–83, 89, 152, 166
Foucault, Michel, 21
Freud, Sigmund, 8, 21–23, 26, 28–32, 42, 50, 53, 56, 58, 66, 78, 101, 116, 116n4, 132, 192, 246–247
Freudian theory/analysis, 26, 26n12, 30, 45, 50–51, 53–56, 58–60, 66, 68, 75, 78, 84, 101–102, 116, 116n4, 120, 132, 144, 144n8, 146, 160, 164–167, 192, 246–247, 252, 258–259
Fukuyama, Francis, 23, 191n23

Gangs, 41, 46–48, 52–55, 58–59, 70–74, 81–83, 142
Gillick competence, 139, 168, 168n16
Globalisation, 3, 8, 10, 12, 20, 43, 175–176, 192, 199, 207, 228–230
Golding, William, 3, 18, 54–58, 67, 90, 149, 253
The Good Son, 19, 154, 165–167, 170
The Great Fire of London, 18, 48, 76–77
Greene, Graham, 3, 18, 52–58, 67, 90

Halloween, 60–61, 152
Hardy, Robin, 3, 61–62
Harrison, Melissa, 3, 20, 37, 213, 219–227
Harry Potter, 14
Harvest, 20, 213–221, 246, 252–253
Hawksmoor, 18, 48, 75–81, 91, 105, 181
Heart of Darkness, 232
His House, 3, 20, 37, 205, 209–212, 246

Hollinghurst, Alan, 3, 18, 45, 47–48, 76, 83–89, 98–99, 110, 118
Home Alone, 166
Horror genre, 3–4, 18, 29–30, 37, 48–49, 51, 55, 57, 59–67, 76–77, 81–84, 89, 92, 95–97, 106, 120, 132, 151–152, 166, 188, 209–212, 250
Houses, 41, 52–53, 56, 58, 65, 71, 77, 90, 182, 187, 209–212; country houses, 27–28, 33, 36, 65, 71, 86–87, 92–107, 104n14, 214, 220–221, 236, 243, 252

Immigration, *see* migration
The Innocents, 3, 3n1, 59–60, 166
Institutions, 1, 6, 8–10, 13–17, 31, 34–35, 42–43, 66, 71, 78, 81–83, 91–92, 104–107, 109–111, 116, 131, 139, 144, 149, 152, 171, 174–175, 177, 180–183, 187–195, 197–198, 201, 212, 215, 218–219, 221–223, 226–227, 233–236, 238, 243–244, 246–247, 254, 257; Definition of "institution," 13–14
The Interpretation of Dreams, 192
Iraq War (2003), 199
Islamist extremism, 15, 206, 208
Islamophobia, 12, 15, 198–199, 206, 208
Islands, 54–57, 62–64, 121, 253
Ishiguro, Kazuo, 3, 5, 20, 23, 37, 173–195, 228–247, 251–252

James, Henry, 3, 59, 95, 166, 176, 205
Japan, 43, 173, 173n1, 175–177, 177n4, 180–193, 182n7, 189n18, 228–229
Jarman, Derek, 3, 19, 23, 110, 112–122, 124–125, 127, 129–133, 252
Jim'll Fix It, 135, 144–147
Johnson, Boris (Prime Minister of the United Kingdom), 200

Keynes, John Maynard, 68, 112
Kubrick, Stanley, 3, 18, 69–75, 129
Kurdi, Alan, 12, 202–203, 206–207, 230–231
Kureishi, Hanif, 208

Labour Party, 35, 45–46, 93, 200
Lacan, Jacques, 22, 25, 25n11, 32; Lacanian thought, 31, 75, 78–80
Leclaire, Serge, 2, 98, 100
Lessing, Doris, 3, 18, 48, 75, 81–83, 89, 152, 166
LGBTQ+ issues, 75, 83–89, 113–115, 225; in history, 111–114, 118, 128–129; moral panics over, 21–22, 30–31, 36, 42–43, 46, 75, 137, 145; Transgender issues, 36, 137
The Line of Beauty, 18, 45, 47–48, 76, 83–89, 99, 110, 118
The Little Stranger, 19, 27, 29, 33, 48, 65, 87, 91–107, 139, 161, 220, 243, 253, 258
Loadsamoney (character played by Harry Enfield), 45, 47, 69
London, 36, 43, 44–46, 50, 52, 55, 76–78, 155, 159, 182, 201–202, 209, 223, 226, 233, 239; 2012 London Olympics, 15
"Loony Left," 41–43, 68, 111, 156
Lord of the Flies, 3, 18, 54–58, 64, 67, 90–91, 127, 149–152, 253

Macaulay, Rose, 3, 18, 50–52, 55, 57–58, 67, 90
Major, John (Prime Minister of the United Kingdom), 149, 149n9
Marlowe, Christopher, 19, 110, 113–133
Masculinity/masculinities, 12, 18, 37, 40–48, 60, 63, 66–70, 89–90, 96, 101–102, 105–106, 159–160, 171, 198–202, 208, 251

Materialism, *see* consumerism
May, Theresa (Prime Minister of the United Kingdom), 173, 192–193, 195, 199, 209
McDowell, Malcolm, 70
McEwan, Ian, 3, 19–20, 37, 42, 45, 47, 112, 136, 138, 140–142, 154–159, 161, 170, 212, 250, 255
Migration, 3, 6, 8, 11–12, 15, 20, 23, 33–35, 37, 49, 87, 89, 174–180, 183–184, 184n13, 186, 190, 192–193, 197–247, 250–251, 253, 256–257; "migration crisis," 174, 202–209, 250; migration within the European Union and "free movement," 15, 64, 198, 200–202
"Moors murders," 141–142
Morrison, Blake, 19, 112, 136, 138, 148–154

"Nachträglichkeit," 95, 100, 106, 135–136, 144, 170–171
National Health Service (NHS), 13–15, 49, 92, 104, 151, 200
Neoliberalism, 5, 8–9, 16–17, 20–21, 23–25, 27–30, 34–35, 37, 40, 45–46, 68, 77–78, 91, 100, 107, 156, 169, 171, 175, 183, 191–193, 198–200, 202, 207–208, 228, 236, 244, 250–252, 254
Never Let Me Go, 16–17, 20, 186, 190, 228, 236–247, 254, 257–258
Notsensibles, 46

The Omen, 60, 81, 152, 166

Pedophilia, 31, 76, 140–147, 1144n8, 157
Paganism, 63–66, 64n8
Peter Pan, 31–32
Postwar period, 9–11, 49, 51, 57, 70, 92, 106–107, 156, 176, 183–184, 252; British postwar social democracy, 35, 68, 70, 92, 104, 106, 111, 159, 178, 183
Protestantism, 65–66, 65n10, 112
Psychoanalysis, *see* psychoanalytic theory

Race/ethnicity, 23, 33, 87, 173, 175, 189, 192, 231; "race riots," 155; racism, 155, 175, 189, 231–235
Reproductive futurism, 5, 7, 22, 24, 28–30, 73, 127, 169, 198, 205–206, 225–226, 239–240, 242, 244, 247, 249, 251, 256
Roeg, Nicholas, 3, 61, 158–159
Romanticism/neoromanticism, 33, 106, 112–113, 138, 162–163, 212–213, 223, 227, 238, 253
Rose, Jacqueline, 4, 31–34, 135–136, 162, 170–171, 203
Rutter, Carol Chillington, 2–3, 33, 139–140, 142–143, 170

Savile, Jimmy, 19, 135, 138, 143–148, 144n8, 154, 171
Schools, 43, 66, 70–71, 83, 111, 139–140, 149, 152, 156, 156n12, 187, 189–191, 206, 226, 229, 233, 243
Second World War, 9–11, 16, 34–35, 49–50, 52, 56, 70, 104, 111, 175–177, 180, 183, 194, 227, 252
Section 28, *see* Clause 28
Sexual violence/abuse, 59, 70–74, 119, 135–148, 150, 170, 208, 218–220
Shanghai, 228–235
Slasher films, 60–61, 152, 166
Spitting Image, 44–45
The Swimming Pool Library, 83–84, 87–88, 98
Szalay, David, 3, 20, 200–202

Teddy Boys, 46–48, 59, 70

Thatcherism, 1, 4–11, 13, 18–20, 34, 39–40, 72, 78, 80, 83–89, 93, 106–107, 110–112, 139–141, 149–150, 156–157, 159–160, 177, 184, 191–192, 194–195

Thatcher, Margaret, 143, 145; cultural representations/fictional depictions of, 16, 46, 154, 160; Thatcher governments, 4, 9, 76, 139, 221; views and policies, 39, 68–70, 72, 140, 143–145, 184, 191–192

Theory, 78–79, 90, 156, 163; opposition to theory, 90, 156, 163; psychoanalytic theory, 26, 26n12, 30, 45, 49–51, 53–56, 58–60, 66, 68, 75, 78, 84, 98, 101–102, 116, 116n4, 120, 132, 144, 144n8, 146, 160, 164–167, 192, 246–247, 252, 258–259; queer theory, 53–54, 58–59, 74, 77, 80–81, 90–91, 102, 110–111, 128–129, 132–133; theories of children and childhood, 4–5, 8, 21–37, 42, 49–50, 53–54, 58–59, 98, 203–206, 254

Thunberg, Greta, 7–8, 137–138

Transgender issues, *see* LGBTQ+ issues

Trojan Horse Affair, 206

Trump, Donald, 137, 206–207

The Turn of the Screw, 3, 43, 59–60, 59n6, 95, 145, 166, 176, 205

United States of America, 4–5, 21–24, 29, 31, 34–35, 46–47, 165, 175–184, 186–187, 189–193, 207, 230, 250–252

University of Sussex, 111, 111n2

"Victorian values," 31, 44, 50, 68, 72, 111, 183, 191

Village of the Damned, 29–30, 59

War on Terror, 23–24, 199, 208, 230

Waters, Sarah, 3, 19, 27, 48, 87, 92–107, 258

Weekes, Remi, 3, 20, 37, 209–212

When We Were Orphans, 20, 23, 37, 228–236, 258

The Wicker Man, 29, 61–67, 139, 218–219

Winnicott, Donald, 32, 49, 51, 55, 58, 90, 101

The World my Wilderness, 50–52, 55–59, 77, 81, 151, 255

Wren, Christopher, 52, 77, 85, 87

Youth cultures/subcultures, 17, 40–42, 45–48, 59, 63, 69–70, 83–84, 89, 159, 191–192

Yuppies, 46–46, 159

www.ingramcontent.com/pod-product-compliance
Lightning Source LLC
Chambersburg PA
CBHW030525230426
43665CB00010B/773